Agnes Sanford and Her Companions

Agnes Sanford and Her Companions

The Assault on Cessationism and the
Coming of the Charismatic Renewal

William L. De Arteaga

WIPF & STOCK · Eugene, Oregon

Mrs. Agnes Sanford, cir. 1950

Contents

Figures | ix

Acknowledgements | xi

Introduction | 1

Part I: How Healing Prayer and the Gifts of the Spirit Went Missing

1 The Early Church: With the Spirit but without a Full Bible | 11

2 Orthodoxy, Heresy, and Revelation: The "Marcion Shove" | 24

3 The Augustinian Norm: The Church without the New Testament Gifts of the Spirit | 29

4 The Reformation and the Tragedy of Cessationism | 38

5 From Cessationism to Secularism | 49

6 Science as Meaning and Hope in Non-Christian Europe | 56

Part II: Clawing Out of Cessationism

7 Revivals and Opposition to Revivals | 69

8 Mary Baker Eddy Gives a Marcion Shove to the Healing Ministry | 80

9 New Thought: True Heresy? | 91

10 Quantum Physics and Christian Spirituality | 99

11 Visualization as Prayer | 112

Part III: The Rise of Christian New Perspective:
A Creative Explosion in Theology and Practice

12 The Anglican Healing Revival: A Proactive Response
    to Christian Science | 123

13 Glenn Clark: Recovering a Hebraic Perspective on
    Effective Prayer | 137

14 Glenn Clark's CFO: From Christian New Perspective
    to Pentecostalism | 155

Part IV: Agnes Sanford: Apostle of Healing

15 Discerning the Path of Christian Healing | 173

16 *The Healing Light*: A Theology of the Energies of God | 192

17 Harry and the Healing of Memories | 206

18 Theologian to the Charismatic Renewal | 221

19 First Theologian of Nature Miracles | 238

20 Two Ministries Carry On | 247

Part V: Reflections

21 Agnes Sanford as Controversial Theologian | 263

22 The Christian Healing Pioneers and the Wisdom of God | 274

23 The Villains of the Story: The Seminaries as Sanhedrin | 285

The Final Word: Jonathan Edwards on Agnes Sanford and
    Her Companions | 297

Bibliography | 303

Subject Index | 321

Figures

1   Prof. Glenn Clark | 169

2   The Rev. Frank Laubach | 169

3   Rufus Moseley | 170

4   The Rev. Ted Sanford, 1942 | 257

5   Agnes and Ted with their car, cir. 1958 | 257

6   Agnes Sanford in Arizona, 1953 | 258

7   Agnes Sanford at her home in Monrovia
with Judith MacNutt, cir. 1980 | 258

8   John and Paula Sandford with author at a
Florida CFO in 1984 | 259

9   Trinity Church Today | 259

10 The Healing Christ stained glass window at Trinity | 260

Acknowledgments

I WISH TO THANK my many Facebook friends who helped and prayed me through some of the difficult stages in the production of this work. Mrs. Susan Brooks Thomas was especially helpful in technical editing, which she did at no charge.

Introduction

AT THE HEIGHT OF World War II an attractive, dark-haired woman in a Gray Lady Red Cross uniform walked the corridors and wards of Tilton Army hospital in Fort Dix, New Jersey. Once a week this lady pushed a goodies cart filled with candy, comic books, and magazines for the wounded soldiers. [1] But she had an additional mission totally unrelated to candies and comics. She was looking for opportunities to pray for the wounded soldiers. She had to do it without attracting the attention of the medical staff. They considered healing prayer "unscientific" and cultic, and it was disallowed in the hospital. But the Gray Lady prowler had a plan. She would stop and engage in a conversation with a soldier and, if the coast was clear, place a copy of *Life* magazine over her hands as she discretely laid hands on and prayed over the soldier's wounds.

Why this Gray Lady had to be secretive about her healing ministry is part of the tragic history of cessationism, the theology that affirms that effective healing prayer ceased after the age of the apostles. Among Protestant mainline churches this erroneous and destructive theory reigned supreme. The hospital staff at Tilton, predominantly Christian, held to this belief, as practically all mainline Christians of the era.

Ironically, the Gray Lady in question was destined to become the most important woman for the revival of healing prayer among the very

---

1. The Gray Ladies were a volunteer service unit of the Red Cross formed during World War I to help at military hospitals in non-medical duties, such as writing letters for incapacitated soldiers and passing out candies and reading materials. They reemerged in World War II to do similar work. For more information on them, see www.redcross.org/museum/history/grayladies.asp

mainline denominations who disbelieved in such prayers. In fact, she and her companions led a great campaign against cessationism and for the restoration of healing prayer and deliverance in the churches. She was also to advocate for the restoration of the gifts of the Spirit which had been recovered by the Pentecostals. This Gray Lady, Mrs. Agnes Sanford, ultimately laid hands on thousands of persons for healing with miraculous effectiveness, not only at Tilton Army hospital, but at many church missions, OSL (Order of St. Luke) events, CFOs (Camps Furthest Out), and other healing events from the 1940s to the late 1970s.[2]

As time passes and it is easier to evaluate her work with historical perspective, it is clear that she was one of the most important and original theologians of the twentieth century. The list of her accomplishments in the field of theology and innovations in healing ministry is astounding.

1. Among the books she wrote on healing, several now stand as classics in the field, especially *The Healing Light* (1947) and *The Healing Gifts of the Spirit* (1966), both of which greatly impacted the early Charismatic Renewal.

2. *The Healing Light* was the first work of Western Christendom to seriously examine the energies of God and light of God as a normal presence and phenomenon for the Christian. Several writers in Eastern Orthodoxy had earlier described this phenomenon, but only as related to contemplative prayer.

3. She pioneered the ministry of inner healing prayer, and taught it to her disciples and companions in the many church healing missions, CFO camps, and OSL missions where she taught and ministered.

4. At a CFO camp she was introduced to Fr. Francis MacNutt, a Catholic Dominican priest. She subsequently discipled him in all that she had learned in healing, deliverance, and inner healing. MacNutt

2. Many of the persons she dramatically healed have passed away, but among those who are still living is the wife of Dean David Collins, Mrs. Ginny Collins. Dean Collins was for several years president of the Episcopal House of Deputies, and fought a "good fight" to keep the Episcopal Church orthodox. Back in 1953 Ginny broke a rib, and had additional severe back problems and pain, then found she was pregnant. Her doctor would not operate for fear of injuring the developing child. Mrs. Sanford laid her hands on Mrs. Collin's head, who then felt a jolt of energy fill her body. She was immediately healed of the back problem and broken rib, and the birth of her baby was an "easy delivery" some months later. A memo about this healing from Mrs. Collins is in the author's possession. The Collins were for years part of this author's home prayer group.

went on to become the principal theologian and writer on healing in the Catholic Charismatic Renewal, and thus passed on her theological legacy to the worldwide Catholic Charismatic Renewal.

5. Several years before the outbreak of the Charismatic Renewal, she and her husband founded the Schools of Pastoral Care, where ministers, priests, and lay leaders were instructed in healing prayer, deliverance/exorcism, inner healing prayer, and the gifts of the Spirit. None of these things were taught at the mainline seminaries of the time, and are often ignored even today. Many of the students taught by the Schools of Pastoral Care became leaders in the Charismatic Renewal, especially after it broke out publically in 1960.

6. At her retirement home in California, she developed and wrote about an active "nature ministry," as in stilling storms and praying for plants. This has been occasionally recorded in Christian history, as in the lives of some Celtic saints, but it was Mrs. Sanford's work *Creation Waits* (1978) that articulated the *first theology* of how to pray nature prayers.

In spite of these achievements, she and her work are not well known among the general Christian public, and there is no published biography of her.[3] This is partially by her own design. She wrote her autobiography, *Sealed Orders*, specifically to forestall misguided biographies about her and her work.[4]

Mrs. Sanford's relative obscurity today is due to several factors. One is that her theological writings, like that of her contemporary Pentecostal brethren, were simply written and based mostly on reflections on Scripture which were formed from comparisons and analogies to her experiences in prayer and the healing ministry. This is very different from the

---

3. Before the publication of this work, the closest thing to a biography of Agnes Sanford was a master's thesis done by Baltz, "Creative Intercessor." This work focuses on drawing out Mrs. Sanford's ties with the Episcopal Church. Fr. Baltz was the rector of St. Jude's Episcopal Church in Marietta, Georgia, where my wife, Carolyn, and I attended from 1983 to 2003.

4. Sanford, *Sealed Orders*. Agnes' intention of avoiding uninformed biographies was related to me in an interview with Dr. Howard Rhys and his wife, Margaret, at the University of the South at Sewanee, on August 13, 1983. Dr. Rhys served there as professor of the New Testament and Greek studies until his retirement. He had also served as the director of the Schools of Pastoral Care, an organization for teaching Christian healing that Agnes Sanford founded (see chapter 19). He and his wife were close friends of Agnes from the 1960s.

expectations people have as to what "serious" theology is supposed to be. These assumptions include that theology must be written by an academically credentialed person, have many comparisons and citations from other theological works, and include references to the latest philosophical trends.[5] Mrs. Sanford did none of this.

But perhaps the more important reason for her obscurity today is that even in her most influential period, 1950–1970, her theology was considered suspicious by many Christians. This stemmed from her theological influences, which included persons such as Emmet Fox and others of the New Thought Movement. For most Christians, New Thought was assumed to be equivalent to New Age and occultism. This was a simplification and wrong assumption, but was believed by many and destructive to Mrs. Sanford's reputation. Truly, Mrs. Sanford's New Thought influences were important in the formation of her theology, but as I labor to make clear in this work, that was *providential influence*. Such heterodox influences in forming new orthodox theology are recurrent events in church history. That is, in certain periods of impasse or theological dryness, the Holy Spirit uses unusual and unorthodox sources to shock and renew the church. I term this process the "Marcion Shove," after a second-century heretic who forced the church to consider that it had a New Testament and not just the Jewish Bible.

This reoccurring relation between heresy and orthodoxy is known in academic circles but *not* normally taught in adult Sunday schools. There, Christian history is most often taught in its sugar-coated version, with heroes and villains, plain and simple. Therefore, it is shocking to most Christians when unorthodox sources and influences are tied to a Christian author. This is what happened to Agnes Sanford with the publication of Dave Hunt's book *The Seduction of Christianity*, which appeared in 1986 and quickly became a runaway bestseller.

Mrs. Sanford's companions and colleagues, such as Professor Glenn Clark and Dr. John Gaynor Banks, both of whom labored to return effective healing to the church, also were influenced by New Thought writers. They developed theologies and parachurch institutions which were hugely important in bringing revival and renewed healing ministries to the mainline churches. Ironically, what they wrote and the institutions they built were often far more *biblically* orthodox and Christ-centered than many of their critics. I give the name Christian New Perspective to Mrs.

5. Smith, "Thinking in Tongues."

Sanford and her companions who traveled with her from New Thought theology to Pentecostalism in the 1950s, and into the Charismatic Renewal of the 1960s. Part III of this book examines the workers and writers of Christian New Perspective and how they laid the groundwork for Mrs. Sanford's theological innovations.

But first I have to take the reader on a truncated course of Christian history. This is done in parts I and II. Part I shows how it was that the New Testament church, which was filled by the Spirit and potent in its healing and deliverance ministry, became the anemic church of the fourth century. The post-third-century church lost its understanding of the gifts of the Spirit and stumbled on with a severely reduced healing ministry. Catholic, Eastern Orthodox, Oriental Orthodox (Coptic), and Protestant churchmen were all at fault in this. Catholics and Orthodox Christians believed that healing prayer was a rare privilege reserved for the very holy, or the responsibility of the saints in heaven. Later, Protestants affirmed that all attempts at healing prayer and exorcism in the church age were inappropriate, even heretical. Chapter 5 traces how disastrous these errors, fastened deep in tradition and theology, were to the church and Western civilization as a whole. Chapter 6 shows how the cultural elites shifted their attention and hope from Christianity to science and pseudosciences such as positivism and Marxism. At the same time, Christian theology, divested of its power to demonstrate the gospel in healings, signs, and wonders (Heb 2:1–4), became a mere parody of itself, as in the "death of God" theology of the 1960s.

Part II does two things. The first, in chapter 7, is to give a brief history of revivals to show that the Holy Spirit strove to bring the church out of its Holy Spirit gifts and healing ministry deficiency, and into the fullness of the New Testament church. Revivals were stymied by churchmen who acted either as biblical Pharisees, and opposed revival because it did not conform to the patterns of orthodox theology, or as Sadducees, who ridiculed and opposed revivals because they disbelieved in the supernatural. The second major theme deals with how the Holy Spirit worked around this blockage and opposition by a new Marcion Shove. Chapter 8 focuses on Mary Baker Eddy and her Christian Science Church as the new Marcionism. Chapter 9 describes its offshoot, and less extreme version, the New Thought movement. Both were heretical and dangerous to the church but, like Macion's theology, had elements of truth within it that the church needed. Chapter 10 shows how modern quantum physics points to the fact that Christian Science and New Thought idealism (mind defines and changes matter) had more truth to them than most Christians realized.

Part III, The Rise of Christian New Perspective, introduces Christian leaders and churchmen who understood that Christian Science and New Thought had something that orthodox Christianity was missing, and began probing and discerning the gap. Chapter 11 specifically highlights Anglican churchmen who established church clubs, called guilds, to bring effective healing prayer back into the churches. Chapters 12 and 13 study the work of Prof. Glenn Clark and his organization, the Camps Furthest Out (CFO), which was the epicenter of Christian New Perspective innovations and influence in America.

All of this sets the stage for the work and ministry of Mrs. Agnes Sanford in part IV. Like others in the Christian New Perspective, she was attracted to New Thought and proceeded with caution to discern its claims. Her work of discernment and journey to effective Christian healing is traced in chapter 14. Chapter 15 discusses her first book, *The Healing Light* (1947), which is the crowning work of Christian New Perspective. It was in this work that the theology of the energies and light of God enters Western Christian thought. Chapter 16 describes Mrs. Sanford's discovery of inner healing ministry. Two other chapters take the story of Mrs. Sanford's ministry to the time when she received the baptism of the Holy Spirit and her writing and ministry took a decidedly Pentecostal turn. This includes her revolutionary work on nature miracles, *Creation Waits* (1978). Chapter 19 highlights two major Christian leaders, the Rev. John Sandford and Dr. Francis MacNutt, who were discipled by Mrs. Sanford and went on to establish important healing and teaching ministries that continue to this day.

Part V reflects on the work and ministries of Mrs. Sanford and her companions. Their theological and ministry innovations are to this day renewing and reinvigorating the way Christians pray and minister. The reader will note that on several critical issues I quote the great Puritan theologian Jonathan Edwards. He was especially fruitful in his theology of discerning whether a movement in the church is truly from God. I allow his thoughts on that issue to be the final word about Mrs. Sanford and the leaders of Christian New Perspective.

My attempt in this book is to reach three audiences at the same time. The first is the general Christian reader who wishes to know more about healing prayer and how it was reintroduced into the church. The second audience is more specialized, and it includes religious leaders, seminary professors and seminarians, Bible students, etc. who are both curious about Mrs. Sanford's work and perhaps suspicious of it. The third audience includes those involved in various healing ministries and especially those who minister inner healing, including theophostic prayer. These specialists have long needed a work describing exactly how Mrs. Sanford came upon and developed inner healing. To serve these various Christian audiences, I have striven to keep the main text as simple and interesting as possible, while providing very ample notes so that the specialist or seminarian can corroborate and do further work on the areas touched by this book.

One last comment: This work barely mentions the *titanic* work of the early Pentecostals, whose pioneer healing ministries were concurrent with the persons from Christian New Perspective. These pioneers suffered unending ridicule and persecution by many in the mainline churches. My original plan for this book included several chapters on Pentecostalism and its heroes, but that would have made the work excessively large. Thankfully, Pentecostalism and its healing component have been well researched in the last decades by a bevy of competent and graced historians.[6] There is need for further research on the exact connections between Pentecostalism and Christian New Perspective, but I leave that to the future.

6. Bundy, "Global Phenomenon."

PART I

How Healing Prayer and the Gifts of the Spirit Went Missing

1

The Early Church

With the Spirit but without
a Full Bible

WHEN THE ROMAN EMPEROR Constantine issued his Edict of Milan in 313, and ended persecution against Christians, it radically changed the course of history. Within a generation Christianity became the established religion of the Roman Empire. Later historians, reflecting on the corrupt and superstitious state of the medieval church, have affirmed that Constantine's actions, and especially the later privileges given to Christianity, were a prime cause of the church's spiritual decline and corruption.[1] This may have some truth to it, but it is also evident that the church's spiritual weaknesses and superstitions, so widespread in medieval times, began earlier than the Edict of Milan.

In fact, many Christian communities of the first centuries did not fully understand or incorporate their true spiritual power or authority. Why this is so is not entirely clear and not well researched. But let me sketch out some reasons why this was so. One reason was that Christians did not have a developed and universally accepted New Testament. While the New Testament was substantially compiled by the end of the second century, there was some resistance to Paul's writings by a minority of bishops.[2] Some sections of the church were reluctant to accept the Book of Revelation, and others doubted the authority of the Pauline "Pastoral

---

1. Burkhardt, *Age of Constantine*. The famous anti-Christian historian Edward Gibbon, in his *Decline and Fall*, is especially scornful of the church's role after Constantine, but believed that the church ruined the empire, rather than that the empire ruined the church!

2. Means, *Ante-Nicene Church*.

Letters." More basically, there was confusion as to equating the New Testament writings with the Old Testament as fully inspired.

Further, there was a fog of sources and resources that the new Christian community had to deal with. This included a large intertestamental library of works, such as the *Book of Jubilees*, the *Ascension of Moses*, etc., that circulated among the early Jewish/Christian communities, and many believed they should be honored as Scripture.[3]

More confusing, several bogus gospels and epistles circulated that claimed to be written by various apostles. Many readers may already be familiar with the much publicized Gnostic *Gospel of Thomas*. In fact, that bogus gospel was quickly rejected by orthodox Christians. However, few are aware of another false gospel that greatly influenced Christian belief, the *Gospel of James*. This document, also referred to as the "Protoevangelium of James," was written as early as 150 by a person who had never been to the Holy Land, and certainly was not the James of the New Testament.[4] It claims to tell the story of Mary's childhood. In this account Mary was set aside as a child to be a temple virgin. Of course there was no such institution in Jerusalem, but the author invented it as a copy of the Roman Vestal Virgins which so influenced Roman spirituality. According to this bogus gospel, when Mary reached puberty she was removed from the temple virgins and Joseph was brought on as her caretaker, but he was too old to have sexual relations with her. This contradicts the plain reading of the canonical Gospels, which give the names of Jesus' younger brothers and cite other sisters of Jesus as born to Joseph and Mary (Matt 1:25; 13:56; Mark 6:3). Even though the *Gospel of James* was later officially rejected, it continued to circulate for centuries. Its distortion of biblical sexuality and its understanding of the Holy Family became widely accepted and not seriously challenged until well after the Reformation.

Further, there was another category of works, less outlandish, such as the *Epistle of Barnabas* and the *Shepherd of Hermes*, that circulated among orthodox communities and were considered by many as scriptural. The *Epistle of Barnabas* was particularly harmful, as it was deeply anti-Jewish. All of this is to say that because the early church did not have a clear, definitive New Testament, some things remained unclear, and others, such as Paul's understanding of the gifts of the Spirit, were

3. On the vast array of intertestamental literature, see Danielou, *Jewish Christianity.*

4. Widely available on the web, for instance, at the New Advent site, http://www.newadvent.org/fathers/0847.htm.

not given the full focus and attention they deserved. Christian leaders and churchmen of the first centuries sometimes stumbled into ideas, doctrines, and liturgical practices that hindered their full appropriation of miraculous gifts, spiritual authority, and effectiveness of the Christian as indicated in the ultimately unquestioned New Testament texts.[5]

The Holy Spirit and the New Testament Church

The New Testament pictures both Jesus' ministry on earth and the church's ministry after Jesus ascended into heaven as powerfully empowered by the Holy Spirit to do miraculous works. Jesus' public ministry began with his baptism by John, where he received the Holy Spirit "without measure" (Matt 3:13–17). After this event Jesus commissioned his apostles, and then his seventy-two disciples, to spread the good news. They and the apostles evangelized while ministering healings and the casting out of demons through the authority of their Master's name.

> As you go, preach this message: "The kingdom of heaven is near." Heal the sick, raise the dead, cleanse those who have leprosy, drive out demons. Freely you have received, freely give. (Matt 10:6–8)

It must be noted that the disciples had this power and authority even before the day of Pentecost and their special empowerment with the Spirit. Also, this commissioning was at the beginning of Jesus' ministry, when the apostles and disciples had an incomplete understanding of Jesus. Most of them considered him as a healing rabbi or a possible Messiah, and possibly a reincarnation of Elisha or another prophet (Matt 16:14), but certainly not the divine Son of God as revealed later.

Further, we can assume that the seventy-two disciples sent out at the beginning of Jesus' ministry (Luke 10) were at various levels of spiritual development. Regardless of their level of spiritual maturity, they all shared the disciples' authority to do the miraculous healings and exorcisms that made proclamation of the kingdom effective (Luke 10:19;

5. The issue of a less than a fully Spirit empowered early church has not been a hot topic among Christian writers and historians. Modern scholars have normally come from the evangelical or liberal persuasion, and would not focus on the issue of the missing gifts of the Spirit due to their theological assumptions. A notable exception is the fine work by the German scholar Campenhausen in his book *Ecclesiastical Authority*. Also useful is the article by Ash, "Ecstatic Prophecy." I am much indebted to these scholars for many of the insights of this chapter.

Matt 28:18–19; John 1:12). This is an important issue. In future centuries this "disciples' authority" would be blighted by the assumption that only those of advanced spiritual attainment, such as monks or other saintly persons, could minister healing or deliverance.

At the dramatic upper room Pentecost event (Acts 2), the disciples received the baptism in the Holy Spirit and were empowered to carry out the proclamation of the gospel with "signs and wonders" that went further than the disciples' authority to heal and cast out demons. The first manifestation of this empowerment was Peter's bold proclamation of Jesus as Lord to the Jewish pilgrims at Jerusalem. His message was miraculously understood by the bystanders in their separate native languages (Acts 2:1–13).

The apostles and disciples continued in coupling of the gospel proclamation with "signs and wonders" and gifts of the Spirit, including healings and resuscitations from the dead. Ananias of Damascus, a simple pious believer, laid hands on Paul and healed him of his blindness (Acts 9:10–18). We are told also that Stephen, the deacon of the Jerusalem church, "did great wonders and miraculous signs among the people" (Acts 6:8).

This gospel-with-miracles union was also central to Paul's ministry to his churches (1 Cor 2:4–5). All this was summarized by the writer of Hebrews, "This salvation, which was first announced by the Lord, was confirmed to us by those who heard him. God also testified to it by signs, wonders and various miracles, and gifts of the Holy Spirit distributed according to his will." (Heb 2:3–4). This included what Jesus had promised his disciples: "I tell you the truth, anyone who has faith in me will do what I have been doing. He will do even greater things than these, because I am going to the Father" (John 14:12).

Doing Theology without the Full Canon of the Scriptures

But a careful reading of the Book of Acts and the Epistles would show neither the nature miracles, such as stilling a storm, nor the miracles of food multiplication. Perhaps the answer to this gap lies in fact that many in the apostolic church did not understand that their disciples' authority extended beyond healing and exorcism. Also, it was Paul who boldly declared every believer to be united to Christ in his body and spiritually blessed and empowered (Eph 1:3). His two prayers for the Christian in the Letter to the Ephesians, (1:16–22, and 3:14–19), combined with his description to his church in Corinth in 1 Corinthians 12–14, give us a portrait of a fully Spirit-empowered Christian community, ministering in the same gifts that came upon the disciples and apostles at Pentecost. But, as we pointed out, Paul's writings were not immediately accepted as Scripture.

The lack of an accepted New Testament weakened the commission of the post-apostolic church to do all that Jesus and the early disciples had done. The four Gospels were circulated quite early among Christians, but were at first seen more as "memory joggers" to the oral proclamation for itinerant evangelists rather than as Scripture. In fact, in the Syrian church, a major component of the early church, the four Gospels were cut down and combined to be more "convenient"—the original "Reader's Digest" Bible.[6]

Paul's letters were written before the destruction of the temple in A.D. 70 and circulated before 150. His letters had been collected, edited, and copied in the "codex" format, and these were then more widely circulated, but not immediately recognized as inspired Scripture. A codex was the early form of a book. It was done on papyrus sheets, the cheap writing medium of the times. This signified convenience, but non-permanence. The Old Testament scriptures, on the other hand, were copied on prepared animal skins and made into rolls. This was expensive, but also signified definite divine inspiration. Thus, for instance, John the Revelator was told at the beginning of his vision on the island of Patmos to "Write on a *scroll* what you see and send it to the seven churches . . ." (Rev 1:11, italics added).

By the time of the Council of Nicaea (325), Paul's epistles were formally and universally accepted by the church as inspirited and worthy of being called Scripture. Before that, a minority faction affirmed that Paul's letters were not fully inspired. Some bishops argued that Paul's letters could not be inspired Scripture because they were written in the common "market" Greek and were inelegant, with awful run-on sentences, etc.[7] Other critics argued that many Gnostic heretics loved Paul's writings, and if these heretics liked his writings so much there must be something wrong with them! Perhaps Paul's accent on visions and spiritual gifts was

6. The "Diatessaron," which was edited and compiled by Tatian the Assyrian (120–80). This work was a major source for the Syrian church until the fifth century. See Schmid, "In Search."

7. Means, *Saint Paul.*

not safe?[8] As we shall see later, it took a heretical challenge to finally force the church to declare that, in spite of their stylistic faults and "mysticism," Paul's letters were indeed Scripture.

The "First Draft" Theology of the Gifts of the Spirit

Thus the earliest theology about the gifts of the Spirit, healing/exorcism, and the spiritual authority of the believer was formed by what could be learned from the oral traditions of the apostles, the direct and varied experiences of the early church with the Holy Spirit, the circulation of some New Testament writings, and other non-canonical writings, and from the Old Testament. The gifts of the Spirit as described in Isaiah 11:2 were particularly important to the early church, as everyone was sure that was Scripture: "And the Spirit of the Lord will rest on Him, the spirit of wisdom and understanding, the spirit of counsel and strength, the spirit of knowledge and the fear of the Lord." For instance, the writings of Justin Martyr (100–165), one of the earliest apologists of the church, explain the gifts of the Spirit in a mix of Isaiah's understanding plus a few that Paul mentions.

> [Christians] are also receiving gifts, each as he is worthy, illuminated through the name of this Christ. For one receives the spirit of understanding, another of counsel, another of strength, another of healing, another of foreknowledge, another of teaching, and another of the fear of God.[9]

The gifts of understanding, counsel, strength, and fear of God seem to be based on the eleventh chapter of Isaiah. The gifts of healing, foreknowledge, and teaching correspond to gifts in Paul's lists, and perhaps the gifts of understanding and counsel might correspond to Paul's mention of the word of wisdom.[10]

But Justin's mix of a New and Old Testament understanding of the gifts of the Spirit was not as universally accepted as it should have been. Unfortunately an Old Testament understanding of the gifts of the Spirit emerged by the third century and reigned supreme until recent times. It is the primary understanding of the gifts of the Spirit in the Roman

8. On the Gnostics' love of Paul's writings, see Pagel, *Gnostic Paul.*

9. Justin Martyr, *Dialogue with Trypho*, section 39.

10. See Kydd, *Charismatic Gifts*, 26–27, for more discussion on this passage in Justin.

Catholic, Eastern Orthodox, and Oriental Orthodox churches. For instance, the Catholic Baltimore Catechism, which was the catechism of American Catholicism for generations was used to prepare children for their first Holy Communion and Confirmation into the 1970s, stated:

> Which are the gifts of the Holy Ghost? The gifts of the Holy Ghost are Wisdom, Understanding, Counsel, Fortitude, Knowledge, Piety and the Fear of the Lord.[11]

This is really unfortunate since, unlike Justin, this list does not include any hint of the New Testament gifts. This shows that the traditional theology on the gifts, formed before Paul's authority was fully accepted, was carried forward by the momentum of "churchodoxy" and uncorrected. Traditional Protestantism has not done any better. With the concept of cessationism, which became central to a majority of Protestantism (see chapter 5), the gifts of the Spirit were relegated to the historical past.

The Galatian Bewitchment

But now back to the early church and Justin (quoted above). Note that Justin incorrectly associated the gifts of the Spirit with human merit: ". . . each as he is worthy." This misunderstanding, that the gifts of the Spirit are to be *earned*, is very natural to human thinking about humanity's relationship with God. We tend to believe of God what is true in human relationships: that we must be "good" to be worthy of a gift. But that is not the gospel, neither in reference to the gift of salvation, nor to the disciples' authority to heal and cast out demons, nor to the gifts of the Sprit. Paul warned his Galatian congregation of falling into this error:

> You foolish Galatians, who has bewitched you . . . ? This is the only thing I want to find out from you: did you receive the Spirit by the works of the Law, or by hearing with faith? Are you so foolish? Having begun by the Spirit, are you now being perfected by the flesh? (Gal 3:1–3)

---

11. Question 177 in the third *Baltimore Catechism*, available online at http://www.catholicity.com/baltimore-catechism. Even the current catechism, issued in 1997, *after* the Catholic Church had experienced thirty years of the Charismatic Renewal, is not much better. It cites Isaiah 11 in full, and discusses "Pentecost" in the church as a historical event, but does not mention Paul and the gifts listed in 1 Cor 12 and 14. See http://www.scborromeo.org/ccc.htm.

To be clear, this is not being critical of Justin. He really was one of the great figures of the early church. But Justin's understandable mistake was repeated many times and many ways by theologians of the early, medieval, and modern church. They had less excuse, as after the fourth century there was much less of the "fog of sources" to confuse Christian writers and theologians. They all had the fully formed Bible with Paul's letters before them. Let us call this belief that spiritual gifts come from merit by its biblical label, the Galatian "Bewitchment."[12]

Healing as Evangelism in the Early Church

Another great hero/saint of the early church was Irenaeus (130–200), martyr and bishop of Lyons. He gives us a clear picture that the early church maintained and practiced the disciples' authority of healing and exorcism widely. Irenaeus had access to Paul's letters and understood the gifts of the Spirit as gifts, and correctly coupled them with evangelization.

> Those who are in truth His disciples, receiving grace from Him, do in His name perform miracles, so as to promote the welfare of other men, according to the gift which each one has received from Him. For some do certainly and truly drive out devils, so that those who have thus been cleansed from evil spirits frequently both believe in Christ and join themselves to the Church . . . others still, heal the sick by laying their hands upon them, and they are made whole.[13]

This was an improvement over Justin, but unfortunately one that was not sustained by the church as a whole. Rather, the thrust of the early church, in the first apologists and theologians, was to stress the use of reason and philosophy in conversion, rather than demonstration of the power of God. To be clear, it is important to give good reasons for one's belief in Christ, as the apostle Peter wrote, "But in your hearts revere Christ as Lord. Always be prepared to give an answer to everyone who

12. We need to note that modern translators mostly use the word *bewitchment* for the Greek *ebaskanen*, which literally means to have received an "evil eye." Paul is saying that the Galatians are in spiritual confusion due to the "evil eye" of the false apostles who have shadowed his ministry and countered the true gospel of grace with that of legalism. Moderns, including translators, don't like to admit that Paul would have believed in such a "superstitious" thing, and prefer milder translations such as "bewitchment." On this, see Elliot, "Evil Eye."

13. Ireneus, *Against Heresies*, cited Frost, *Christian Healing*, 104.

asks you to give the reason for the hope that you have. But do this with gentleness and respect" (1 Pet 3:15). But a good reason without a demonstration of the power of God is itself an unbalanced Gospel (Heb 2:1-4).

The Galatian Bewitchment as Model Theology: Monasticism

The Galatian Bewitchment almost reached the status of an official doctrine with the development of Christian monasticism. This movement was birthed with the life of St. Anthony of the desert (251–356). In truth, monks were often baptized in the Holy Spirit, though they did not use that vocabulary. This happened through persistent, laborious prayer, much in the manner of the Old Testament prophets (Matt 11:12).[14] As Christians, they had the disciples' authority for healing and exorcism. The laypersons who came to them for spiritual advice or healing were astounded that these holy men could heal and cast out demons. But because the Galatian Bewitchment was already universally accepted, these laypersons did not understand that they had the same authority, or that persons in their own parishes had similar but hidden spiritual gifts.

Unfortunately the early monastic movement was also captivated by the Stoic concept that pain and illness were to be accepted bravely, and without striving for healing. To be fair, a few Scripture verses could be cited to support this, as in Paul's "thorn in the flesh" (2 Cor 12:7). In addition, it is central to the Christian Scriptures that every believer take up a cross and share the sufferings of Christ (Matt 8:34; 2 Cor 1:5–7; Phil 3:10). However, an absolute connection was made between the sufferings brought on by illness and the believer's sharing of Christ's sufferings. This concept of illness as redemptive suffering subordinated the many Scripture passages which showed that illness was brought on by demonic oppression and an evil to be countered by the church's ministry (Luke 13:16, for example).

As a result, monks were willing to pray for healing for the visitors who came to them, but they were not anxious to receive healing prayer

14. That many monks and nuns have had the spiritual gifts is witnessed to by the work of the renowned dean of Pentecostal historical scholarship Dr. Vinson Synan. As a boy he was brought up to believe that the Catholic Church was the "whore of Babylon." But along the way to his PhD in church history he did a careful study of medieval Catholic literature. Dr. Synan came to understand that prevailing prayer of the monks and nuns in the monasteries was the normal way of receiving the baptism of the Spirit until the advent of Pentecostalism. See Synan, "Mystical Tradition."

for themselves. One of the great healer monks, Benjamin of Nitria, suffered a long and painful illness from dropsy but refused healing prayers so that he might partake of the sufferings of Christ.[15] In essence, the monks inverted the Scriptures, making the normative biblical attitude toward healing the exception, and the exception, redemptive suffering, the normative. This inversion was passed on to subsequent Christian theology. It became the perfect alibi for those Christians who lost their faith expectancy for healing prayer. All illness could then be assumed to be from the Lord and for the purpose of redemptive suffering.[16]

Even more of a distortion of the Bible was the confusion that holiness was to be acquired through ascetical practices. This was the Galatian Bewitchment in its extreme form. This was plain in the writings of Athanasius (296–373), bishop of Alexandria and defender of Trinitarian theology. He wrote an immensely influential biography of St. Anthony. In it he lauds Anthony for his stern ascetical practices, his constant fasting, etc., including the fact that he never bathed or washed his feet.[17]

Humility Trumps the Spiritual Gifts

Anthony warned his fellow monks not to be puffed up with pride because of their spiritual gifts, which is a valid point.[18] However, this warning became a central theme of subsequent monastic literature. This was stressed by John Cassian (360–435). Cassian visited and lived in several monasteries in Egypt and Syria and then founded the first monasteries in Europe on those models. Cassian's sermons and discourses on the spiritual life, *The Conferences*, laid the foundations of European monastic theology. One of his conferences was on the gifts of the Spirit and healing/deliverance.

> Finally, the Author Himself of all miracles and mighty works, when He called His disciples to learn His teaching, clearly showed what those true and specially chosen followers ought

15. Palladius, *Lausiac History*, section 12.

16. Frost, *Christian Healing*, 189.

17. Athanasius, *Life of Antony*, ch. 47. The "virtue" of not bathing was called *alousia*. On the issue of cleanliness and the Christian, and how the Puritans restored sanity to this issue, see Winner, "Cleanliness and Godliness."

18. Athanasius, *Life*, chapter 38. Indeed many modern Pentecostal and charismatic ministers have fallen into vainglory through being impressed by their gifting in healing and the other spiritual gifts.

chiefly to learn from Him, saying: "Come and learn of Me," not chiefly to cast out devils by the power of heaven, not to cleanse the lepers, not to give sight to the blind, not to raise the dead: for even though I do these things by some of My servants, yet man's estate cannot insert itself into the praises of God, nor can a minister and servant gather hereby any portion for himself there where is the glory of Deity alone. But do ye, says He, learn this of Me, "for I am meek and lowly of heart." For this it is which it is possible for all men generally to learn and practice, but the working of miracles and signs is not always necessary, nor good for all, nor granted to all. Humility therefore is the mistress of all virtues, it is the surest foundation of the heavenly building, it is the special and splendid gift of the Savior.[19]

Although Cassian affirmed the reality of miracles and supernatural signs, his teaching watered down the plain biblical understanding of the gifts.[20] Paul urged that Christians should be ambitious to receive them (1 Cor 14:1) and that the gifts were for the corporate good of the Christian community (1Cor 14: 1; 1 Cor 12: 7). Similarly 1 Peter 4:10 declares, "As each one has received a special gift, employ it in serving one another, as good stewards of the manifold grace of God." Little of this made it in Cassian's writings or in monastic theology.

Cassian's gifts-cautious theology was accepted as orthodox and spread through the new monasteries in the Latin church of the West. More than a thousand years later, his gift-cautious theology was codified and reinforced by the famous Spanish mystic St. John of the Cross (1542–1591). St. John was given the title "Doctor of the Church" by the Catholic Church, and like Cassian taught that any spiritual manifestations, such as visions or gifts of healing or prophetic utterance, would *endanger* the believer's quest for spiritual perfection.[21]

In the Eastern branch of Christianity, what became the Greek Orthodox Church and the national churches it spawned, the gifts of the Spirit and healing/deliverance had a different route to marginalization. Several of the fathers of the Eastern church had strong biblical views of

19. John Cassian, *Conferences*, no. 15, online at http://www.newadvent.org/fathers/350815.htm.

20. To my knowledge, the Episcopal priest and scholar Morton Kelsey was the first person to seriously challenge Cassian on his theology of the gifts. See his *Healing and Christianity*, ch. 8, "Healing in the Victorious Church." This work is a pioneer classic of the charismatic movement.

21. See especially his *Mount Carmel.*

the importance of the gifts.[22] Gregory of Nyssa (336–394), perhaps the greatest of the Eastern fathers, was especially clear in his understanding and encouragement of the gifts of the Spirit as belonging to the Christian community.

But again the Galatian Bewitchment asserted itself. For Gregory of Nyssa the gifts were not understood as gifts, but as the *rewards* of a sanctified life, with an eye to "perfection," and again without Paul's understanding of the gifts as essential to the Christian community.

> . . . even if someone receives the gifts which the Spirit furnishes (I mean the tongues of angels and prophecy and knowledge and the grace of healing), but has never been entirely cleansed of the troubling passions within him through the charity of the Spirit . . . he is still in danger of failing if he does not keep charity steadfast and first among his virtues.[23]

With time, the gifts of the Spirit became restricted to those in the monastic life as a sign of great holiness.[24] Thus, in the church, both East and West, the gifts of the Spirit and healing were shut off from the daily life of the parish life and from ordinary laypersons.[25] To be clear, the gifts of the Spirit and healing/exorcism did continue in the Catholic, Oriental Orthodox, and Eastern Orthodox Churches throughout their history, but they were limited mostly to the clergy or members of religious orders.

As witness to the terrible blight this brought on to the church, let me quote but one instance of many that could be cited. The Rev. Dr. Francis MacNutt, now recognized as one of the founders of the Catholic Charismatic Renewal, and one of its principal healing theologians (see chapter 19), recalled from his pre-charismatic days:

> . . . when I entered the Dominican Order and read the lives of the saints with all the fervor of the novitiate days, I couldn't help but wonder why they seemed to have so much success going around healing the sick through their prayers, while we were never encouraged to pray for such things. We got the impression

22. Stephanou, "Early Church." This article was written at the dawn of the Charismatic Renewal. The author, a Greek Orthodox priest, rightfully shows that the gifts of the Spirit were foundational to Orthodoxy theology, and looked forward to a general renovation for the Orthodoxy churches by the Holy Spirit. That did not happen. The renewal was suppressed by the Orthodox hierarchy and labeled heretical.

23. Gregory of Nyssa, *Mode of Life*, 131.

24. McDonnell, *Christian Initiation*, 252, 321.

25. Stephonou, "Early Church," 142.

that praying for healing was presumptions, like pretending to be a saint—which I certainly was not. We were not worthy of extraordinary manifestations of God's power.[26]

Fr. MacNutt had to learn effective healing prayer from Mrs. Sanford and Protestant charismatics such as the Rev. Tommy Tyson later in his life. This echoes an experience in my family that happened in the early 1970s. I took my mother to a conference on healing where she received that gift, and helped pray for and heal several persons while she stayed with me in Georgia. On her return to Puerto Rico, she attempted to lay hands on and heal her ailing aunt, a very traditional Catholic, who rebuffed her as presumptuous. She felt humiliated by this rebuke, and it was several years before she again prayed for anyone for healing.

26. MacNutt, *Healing*, 10.

2

Orthodoxy, Heresy, and Revelation

The "Marcion Shove"

IN THIS CHAPTER[1] WE need to discuss a controversial topic: God's sovereign use of non-believers and heretics to further revelation or to correct the people of God from their errors.[2] Many Christians assume that God and his Spirit speak only through his chosen people: prophets in the Old Testament and orthodox Christians in the church age. In fact, it is the heathen or the heretics who at times have the first word about a spiritual situation or issue.

Just one biblical example among many is the incident of a heathen king speaking and working the will of God, described in 2 Chronicles 35 and 2 Kings 23. Josiah, king of Judah, drove out the mediums, ended every form of idolatrous worship in his kingdom, and repaired the temple. He was one of the great righteous kings of the Old Testament. Scripture says, "And before him there was no king like him who turned to the Lord with all his heart and with all his soul and with all his might, according to all the law of Moses; nor did any like him arise after him" (2 Kgs 23:25).

However, his reign ended before its time because he did not stop to discern the voice of the Lord. Neco, pharaoh of Egypt (a pagan and an idolater), was at war with Babylon and requested safe passage for his army through Judah. Josiah had his hackles raised and, without consulting the Lord, challenged Neco's intrusion. Neco assured Josiah that God had sent him to fight the Babylonians, not the Jews.

---

1. This chapter is modified and expanded from chapter 13 in *Quenching the Spirit*, "What Does a Heretic Know About Truth?"

2. The best work on both the destructive and creative role of heresy is Brown, *Heresies*. See also the insightful article by Einar, "Orthodoxy and Heresy."

But as Scripture records, Josiah did not "listen to the words of Neco from the mouth of God, but came to make war on the plain of Megiddo" (2 Chr 35:22). As a result, Josiah lost his life in battle, and the crown of Judah passed on to an ungodly king who returned to idolatry. The godly king did not discern the providential task of the Egyptian Pharaoh, who had in fact correctly heard the voice of God.

The New Testament echoes this irony of revelation in the history of Josiah and Neco. Those who were especially waiting for the Messiah, the Pharisees, and therefore should have received Jesus, did not. Many Gentiles, whose minds were on other matters, received and proclaimed him. Throughout the Gospels it was often the heathen, such as Roman centurions or the Canaanite woman with the demon-possessed child, who had the strongest faith in Jesus, while most of the Jewish religious leaders remained skeptical. For instance, it was a Roman centurion at the crucifixion who blurted out, "Surely this was the son of God!" (Matt 27:54).

New Testament writers were not reluctant to affirm the truth of God when it was discussed in heathen sources. Paul began his speech to the Gentile crowds in Athens by quoting their own poets (Acts 17:22–28). In this case Paul understood that the Greeks' natural theology could be a starting point for the gospel. A quotation in the letter to Titus (1:12) comes from the Oracles of Memander. In these cases Paul was not concerned about the pagan origins of the sayings; rather he used whatever truth there was in them and incorporated them to spread the gospel.

Revelation and Heresy in the Church Era

Christians are generally comfortable with the idea that God still speaks to the church through an occasional prophet. Most Christians would agree, for example, that the reformer Martin Luther was a prophet to the church of the 1500s, or that Martin Luther King Jr. was a prophet of the twentieth century. From our perspective, these individuals were correct about foundational issues, though their shortsighted contemporaries often ridiculed them as deviant. Indeed, what marks a prophet is the sound (orthodox) doctrine he derives from both the spirit and the letter of biblical revelation. In contrast, many churchgoers and clergy often hold a more comfortable and superficial view of what is orthodox, believing orthodoxy to be equivalent to their current group or denominational creed. I call this "churchadoxy."

At times, heretics in the church era have played a similar role to the truth-bearing heathen in biblical times. They have been used by God when the majority of Christians have been too stubborn and comfortable in their churchadoxy. Dr. Harold O.J. Brown, professor at Reformed Theological Seminary in Jackson, Mississippi, demonstrated in his now classic book, *Heresies: The Image of Christ in the Mirror of Orthodoxy and Heresy From the Apostles to the Present*, just how extensively heretics have forced the church into the discovery of its deepest truths.[3] Specifically, many of the great doctrines of the church were forged as responses to initial heresies, and most often incorporated fragments of truth first brought to light in non-biblical ideas.

For instance, from the second century the person of Jesus was subject to all sorts of explanations. Among the most damaging and erroneous was the explanation of the Docetists, who believed that Jesus was a ghost-like being, not an incarnate person. Some claimed that Jesus was God but not man, or inversely, man but not God. In any case, these fragmented views forced the church to think about the person of Jesus and to come to its scripturally balanced understanding of Jesus as God-man.[4]

Marcion as Heretic and Prophet

Perhaps the most important example of this "heresy proceeds orthodoxy" process occurred in the development of the Christian Bible. During the first centuries of the church most bishops were content to consider the Old Testament as the church's Bible, and entertain the Gospels and Epistles as "good reading" but not as Scripture equivalent to the Old Testament. A heretical movement led by Marcion of Sinope (c. 85–160) forced the church to understand that there was indeed a new body of Scripture—the New Testament.[5]

3. Brown, *Heresies*. Dr. Brown received a PhD from Harvard in Reformation studies and served many years as professor of systematic theology at Trinity Evangelical Divinity School, one of the great evangelical institutions of America. Brown's central thesis, that heresy precedes and leads to orthodoxy, is explained in less technical terms in the recent book by Gonzales, *Armchair Theologians*.

4. Brown's insight is that heresy at times precedes orthodoxy was not entirely original. This process was studied before him by the Catholic monk-theologian Dom Odo Casel. Casel calls the relationship between heresy and truth "shadow truth," that is, heresy is like a shadow that comes before the arrival of the real. See Casel, *Christian Worship*.

5. A good introduction to the difficult relationship between Marcion and our

Marcion's theology was both destructive and insightful. It was destructive and truly heretical in a cluster of ideas. He believed that the Old Testament was not Scripture. He believed that the God of the Old Testament was a "lesser god"—a platonic "daemon," or demigod. It was this god that created the material order. For Marcion, the material world, including all sexuality, was an evil entrapment. Members of his congregation had to pledge to celibacy as a way of escaping the world's sensual enticements.

To affirm his point that the god of the Old Testament was a mere daemon, Marcion cited the instances in the Old Testament when the Lord commanded the slaughter of various Canaanite peoples, including women and children (as in Deut 7:1–2.) Indeed, this is an issue that troubles many to this day. Thus for Marcion, the god of the Old Testament could not be the same loving "Father" of Jesus.[6]

On the other hand, Marcion believed the true Scriptures, the real and only Bible, were made up of the Gospel of Luke and the letters of Paul. Further, believing that the Holy Spirit inspired him, he edited Paul's letters and Luke's Gospel to exclude any positive connections between Christianity and Judaism. He believed the Jews to be the creation of the daemon of the Old Testament and not worthy of respect. Marcion was the great anti-Semite of his age. All of this made Macion truly a dangerous heretic.

But notice that Marcion had a firm hold of an important truth before the rest of the church. The letters of Paul were indeed Scripture, and the church did indeed need to recognize the New Testament. Further, as the great historian of the early church Adolf von Harnack noted, Marcion had a better understanding of justification by faith in Jesus than most of his orthodox contemporaries. His stress on Paul's letters led naturally to this. He was, in a sense, the Martin Luther of the early church.[7] Thus, Marcion was both dangerously mistaken but also insightful and prophetic—*at the same time.*

Bible is Miller's article "Our Bible."

6. Significantly, this argument is voiced by many liberal theologians who may not go as far as Marcion but functionally dismiss the Old Testament as irrelevant to Christian life. See Gussai, "Old Testament." Note also the excellent trilogy of articles on this difficult issue of God insisting on the elimination of the Canaanites in the July/August 2013 issue of *Christianity Today.*

7. Harnack, *Marcion.* Some scholars have argued that the writer of the Pastoral Epistles (1 and 2 Timothy and Titus) was similarly a "pre-Marcion" in so far as the Old Testament has little relevance for the Christian. See Wolfe, "Pastoral Epistles."

The more orthodox bishops and the rest of the church were right about the Old Testament as Scripture, but they were also slow in accepting Paul and the rest of the New Testament writings as equally inspired. Both sides were partially right and partially wrong. As it worked out, in combating Marcion's opinion about the Old Testament, the church hastened its dialogue about the role of these new "good readings" and eventually accepted Marcion's basic position on Paul.

An acceptance of Marcion's whole system would have had devastating consequences on the church, both theological and practical. Without the Old Testament sense of law, righteous behavior would have been impossible to discern or establish. And with his sexual policy the church would have faded into oblivion, much like the nineteenth-century Shakers. In summary, Marcion's heresy gave the orthodox bishops a "shove" into doing what they should have done: accept the reality of the New Testament.

3

The Augustinian Norm

*The Church without the New Testament
Gifts of the Spirit*

St. Augustine of Hippo (354–430)

PERHAPS THE MOST IMPORTANT figure in the formation of Western theology was St. Augustine, bishop of Hippo (now called Annaba, in Algeria).[1] Augustine not only sketched out what became orthodox Roman Catholic theology, but his writings were read and revered by Martin Luther, John Calvin, and other Protestant reformers. In a sense, he is the father of both Catholic and Protestant theology.

Augustine was raised a Christian and educated in the Hellenistic and Roman learning of his day. He showed special talents in literature and philosophy. He was especially influenced by the philosophy of Neo-Platonism and its leading proponent, Plotinus. This philosophy stressed an otherworldly form of philosophical spirituality, with rituals and magical forms to enable the seeker to separate from the attachments of the senses and unite with the "One," i.e., God. As a young man Augustine also explored several non-Christian cults, and settled into the Manichaean religion and a sexually permissive life. Providentially, he experienced a dramatic conversion and returned to the religion of his childhood.

Augustine then dedicated all of his classical learning and talents to the service of Christianity. Augustine made many original contributions to Christian theology, including his massive work on the Trinity, which became the reference point for Western orthodoxy on this topic. This

---

1. This chapter is expanded and modified from chapter 5, "Truth and Error in the Catholic Ministry of Healing," in *Quenching the Spirit*.

work focused on the persons of the Godhead and their relationship with each other—important issues indeed. Unfortunately, he followed the earlier tradition of the church and understood the gifts of the Spirit in terms of Isaiah 11:2. In Augustine's work *On the Sermon On the Mount*, he drew parallels between the gifts of the Spirit according to Isaiah and the Beatitudes of the Sermon on the Mount. Nowhere in this or his other writings are the gifts discussed in reference to Paul's description or how they operate in the Christian community.[2]

Augustine's Theology of Healing

Augustine's early writings dismissed the ministry of healing as improper for Christians. In one of his first books, *On the True Religion*, he wrote with typical philosophical conceit, "These [healing] miracles were not allowed to last until our times lest the soul [of the believer] ever seek visible things and the human race grow cold because of familiarity with those things whose novelty enkindled it."[3] Similarly, in another early work Augustine reasoned that the Gospel miracles were performed to give Jesus the public authority that was necessary to convince the multitude.[4] This implied that more philosophical or "spiritual" Christians had no need of miraculous evidence—again a negation of Hebrews 2:1–4.

This belief that miracles and the healing ministry ceased after biblical times is called cessationism. In this view the purpose of miracles was to authenticate the authority of the Old Testament prophets, or Jesus and his apostles. Missing in cessationist theology is an understanding of healing as a sign of God's compassion or the miraculous as a mark of the kingdom (Mark 8:2; Luke 9:1–2). The idea of cessationism originated well before Augustine. It can be traced to Jewish rabbinical commentaries that preceded the Christian era. Some rabbis were concerned that since the times of Haggai, Zechariah, and Malachi there had not been an authentic prophet in Israel. Several ideas were proposed to explain why this was so, such as the lack of piety among the population. In the second century some Christian writers used this rabbinical speculation to assert that the Holy Spirit had been withdrawn from the Jews and passed on

2. Augustine, *Sermon on the Mount*.

3. Augustine, *On True Religion*, 25, 47.

4. See Kelsey's excellent study of Augustine's healing theology in his *Healing and Christianity*, ch. 8, "Healing in the Victorious Church."

to the Christians.[5] By the third century a few Christian apologists used cessationism as an explanation for the apparent *rarity* of healing miracles and gifts of the Spirit in the Christian community. Augustine adopted this view as a new Christian and maintained it most of his life.

However, about six years before he died Augustine rejected cessationism. This happened when he noted that a young man afflicted by epilepsy was miraculously healed at the beginning of an Easter service at his church. That caused him to investigate other reports of healings.[6] By the time he came to write his last works, *City of God* and *The Retractions*, he enthusiastically affirmed the continued healing ministry of the church. In *The Retractions* he explained that miracles were still common in the Christian community, although he had not seen some of the more spectacular miracles of the apostolic age, such as people healed by the mere shadow of an apostle (Acts 5:15): "I myself had recently learned that a blind man had been restored to sight in Milan . . . and I know about some others, so numerous even in these times, that we cannot know about all of them nor enumerate those we know."[7]

Augustine's final theology of healing is found in *The City of God*, completed four years before his death. He describes the healing ministry that flowered in his diocese after his acceptance of healing prayer. From his personal experience he speculated on how cessationism crept into Christian writings. Christians were shy about telling of their own healings, believing it a matter of humility. Thus, although everyone knew the Gospel accounts of healing, few heard of their own neighbors' healings. As bishop he determined to remedy this and insisted that persons miraculously healed give a witness in church. Two years before he wrote the *City of God* he began a record of healing miracles within his diocese. In that short time seventy healings were recorded. Augustine only wrote about those healings he could personally verify. Several occurred during the administration of baptism, including complete healings from hernia and gout. In one case a woman with advanced breast cancer had a dream in which she was told to go to the next baptismal service and have a newly baptized person pray for her. She did so and was instantly healed of the cancer.[8]

---

5. Greenspan, "Prophecy Ceased."

6. Kelsey, *Healing and Christianity*, 186–87.

7. Augustine, *Retractions*, 1.11.7.

8. Augustine, *City of God*, 22.8.

The Philosophical Distortion of the Healing Ministry

But Augustine also believed in the healing power of relics to evoke the intercessory powers of martyred saints. This type of petition was the major element in his theology of healing. In several churches of North Africa the divided bones of St. Stephen, the martyr of Acts 7, were believed to have been interred, and were the subject of veneration and pilgrimages.[9] The evangelical[10] reader would find this aspect of Augustine's theology to be superstitious, or more pagan than Christian. In reality, the idea of relics is *partially true and partially wrong*. It is an exaggeration of a scriptural truth by way of classical Greek philosophy.

Many passages in the Bible show how the power and energy of God can flow through matter, especially cloth and clothing. One of the clearest examples is God's instruction to Ezekiel about the rite of the temple, specifically about the duties of the priests as they exit the sanctuary.

> And it shall be that when they enter at the gates of the inner court, they shall be clothed with linen garments...And when they go out into the outer court, into the outer court to the people, they shall put off their garments in which they have been ministering and lay them in the holy chambers; then they shall put on other garments that they may not transmit holiness to the people with their garments (Ezek 44:17–19)

The fact that touching a spiritually charged garment can release spiritual energy/power to sanctify was repeated in the well-known New Testament story of the woman with the issue of blood (Luke 8:42–48). It is especially instructive that Jesus felt "power" leave him when the ill woman touched him: "But Jesus said, "Someone touched me; I know that power has gone out from me" (v. 46). Also, in Acts 19:11–12 Paul's aprons and handkerchiefs contained so much of God's power that they were taken to the sick for healing and exorcism.

Augustine's belief in the healing power of Stephen's bones was understandable based on these scriptures, but especially on an incident described in 2 Kings 13. In that incident Elisha the prophet had died, and his bones

---

9. On the very early cult of St. Stephen, see Bovon, "Christian Martyr."

10. "Evangelical" has a broad meaning today, but here I am using it in the context of its opposite, liberal Christianity. Evangelicals consider the Bible as inspired by God and truthful, believe that the miracles and supernatural events described really happened, and hold that a person must come into a personal relationship with Jesus ("born again") to be truly Christian.

lay exposed in a pit. A burial party passed by but was suddenly attacked by marauders, and the body of the dead man was dumped into Elisha's pit. When the man's body hit the prophet's bones the man came back to life (2 Kgs 13:20–21). Elisha's bones had retained God's energies, and this was discharged as the body of the dead man touched it. Augustine assumed that the bones of Stephen would have similar healing qualities.

From a purely biblical perspective, Augustine's assumption was possible. However, a flaw in his philosophical assumptions allowed a valid biblical truth—that matter can carry the *energies of God*, even resuscitation power—to be exaggerated to the point of untruth. Augustine's error had to do with the philosophical assumptions of Greek philosophy. The main concern of the major Greek philosophers was how things are similar (the problem of universals). Permanence was considered a reflection of "the good," but change a degeneration of the good. The central concept of Plato's philosophy was his ideal "forms," which were eternal and changeless. Similarly, in the philosophy of Aristotle (the more materialist school of thought) the concept of changeless "essence" was central. Both related to the *permanence* of things. In contrast, Hebraic thought had a better appreciation of change and motion, although it was less philosophically sophisticated.[11]

Augustine and other Christian theologians of his age held the assumption that the changeless and eternal are good, while the temporary and changeable debase the good. When they read about the healing power of Peter's aprons or Elisha's bones, they understood them as being holy in "essence" and "form." This would be a permanent characteristic given to matter by its association with a holy person. They did not understand that the healings resulted from a spiritual *energy* that was discharged. This lack of an adequate theology of energy has afflicted Roman Catholic theology up to modern times. To this day Catholics define relics as "objects sanctified by contact with his [the saint's] body."[12] Notice the definition uses the word "sanctified," a permanent characteristic, not "energized," which is temporary but more biblically accurate.

---

11. I owe this insight into Greek philosophy to Popper's classic work *Open Society*, vol. 1, *Spell of Plato*. On the more open Hebraic view of change, see Boman, *Hebrew Thought*.

12. *New Catholic Encyclopedia*, "Relics." One wonders how much sounder traditional theology might have been if the philosophical fashion at the time of Augustine had favored the pre-Socratics, especially Hereclitus, who understood change and energy as centrally important.

Ironically, the original Greek text of the New Testament scriptures, written in the market Greek of the era, possessed an entirely adequate vocabulary for spiritual energy. The words used by New Testament authors for the energies of God are *dunamis*, which simply means power, and *energia*, which means energy. New Testament writers used these words to describe God's energies at work on earth in healing diseases or transforming character, as in Paul's mention of Christ's *energia* in his life: "We proclaim him, admonishing and teaching everyone with all wisdom, so that we may present everyone perfect in Christ. To this end I labor, struggling with all his *energy*, which so powerfully works in me" (Col 1:28–29, italics added).

Early Christian theologians dedicated much thinking to God's personhood and essence, and the complications of the Trinity (all eternal, permanent characteristics of God), but it developed little or no theology for God's *dunamis* and *energia*.[13] An adequate theology of grace should have dealt with these, but this did not happen. (The exception is found in some of the later literature from the Greek Orthodox Church which examined the "divine energies" as part of the experience of mystical prayer.)[14]

An understanding of God's *dunamis* was so neglected in Western theology that the translators of the King James Version of the Bible used the word *virtue* for *dunamis* in Luke 6:19. It seemed to them that it would be crude to say that Jesus felt "power" leaving him, so they moralized it to say "virtue." As we shall see, when Mrs. Agnes Sanford wrote about the healing energies of God in the 1940s as "healing light" she was considered a heretic for this by many Christians. This was not because what she wrote was unbiblical, but because it was not found in traditional theology (see chapter 16).

The tragedy of this philosophical misunderstanding—that relics have an eternal rather than temporary deposit of God's energies—meant that the church (both East and West) would settle for a sub-biblical mode of healing ministry. Its clergy would often "expose" a relic to a sick person, or process with a statue and relic in times of plague or illness, rather than do the biblically mandated acts of laying on of hands or anointing with oil by elders in faith. Those were the things that could really and regularly transmit God's healing energies.

13. Bradshaw, "Divine Energies."

14. Zimany, "Divine Energies." More accessible is the article by Mathews-Greene, "Eastern Orthodoxy."

Augustine also missed a cue about the disciples' authority when he did not pursue the fact that even newly baptized Christians had healing authority, as he discovered in the case of the woman with breast cancer. Had he followed this lead it might have ended the reign of the Galatian Bewitchment, which was to blight Catholic theology even to the present day.

Healing in the Middle Ages

With Augustine's theology as normative, the disciples' authority to heal by prayer and the laying on of hands, and do deliverance by command, did not fare well in the Middle Ages. The command to heal and cast out demons became the domain of the clergy, with healing ministry only rarely exercised by the laity. The healing ministry, outside of the use of relics or statues, was divided into two parts: anointing with oil, which was given the favored status of a sacrament, and exorcism, which was simply called a rite. Both were reserved for the clergy. The division into anointing and exorcism had some practical value, although if one studies the Gospel accounts of the ministry of Jesus that type of division is not apparent. Rather, Jesus healed the afflicted by either curing an illness or commanding an evil spirit to leave, depending on the presenting situation.

Later, confusion developed in believing that exorcism was always for very serious demon "possession" (as depicted in the movie *The Exorcist*). Thus, in later Catholic theology there was no ministry of casting out of minor spirits, as when Jesus cast out the spirit of infirmity in the crippled woman (Luke 13:10). Today such an action, which many Spirit-filled laypersons do regularly, is usually called deliverance. Catholic exorcism ministry was serious and unusual, and later codified to require permission by the local bishop.[15]

Mostly, healing degenerated into a cult of relics and pilgrimages. Many readers who studied *The Canterbury Tales* in an English class may remember Chaucer's description of the Pardoner. A pardoner was a traveling clerical official who sold remission for punishment in the afterlife (purgatory). Chaucer's Pardoner carried bottles of pigs' bones and bits of rags, which he publicized to be relics of great saints. He hypocritically told church audiences that those bones and rags would heal all of their ailments as well as those of their animals.

15. The Catholic exaggeration of the hero role of the priest in exorcism is shown in the bestselling book by Martin, *Hostage to the Devil*.

What happened to the practice of anointing with oil for healing was especially tragic. The early church understood the passage in James 5:14–16 as a commission to pray for physical healing and the possible sins that may lie at the base of the illness—the plain meaning of the passage.

> Is any one of you sick? He should call the elders of the church to
> pray over him and anoint him with oil in the name of the Lord.
> And the prayer offered in faith will make the sick person well;
> the Lord will raise him up. If he has sinned, he will be forgiven.

During the first centuries of the church's existence many healings were done in this way. However, in the ninth century the biblical mandate for healing through the anointing with oil was severely damaged. Theodult of Orleans (bishop of Orleans 798–818) proposed that the main function of the sacrament of anointing the sick was to impart a sanctifying grace. This grace supplemented the grace of the sacrament of penance. In a pastoral letter to his priests, Theodult instructed his priests as to the proper form of administering and understanding the sacrament: "When the sick man has been anointed in the way that has been set forth, let him be enjoined by the priest to say the Lord's Prayer and the Creed, and to commend his spirit into the hands of God, and to fortify himself with the sign of the cross, and to bid farewell to the living."[16] Thus anointing with oil was no longer understood or practiced as an effective healing prayer. Rather, it was transformed into a rite of happy death and last rites for a terminally ill person. The sacrament promised the person to bypass the torments of purgatory and go directly to heaven.

The errors of the Galatian Bewitchment and the quest for individual perfection via humility produced a double bind of ineffectiveness in the healing ministry. If a Catholic layperson felt he or she had a gift of healing (the disciples' authority), it should not be exercised because he or she had no ordained office, and in any case it was a threat to humility. If the person exercised it, he or she was not humble, and therefore not truly sanctified. Thus, the layperson's ministry was most probably invalid, or possibly due to witchcraft.

Far safer to a person's humility was healing prayer through the intercession of the saints, especially Mary. If the saints produced a healing miracle it would not endanger the humility of the petitioner. As the Protestant critique pointed out, this was both unbiblical and perilously close

---

16. Puller, *Anointing of the Sick*, 105. This classic work documents the effective use of anointing in the early church and its tragic decline into a non-healing rite.

to spiritualism.[17] Indirect petition through the saints also made it difficult for the Christian to exercise direct faith expectancy. The prayer of petition, though certainly a valid form of Christian prayer, is not the direct prayer of faith to the Father that Jesus urged upon the disciples (Matt 17:20).

17. See John Calvin's fine insight into this in his *Institutes*, 1.7.1–2.

4

The Reformation and the
Tragedy of Cessationism

When Martin Luther, an Augustinian monk, nailed his Ninety-Five Theses on the church door in Wittenberg (1517), Catholicism was in a quagmire.[1] It was deeply wounded by sub-biblical traditions and practices. Unfortunately, the reformers' dream of returning the church to biblical standards was more difficult than they imagined. This was partially due to the fact that both reformers and Catholics were educated into, and influenced by, a Christian theology that minimized the understanding of the gifts of the Spirit and the value of healing and deliverance as demonstrating the gospel.

Luther's positive and transforming insight was that Christianity was at its core faith based, not works based. He had no intention of forming a separate church, and merely wanted to bring the Catholic Church back to its biblical senses.[2]

1. An early version of this chapter appeared as chapter 6, "The Reformers Overreact to Catholic Error," in *Quenching the Spirit*.

2. In the long run Luther succeeded. Note that contemporary Catholic theologians agree with the core of Luther's understanding of faith and justification. On this see the amazing article in the Catholic journal *First Things*, "Call to Holiness."

Reaffirming Cessationism: The Great Setback[3]

Although St. Augustine was the most cited and trusted of the church fathers for Luther, Calvin, and other reformers, his works were read selectively. Augustine's general theology was accepted as the norm for orthodoxy, especially since Augustine had developed an excellent understanding of salvation by grace and faith, and had a strong doctrine of predestination. But Augustine's later appreciation of the healing ministry was ignored. His healing theology, including his belief in relics, was seen by the reformers as the source of the Catholic abuses and superstitions that they knew so well. Augustine's original cessationist theology seemed to fit the reformers' goals of cleansing the church. If healing and the gifts of the Spirit belonged only to the apostolic church, then the corrupt practices of pilgrimages, relic worship, votive candles, etc. were the natural result of attempting to move in the spiritual life without God's grace.

Martin Luther was the first of the reformers to reconsider resurrecting Augustine's cessationist theory. Luther's thoughts on healing and deliverance were not consistent. On the one hand he initially favored Augustine's early views of cessationism in regards to healing prayer, but on the other hand he eventually did come to believe in the reality of deliverance prayer for demonic oppression. He famously threw an inkbottle at the devil on one occasion, and several times effectively did deliverance ministry. He wrote to his pastor friend Bernard Wurzelmann in 1535, "About ten years ago we had an experience in this neighborhood with a very wicked demon, but we succeeded in subduing him by perseverance and unceasing prayers and unquestioning faith. . . . By this means I have restrained many similar spirits in different places."[4]

Like Augustine in his last years, Luther also came to believe in healing:

> If the physicians are at a loss to find a remedy, you may be sure that it is not a case of ordinary melancholy. It must rather be an affliction that comes from the devil, and this must be counteracted by the power of Christ with the prayer of faith. This is what to do, and what we have been accustomed to do; for a

3. On cessationism see my work *Quenching the Spirit*, chapter 6, and an excellent work on Calvin's cessationism, Langstaff, "Temporary Gifts." An article based on Langstaff's work and incorporating new material on Luther's role in cessationism is Hejzlar's, "John Calvin."

4. Luther, *Spiritual Counsel*, 42.

cabinetmaker here was similarly afflicted with madness and we cured him by prayer in Christ's name. Accordingly you should proceed as follows: Go to him with a deacon and two or three good men. Confident that you as pastor of the place, are clothed with the authority of the ministerial office, lay your hands upon him and say, "Peace be with you, dear brother, from God our Father and from our Lord Jesus Christ." Thereupon repeat the Creed and the Lord's Prayer over him in a clear voice, and close with these words: "O God, almighty Father, who has told us through thy Son, 'Verily, verily I say unto you, Whatsoever ye ask the father in my name, he will give it you.'" . . . Then, when you depart, lay your hands upon the man again and say, "These signs shall follow them that believe; they shall lay hands on the sick, and they shall recover."[5]

Philipp Melanchthon (1497–1560), colleague of Luther, and the Reformation's first systematic theologian, went further. He believed that the healing ministry "remained in the church also later, [than the apostles] and it is certain that many are still healed by the prayers of the church."[6] This common sense approach, which could have been developed into a Reformed theology of healing, was tragically overwhelmed by the greater prestige of John Calvin's opinions.[7]

In fact, it was John Calvin (1509–1564), the great Reformed systematic theologian and Protestant leader of Geneva, Switzerland, who converted cessationism from a debatable theory into a core Protestant doctrine.[8] Calvin's father held administrative posts in the church, and through connections was able to provide for an excellent education for his academically precocious son. During his studies he came under the influence of humanist scholars. Humanism was a movement of the late Renaissance that admired and sought to reintroduce Greek philosophy and classical Greek and Roman art forms into Christian culture. The humanists especially revered the philosophy of Plato, which they believed to be superior to that of Aristotle's, which was at that time in fashion through the theology of St. Thomas Aquinas.

5. Cited in Hejzlar, "John Calvin," 52.

6. Ibid., 45.

7. Why this is so is unclear. Recently there has been good scholarship on Luther's ultimate acceptance of the healing and deliverance ministry; see Foller, "Luther on Miracles." But to my knowledge there is no study on why and how the healing ministry was disconnected (or perhaps never fully accepted) in the Lutheran churches.

8. Kelsey, *Healing and Christianity*, 220–23.

Calvin early on adopted Augustine's cessationism, and rejected his later corrections. Why this is so is unclear. Certainly his dislike for Catholic abuses in the healing ministry was a factor. But another factor may have been his enchantment with Platonic philosophy, which disdained the body as an entrapment to the spirit. In his *Institutes* he often referred to the body as prison and "our tabernacle, unstable, defective, corruptible, fading, pining, and putrid."[9] In singularly Platonic tones he wrote:

> If heaven is our country, what can the earth be but the place of exile? If departure from the world is entrance into life, what is the world but a sepulcher. . . . If to be freed from the body is to gain full possession of freedom, what is the body but a prison? . . . Thus when the earthly is compared with the heavenly life, it may undoubtedly be despised and trampled underfoot.[10]

Certainly there are passages in Scripture that support a yearning for heaven, but like the monks of Egypt, Calvin's accent is more Platonic than biblical. There is no notice or joy in the possibility of physical healing and the celebration of good health. Perhaps because Calvin was never in good health as an adult it was difficult for him to accept that God could heal anyone else in the present age. In his commentaries on the Scriptures Calvin constantly stressed how the gospel was healing to the soul, not the body.[11]

Calvin argued many times against any continued ministry of healing, the gifts of the Spirit, or of the any miraculous events in the life of the Christian. Calvin wrote in his famous *Institutes*:

> But that gift of healing, like the rest of the miracles, which the Lord willed to be brought forth for a time, has vanished away in order to make the new preaching of the gospel marvelous forever. Therefore, even if we grant to the full that anointing [for the sick] was a sacrament of those powers which were then administered by the hands of the apostles, it has nothing to do with us, to whom the administering of such powers has not been committed.[12]

---

9. Calvin, *Institutes*, 3.9.5

10. Ibid., 3.9.4.

11. Hejzlar, "John Calvin," 38.

12. Ibid, 5, 19, 18. The contemporary Calvinist scholar Paul Elbert attempted, but failed, to show that Calvin was accepting of the gifts of the Spirit for all Christians. See especially pp. 242–44, where Elbert admits that Calvin misunderstood the gifts of the Spirit as graced natural mental gifts, missing the element of the supernatural.

Unlike Luther and Melanchthon, Calvin even disallowed the ministry of exorcism and deliverance. In this, his hatred for things Catholic led him to believe that the Catholic ritual of exorcism was "nothing else than feats of dexterity, in which Satan pretends to fight with himself."[13] Calvin also ridiculed the Catholic sacrament of extreme unction as a useless, human-invented ritual:

> And for what greater reason do they [the Catholics] make a sacrament out of this unction than out of all the other symbols mentioned to us in Scripture?...Why is not clay made of spittle and dust a sacrament? But the others (they reply) were individual examples, while this was commanded by James. That is, James spoke for that same time when the church still enjoyed such a blessing of God. Indeed, they affirm that the same force is still in their anointing, but we experience otherwise. . . . James wishes all sick persons to be anointed (James 5:14); these fellows [the Catholic priests] smear with their grease not the sick, but half-dead corpses when they are already drawing their last breath, or (as they say), in extremis. If in their sacrament they have a powerful medicine with which to alleviate the agony of diseases, or at least to bring some comfort to the soul, it is cruel of them never to heal in time. James would have the sick man anointed by the elders of the church; these men allow only a priestling as anointer.[14]

In regard to the other gifts of the Spirit, such as prophecy and the word gifts such as tongues, words of wisdom, and knowledge, Calvin was again negative in the absolute. Actually, there is not a single direct statement about the word gifts of the Spirit in his *Institutes*. Instead he used the phrase "evident powers" of the Spirit to indicate the original apostolic gifts described in Acts. What he had to say about the cessation of the "evident powers" is gleaned from his discussion of the Catholic sacrament of confirmation, where a Catholic bishop lays hands on the person for the intention of receiving the gifts of the Spirit:

> If this ministry which the apostles then carried out still remained in the church, the laying on of hands would also have to be kept. But since that grace has ceased to be given, what purpose does the laying on of hands serve? . . . In what respect, then, will these actors [Catholic bishops] say they are following

13. Cited in Hejzlar, "John Calvin," 48.
14. Calvin, *Institutes*, 5.19 and 21.

the apostles? They should have brought it about with the laying on of hands, in order that the evident power of the Holy Spirit might be immediately expressed. This they do not accomplish.[15]

These passages reflect both the truth and tragedy of the Reformation's critique of Catholicism. Calvin's critical observations are mostly true. Nothing manifested and no gifts of the Spirit were evident when a bishop placed hands on a person for confirmation. Similarly, the sick were no longer healed in the sacrament of extreme unction.

But Calvin could not see past the Catholic abuses and distortions to the Bible's original intentions. There is no evidence that Calvin ever attempted a simple laying on of hands or an anointing with oil in faith for healing. He assumed cessationism to be correct. From that assumption Calvin developed his systematic theology on the core doctrines of Augustine, some of the church fathers, and the Bible. But with cessationism at its core, he doomed Protestantism to a long period of spiritual incompleteness and weakness.

Radical Cessationism

Calvin extended cessationism from an understanding that healing and miracles are no longer operative to a broader concept that practically all spiritual experiences, such as the receiving of dreams and visions, are not proper for the current age. This expansion happened although Calvin had an appreciation for some of the Christian mystics, and in fact quoted the mystic Bernard of Clairvaux more than any other source except Augustine. But Calvin was anxious that Protestantism not imitate the Catholic mystical tradition of spirituality.[16] Like healing prayer, Catholic contemplative prayer had at times become debased to a point where many monks and nuns were confusing the frequency or vividness of spiritual experiences with progress in the spiritual life. Combined with the ascetical tradition of monasticism, this produced a form of spirituality that at times lacked discernment and even common sense.

Calvin's agenda was that the Reformed Christian be a person anchored in the Bible, and that the ministers "strengthen consciences by teaching things true, sure, and profitable."[17] This is the opposite of mysti-

---

15. Ibid., 5.6.3.

16. Harkness, *Mysticism*, 124. See also Hoffman, *Luther*.

17. Calvin, *Institutes*, 1.14.4.

cism, which tends to be fuzzy and irrational if not properly grounded in Scripture and discerned. To this day, many evangelicals, the inheritors of Calvin's Reformed theology, tend to use the tem term "mystical" only in its negative sense, to indicate confusion caused by undiscerned and illusionary spiritual experiences.[18]

At the same time, Calvin accepted the contemporary Catholic philosophical understanding pertaining to the mind and soul. This was the Christian realism of St. Thomas Aquinas (1225–1274). St. Thomas based his theology on the materialist philosophy of Aristotle, who stressed the role of the five physical senses as the only way of understanding the world. In deference to Catholic mystical tradition, St. Thomas Aquinas accepted the spiritual abilities (faculties) of the soul and the "graces of prayer" (Catholic terminology for the gifts of the Spirit). However, those graces were given only brief attention in St. Thomas's writings. By the time of the Reformation, St. Thomas' theological system (and its Aristotelian assumptions) was predominant in the universities. It was these assumptions about the mind and psychology that both Luther and Calvin learned as young men.

Unlike St. Thomas, Calvin felt no need to give legitimacy to the spiritual gifting of individuals or the Catholic understanding of the graces of prayer, i.e., the gifts of the Spirit. Calvin's purposes of reforming Christendom and downplaying the Catholic mystical tradition were better served by accepting the five senses and reason, the Aristotelian/St. Thomas model, as the only reliable way to know truth. Thus, for Calvin the only manner in which one could discern God's will and voice was in the reading of Scripture and through the inner witness of the Spirit. In fact, practically the only spiritual experience permitted to Christians by Calvin's cessationism was the experience of being converted and the inner witness of the Spirit in that process.

Calvin's five-sense cessationism was also related to one of his core theological understandings, which was influenced by St. Augustine. This was the concept of original sin and how this sin affects humankind's reasoning and understanding. It is called the theory of "total depravity," and it became one of the distinguishing doctrines of orthodox Calvinist

18. It is only with the recent prophetic wing of the charismatic movement that the word *mystic* is acquiring a renewed positive meaning among Protestant Christians. That is, a mystic is one who has spiritual experiences that *can* be from the Holy Spirit, and every Christian is encouraged to discern their dreams, visions, and spiritual experiences, just as in the Bible. See Crowder, *New Mystics*.

theology. It states that human beings cannot in any way come to God, hear his voice, or understand the gospel without God's special, "prevenient" grace. Without predestination into the church, people are hopeless and totally cut off from God to the point that they cannot hear from God. This of course is contradicted by the many instances in the Scriptures in which heathen hear or discern God's voice (discussed in chapter 2). An added New Testament example is the instance when Pilate's wife had a dream warning her of Jesus' innocence (Matt 27:19). We will discuss this further in chapter 18 with regard to Agnes Sanford's theology of the gifts of the Spirit.

Calvin's five-sense cessationism unintentionally destroyed the capacity for discerning spiritual phenomenon. That is, the exercise of discernment implies that spiritual experiences (visions, dreams, prophecies, and so forth) can be from multiple sources—the Lord, the demonic, or the human mind—"flesh" as Paul termed it. In Reformed theology no present-day "mystical" experiences can be of the Lord, so that direct spiritual experiences are either delusions of the mind (called "enthusiasm") or from the devil.

Faith without Analogous Experiences

Protestant theologians settled for what might be called the cessationist hermeneutic. They accepted that miracles happened in biblical times, but believed that those miracles can only be verified by faith in the biblical records, not present-day analogous experiences. The whole book of Acts (and 1 Corinthians and Hebrews 2:1–4) became history, not model. Its miracles ceased to be a pattern for the living church. This hermeneutic avoided the superstitions, exaggerations, and myth-making of Catholicism, but at a terrible cost. Cessationism robbed Protestants of an important means of biblical verification, analogous spiritual events. Protestant ministers expected Christians to believe every miraculous event in the Bible but to reject as superstition any present-day evidence for the miraculous. This non-analogous way of thinking is contrary to the way people normally think, which is from the known to the unknown, and from partial knowledge to fuller knowledge.[19] If Christians cannot experience and

19. On the importance of analogous knowledge in spiritual matters, see Foster, "Piaget and Parables."

see local miracles of healing and the gifts of the Spirit, then they cannot fully understand the biblical record.

Cessationist theologians often justified their non-analogous hermeneutic by citing Jesus' reproof to Thomas for not believing in his resurrection: "Blessed are they who did not see, and yet believed" (John 20:29). However, Thomas witnessed many of Jesus' miracles, including several resuscitations from the dead. Thomas was reproved because he would not extend his faith after having much evidence of Christ's power and authority.

The importance of analogies in faith is clearly demonstrated by an article in *The British Medical Journal* by Dr. Rex Gardner, a gynecologist and medical missionary. Dr. Gardner meticulously researched the work of Venerable Bede (673–735), *A History of the English Church and People.* Bede was the great monk-historian of the early English and Celtic church. Dr. Gardner compared Bede's reports of healing miracles with similar cases of healing prayer in his own ministry and that of other medical missionaries. Gardner found parallels for Bede's reports of healings from such things as severe construction accidents and fatal diseases on the contemporary mission field. For modern healing miracles he was also able to get follow-up information and verification. As a medical doctor his analysis is especially impressive, as he could authoritatively declare which healing cases were recoveries outside the realm of natural possibility.[20]

As far as Dr. Gardner could tell from modern verified experiences in healing prayer, nothing in Bede's accounts of healing prayer was improbable or more miraculous than what is ministered through the faith-filled prayers of contemporary Christians. He concluded that modern historians have been biased by materialist assumptions in dividing Bede's work into "good history," as when Bede recorded the political and social events of this time, and "religious myths," as when Bede recorded healing miracles within the Anglo-Celtic community.

The point is that a known miraculous healing in the present verifies by analogy a similar recorded healing in the past (including biblical miracles). That type of encouragement and verification is impossible when either biblical events or miracles of the early church are limited or dismissed with cessationist theology. The cessationist hermeneutic destroys the ability and faith expectancy of the Christian community to

---

20. Gardner, "Miracles of Healing."

pray in faith for the miraculous, and thus such Christian communities are cut off from analogous verification of Biblical miracles.

Non-Cessationist Protestantism?
Healing Prayer at the Birth of Anglicanism

During the complex and bloody process of the English Reformation, there was a moment when cessationism was challenged and healing prayer revived. It happened through a committee of churchmen and scholars who formulated the first set of guiding principles for the newly independent Anglican Church. The document they produced was called *The Bishop's Book* (1537). Among its provisions was a reformation of the Catholic rite of extreme unction to bring it in harmony with the Bible and the practice of the early church. Citing James 5:14–16, *The Bishop's Book* declared anointing to be "a very godly and wholesome medicine or remedy to alleviate and mitigate diseases and maladies, as well as of the soul as of the body of Christian men."[21] This was plainly both anti-cessationist and critical of the Catholic view of "extreme unction" that had no healing expectancy.

A few years later Henry VIII, who was well read in theology, revised *The Bishop's Book* and affirmed anointing of the sick as a healing sacrament.[22] These reforms were carried forward to the first *Book of Common Prayer* (1549). The priest was directed to pray:

> Hear us, almighty and most merciful God, and Savior: Extend thy accustomed goodness to this thy servant, which is grieved with sickness: Visit him, o Lord, as thou diddest visit Peter's wife's mother, and the Captain's servant. And as thou preservest Thobie [Tobit] and Sara by thy Angel, from danger: So restore unto this sick person his former health, (if it be thy will), or else give him grace so to take thy correction, that after this painful life ended, he may dwell with thee in life everlasting. Amen.[23]

This was what the reformers, Calvin and the others, should have done about healing prayer: correct Catholic abuses and exaggerations by returning to the original biblical intention and the practice of the early

21. Cited in Gusmer, "Anointing of the Sick," 263.

22. Ibid.

23. The entire first *Book of Common Prayer* is available online at http://justus.angli-can.org/resources/bcp/1549/BCP_1549.htm.

church. As the Anglican scholars and divines demonstrated, this was do-able. Unfortunately, this true Reformation lasted only a short season. The more radical reformers within the English church were suspicious that the modified rite of anointing was too close to Catholic "superstitions" and should be totally eliminated.[24] Archbishop Cranmer, leader of the Reformation in England, invited the eminent German Reformed theologian Martin Bucer to assist in reviewing *The Book of Common Prayer*. Under Bucer's influence cessationism was reaffirmed, with the result that in the 1552 edition of *The Book of Common Prayer* the rite of anointing was eliminated, and tragically not restored until the 1928 version. Protestantism continued in its destructive way of doing church without healing prayer and the gifts of the Spirit.

24. For a detailed account of the triumph of cessationism in the English Reformation, see Kester, "Charismata in Crisis."

5

From Cessationism to Secularism

THE REFORMATION, WHICH WAS begun by Luther as a challenge to debate with the papal representative, became within a few decades a war between Catholics and Protestants.[1] Each side tried to save the other from the heresy by battle or torture. The first battles took place in France between Catholics and French Calvinists (Huguenots) and culminated in the widespread slaughter of Protestants, the St Bartholomew's Day Massacre of August 1572.

Decades later there followed one of Europe's bloodiest and cruelest wars, the Thirty Years War (1618–1648). This was fought mostly in what is now Germany. It resulted in such enormous devastation and left so few adult males alive that the Catholic Church temporarily lifted the restriction on polygamy in the Catholic sections of Germany and Austria in order to repopulate the wartorn areas. Finally, when both sides were exhausted, they signed a treaty to lay low and let the others be, the Treaty of Westphalia (1648). It is not strange that by the end of the Thirty Years War many reasonable persons were cynical about Christianity. The kingdom of God had become the reign of doctrinal contention and war.

Some Enlightenment thinkers and philosophers concluded that Christianity was a disposable and barbaric leftover from the middle Ages. Voltaire, the preeminent Enlightenment anti-Christian thinker, spent his adult life criticizing "the infamy," the church. His famous short novel *Candide: or, All for the Best* (1759) tells the story of a young man seeking peace but running into disasters such as the Inquisition in Portugal,

1. This is a highly modified version of my earlier chapter "The Fall of Christianity in Europe," chapter 7 in *Quenching the Spirit*.

49

which tortured and killed many innocent persons. The punch line was that Christianity was useless to bring happiness or peace, and the best thing was to "tend your own garden" and leave the other side alone.

The Gifts Deficient Church and the Secularization of Europe

The doctrines of cessationism, on the Protestant side, and the Galatian Bewitchment, on the Catholic side, had created a Christendom that had little spiritual power to authenticate the gospel of Jesus Christ as mandated in Hebrews 2:1–4. The tragic consequences of this are only now obvious: the decline and fall of Christianity in Europe.

This happened as the Protestant churches attempted to maintain their faithfulness to the gospel but denied the need for analogous spiritual experiences, i.e., the gifts of the Spirit, healing prayer, and miraculous acts. Cessationism made Christian life and belief easy prey for atheist and deist Enlightenment intellectuals who were looking for ways of "freeing mankind from the shackles" of revealed religion. The English philosopher David Hume (1711–1776) exposed the fundamental weakness of cessationism by bringing it to its logical conclusion: since no miracles are observable in the present (because the Christians he knew never prayed in faith for healing or the miraculous), none ever took place in the past. Thus, biblical miracles were myths.

Hume's most important book, *An Enquiry Concerning Human Understanding* (1748), was a major turning point in European history. It banished belief in the miraculous from the thinking of European elites. After its publication, intellectuals could not easily or publicly declare belief in miracles, in either the biblical or church age. Not that this was all due to Hume. The process of banishing spiritual reality from the court of public discussion had started before him. However, Hume summarized the Enlightenment's anti-religious attitude and capped it with his own genius for logical reasoning.[2]

Hume well understood the importance of analogies in human reasoning and thought. In his writings he used the logic of analogy in equating the Gospel miracles with the folktales of old, such as those recounted

---

2. See the classic work by the great Jewish historian Gay, *The Enlightenment*, for an understanding of the central role that anti-Christianity has in later Enlightenment thought. For a detailed study of this radical anti-Christian and atheistic core of the later Enlightenment, see Blom, *Wicked Company.*

by the ancient Greek historian Herodotus. He had mixed outlandish tales of monsters, omens, and the like with valid historical events.

> It is strange, a judicious reader is apt to say, upon the perusal of these wonderful historians, that such prodigious events never happen in our days. But it is nothing strange, I hope, that men should lie in all ages.[3]

Hume's attack on the miracle of the Bible provoked a heated response from Christian apologists. Protestant theologians attempted to pick apart his logic. They stressed that observation and experience are not universally truthful, as experience never determines with certainty the whole range of reality. One Christian writer cited the true story of the first Dutch ambassador to the king of Siam to illustrate this point. It seems that the ambassador was recounting Dutch history to the king when the ambassador told of a winter battle when soldiers crossed a frozen river. At that point the king, who had never seen ice or snow, became incensed. He shouted that "solid water" was not possible, concluded that nothing that the ambassador had told was true and threw him out of court.[4]

It was fine that Christians made the point that experience does not determine all truth. But note that Hume's Protestant critics granted him the central assumption, that no miracles could be observed in the present. Cessationist theology created a culture where no faith-filled prayers for healing, exorcism, or miracles would be attempted by the pious Protestant, and thus none could be observed. No analogous evidence, as Dr. Rex Gardner presented, could be brought to bear against Hume's argument. European Protestantism ultimately became a ghost-like faith because of the lack of support from any present-day miraculous experiences.[5]

Protestant Christianity and the Liberal/Conservative Divide

After Hume and other Enlightenment thinkers had challenged Christianity on the miraculous, European Protestantism separated into two camps. One was of the theological conservatives, who maintained the cessationist hermeneutic at all cost. The other camp was that of the liberals, founded by Friedrich Schleiermacher (1768–1834). It was he who attempted to

3. Hume, "On Miracles" in his *Human Understanding*.

4. For a survey of the Hume controversy see Burns, *Great Debate*.

5. For a magnificent study of the relationship between the denial of miracles (cessationism) and the decline of Protestantism in Europe, see Keller, *Miracles in Dispute*.

accommodate the gospel to Hume's logic. In his most important work, *On Religion* (1799), Schleiermacher decided that the acceptance of the miracle accounts in Scripture was improper for enlightened believers, and he outlined a radical method of biblical interpretation, the "myth hermeneutic," to accommodate to the times. In this interpretation the miracles in the Bible were seen as myths that had "deep meaning" but never occurred historically.

Schleiermacher's good intentions had disastrous results. It created a form of Protestantism that was fundamentally Sadducaic. That is, like the biblical Sadducees who disbelieved in the supernatural, such as angels, the promise of the resurrection, etc., but enjoyed control of the temple, Schleiermacher created a religion of theology and worship without reference to the supernatural in the world. The modern biblical scholar and theologian Rudolf Bultmann (1884–1976) popularized this interpretation and called it "demythologizing." But all the elements of it were present in liberal theology a century before he was born. The illogical and circular nature of the myth hermeneutic is seen in Bultmann's attitude to the healing ministry. When questioned about the public healing ministry of Johann Blumhardt (1805–1880), Bultmann called it a "legend" and an "abomination" to Protestantism. Of course he made no effort to see if there was any evidence for the miraculous in Blumhardt's well-documented ministry.[6]

In fact, Johann Blumhardt was a German pastor who discovered the authority and power of the believer to heal and cast out demons, in spite of the theology he had been taught. Like several other pastors in the Protestant tradition, his healing gift broached naturally in the course of ministry.[7] In the 1840s he established a healing spa home, a place where persons could come for healing and prayer. His institution was under close scrutiny by government officials, skeptics and Christians alike. No one denied that many healings took place, though the critics believed they were only "psychosomatic cures."[8] Bultmann illustrated the blindness and illogical nature of the myth hermeneutic in his critique

---

6. Bultmann, "A Rely," in *Kerygma and Myth.*

7. For instance, the earlier healing ministry of Pastor Michael Haykin. See Knolly, "Michael Haykin."

8. Kelsey, *Christian Healing*, 236–37. For a fuller description of his life, theology, and ministry, see Krüger, "Johann Christoph Blumhardt." For a description of Blumhardt's theology as well as citations to German primary sources, see Kydd, *Healing Through the Centuries*, chapter 3, "J. C. Blumhardt."

of Blumhardt: since miracles never happen, no evidence for miracles in the present will be investigated or entertained, period.

Generations of the most educated Protestant theologians have followed Bultmann's destructive methodology and staffed the mainline seminaries. It is a data-avoidance methodology disguised with sophisticated vocabulary, and seemingly authenticated by citation among themselves, but not looking at any evidence outside of their immediate circle.[9] In the course of two centuries, liberal/Sadducaic theology ran its tragic course of attempting to "save" the gospel by accommodating to the assumptions of the Enlightenment, and became instead a destroyer of Christian faith. Without belief in the miracle accounts in Scripture, the claims of Jesus as Son of God could not be upheld. But the miracles of Jesus were difficult to believe without the analogies of present-day miracles.

Early on the evangelicals rightly saw that accommodating liberal theology to the Enlightenment through the myth hermeneutic was a Trojan horse. However, because evangelical scholars could not, and would not, point to any contemporary miracles or gifts of the Spirit, their witness against the myth hermeneutic was mostly ineffective. Further, by not dealing convincingly with the serious issues raised by Hume, Voltaire, and anti-Christians thinkers, evangelicals paid the price of losing the intellectual classes. Especially after the disastrous Scopes Trial in America, which pitted the Bible against evolution, evangelicals came to be seen as anti-intellectual and anti-scientific.[10]

The Fall of European Christianity

The cessationism-to-Sadducaism process (i.e., not believing in the supernatural) left Europe, once the center of Christianity, in the spiritual darkness of the post-Christian era. Europe's magnificent cathedrals and churches now stand mostly as museums, and Sunday attendance in European nations rarely exceeds 7 percent of the population. In Denmark, the home of the brilliant and ironic theologian Soren Kierkegaard, Sunday attendance at church barely reaches 3 percent, although a majority of Danes

9. On the issue of academic theologians and sociologists not fairly looking at evidence for the miraculous and the occurrences of faith, see Greeley, *Unsecular Man*, "Introduction."

10. There have always been notable exceptions to this, as in the churchmen of the "Princeton Theology," who attempted to reconcile science and revelation in the nineteenth century, and in our time the work of Francis Schaeffer and others.

are nominally Christian and pay taxes to the state-supported Lutheran Church. Practicing Christians in Denmark are often shunned socially, especially in the universities.[11] In the German city of Wittenberg, where Luther began his protest against papal indulgences and other unbiblical practices, the majority of the people are outright atheists, and Protestants make up less than 10 percent of the population.[12] In Holland it is now common for pastors to be open unbelievers. They "do church" as an effort of bringing some kindness and love to the world, but without belief in either God or the afterlife. A perfect Sadducaic Christianity indeed![13]

The noted Catholic historian Hilaire Belloc, writing before World War II, commented on the Protestant decline in Northern Europe and its failure to effectively counter Nazism and Communism. He correctly ascribed Protestantism's decline and impotence to the influence of Calvinism (cessationism) and called Calvinism a "failed heresy." His point was that although Calvinism was effective in critiquing Catholicism it could not by itself maintain the gospel faith in the long run.[14]

Belloc, however, was too optimistic about Catholic Europe. He died in 1953 before a similar Catholic decline was obvious. Although Spain, Italy, and other Catholic countries in Europe did not decline to faithlessness as quickly as Calvinist and Lutheran Northern Europe, their decline did come, and proceeded rapidly once it started. Had Belloc lived two decades longer he would have seen that maintaining the Christian faith in competition against secularism with the Catholic Galatian Bewitchment and its gifts-suspicious theology was as ineffective as Protestant cessationism. Cynics and secularists can dismiss the rare Catholic miracles events as rumors, instances of abnormal psychology, or psychosomatic cures. Catholicism in Europe is becoming a "hallow church" with ever-shrinking congregations and an ageing and numerically inadequate priesthood.[15]

That the cessationism-to-Sadducaism process did not go as far or as quickly in the United States was mostly because of God's grace in pouring on America waves of revival. The revivals provided fresh impulses of the

11. Sommerville, "State of Denmark."

12. Berg, "Luther's City."

13. Pigott, "Dutch Rethink Christianity."

14. Belloc, *Great Heresies.* Compare with the insight of the greatest philosopher of history, and a Christian, R. G. Collingwood, who affirmed that the spiritual vacuum created by liberal Christian theology set the stage for the Nazi movement. See Gilman, "Religious Sources."

15. See the article in *The Economist,* "The Void Within."

Holy Spirit's presence and power upon believers in America. America also received large numbers of Quakers, Moravians, Pietists, and other non-Calvinist Protestants as immigrants. These were the very denominations that had an appreciation for the experiential/spiritual dimension of Christianity. Similarly, the Methodists, the most numerous and influential denomination of America in the nineteenth century, were an experiential, almost Pentecostal, denomination well into the first decades of the twentieth century.

Having said this, it is also becoming increasingly clear that the mainline denominations of the United States, such as the Episcopalians, Presbyterians, Congregationalists, Lutherans, Disciples of Christ, and Methodists, are undergoing rapid contraction similar to the general decline of European Christianity. These are the denominations whose seminaries were captivated by liberal theology and its demythologizing Sadducaism. With cessationism at their core, the mainline denominations in the United States have gone from 50 percent of the population in the 1950s to about 9 percent today. They are shadows of their former selves, having aging congregations and propped up by endowment monies from the past generation. They often have lovely churches and large properties, but mere memories of influence and political power.[16]

The Enlightenment and its aftermath eroded the spiritual goals, purposes, and hopes of human life that were central to the Christian Europe since the fifth century. But humanity cannot live without those things for very long, and thus new ideologies and movements arose to deliver what Christianity no longer credibly supplied. This will be the subject of our next chapter.

16. Bottum, "Protestant America." Like Belloc, Bottum is overly optimistic about Catholicism. Roman Catholicism in the United States seems numerically robust principally because of the massive influx of Hispanic Catholics. Millions of non-Hispanic Catholics have migrated to evangelical or Spirit-filled denominations, or into agnosticism and atheism. This continues at a rate of about 100,000 persons per year. See Castaldo, "Catholics Come Home?"

6

Science as Meaning and Hope in Non-Christian Europe

AFTER THE DE-CHRISTIANIZING IMPACT of the Enlightenment, Europeans began the long, futile search for moral anchorage and purpose in life. The philosopher Friedrich Nietzsche (1844–1900) proclaimed at the end of the nineteenth century that "God is dead!" He meant by this that educated Europeans no longer really believed in God or Christianity.[1] Rather, they went through the motions of Christian life, as in baptizing their children, occasional church attendance, etc., because it was demanded socially, or was part of their cultural identity.[2]

Nietzsche gave the most insightful analysis of the times. But ultimately, the chief secular alternative to Christianity was developed by the philosopher Friedrich Hegel (1770–1831). His philosophical system presented a counterfeit Holy Spirit called the "spirit of history." With Hegel's philosophy a person could align himself with the direction of history (that is, correct politics) and fulfill his moral destiny. In the twentieth century humankind suffered grievously from Hegel's counterfeit Holy Spirit. Hegelian philosophy wed to Nietzschean philosophy led to Fascism and Nazism (the Hegelian Right). United to radical economic thought and utopianism, it produced Marxism and Communism (the Hegelian Left).[3]

1. This happened also among many of the intelligentsia of England and the United States, though it was delayed, and to a lesser extent. See Lundin, "Old Pieties."

2. Especially his work *The Gay Science* (1887). "Gay" meant joyous at that time, not homosexual.

3. This is described in secular terms in one of the great works of twentieth-century philosophy, Popper's *The High Tide*.

56

Both systems created hatred, war, and genocide as their enemies were relegated to what Karl Marx termed the "dustbin of history," and thus had no rights.

Science as Salvation[4]

For many secular Europeans, science and scientific progress became the chief source of hope that fed into and became part of Hegelian spirit of history. This was given definition by Auguste Comte (1798–1857), who developed an influential philosophical system called "positivism." He believed humanity was progressing from its primitive theological stage in which people believed in religions of various sorts, through to the metaphysical stage, meaning speculative philosophical systems, to its final and glorious stage, the scientific era. This stage, scientific thinking, which Comte termed the religion of humanity, would ensure progress and ever-growing happiness. This fantasy was actually quite influential in the Victorian period.[5]

Indeed, science had accomplished astonishing things since the beginning of the seventeenth century. For instance, chemistry had morphed out of the occultism of alchemy into an industry-transforming science with new elements discovered and chemical processes understood. The beginning of the nineteenth century saw the invention of steam engines for trains and ships, and ushered in the beginning of the electronic age with the telegraph. Humankind's knowledge about the physical universe through astronomy and physics achieved tremendous strides also.

For us, in the twenty-first century, the union of science and moral progress as believed by the positivists seems ludicrous. We have passed through wars that science helped make the most destructive in history. Most of us would agree that science can make things more convenient, but does not make the world any better in a moral sense. But for many

---

4. On the philosophical and logical pretentions of science as salvation, see the works of Mary Midgley, professor at Newcastle University and an atheist, especially her *Evolution as Religion*.

5. Comte and his positivism made an significant impact on the elites of Brazil, who loved reading French philosophy. They chose as Brazil's national motto Comte's much-used phrase "order and progress" and placed it on their flag. For a masterful Christian reflection on the optimistic delusions of positivism, see Lubac, *Atheist Humanism*.

persons in the nineteenth century it seemed there was no limit to the moral good and happiness that science would achieve for humankind.

Part of the illusion of "science as salvation" was that science itself was not well understood, even by the educated public. Science was seen and defined as an authoritative system, such as physics, chemistry, and astronomy, that gave true, quantifiable information. Every discipline tried to come under the umbrella of science and in its glory and prestige. Several systems that were not science but presented themselves as such impacted American and European cultures to their roots.

The most powerful and ultimately most destructive, in terms of human lives lost and tormented and prosperity ruined, was Marxism. Karl Marx (1818–1883) built his speculations on positivist assumptions and claimed the system he developed was both scientific and identical with the Hegelian spirit of history. His mix of quasi-religion, philosophy, and economic theory gave his disciples an assurance, identity, motivation, and purpose of life that Christianity gave in former centuries.[6] Marx made firm predictions that a new era was to break out, helped by the inexorable spirit of history and led by industrial workers revolting against capitalist exploiters and the bourgeois. In fact, where communism came to power it did so through a coalition of peasants and radicalized intellectuals.

In the 1900s Eduard Bernstein, a Social Democrat politician, attempted to modify Marxist theory because it was not developing as prophesied. He was quickly denounced by the orthodox Marxists as a reactionary and "revisionist." The word revisionist came to have the same meaning as heretic: a person with no reasonable argument and no rights. In the torture cells of Stalinist Russia and its gulags, these secular heretics died by the hundreds of thousands in a new Inquisition that had far less mercy or procedural justice than the Catholic one. Regardless, rationalizations are easy to put in place, and Marxists' claims to scientific validity continued until recent times.[7]

The second major movement that claimed scientific status was Sigmund Freud's psychoanalytical movement. Freud claimed he had developed the science of the human mind. Certainly it was an elaborate system, and gave explanations for human decisions and behavior. But

---

6. On this see the secular writer Lilla's "Our Libertarian Age."

7. Marxism's ability to beguile and attract even after the fall of European communism in such places as central India and Venezuela is due in part to its counterfeit (demonically driven) spirituality.

explanatory systems are not necessarily science, and Freud's system was muddled and injured by his own character flaws and search for fame.

It took over seven decades for psychoanalysis to be finally exposed as a mix of quackery, untestable theories, and some good insights.[8] Freud had been criticized since his first publications, but built up a professional following and many devotees in academic circles who quite effectively marginalized serious criticism. The turning point against Freud came long after his death. It was a series of review essays in the *New York Review of Books*, the icon of American liberalism, that appeared in 1993–1994. These articles laid out various strands of irrefutable research that proved that Freud was fundamentally a fraud. For instance, his famous Oedipus complex masked what he knew of the reality of childhood sexual abuse.[9]

But that was in the 1990s. All throughout the twentieth century academic thinkers in America were captivated by Freud. Several combined both Marx and Freud into a unified critique of Western civilization. They succeeded, and greatly contributed to the chaos, destructiveness, and moral decline of our present era.[10] The continued hold of Freudian theories is astounding. For instance, in the blockbuster movie *Titanic* (1997) the background hero is Freud, who is part of the dinner conversation, and his sexual liberation is acted out in the protagonists.

The third movement, and perhaps least destructive of the three, was Mary Baker Eddy's Christian Science movement. We will examine its pretensions, as well as its positive role in awakening the Christian churches to their healing ministry later in chapter 8.

The Real Meaning of Science

We now understand that none of these three movements were sciences in any meaningful sense. Rather, they were elaborate intellectual constructs

---

8. A superb short critique of Freud and his psychoanalytical movement is found in Cromartie, "Freud Analyzed."

9. Oakes "Unauthorized Freud." On the damage done by Freud's theories, see Torrey, *Freudian Fraud*.

10. For instance, the works of Erich Fromm, now mostly forgotten, but in the 1960s deeply influential. See his *Beyond the Chains* (*really*, don't bother unless you have to for educational reasons). Another of the immensely destructive intellectuals was Norman Brown. Again, don't bother unless you need to, but see Brown's disastrously influential *Life Against Death*.

and mythologies that made great promises. They succeeded for various time periods because they had tremendous motivational powers.

The man who did the most to identify and separate science from pseudo-science was Karl R. Popper (1902–1994). He is a person who will probably be remembered as one of the greatest philosophers of the twentieth century.[11] We need to look at his clarification of the nature of science because it will play an important part of our discussion of Christian Science and the development of the Christian healing movement.

Popper was born in Vienna and brought up as a Lutheran, although later in his life claimed to be only an agnostic—the common result of the cessationism on a brilliant thinker who never saw any analogous evidence for biblical miracles.[12] As a young man in post–World War I Vienna, he investigated both Marxism and the psychoanalytical movement, and he joined both groups. In fact, he studied directly under Karl Jung (1875–1961), one of the original disciples of Freud and a founder of a rival wing of psychoanalysis called "analytical psychology." But Popper was disappointed to see that in both Marxism and psychoanalysis there were tendencies to ignore evidence that did not fit into their theories.

On the other hand, Popper was greatly impressed by Albert Einstein and his new theory of relativity. Einstein's equations showed that matter and energy interacted, e.g., that light was influenced by mass. This was a radical and controversial idea at the time. Einstein proposed an experiment to prove this. His equations showed that the light from distant stars is bent as it skims past the sun. However, this is impossible to observe due to the sun's corona, but it would be possible to observe and picture during a solar eclipse.

In 1921 several teams of British astronomers traveled to remote areas of the world to photograph just such an eclipse. They reported that indeed starlight was deflected as it came near the sun (it shifted to the red spectrum). Relativity was verified by a specific test. Inversely, Einstein's astronomical test could have proven him wrong. The news made headlines all across the globe.

---

11. An excellent summary of Popper's philosophy and political thought can be found in the article on him in the *Stanford Encyclopedia of Philosophy*, online at http://www.plato.stanford.edu/entries/popper/. Popper can also be seen as one of the great thinkers of political philosophy. His classic work on the field, *Open Society*, has gained increasing influence in recent decades, after being largely ignored for many decades by the Marxist intelligentsia of the West.

12. Popper wrote an excellent autobiography, *Unended Quest.*

The manner in which Einstein presented his theory and sought to have it tested deeply impressed Popper, especially in comparison with what he had observed in Marxism and psychoanalysis. Popper then turned his attention to what made science scientific. He presented his conclusions in a seminal book, *The Logic of Scientific Discovery*, first published in 1934 in German.[13]

Popper saw that science was fundamentally a methodology for expanding and correcting knowledge. It depended on the creation of new hypotheses for this expansion to take place. These hypotheses are tested to attain ever-closer approximations of the truth. Scientific theories are never definitively proven true. Rather, they are stabilized as close to the truth with rigorous tests, but there is always the possibility that some new hypothesis will generate a new test to overthrow present theory. Testing and refutation are at the heart of science.

For Popper, to be truly scientific a theory must go through some test in which it may be disproven. Einstein's suggestion of photographing an eclipse put his theory in jeopardy. Had the photographs shown no shift in the starlight, his theory and equations would have been proven wrong or at least incomplete. This ability to be disproven is what Popper called "falsifiability," a rather awkward but useful word. It is precisely this characteristic that pseudo-scientific theories like Marxism, psychoanalysis, and Christian Science do not have. Pseudo-sciences *rationalize* failed predictions rather than admit that part of their theories may be wrong. We need to keep this in mind when we study the claims of Christian Science and New Thought as "scientific" movements.

The Decades of Theological Destructiveness and the Age of DOG Theology

By the 1960s and the decades after, mainline theologians and church elites believed that their denominations represented the end product of the most modern and the best of Christianity. Many theologians of the era also claimed not only the mantle of modernity but of science as well. For instance, the department chairperson and professor at the prominent mainline seminary I attended in the 1980s claimed that his theological

13. Popper, *Logic of Scientific Discovery*. This is a specialized text, written with many equations and best left to those in the field of philosophy and science. His ideas are presented in a readable form in Popper's later works, especially *Conjectures and Refutations* and *Objective Knowledge*.

writings were "scientific" because he followed "Marxist principals of analysis" and because, like his colleagues, he had banished all considerations of the supernatural from the Bible and church history. He was also an unashamed atheist.[14]

At the same time, the mainline leadership understood that their churches were losing members and needed to change in some way. In their amnesia and disdain about real revivals of the church such as the Faith Cure movement and Pentecostalism (see chapter 7), and not understanding that the churches were under the curse of cessationism, the elites believed the way forward was to incorporate the latest modes of philosophy, psychology and social service in order to "fix" the church and prepare it for the future.

Indeed, the 1960s was a hinge point in modern history. In America the post-World War II consensus of anti-communism was ridiculed and overthrown by the academic left, and their student radicals, who looked at the Vietnam War through Marxist eyes, shouted, "imperialism!" Secularization and Freudian sexual "liberation" became mainstream, as modeled in the Woodstock festival. It all seemed so liberating. AIDS and other STD epidemics, and the devastating emotional and spiritual effects of sexual permissiveness on women, were decades in the future.[15] It was the age of spiritual, moral, and political anarchy.[16]

The Sadducaic theology (theology without the supernatural) of the 1960s, and much the rage, was Death of God theology. It is truly identified by its acronym, DOG theology. DOG theologians noticed that even in America Christianity was becoming increasingly irrelevant to more and more people. Nietzsche had seen this in nineteenth-century Europe, and he was adopted as the great prophet and wise man of DOG theology. This pack of theologians affirmed, like liberal theologians before, that the miraculous was mythical, and the Bible merely a collection of interesting writings that were comparable with other religious texts.[17]

14. In the same vein, I remember that as an undergraduate at Fordham University (Catholic) in the 1960s theology was referred to as the "queen of the sciences." I am not sure too many took that seriously other than some of the older faculty. This claim had something to do with the systematic attention to Church doctrines and papal encyclicals.

15. See the seminal book by Shalit, *Return to Modesty*.

16. There is a vast literature on the destructiveness of the 1960s generation. For a succinct discussion and key books see Larsen's article, "Imagine There's No Christendom."

17. Among the most important DOG theologians were Harvey Cox of Harvard

Perhaps he most influential DOG theologian was John A. T. Robinson, a biblical scholar and an Anglican bishop in England, and author of the bestseller *Honest to God*. Robinson claimed that for Christianity to be relevant in the modern world one had to honestly admit that the supernatural does not exist. Even the clergy have to be honest about this. He suggested that Christians should stop talking about God!

> "[W]e should do well to give up using the word "God" for a generation, so impregnated has it become with the way of thinking [miracles and the supernatural] we have to discard if the Gospel is to signify anything."[18]

The "anything" Robinson had in mind was to focus on social work to demonstrate the love of God. God, in fact, was no longer to be worshiped as person, but sensed in a pantheistic understanding.[19]

Robinson and other DOG theologians made much of their honesty in revealing their faithlessness. But really just the opposite is true. Behind the often sophisticated language of DOG theologians lay a deep dishonesty. They did no due diligence in examining any evidence for the miraculous in the larger Christian community. In a massive dose of snobbism and Sadducaism, they merely confirmed their faithless opinions by consulting with like-minded academics and clerics. The "peasants" in the outer realms who believed in healing and the miraculous, like the Pentecostals, were assumed as mistaken, and thus there was *no need for fact checking.*

True honesty and integrity would have demanded that DOG theologians investigate past their academic fire hydrants and sniff out the truth.[20] They could have encountered groups like the Guild of Health (in

---

Divinity School, Anglican Bishop John A. T. Robinson, and academic theologian Thomas J. J. Altizer, who worked out of Emory's Candler Seminary and did much to radicalize that faculty. The leadership of the DOG theologians mostly came from the Anglican (UK) and Episcopal Churches (USA). Not surprisingly, these churches fell into huge membership loss and disintegration by the twenty-first century. Cox has been the only one to admit he was wrong, and in his *Fire from Heaven* (1995) outlined the effectiveness and amazing growth of the Pentecostal/charismatic churches worldwide. Indeed, *Fire from Heaven* reminds one of St. Augustine's *Retractions*. On Harvey Cox's spiritual journey from Sadducaic liberalism to accepting Pentecostalism, see Hollenweger, "From Heaven."

18. Ibid., 8.

19. Robinson's pantheism is only hinted at in *Honest to God* but is clear in his subsequent writings. See Brierlen, "Review."

20. The reader may be surprised at the contempt I express for DOG theologians,

England) or the Order of St. Luke (in America) doing healing missions, or hundreds of Pentecostal churches that would have demonstrated God's presence and the gifts of the Spirit. The eminent sociologist Andrew Greeley, a Jesuit priest, noted the flawed methodology of DOG and other cessationist theologians in his work *Unsecular Man,* and took it to task.

> [O]ne does not analyze contemporary religiousness by limit-
> ing oneself to the university campus. Such a statement seems
> so obviously true as to be unnecessary, and yet most essays on
> contemporary religion have not looked at the religiousness of
> what one could call, using the currently fashionable phrase, "the
> silent majority." If substantial segments of the population are
> still involved in religious activity, they are dismissed either as a
> residue of the past or . . . not "authentic."[21]

Naturally, Greeley was not much noticed in academic circles.

In 1966 *Time* magazine published the infamous issue entitled "Is God Dead?," which featured the DOG movement in a favorable light—as the next big advance in theology.[22] When I attended seminary in the 1980s DOG theology was still highly respected, although by that time it was clear nothing fruitful had come of it, and liberal theology moved on to political and gender radicalizations of various sorts.[23] Just how many millions of Christians were led by this Sadducaic heresy to total unbelief and apostasy is impossible to tally this side of eternity. But their influence was massively destructive.[24]

However, unknown to most Christians, 1960 saw a new revival break out that was not limited to any one denomination, or even to Protestantism. This was the Charismatic Renewal. This revival was the product of decades of ferment, and had its origins in a Marcion Shove that reminds one of the first centuries of Christianity. The Holy Spirit had been engaged in this revival via Pentecostalism and a less noticed second front for over fifty years to bring another great wave of

---

and perhaps think, "This is not Christ-like." But compare with what Jesus said about the false religious teachers of his age (Matt 23:27).

21. Greeley, *Unsecular Man,* 7.

22. *Time,* August 6, 1966. The lead article is entitled "Towards a Hidden God."

23. Note how DOG theology was still taken seriously; see Slee, *Honest to God.*

24. Note the autobiography of popular movie and TV star Dick Van Dyke, *My Lucky Life.* Without irony or sadness, Van Dyke cheerfully relates his devout Christian boyhood and adulthood that came to an apostate end through his readings of DOG theologians and his personal friendship with Bishop Robinson.

revival to the church. But before dealing with this second front we need to describe in briefest terms possible the frustrating course of revivals in the church age.

PART II

Clawing Out of Cessationism

7

Revivals and the Opposition to Revivals

THE HOLY SPIRIT CONSTANTLY strives to bring the church into conformity with the pattern of the Spirit-empowered church that would reflect the pattern of holiness and power of the Spirit-filled apostolic church.[1] The Spirit does this within the bounds of love and respect for human freedom, including allowing for serious mistakes. For instance, God could have posted an angel next to John Calvin so that every time he thought of cessationism he would have been hit by a migraine headache. This would have avoided much tragedy and loss, but that is not God's way of respecting our freedom.

Rather, the Spirit moves through prophets and revivals to guide the church out of its mistakes and into its destiny as the empowered, spotless Bride of Christ. As in biblical times, prophets are often ignored or ridiculed, and sometimes burned at the stake. Also, every revival has its imperfections and often falls into error and exaggeration (the Wesleyan revival of 1740s to 1800 may be an exception to this). At times the failure of revivals was due to the weakness or failures of the revival's prophetic leaders. Other times it was due to not having in place "elders" to judge and limit prophetic utterances, as mandated by Paul in 1 Corinthians 24:29.

An example of the latter case is the Montanist revival (roughly A.D. 170–350). This group reintroduced the church to active prophecy and the gifts of the Spirit. But it was flawed by a moral legalism that asserted that those Christians who broke under Roman torture or persecution and

---

1. The main elements of this chapter are derived from two chapters of *Quenching the Spirit*: chapter 9, "Evangelical Healers of the 1800s," and chapter 10, "The Healing Revival Destroyed by Victorian Pharisees."

renounced their faith could not be readmitted into church fellowship. The majority of bishops thought to the contrary, and allowed repentant apostates to return to full communion after suitable penances.

The Montanists had several prophets who prophesied that very soon Jesus would return to establish a New Jerusalem at their hometown, Pepuza, a tiny village in what is now central Turkey. That did not happen, and the Montanists separated into a legalistic denomination of early Christendom, and faded out by the fifth century.[2]

The pattern of poorly discerned prophetic utterances has ruined or marginalized several revival movements. One in the 1830s had especially great potential: the Irvingites, or as they called themselves, the Catholic Apostolic Church. This group experienced a Holy Spirit infilling and recovered an understanding and use of the gifts of the Spirit, including tongues. Their prophets prophesied that Jesus would return very soon, and *definitely* before the death of their last founding apostle. This apostle died in 1901, and the denomination declined after that.[3]

But revivals are most often stymied by the opposition of *orthodox churchpersons* who do not recognize the presence of the Spirit in a revival. Just like the Pharisees of the New Testament, these orthodox churchpersons are so enamored with their present theology and church practice that they cannot believe that God is moving in new ways or among some group that is not their own.[4] Such Pharisaic opposition occurred in the seventeenth and eighteenth centuries with a cluster of interlocking revivals that was called by historians the Transatlantic Evangelical Revival.[5] This was a series of revivals and revived groups that arose a century after the Reformation, and included such groups as the Moravians, German Pietists, Scottish Presbyterians, Dutch Calvinists, English Methodists, and those congregations involved in the American Great Awakening. These revivals did not go so far as to bring back the gifts of the Spirit or healing, although several brief incidents within these revivals did point in that direction. But the Methodist revival, and its later derivatives in the American Holiness movement, prepared the way for Pentecostalism and the fullness of the gifts of the Spirit.

2. On the Montanists, a fair and charitable assessment of them is given in the classic work of pre-Pentecostal revivals, Knox's, *Enthusiasm*, chapter 3.

3. Some Irvingite congregations still survive. On the history of this denomination, see Flegg, *Gathered under Apostles*.

4. I examined this issue extensively in my work *Quenching the Spirit*.

5. See for example Lambert, *Pedlar in Divinity*.

Our understanding of these interlocking evangelical revivals has been revolutionized in recent decades by the magisterial work of Dr. William R. Ward (1925–2010) of the University of Durham.[6] Ward's scholarship showed that the Evangelical Awakening was not just a transatlantic event of New England and United Kingdom reformers, but involved early origins in various parts of Central Europe. Ward showed that the leaders of these revivals were universally reacting against the formality and dogmatic/theological emphasis of Protestantism which gave scant attention to heart religion and individual piety.

Ward also discovered that these leaders were stimulated into their evangelicalism by influences that would now be called heretical. Especially influential were the esoteric/occultist theories of the alchemist Paracelsus (1493–1541). His theories were believed to be valid and a model of relating theology to the physical world. Also deeply influential was the work of Giovanni Pico della Mirandola (1463–1494), who attempted to reconcile the Jewish Kabbalah, an occultist and mystical form of Judaism, with Christianity. Also influential was Jakob Bohme (1575–1624), who believed that humanity was created as an androgynous being, and split into two sexes after the fall. The spiritualist Emanuel Swedenborg (1688–1772) was also widely read by many evangelicals of the era, including George Whitefield, the major evangelist of the Great Awakening.[7]

Plainly, what Dr. Ward's scholarship demonstrates is a Marcion Shove. That is, that irregular or heretical ideas and persons stimulated an orthodox, biblical, and creative response at a time of church self-satisfaction and formalism. Dr. Ward did not use the term "Marcion Shove" but clearly traced how the leaders of evangelical revivals were able to draw out of the unorthodox and heretical influences an *impulse* to reform Protestant Christianity into something more heartfelt, and conform it closer to its New Testament model. Their knowledge and love of Scripture allowed them to filter out those specific ideas that were dangerous to the church, just as the bishops of the early church discerned the truth and errors in Marcion. I stress this here because we will see another example of the Maricon Shove when we study the leaders of Christian New Perspective, including Mrs. Agnes Sanford.

This is a book that focuses on Mrs. Agnes Sanford and her companions, not on the history of revivals. But to understand why her biblically

6. Noll, "Rewriting the History."
7. Ward, *Early Evangelicalism.*

sound theology and her discovery of inner healing was so fiercely opposed and slandered, we need to say something more about Pharisaism, the tendency of orthodox churchpersons to oppose revival. The best way to do that is to look very briefly at the Great Awakening, and compare its Great Theologian, Jonathan Edwards, with its Great Pharisee, Charles Chauncy.

Jonathan Edwards Triggers and Discerns the Great Awakening

The First Great Awakening began at Jonathan Edwards' church in Northampton in 1734. It was triggered by a sermon series about damnation and salvation. The sermons led many to awaken from their nominalism to become truly born again Christians. Edwards wrote a letter to a colleague in Boston describing how it happened. This was then expanded into his first public piece on revival, *A Faithful Narrative of the Surprising Work of God in the Conversion of Many Hundred Souls in Northampton* (1736), now often called simply "Faithful Narrative."[8]

Edwards emphasized how conversion and the intense sense of God's presence affected the body in strange ways. Abigail Hutchinson, a person profoundly converted and sanctified by the revival, would at times faint away while talking of her experience with God. On one occasion during a home group meeting.

> . . . some asked her concerning what she had experienced; and she began to give an account, but as she was relating it, it revived such a sense of the same things, that her strength failed; and they were obliged to take her and lay her upon the bed.[9]

The revival subsided by 1735, although the people touched by it remained fully converted. In 1739 George Whitefield, the great English revivalist, came to the Colonies. Under his anointed preaching, revival became widespread in all the colonies, with many of the bodily agitations, faintings, and emotional outcries becoming common. This caused some concern and criticism among the clergy, and Edwards wrote the *Distinguishing Marks of a Work of the Spirit of God* (1741) to answer some of these concerns. In that important work he affirmed that the exercises, the bodily manifestations that often accompany revival, often bear good

---

8. Edwards, *A Faithful Narrative.*

9. Ibid., section 2, 360.

fruit as in manifest conversion. But they can also be counterfeited, or merely self-induced. Thus bodily exercises themselves are not proof of the presence of the Holy Spirit. Rather, one has to judge the exercises by the fruit of real change and spiritual progress of the persons and congregations affected by revival.

The Rev. Edwards developed criteria based on Scripture to assess the fruit of revival and see if it was truly from God, regardless of the intensity or lack of intensity in the exercises. These were five general criteria for discerning if revival and its accompanying exercises were truly from the Holy Spirit:

1. When the operation is such as to raise their esteem of that Jesus who was born of the Virgin, and was crucified without the gates of Jerusalem; and seems more to confirm and establish their minds in the truth of what the gospel declares to us of his being the Son of God, and the Savior of men; is a sure sign that it is from the Spirit of God.

2. When the spirit that is at work operates against the interests of Satan's kingdom, which lies in encouraging and establishing sin, and cherishing men's worldly lusts; this is a sure sign that it is a true, and not a false spirit.

3. The spirit that operates in such a manner, as to cause in men a greater regard to the Holy Scriptures, and establishes them more in their truth and divinity, is certainly the Spirit of God.

4. Another rule to judge of spirits may be drawn from those compellations given to the opposite spirits . . . "The spirit of truth and the spirit of error." These words exhibit the two opposite characters of the Spirit of God, and other spirits that counterfeit his operations. And therefore, if by observing the manner of the operation of a spirit that is at work among a people, we see that it operates as a spirit of truth, leading persons to truth, convincing them of those things that are true, we may safely determine that it is a right and true spirit.

5. If the spirit that is at work among a people operates as a spirit of love to God and man, it is a sure sign that it is the Spirit of God.[10]

___

10. Goen, *Great Awakening*, 253. These are an abbreviation of the points in section 2 of Edward's *Distinguishing Marks*.

By this time there was considerable excess among other and often intemperate revival preachers. One revivalist believed he could discern the spiritual state of a church pastor, as to whether he was truly converted or a false believer. His negative judgment would prompt the congregation to remove that pastor from the pulpit. This caused much resentment among the clergy towards the revival.

In Edwards' next work, *Some Thoughts Concerning the Present Revival of Religion in New England* (1743), he aimed at allaying the fears and resentments of the clergy by informing them of the overall benefits of revival in spite of its faults and indiscreet preachers. In this work he urged that revival must be judged as a *whole and not by its extremes.*

> Another foundation-error of those who reject this work, is, they are not duly distinguishing the good from the bad, and very unjustly judging of the whole by a part; and so rejecting the work in general, or in the main substance of it, for the sake of some accidental evil in it.[11]

Edwards again pointed out how often and how many churches had truly experienced good fruit in revival worship and enthusiasm for the Christian life. He affirmed that revival exercises, although strange, such as Abigail Hutchinson's faintings, often bore much good fruit in the long run. He also pointed out that exercises such as the fallings had occurred before, as in the Scottish Presbyterian Revival of the 1600s, and were continuing in his time.[12] Edwards repeated and expanded this message, in his last and now classic work on revival, *A Treatise Concerning Religious Affections* (1742). By the time it came out, revival was under severe attack, principally by the writings of the renowned Boston pastor Charles Chauncy.[13]

The Rev. Chauncy did precisely what Edwards warned not to do. Chauncy collected letters only from clergy antagonistic to the revival. He made an arduous horseback circuit of New England on which he gathered every story of exaggerated exercises, imprudent sermons, and tactless acts of extremism and cobbled them together as a picture of the revival. That work, called *Seasonable Thoughts on the State of Religion in New England* (1743), greatly pleased the now frightened clergy. It pictured the Great Awakening as an uncontrolled orgy of emotionalism and

11. Edwards, *Some Thoughts*, section 3, 371

12. Ibid., 370.

13. See my detailed discussion of Chauncy in *Quenching the Spirit*, chapter 3, "The Great Awakening Quenched."

theological error. It outsold all of Edward's works and effectively put an end to the Great Awakening.[14]

We should note that a significant minority of clergy understood what Edwards had said and recognized the good fruit that revival had brought to their churches. This faction was called the New Lights. They passed on Edwards' writings to the next generation, so that when the Second Great Awakening occurred (1801–1830) the revival preachers understood the exercises in Edwards' sense and were not disturbed by them or stopped by the inevitable Pharisees of the time. The Second Great Awakening succeeded marvelously in transforming America from a deist country (as its president Thomas Jefferson had become) into a majority-evangelical nation.[15]

The opposite happened with the Pentecostal Revival at the beginning of the twentieth century. By that time, Edward's writings were passé and not read by the clergy or taught in seminary. Thus, when the Pentecostals began manifesting body agitations and fallings it was incomprehensible to its critics and the new Pentecostals were derided as "Holy Rollers," a disparaging moniker that stuck.[16]

We will get back to Edward's discernment criteria as to whether a movement is from God or not when we evaluate the work of writers and leaders of the Christian New Perspective, and especially the ministry of inner healing that Agnes Sanford birthed. Space restrictions must limit our descriptions of the revival versus the Pharisee syndrome. But we do need to point to two revival movements that impacted the healing ministry and its recovery: the Faith Cure movement of the 1880s, and the Pentecostal Revival that began at Azusa St. in 1906.

The Faith Cure movement is much less known today than Pentecostalism, but it must be considered an indispensable precursor to the Azusa St. Revival and the Pentecostal churches it birthed. The Faith Cure movement was led by Dr. Charles Cullis (1833–1892), a homeopathic physician from Boston and pious Episcopalian. He was led by compassion to found a rest home for destitute and dying tuberculosis patients, something not uncommon in the era. However, he was providentially led to discover that faith-filled prayer could cure many of them of their

14. Chauncy, *Seasonable Thoughts*.

15. The Second Great Awakening is not as well known as the First, but was perhaps more significant in its overall effect on American religion and character. See Conkin's *Cane Ridge* and my own work, *Forgotten Power*, chapter 7.

16. McDermott, "The Great Divider."

fatal disease. Protestant ministers of various denominations, such as the Baptist A. J Gordon, noticed his work and joined the healing movement.

By the 1880s the ministers of the movement were having healing conventions at Old Orchard Beach in Main where healing prayer was taught and ministered at healing lines with anointing and laying on of hands. A bevy of solid, biblically based books on healing prayer came out of this revival, authored by Dr. Cullis, Gordon, and others.[17] But it must be mentioned that some of the works espoused a no-medication doctrine, that is, that taking medicine or seeking medical assistance is contrary to the faith needed to receive divine healing. Dr. Cullis, of course, had no part in this development.

The Faith Cure movement attracted much publicity at its height, much of it favorable, as there were indeed many persons who were miraculously healed during this period. It was a moment when cessationism in America could have been overthrown. However, another great Pharisee came to the fore. He was James Buckley, the editor of the *Christian Advocate*, the prestigious national Methodist journal. Methodism was in this period the largest single Protestant denomination in America.

Buckley relentlessly attacked the Faith Cure movement as occultic and heretical, claiming it was no different from the heresy of Christian Science. He derided its healings as psychosomatic and minor. He focused on the no-medication doctrine and its fallacy. Together, his articles in the *Christian Advocate* and his book *Christian Science and Other Superstitions* did what Chauncy's work had done a century and a half before: it defamed and crippled a great move of God.[18]

Thankfully, the discoveries of the Faith Cure movement were passed on to the Pentecostal Revival at the turn of the century. This happened because many of the Faith Cure healing evangelists were still alive at the time of Azusa St. and seamlessly stepped into Pentecostalism.[19] Unfortunately, many in the emerging Pentecostalism accepted the no-medication doctrine, and thus even to this day there are incidents of persons dying from entirely curable diseases for lack of available meditation.

The Pentecostal Revival itself should be considered as the most successful revival of Christendom since the Reformation. It recovered the use of the gifts of the Spirit and made them a part of *normal* Christian life. The

17. Just to cite two: Cullis, *Faith Cures*, and, A. J. Gordon, *Ministry of Healing*.

18. Buckley, *Other Superstitions*.

19. Albrecht, "Carrie Judd Montgomery."

rise of Pentecostalism, its opposition, and its consistent slow growth in the face of jeering critics has been well documented.[20] The critics of the period were able to point to an embarrassing mistake of some Pentecostals, including its founder, the Rev. Charles Parham. He believed that the tongues spoken in his revivals were the tongues described in Act 2, where Peter gave a sermon that was understood in many languages. The Rev. Parham did not understand that what manifested was the tongues described in 1 Corinthians 12–14, which Paul described as a heavenly language for use in intercessory prayer and prophecy. Parham sent out missionaries with no language training on the assumption that they would preach in tongues and the natives would understand. That did not happen, and Pentecostals were ridiculed. But again we should note that the critics of Pentecostalism did not apply Jonathan Edwards' criteria of judging the *whole movement*, nor did they notice how Pentecostalism revived the healing movement, or that many congregations grew in evangelization and ministry. Rather, the critics but focused on Pentecostalism's immaturities.

There was no single person to earn the title of the Great Pharisee of Pentecostalism, although there were many contenders. One book of this period, however, deserves mention for its effectiveness in quenching Pentecostalism and for affirming cessationism: *Counterfeit Miracles*, which to this day is still used by many cessationists as a prime resource.[21] Its author, Benjamin B. Warfield, was part of the Princeton theology which battled for biblical inerrancy and against liberal theology. In those he did well, and so also in advocating a reasoned and moderate response to Darwinism. This makes his attack on the Faith Cure movement and Pentecostalism all the more tragic.

Healing as Heresy

By the time Buckley, Warfield, and others had finished their critique of the Faith Cure movement and later Pentecostalism, healing had been classified as heresy and illusion. Those who strongly held to healing prayer

20. To cite just two of the classics of Pentecostal history, Synan, *Holiness-Pentecostal* (1971), and Dayton, *Roots of Pentecostalism* (1987).

21. Warfield, *Counterfeit Miracles*. On its continued citation by present-day cessationists, see MacArthur, *Strange Fire*, 313. See my review of this intemperate work, "Parody of Jonathan Edwards's Theology." For a detailed critique on Warfield's work see Ruthven, *Cessation of Charismata*. Ruthven's work is a classic of Pentecostal scholarship.

were heretics, and the religious communities to which they belonged were not really part of the Christian church at all, but cults. Therefore, they were not to be studied or valued as part of the kingdom of God.

This is demonstrated in the work of a prominent Christian scholar of the time, William Warren Sweet. He became dean of the divinity school at the University of Chicago and attracted an excellent faculty of church historians who wrote volumes of what became the accepted version of American Protestant history. Dr. Sweet published the first edition of his influential *The Story of Religion in America* in 1930, which continued to be reissued and revised for thirty years.[22] In Sweet's vision, mainline Protestant Christianity was the Christianity of America. He paid attention to the fundamentalist-versus-liberal debates, church expansion, and missionary activities of the Protestant churches. But neither the American Lutherans nor the Roman Catholics received much coverage in spite of their large numbers. The *Pentecostals received no notice*, and, similarly, the Faith Cure movement was not mentioned.[23]

Paul Chappell, who wrote a dissertation on the Faith Cure movement, or, as he termed it, the Divine Healing movement, noted in 1983 how the Faith Cure had been written out of American church history:

> Divine healing has been one of the most fascinating, yet controversial themes to develop in the modern history and theology of the American church. It has also been one of the few significant developments in the American church which has remained almost completely unexamined by church historians.[24]

At a workshop I was giving on Agnes Sanford, a minister asked me if Mrs. Sanford had been influenced by the Faith Cure literature or the literature of Pentecostalism. In an off-the-cuff answer I said, "No, because there was no Google at the time." That seems flippant, but it points how things have changed since the 1930s, when Mrs. Sanford began her investigation into healing prayer (chapter 15). Now anyone can do a Google search for "healing prayer" and come up with an astounding number of hits (over 21,000,000!) from orthodox Christian, unorthodox, or cultic sources, find a satisfactory title, and easily get it if it is in print.

---

22. Sweet, *Religion in America* (1930).

23. On the problem of selectivity and poverty of coverage of American church history, see the fine article on Sweet by Ash, "American Religion."

24. Chappell, "Divine Healing," 358.

But this was not even imaginable in the 1930s. Further, Mrs. Sanford and her husband Ted were missionaries to China and came to the
United States in 1928. They had no knowledge of the controversies about
the Faith Cure or Pentecostalism, and by then few mainline Christians
considered Pentecostal healing literature as anything but cultic. Faith
Cure and Pentecostal books would not have been available in even the
finest bookstores of the era, no more than a New Age book can be found
in a Christian bookstore today. In fact, there were very few bookstores
in America prior to World War II, and it was not uncommon for small
cities to have no bookstores at all. The expansion of a large middle-class
reading public, and bookstores to service them, really began after World
War II.[25] The literature of Pentecostalism and its healing ministries were
sold mainly by traveling Pentecostal evangelists at their services, where
no mainline Christian dared attend.

Thus Mrs. Sanford, Professor Glenn Clark, and the other pioneers
of Christian New Perspective, whom we will examine with care, had to
start from scratch. They began from the Bible and from sources of the
then popular the readily available literature of Christian Science and
New Thought (explained fully in the next chapters), where they did a
Marcion Shove as they discerned that literature. We will note that in doing so they had to reinvent the basics of healing prayer, and waste some
time and effort, but they also went into areas of healing that were original and would not have come as a linear development from Faith Cure
and Pentecostalism.

One clear advantage that Mrs. Sanford and most Christian New
Perspective leaders and authors had was that they did not have much
opposition from the Pharisees of the era, at least in the beginning of
their ministry years. That is, they operated in parachurch organizations
such as the Camps Furthest Out (CFO) and the Order of St. Luke (OSL),
where Pharisees were not likely to show up or be influential if they came.

---

25. WWII played a critical role in expanding the reading public, via cheap pa-
perbacks made available free to GIs. After the war there was a rapid multiplication of
bookstores and other book outlets. See Appelbaumser, "Gave Away."

8

Mary Baker Eddy Gives a Marcion Shove to the Healing Ministry

The Idealist Sects

WE NOTED HOW THE Holy Spirit sought to awaken the church through various revivals within orthodox churches and groups. In the following chapters we will examine how the Holy Spirit simultaneously brought revival and biblical recovery through a second front, that is, heretical groups that arose in America in the mid-nineteenth century. These groups are commonly referred to as the metaphysical sects or the metaphysical movement.[1] They may be better termed the "idealists sects," as they all believed that mind was superior to, and ruled, matter. The more extreme of the sects believed that matter was an illusion.[2]

1. The term "metaphysical movement" has caused some confusion, as it can be mistaken for the sub-discipline of philosophy called metaphysics, which deals with how we know and how the mind understands categories. I have seen this confusion in less-than-well-informed anti-cult writers who lament that "Metaphysics is often taught in college!"

2. In European history there have been various "idealist" philosophies and philosophers who have given the mind and thought prominence over the material world. Plato is the best example. In the eighteenth century there arose a group of Christian British idealist philosophers, bishop George Berkley being the most famous. Berkley reintroduced idealism into popular discourse and attempted to counter the materialist and realist drift of European philosophy. Berkeley's arguments were highly technical and had no pastoral consequences in ministry. These idealist philosophers did little to stem the materialist and atheistic drift of modern philosophy. On this see Sell, *Philosophical Idealism.*

The idealist sects began through writers and philosophers, and then became a healing movement through the Mind-Cure pioneers of the 1860s, who taught various ways of healing through mind power. Out of the early Mind-Cure movement developed Christian Science and later New Thought, which included Unity Christianity, it's most prominent group.[3]

It is important to remember that the idealist sects arose at a time in America when the Bible was at the center of literacy, education, and opinions to a degree hardly imaginable today. Common to many persons of the idealist sects was a desire, driven by a common-sense reading of Scripture, that the church should be more than the powerless and healing deficient institution that cessationism had made it. Warren Felt Evans, the well-educated spokesman of the early Mind-Cure movement, and a former Methodist minister, wrote:

> May an age of living faith and spiritual power succeed the present reign of materialism and religious impotency, so that the so-called miracles of history may be reproduced as the common facts of our age.[4]

Gnosticism in the Idealist Sects

These idealist sects had neither Pharisees nor Sadducees within them to tell them that healing and spiritual phenomenon were either impossible, only for another age, or the product of delusion. However, it is easily discerned that these idealist sects were influenced by a (demonic) spirit of Gnosticism. Gnosticism is the very opposite of Pharisaism and Sadducaism. Whereas these tend to believe too little about spiritual realities and miracles, the gnostics tend to believe everything and anything, and thus open themselves to demonic influences.

Within the idealist sects there was a conflict between the biblical endowment common to its founders, and the demonic-Gnostic spirits which strove to ruin that legacy. For the most part the Gnostic element prevailed, although in our study we will center on those persons and groups who discerned and prayed their way through the Gnostic elements.

3. The standard histories of the idealist sects are Judah, *Metaphysical Movement*, and Braden, *Spirits in Rebellion*.

4. Evans, *Mental Medicine*, iv.

Of the idealist groups, Christian Science was perhaps the most heretical and extreme, and Unity Christianity the least. Professor Glenn Clark, whose work we will study later, termed them the "impatient sects."[5] Clark meant that in their quest to move the Christian churches out of their deadening cessationism they lost patience and walked away from the mainline churches, and sadly, their historic, creedal doctrines.

The original inspiration for those in the idealist sects were the writings of Ralph Waldo Emerson (1803–1882). Emerson is remembered mostly for his essays and as the founding father of transcendentalism.[6] Deeply dissatisfied with the Calvinist orthodoxy of his New England, he became a Unitarian minister. Emerson encountered idealist philosophy through sources that included ancient philosophy (Plato and the neo-Platonists) but also readings from Eastern religions. His lifelong quest was to make the idealist perspective the basis of spiritual renewal.

Idealism as Healing: The Mind-Cure Movement[7]

The person who really turned idealism from a philosophical discussion into a practical healing movement was a clockmaker, Phineas Quimby (1802–1866).[8] Quimby received a scant education, but loved to read and had an inquisitive mind. Sickly from his youth, Quimbly was healed by a traveling French hypnotist. He then read about hypnotism and took up therapeutic hypnotism himself. He developed a healing procedure in which he hypnotized his patients and gave them healing suggestions and affirmations, after which many became well.

At the same time, Quimby developed a passionate hatred for doctors and a disdain for Christian churches and their ministers. He believed his healings were all due to the powers of the mind and had nothing to do with religion, or God's grace, etc. From a modern perspective, Quimby's dislike for doctors was quite understandable, as medical practice at the time was often little more than quackery, with such things as leaching, bleeding, and caustic mustards the most commonly practiced "remedies."

5. This is also the theme of Braden's *Spirits in Rebellion*.

6. On Emerson and the transcendentalists see Schmidt, *Restless Souls*.

7. Parker, *Mind Cure*.

8. See a brief biography by his son, George A. Quimby, "Phineas Parkhurst Quimby," online at http://www.ppquimby.com/gquimby/biography.htm. An insightful article on Quimby is Poterfield, "Native American."

Today, many evangelical Christians believe that hypnotism is a form of witchcraft and thus automatically sinful. The biblical evidence for this is analogous at most. On the other hand, the Catholic Church allows hypnotism under certain circumstances, as in pain control. The truth is that hypnosis can immobilize a person's fear, which makes hypnotism effective in eliminating many psychosomatic illnesses and some forms of pain. However, experience has indicated there are indeed spiritual and emotional dangers in hypnotic procedures, as many evangelicals often affirm.[9]

Quimby's accidental discovery of the deeper levels of the human mind paralleled what was happening in Europe under such physicians as Anton Messer and Jean-Martin Charcot. These led to Freud's theory of the unconscious which has so influenced the modern world.[10] Quimby did not go in that direction, but developed a theory of mind inspired by the idealism of Emerson and the transcendentalists and based on what he experienced in his hypnotic practice. It was a loose system of ideas written down in several essays. These were circulated among his followers but not published until well after his death.

Quimby's system was a grandiose radical idealism. For Quimby the mind was all, and matter unimportant. Illness was caused by erroneous ideas, and thus could be healed by correct and positive ideas given through hypnotic suggestion. Further, he believed that what he had discovered about the mind was absolute science, and a manifestation of God. He claimed his system to be the key to all human happiness and fulfillment. Quimby's system was influential mostly through persons who came to him for healing, such as Warren Felt Evans, the Dressers, and especially Mary Baker Eddy.

Mary Baker Eddy: The Marcion of the Nineteenth Century?[11]

The best known, and most influential of the Mind-Cure sects was Christian Science. Founded and ruled by Mary Baker Eddy (1821–1910), the

9. Note the balanced position on this topic by evangelical psychologist Gary Collins, *Magnificent Mind*, chapter 15, "The Hypnotic Mind."

10. Ellenberger, *The Discovery*.

11. The literature on Christian Science is vast. A standard and well-balanced source is Gottschalk's *Christian Science*. The writings of Robert Peel, a Christian Scientist himself, give many details of Mrs. Eddy's life but are unfortunately largely uncritical of her. See for example his *Spiritual Healing*. Mrs. Eddy's propagandistic autobiography is her brief *Retrospection and Introspection*.

sect grew to have a worldwide following and survives to the present time. Mrs. Eddy's principal book, *Science and Health with Key to the Scriptures* (first ed. 1875) became the sect's second Bible, as the *Book of Mormon* is a second Bible to the Mormons. To this day the Christian Science minister (called "reader") does not give sermons; rather, he or she reads sections of the Bible alternately with readings of Mrs. Eddy's commentary on the biblical passages read.

Mary Morse Baker had a happy childhood in a household where her father was a strict Congregationalist and her mother a particularly devout and prayerful woman. However, subsequent years were filled with tragedy and disappointment. Her first husband died shortly after the birth of their only child, and, due to lack of means, she had to have the boy raised by others. Later her second husband abandoned her. This was then followed by years of illnesses.

During her long illness she read much, including transcendentalists and some spiritualists' works. She also took up homeopathic medicine. In its medications Mary received some alleviation of her sufferings. But Mrs. Eddy had an astute mind, and suspected that the tiny quantities of active ingredients in the homeopathic potions were not the real source of healing. She actually experimented with sugar pills as placeboes to test her suspicion. She found that they had the same positive effects as the homeopathic medications.[12] She concluded it was the belief in the patients' mind that was the real healing agent. With this discovery Mrs. Eddy became convinced that the idealist understanding of the power of the mind was correct.[13]

For more complete healing Mrs. Eddy moved to Portland, Maine, for hypnotic treatments from Phineas Quimby. She received much relief from his treatments and stayed to become one of his disciples. During her stay with Quimby she read his manuscripts and learned his techniques and theories. It is now quite evident that the core of what became Mrs. Eddy's Christian Science was in fact a reformulation and plagiarism of Quimby's writings.[14] The plagiarism from Quimbly became clear when the original Quimby manuscripts were published in 1921.[15] Mrs. Eddy had died a decade earlier, and as with most sects, the Christian Scientist

12. Eddy, *Retrospection and Introspection*, 33–34.

13. Eddy, *Christian Healing*, 11–12.

14. Wilson, "The Origins."

15. Dresser, ed., *The Quimby Manuscripts*. On this issue see Judah, *Metaphysical Movement*, 270–72.

members had become loyal to their founder beyond the power of reason or reproof, and they refused to accept the plagiarism accusation. Rather, they have steadfastly maintained that Mrs. Eddy system was a divine revelation and totally original.

Mary Baker Eddy plagiarized and wrote *Science and Health* with the affectations of the age. That is, like many, she imitated the convoluted writing and bombast of the philosopher Friedrich Hegel.[16] The result was that the first edition of *Science and Health* was an unreadable mishmash. Her disciples had to take the work and edit it several times. The final version (1906) is understandable if pursued with concentrated effort.[17]

Mrs. Eddy did have important differences with the Quimby system. For one, she did not share her teacher's disdain for the church or Christianity. To the contrary, Mrs. Eddy believed herself a devout Christian, and saw herself as a great reformer, like Martin Luther, sent by God to bring the church back to its senses and into its healing ministry. (In her later years her vanity turned to megalomania and she saw herself as co-equal with Jesus.)

Mrs. Eddy also rejected the hypnotic technique used by Quimby. She instead substituted for it affirmations and denials such as, "God is Good, God is All," and inversely, the belief that sickness is an illusion and unreal. The Christian Science healer, called a practitioner, was trained in this radical idealism. If a person came in with a cancerous tumor, the practitioner would affirm the tumor unreal, and that only God's goodness and perfect health were truly real. The practitioner would also exhort the patient not to fear, and to totally trust in God for his or her healing. The practitioner disciplined his or her mind to avoid negative thoughts about the patient as he lifted the patient to God, and visualized the patient as well.

In the Christian Science system, healing, spiritual growth, and even salvation come to the seeker through correct knowledge, i.e., Christian Science doctrines and principles of thought. To the degree that the person

16. Mrs. Eddy did *not* copy *Science and Health* from a manuscript by the Hegelian philosopher Francis Lieber. That accusation was made in the 1930s and was the product of a crude forgery and extortion plot directed against the then rich First Church of Christian Science. As astute an anti-cult writer as Walter Martin accepted this fraud, see his *Christian Science*. On the false association with Lieber see Johnson, "Historical Consensus."

17. Imitation of Hegelian bombast and writing style was common in the era. For instance, many Civil War memoirs and battle accounts were plagued with this problem. In contrast, Ulysses S. Grant's famous *Personal Memoirs* (1885–86) were written in simple, humble, and readable style, and became a sensational bestseller.

understands that God is All, and he or she is part of God, to that degree the person will grow spiritually and acquire perfect health. Mrs. Eddy's system was a sloppy pantheism in spite of denials by its founder.[18] Evil, sin, and ultimately death are to disappear from the life of the Christian Scientists as they progress into the knowledge and participation of God and Good. Jesus Christ was an embodiment of the divine principle, the first and perfect Christian Scientist, but not any more God than all of us.[19]

Mrs. Eddy taught that Jesus' blood sacrifice was irrelevant to humanity's sin problem and merely an example of selflessness:

> The efficacy of Jesus' spiritual offering is infinitely greater than can be expressed by our sense of human blood. The material blood of Jesus was no more efficacious to cleanse sin when it was shed upon "the accursed tree," than when it was flowing in his veins as he went daily about his Father's business. His true flesh and blood were his Life, and they truly eat his flesh and drink his blood, who partake of that divine life.[20]

All of this made Christian Science truly a Gnostic heresy. This denial of evil as real is philosophically simple and psychologically satisfying. It does wonders for self-esteem to think one is above all evil and sin. However, the evil and sinfulness of our fallen world keep butting in. Mrs. Eddy's last years were a pathetic attempt to postpone and hide her infirmities. She had a most intrusive toothache, which no amount of affirmation/denial could heal, and ultimately had to go to a dentist. In 1910, at the ripe old age of eighty-nine, she shocked her most devoted disciples by dying. They thought it certainly would not happen to her.

Early on, Mrs. Eddy naively expected the churches to accept her doctrines and healing techniques. Most churchmen of the day quickly saw Christian Science as heretical, though many did so for the wrong reason. Many conservative churchmen labeled Christian Science as heresy simply because it taught *healing*. Others noted Mrs. Eddy's adamant stand against medication and even proper body hygiene and saw Christian Science as not only a cult but a danger to the community.[21] Actually, it was Catholic scholars, educated in the history of the church's early

18. Eddy, *Versus Pantheism.*
19. Eddy, *Science and Health*, 473–75.
20. Ibid., 25:3–9.
21. Cunningham, "Impact," 887.

battles against heresy, who immediately and correctly labeled Christian Science as a new form of gnosticism.[22]

Like Quimby, Mrs. Eddy stressed that her system was scientific. Significantly, she defined science in the terms of the contemporary usage (and out of Webster's Dictionary) as "knowledge, duly arranged and referring to general truths and principals on which it is founded . . ."[23] *Science and Health with Key to the Scriptures* attempted to be scientific by establishing a consistent doctrine and arranging it is a systematic way. The healings it produced were believed to authenticate the whole system.

Christian Science as Partially Right

Granted that the core doctrines of Mind-Cure and Mary Baker Eddy's Christian Science are Gnostic and heretical, we must now ask the key question of any heretical system: Were there elements within it that were partially right? The Christian's evaluation of Christian Science (and other idealist sects) then takes a considerably different tone that of most of its evangelical anti-cult critics.

First and most obvious: Mind-Cure and Christian Science were correct in advocating radical anti-cessationism. The healings described in the New Testament are indeed to be practiced today. The orthodox Protestant churches were *destructively wrong* on this issue.

Second: Christian Scientists practitioners did indeed minister many healings, and still do today. It may bother some Christians that heretics have any spiritual power, but heresy does not negate faith expectancy that God will act for the good. We should note that Jesus credited certain semi-pagans with greater faith than the children of Israel, as for instance the Syrophoenician woman of Matthew 15:21–28 and the centurion with the sick servant (Matt 8:10).

Agnes Sanford understood this from a personal experience. In her life she had transited from Presbyterian cessationism to New Thought and finally into Pentecostalism. She reflected on her early friends in New Thought and Christian Science and believed that the reason they healed effectively was that many of them were *faith-filled monotheists*. That is, that although many Christian Scientists were indeed not Christian, they did believe in one God who would answer prayer. They thus had the same

22. Gottschalk, *Christian Science*, 91.

23. Eddy, *Yes and No*, 9–10.

access to answered prayer as an Old Testament Jew.[24] In contrast, Mrs. Sanford noted that cessationist Christians, who had a biblically accurate view of Jesus as Savior and Son of God, had *no faith for healing*, and thus zero effectiveness in this ministry.

Third: Quimby, Mrs. Eddy, and the other Mind-Cure advocates were at least partially right about the power of the mind to heal. Again, this is difficult for some evangelicals to accept, brought up as they were on five-point Calvinism and its radical philosophical realism. In that theology the mind does not interact with matter. But study after study has documented that the placebo effect does bring about some healing. Also, many mind-body studies in last decades have shown the importance of optimism and visualization as resulting in real healing. It seems simply true that God designed both the body and mind with a natural ability to heal.[25] Mind-Cure and Christian Scientists tapped into this, but orthodox Christians knew nothing about it.

Fourth: The affirmation/negation technique, the core of the Christian Science approach, is scriptural. It is *one* way of healing among many used by Jesus to heal and raise the dead. We will show the biblical evidence for this after our discussion of Jesus' healing of Jairus' daughter (Matt 9:18–26; Mark 5:21–43; Luke 8:40–56) and its relation to quantum physics and idealism later in chapter 10.

The Spread and Influence of Christian Science Churches:[26]

The early growth of Christian Science was phenomenal. Precise numbers may never be known, as Mrs. Eddy was secretive about the statistics of her church. There were, however, hundreds of thousands of adherents by the turn of the century. It is difficult for Christians in the twenty-first century to understand both the attraction and influence that Christian Science had at the end of the nineteenth century. We now have many churches where healing ministry is effective. But imagine the dilemma

24. On this point see Sanford, *Behold Your God.*

25. There is a large body of literature on this issue. Among the most interesting is the cover story of the February 12, 2009 issue of *Time*, Kluger's "Biology of Belief," which shows how people of various religious beliefs have better medical outcomes than secular persons precisely because they believe they will. See also Collins, *Magnificent Mind.*

26. This section is based on the research of Dr. Cunningham, presented in his article "The Impact."

of a Christian mother with a deathly sick child in the 1880s. She could ask her Baptist, Methodist, or Presbyterian minister to pray for the child, and he would pray some pious prayer about having the "strength to endure" what God willed, i.e., the death of the child, etc. Or she might go to a Christian Science practitioner whose prayer had faith expectancy for healing, and had a chance for healing.

Aside from this main reason, its effective healing ministry, many Christians were attracted to Christian Science and other idealist sects because they seemed to reflect the latest in human knowledge and progress. The philosophies of German Idealism, as in the philosophers Hegel, Fitch, etc., and American transcendentalists were in the conversations of the educated classes, as well as the new, distinctly American philosophy of pragmatism, which stressed the utility of ideas.[27] Christian Science seemed to combine both modes of thought. It was idealist in its philosophy and pragmatic in its promise of healing here and now. The magazine revolution of the 1890, spurred by better printing presses, helped fuel the spread of Christian Science. Editors learned quickly that articles on Christian Science, personal testimonies to miraculous healings, and Mrs. Eddy were among the hot topics of the age.

Another major factor, not often noted, is that *Science and Health* was only vaguely comprehensible, and thus its heretical nature obscured to the normal Christian inquirer. Many, like Christians of all ages, understood the New Testament's plain command to heal the sick but had suppressed it in deference to their denomination's acceptance of cessationism. Reading about Christian Science was a release to many that the plain reading of Scripture was the right one, and not cessationist rationalizations. In its first expansive decades many Christians in the pews accepted Christian Science, or sympathized with it without leaving their home denominations.[28]

By 1910 there were over one thousand Christian Science church buildings in the United States, and other countries experience similar growth. An article in the *London Times* wrote with alarm,

27. Americans had at this time one of the great idealist philosophers of the modern world in the person of Josiah Royce (1855–1916), a friend of William James, the founder of pragmatism.

28. Cunningham, "Christian Science," 891. This is analogous to what happened in the 1970s when many Christians came into the Charismatic Renewal and went to its prayer groups, but remained in their own, sometimes hostile, congregations.

Clergymen of all denominations are seriously considering how to deal with what they regard as the most dangerous innovation that has threatened the Christian Church in this region for many years. Scores of the most valued church members are joining the Christian Science branch of the metaphysical organization, and it has been thus far impossible to check the defection.[29]

Not all clergy were as negative. Some saw some good in Christian Science and its emphasis on positive faith. The Rev. Lyman Powell, a well-respected cult investigator, rightly discerned the issue:

But the fact remains that Mrs. Eddy and her followers identified themselves, as have no other people in the world, with the religious and philosophical revolt against materialism, and if as years go by they prove wise enough to eliminate the crass and the crude, the foolish and the dangerous, and to profit by criticism, not all of which has been ill-natured and disrespectful, which they have of late received, Christian Science may become a blessing to the world.[30]

The Rev. Lyman's hope that Christian Science would heed some of its more constructive critics was not fulfilled. In fact, as the new century progressed Mrs. Eddy turned increasingly authoritarian and deaf to correction of any sort. But this in turn caused many of its adherents to leave the mother church and form new groups, some of which did in fact develop as corrected and moderate forms of Christian Science. These indeed ultimately blessed the whole of Christendom. To these Christian Science–engendered groups and individuals, called New Thought, we will now turn.

29. *London Times*, May 26, 1885, cited in Cunningham, "The Impact," 891.
30. Cited in Cunningham, "The Impact," 905.

9

New Thought: True Heresy?

IN THE 1890S THE term New Thought began to be used for those groups that had either originated in Mind-Cure or separated from Christian Science.[1] New Thought groups began with Christian Science idealist doctrines and the healing techniques of denial and affirmation, but quickly formed their own derivations and even new vocabulary. An example is their use of the word "vibration" to indicate the essence of a thing or unity of thought. This derived from the discovery, astounding to many, of electromagnetic radiation and radio waves that vibrate throughout the universe.[2]

By the end of the first decade of the twentieth century, New Thought was a major religious, business, and life-success motivational movement. Many of the groups were functioning as parachurches, that is, having their own meetings and organizations, but with most of their members attending traditional Christian churches for Sunday worship. Some, however, were completely separated from Christian churches. In 1914 many New Thought leaders joined in an umbrella organization, the International New thought Alliance (INTA). Most of those involved backed off from

1. On the New Thought movement see Judah and Braden, cited in the previous chapter, and also Dresser, *New Thought*.

2. Most Christians laugh at the usage of "vibration" in New Thought and later New Age writings. It may be nonsense, but if the new string theory of subatomic particles proves to be correct, it may be another case of heretics having it right before orthodox Christians. In string theory the universe is built on tiny strings (much smaller that atomic particles) that vibrate at different frequencies and thus create the multiplicity of matter. Thus the whole universe is a vibration. For a layperson's presentation of string theory and vibrations, see Greene, *Elegant Universe* and "Hanging."

the extremes of Christian Science in denying evil or the importance of the material world. In fact, as motivational writers they often stressed the enjoyment and acquisition of material things.

It is convenient to divide New Thought into two camps. On the one hand were the universalists. These persons believed that all religions are inspired, and that there are many spiritual leaders, "avatars" or "masters" equivalent to Jesus in their spiritual development and ability to bring enlightenment to the world. This section of New Thought became what is today the New Age movement, with all its Eastern religion and occult (demonic) attachments.

The other part of New Thought was made of individuals who considered themselves Christian and upheld the primacy of the Christian Bible. We will call this group the "Bible-affirming" wing of New Thought. Even these persons were often influenced by the Gnosticism of the original sources of the movement. This side of eternity it is impossible to say who among these were *really* Christian and who were deluded as to their status. Some were like Mrs. Eddy, who often quoted the Bible, but allowed Gnostic ideas to override the basic Christian doctrines of sin and repentance, the cross, and Jesus as only begotten Son of God. Others, in any fair estimate, were really Christian, but had irregular ideas and vocabulary.[3]

In discussing this issue we must remember that traditional Christianity has long been harsh in limiting who really is in the Body of Christ. I recall that, as a good Catholic youth in the 1950s, I was taught that practically all Protestants went to hell. My wife, raised Baptist, believed the same thing about Catholics. To the contrary, Paul's baseline definition of a Christian in Romans 10:9–10 is very generous:[4]

> That if you confess with your mouth, "Jesus is Lord," and believe
> in your heart that God raised him from the dead, you will be

---

3. There is an analogous issue in evaluating if Mormons are truly Christian. See the interesting article on the evangelical-Mormon dialogue, Ostling, "Improbable Dialogue."

4. Andrew F. Walls, who has resided in Africa for decades and is an expert on modern missions, gives some insight into the essential characteristics of Christian believers. He has studied the emerging native churches in Africa, many of which have no ties with the historical churches of Western Christianity, and often little awareness of the historic creeds. Among these very vibrant churches he finds a certain "Trinitarian" commonality. They all adhere to the "God of Abraham, Isaac and Jacob" (recognize the whole Bible and the God of the Old Testament), recognize Jesus as his Messiah, and experience the living presence of Jesus' Spirit. See Yerxa, "On the Road," and also Wells' major work *Cultural Process*.

saved. For it is with your heart that you believe and are justified,
and it is with your mouth that you confess and are saved.

However, even this definition excludes Mrs. Eddy and many others
in the idealist sects who believed that the bodily resurrection of Jesus was
a crude doctrine. It would also exclude those of the universalist wing of
New Thought who saw Jesus as a teacher, not the Lord. (Ironically, there
are many liberal Protestants found among the mainline denominations
who believe just as little about Jesus, but have never been excluded from
their churches or influential seminary posts.)

It is necessary for our study to mention a few of the figures and
institutions of the Bible-affirming wing of New Thought. These persons
ultimately proved to be influential on the church as a whole. Much of this
was done by influencing a second generation of writers and leaders who
took some of their insights, but weeded out the Gnostic ideas found in
New Thought.

Unity School of Christianity[5]

Perhaps the most enduring and influential of the New Thought churches
was the denomination founded by Charles Fillmore (1854–1948) and
his wife, Myrtle (1845–1931). Charles was a real estate agent; she was
a graduate of Oberlin College, and a devout Christian. Myrtle had been
sick on and off from childhood, and after her marriage was diagnosed
with tuberculosis. By 1886 Myrtle was at the point of death. She went
to hear a passing New Thought lecturer and learned the basic pattern of
affirmation and negation. She applied it to herself by repeating, "I am a
child of God and therefore I do not inherit sickness."[6] She immediately
improved and was totally healed within months. This caught Charles'
attention and he began studying Christian Science, New Thought writers, and the literature of world religions. He attempted to synthesize
it all under a Christian umbrella with Jesus as Lord and the Bible as
the central text.

Unlike Christian Science, Unity did not develop as an authoritarian
sect. In fact, the first literature published by Unity was from the hand of

---

5. My chief sources on the Fillmores are Freeman, *Household of Faith*, and
D'Andrade, *Charles Fillmore*.

6. D'Andrade, *Charles Fillmore*, chapter 6 has an excellent account of her healing.

another New Thought author and faith healer, Emily Caddy, whose work *Lesson in Truth* became the theological basis of Unity.[7]

Unity was several steps removed from the extremism of Christian Science. Charles plainly believed, for instance, in the real, physical resurrection of Jesus.[8] Medicine was accepted as a normal adjunct to healing prayer. Charles and Myrtle also rightly discerned that spiritualism was a demonic entrapment. Significantly, Charles withdrew Unity from the INTA when that group accepted spiritualists.[9]

On the other hand, Unity never totally separated from the universalist influences of New Thought. Although the Bible and Jesus were given preeminence, the exclusive claims of Jesus as God-man and sin redeemer are not absolutely clear. Charles also accepted the Gnostic doctrine that sexual activity weakened spiritual power and advised married couples to abstain as much as possible. Like Mary Baker Eddy, he believed he and others in Unity could attain bodily immortality through absolute abstinence and positive thinking:

> Through the sins of the sex life (casting away of the precious substance), the body is robbed of it essential fluids and eventually disintegrates. The result is called death, which is the great and last enemy to be overcome by man. Immortality in the body is possible to man only when he has overcome the weaknesses of sensation, and conserves his life substance.[10]

Unity also stressed the doctrine of reincarnation. In fact, Charles Fillmore believed he was a reincarnation of the apostle Paul.[11] Many Christians affirm reincarnation to be a true and serious heresy, citing Hebrews 9:27. This has much truth, but it is perhaps better to view it as a serious irregular idea. Reincarnation does have a *biblical echo* in the Elijah-John the Baptist connection described in the Bible (Mal 4:5; Matt 17:10–13 etc.).[12] If the Elijah-John the Baptist connection is not personal reincarnation, but a strong and specific spiritual tie (as indicated in Luke 1:17), do people living today have similar connections? This segment of biblical revelation has not been adequately elaborated in traditional

7. Caddy, *Lessons in Truth*.

8. Fillmore, *Atom-Smashing Power*, 146–47.

9. Fillmore, *Christian Healing*, lesson 10, no. 14.

10. Fillmore, *Twelve Powers*, 23.

11. Braden, *Spirits in Rebellion*, chapter 7.

12. See also Pss 16:10; 30:2–3; 49:15; 103:1–5; 116:2–7.

Christianity. Interestingly, it was accepted as fact by Gregory of Nyssa, the giant of the church fathers, who believed such a relationship existed between his own sister, Macrina, and an early Christian martyr, Thecla.[13] In any case, not having a stable, understandable explanation of the Elijah-John the Baptist connection within orthodox Christianity exposes every generation of Christians to speculate about reincarnation, though most generally only privately.[14]

Emmet Fox (1886–1951)[15]

Emmet Fox was born the son of a well-to-do English physician and member of Parliament, and a pious Roman Catholic mother. Very devout as a child, he received the gift of healing at six years of age, but at the time could receive no guidance for its use from either Catholic or Anglican clergy. At his Catholic confirmation he saw in a vision that when the bishop laid hands on the recipients tongues of fire fell down on them.

Without orthodox guidance on these matters he gravitated to the idealist sects, first to Christian Science and Divine Science (an offshoot of Christian Science) and then Unity. Fox formed his theology from all these sources, from his reading of Scripture, but also from fellowshipping with the Quakers. He believed that the Quaker practice of silent worship and their doctrine of pacifism made them the closest denomination to biblical Christianity.

His theology was quite close to that of Unity, believing, for instance, in Fillmore's claim that the second coming of Christ was a spiritual event, not a physical one. Fox also strongly believed in reincarnation. For instance, he believed that Moses derived his spiritual power and wisdom from previous incarnations.[16]

On a more positive note, like Fillmore, Fox saw Jesus as the sin bearer of our race (more on this in chapter 17) and upheld the Hebraic perspective that material life on earth is both good and spiritually significant, as against the Christian Science view of the material world as

13. Gregory of Nyssa, *Life of Macrina*, 164–65. I discuss this in the first book I wrote (and wish I could rewrite), *Past Life Visions*.

14. Barna Group, "American Describe."

15. Fox's biography was written by his friend and published shortly after Fox's death: Gaze, *Emmet Fox*.

16. Fox, *Ten Commandments*, 24, 58.

illusion. Fox's *Sermon on the Mount* became the influential classic because its subject matter lent itself to the valid insights of the New Thought perspective.[17] *The Sermon on the Mount* describes the Bible miracles as absolutely reliable, and Jesus' teachings as "this-worldly" (Hebraic) and totally realistic and applicable.

In 1931 Fox began pastoring one of most successful New Thought churches in America, the Church of the Healing Christ. It was based in New York City, where it met in large venues such as Carnegie Hall to accommodate the crowds drawn to hear his motivational sermons and experience his healing meditations.

Fox was vastly influential in his generation, even among many traditional Christians. For example, his *Sermon on the Mount* was on the suggested reading list for new Alcoholics Anonymous members. Noman Vincent Peale took many of his motivational and faith ideas and repackaged them into his more orthodox "positive thinking" theology. Dr. Peale wisely rejected Fox's Gnostic entanglements and theories of reincarnation. Peale's *The Power of Positive Thinking* was the single most read motivational book of the 1950s and 1960s, with about twenty million copies printed worldwide in fourteen languages.[18] It took from Fox the this-worldly belief that prayer and faith would change a person's everyday life, and the belief God was our ally in our struggles and would often provide miraculous answers to prayer.

Peale was also influenced by Unity literature. In 1945 he founded *Guideposts* magazine, inspired by the Unity business and inspirational magazine, *Good Business*. *Guideposts* followed the *Good Business* format of positive testimonials of the power of God to help in the business environment and everyday life.[19] *Guideposts* became the largest circulated Christian magazines of all time, with about four and a half million subscribers. Peale in turn mentored Robert Schuller, who for decades produced and preached in the internationally television broadcast *Hour of Power*.[20] Thus New Thought insights into faith for successful living came to mainstream America (and the world) via books, radio, and television

---

17. Fox, *Sermon On.*

18. Peale could not get it published under its original title, *The Power of Faith*, because that was similar to other works. Dozens of other books flowed from Peale's typewriter in the following decades.

19. Compare *Guideposts* with the collection of *Good Business* articles published in Unity school of Christianity's *Marketplace*.

20. Vaskuil, *Robert Schiller.*

by two of its most famous evangelical preachers. We will note Fox's influence on Agnes Sanford later in chapter 15.

Frederick L. Rawson (1859–1923) [21]

The last figure we must look at in this section is much less known today. He was a distinguished English scientist and engineer. Frederic L. Rawson designed Britain's first electric train line, and was a successful businessman. As a scientist and electrical engineer, Rawson became aware that the early experiments in particle physics were pointing to idealist conclusions, i.e., that mind had power over matter. His insight came decades before the idealist understanding was widely accepted among scientists in what became known as the Copenhagen interpretation of quantum physics (see chapter 10 below).

In the 1880s Christian Science had come to England and *The London Daily Mail* commissioned Rawson to investigate it and do a report for its readers. What Rawson found deeply impressed him. Here was a system of healing which seemed to combine Christianity with the idealist principles that were becoming scientifically provable. Rawson joined Christian Science, but soon clashed with its authoritarian and dogmatic ways. But not before he mastered its negation/affirmation type of prayer, and experienced successes with it. Not unnaturally, he also accepted Mrs. Eddy's belief that true Christianity should be scientific.

As an independent practitioner, Rawson combined what he learned from Christian Science with a fundamentalist form of Christian theology called Anglo-Israelism. This brand of fundamentalism held to the essential elements of the gospel but had an attached ethnic vanity. It claimed that the Anglo-Saxons tribes that invaded England were part of the Ten Lost Tribes of Israel. These tribes had inherited all of the promises of Scripture in regards to prosperity, health, and well-being. This explained why England and America were so prosperous and sincerely Christian. This bit of ethnic vanity may be ridiculous, but it is really not a soul-destroying heresy in any sense. At the time, it was popular among the English upper classes and was held many persons in Victorian America.

It is easy to dismiss Rawlson's book *Life Understood*, with its Anglo-Israel assumptions and its exaggerated Christian Science idealism. But it did have much to commend it. It was the first major work to deal with

---

21. A brief biography of Rawson in found in Braden, *Spirits in Rebellion*, 432–44.

the theological implications of what would become known as quantum mechanics. Rawson was the first to suggest that prayer was a form of energy that might be ultimately measured and its laws understood. Like others in New Thought, Rawson believed in the "this-worldly" power of prayer to radically change the course of world events, and bring God's will on earth to pass, as in the Lord's Prayer. He wrote:

> True prayer is solely due to the action of God. This action is the Holy Ghost, or Divine Science . . . which is the action of God on the real man that makes man what he is, namely, the knowledge or conscience of God, or in other words, God's power thinking his own ideas.[22]

When World War I broke out (1914) Rawson organized a campaign to pray for the troops with his method. In 1916 he began a magazine called *Active Service* which centered on teaching the public how to effectively pray for protection for their husbands and sons on the front. Rawson's followers testified to many successes, including one company commander who claimed to have lost no men in a year of front-line combat. It is now impossible to prove if his method of prayer was any more effective than the prayers of traditional Christians. In any case, British casualties in the war were as awful as the other major powers. We will note Rawson's influence on Professor Glenn Clark later in chapter 13.

22. Rawson, *Life Understood*, 236.

10

Quantum Physics and Christian Spirituality

The Discovery of the Idealist Basis of the Universe[1]

As F. L RAWSON understood and prophesied, and just when Christian realism and secular materialism were most influential, the very foundations of these philosophical systems were being undermined by emerging discipline of subatomic physics (quantum physics). Discoveries in this field made realism and materialism obsolete as descriptions of the physical universe. In fact, what the physicists discovered was that the foundations of the physical world were idealist, that is, mind interacted with matter, and matter could not fully exist without mind.

These discoveries had tremendous implications in reference to Christian Science and the various New Thought groups we have been discussing. Although the new scientific discoveries in no way justified their claims that matter was unimportant, they do show that they were closer to the truth ("partially true") than their orthodox Christian critics imagined.

---

1. This chapter is a lightly revised version of chapter 12 in *Quenching the Spirit*, "The Spiritual Side of Quantum Physics." For readable introductions to the concepts discussed in this section, see Gribbin, *Schrodinger's Cat*, Wolf, *Quantum Leap*. For a historical overview see Gamow, *Thirty Years*, and Segré, *Faust in Copenhagen*. For an excellent general discussion of how discoveries in modern science have challenged the materialist and atheistic assumptions of eighteenth- and nineteenth-century science, see Barr, *Modern Physics*. A most interesting article on the theological implications of the "uncertainty principal" is Johnson's, "Does God Play?"

The quantum physics revolution began as a result of attempts to study the nature of light. Early experiments had demonstrated that light was a wave. Later, however, other experiments demonstrated that light also behaved as a particle. It soon became apparent that light could be proven to be either a wave or a particle, depending on the experiment that was structured.

This concept, that something can manifest in a seemingly contradictory manner, is called complementarity. It became a fundamental concept of the new quantum physics.

Through further experiments an astounding discovery was made. If any person observed a beam of light during a simple two-hole experiment, the wave manifestation collapsed, and the light became a particle *merely by being observed*. The presence of the observer changed the results of the experiment! Without observation the beam of light existed in a ghost-like state, with potential for either a particle or wave but settling in neither. It would eventually manifest as a wave if it remained unobserved.[2] This all but shattered the fundamental assumptions of materialist-realist science (and Christian theologians such St. Thomas Aquinas and John Calvin) that nature operated independently of the mind.

Mathematical and experimental work done by Max Planck, one of the pioneers of quantum physics, discovered that the power of the mind to influence matter by observation had a mathematical expression in the central equation of quantum physics: $E = \hbar f$. The critical item of this equation is the $\hbar$, the energy value of mind observation that breaks the wave manifestation of light into a particle. The $\hbar$ is also called Planck's constant, and its value (wattage, as in *real* energy) is one of those tremendously small numbers only mathematicians understand, but a real wattage nonetheless.

Later it was realized that the universe could not exist as we know it with much variation in $\hbar$. If $\hbar$ were a smaller value, the wave function would not break, and this would make, among other things, vision impossible. On the other hand, if the value of $\hbar$ were *slightly* higher, then every thought would dramatically and dangerously alter matter. That nature is so delicately balanced for our good is now called the anthropic principle, or sometimes the fine-tuned universe. It seems that from the very instant of the Big Bang (the assumed moment of creation) many

---

2. Explained clearly in Gribben, *Schrodinger's Cat*, 166–69.

things went exactly right to allow for intelligent (and spiritual) life in the cosmos.[3]

By the 1920s there was a great debate among informed scientists as to what the discoveries in quantum physics meant. The mathematical equations which demonstrated these findings were producing startling advances in electronics and physics. In fact, the electronics industry would not have come about without quantum theory. However, many of the scientists who were at the forefront of these discoveries were disturbed by the philosophical implications. They had been educated as materialists and realists, yet everything in quantum physics suggested that at the atomic level the universe operated by idealist principles— that mind had influence on the behavior of matter.

Erwin Schrodinger, one of the great scientists and mathematicians of the era, explained the idealist conclusions of quantum physics with a parable which came to be known as the paradox of Schrodinger's cat. A cat was placed in a sealed box with a vial of poison gas, and the gas had exactly a 50 percent chance of being released and the cat killed. Schrodinger explained that before the box was opened the cat was in a ghost-like state, neither dead nor alive. The event of opening the box and observing the cat created the definite dead or live cat, just as the observer triggered the light wave to become particles in the two-hole experiment.

Idealism and the Copenhagen Interpretation

For decades there was a contentious debate among scientists as to the implications of quantum physics. This reached a climax at a conference in Dr. Niels Bohr's institute in Copenhagen, Denmark. Dr. Bohr (1885–1962) was brought up in a devout Lutheran household, and later was deeply influenced by the writings of Soren Kierkegaard. Bohr created at his physics institute a place that reflected his Christian character. It was an institute of the greatest scientific excellence and integrity made possible by cultivating an atmosphere of openness and communication. At Bohr's institute conflicting ideas and theories could be debated with great

---

3. See Leslie, "How to Draw Conclusions," 297–12. The seminal book on the discovery that our universe is fine-tuned for our benefit is Barrow and Wheeler, *Cosmological Principle*. This book is written in mathematical language with equations that only a science or math major could understand. For a detailed review in understandable English of this most important source for the idea of intelligent design, see Halberg, "Barrou and Tipler's."

passion, while maintaining mutual respect and fellowship. The scientists and their graduate assistants would even take time during the yearly conferences at his institute to do witty dramatic skits to poke fun at each other and enliven the sessions.[4]

In 1927 the chief physicists and scientists of the era met again at Bohr's institute and discussed the meaning of the new physics. Bohr was an enthusiastic supporter of the idealist implications, regardless of how little sense the discoveries made in terms of traditional Western realism. Bohr's view, called the Copenhagen interpretation, steadily won the arguments among scientists by virtue of its mathematical and experimental triumphs.

Modern scientists now side with the Copenhagen interpretation and accept, to one degree or another, the idealist view of matter as interactive with the mind. Fresh experimental evidence continues to be found verifying the importance of observation as a factor that influences matter, and Bohr's Copenhagen interpretation won over all objections to it.[5]

However, many scientists are wary of attempts to expand the discoveries of quantum mechanics from atomic and subatomic interactions to the ordinary world. The argument from these scientists is that there is no direct evidence that ordinary matter, matter made up of billions of atoms together, can operate with the laws of subatomic particles. Similarly, they claim that expanding quantum rules to the realm of psychic or spiritual events is not legitimate.[6] This line of reasoning is advocated by those scientists of the realist materialist tradition who are still disturbed by any evidence that calls into question the assumptions of a mechanical and God-empty universe.

On the contrary, the evidence is mounting that under some circumstances ordinary matter operates with the mystical properties of quantum physics. For instance, scientists have designed certain electronic devices of up to half a centimeter long to operate as a single atomic entity.[7]

4. On the wonderful openness and playfulness of Bohr's institute see Segrè, *Faust in Copenhagen*.

5. Albert, "Was Einstein Wrong?"

6. Rae, "Extrasensory Physics."

7. Gribben, *Schrodinger's Cat*, 23.

Quantum Physics as Natural Theology

Some of the theological implications of quantum physics have made it into mainline Christian literature—it should have begun with Rawson's *Life Understood* a century ago.[8] In the last decades the writing of noted physicist and Anglican priest Fr. John C. Polkinghorne (b.1930) on the theological implications of quantum physics have gained wide credence and circulation. This came, unfortunately, half a century after the main discoveries of quantum physics were clarified in the Copenhagen interpretation.

Even worse, these Christian writings were published *after* non-Christian writers launched several popular explanations of quantum physics based on Eastern mysticism. The most important of these was Fritjof Capra's work *The Tao of Physics*, published in 1976, which became a bestseller. This book drew explicit parallels between quantum physics and doctrines of Eastern mysticism. This book, though filled with many useful insights, gave many Christians the impression that quantum physics is a branch of Eastern occultism. Several other books in this vein have followed.[9] When the first edition of my work *Quenching the Spirit* was undergoing translation into Spanish (1993), its first translator resigned from the project when he saw my chapter on quantum physics, believing the book was thus necessarily occultist!

Even secular critics have observed that this crop of quantum-physics-as-Eastern-mysticism thinking has been little more than speculative. What has really been accomplished in the quantum revolution is the destruction of the traditional naive realism of science.[10] These Eastern interpretations should be viewed as temporary hypotheses filling in the vacuum in spiritual understanding created by Western materialism and its theological cousins in liberal theology and DOG theology.

The importance of the observer has produced some wildly speculative theories in these writings. Some researchers now claim that the universe is only possible because *we* observe it, and even its creation was due to our present observation of it![11] Another example of speculative

8. See the lead article, "Dissenting View," in *Christianity Today*. The presentation was sketchy and timid.

9. For example, Zukav, *Dancing Wu*.

10. McCance, "Physics Buddhism," published in *Zygon*, the premier Christian journal dedicated to studying the relationship between Christianity and science.

11. Rothman, "What You See."

interpretations is the many universes theory. In this view every time a person makes a decision, as in opening the door to Schrodinger's box, the universe splits into both possibilities, one with a dead cat, another with a live one. This happens in infinite repetition as each human being creates new universes every time he or she makes a decision.[12]

The Eastern mystical interpretations given by Capra and others are plausible because the spiritual implications of quantum physics are of a general nature. They can be interpreted in terms of many religious systems and belong to a category that the Christian tradition calls natural theology, that is, theology that can be discerned without specific recourse to revelation, as Paul indicates in Romans 1:19–20.[13] By its very nature, natural theology is incomplete and subject to misguided interpretations. For example, Paul pointed out that creation points to a creator (Rom 1:20), yet creation gives only a natural theology of God, not the specifics of God as a loving Father. This comes from revelation. Natural theology without the specific correction of Scripture can drift into incorrect conclusions or dangerous models, as in the Greek father-god Zeus, who lusted after and fought with lesser gods.

Quantum Laws and Biblical Spirituality

Thankfully, Christian theologians are finally dealing with the theological implications of quantum physics. As a result, new areas of understanding and appreciation of the Scriptures have opened. However, to claim that quantum physics proves this or that doctrine of the Bible is to err in the same way that the Eastern mystical school of quantum writers has erred. The theories of quantum physics simply show that the philosophy of radical materialism, which has been used to support cessationist theology, is inadequate to explain reality. However, to view miracles simply in terms of quantum physics misses the point.

What follows must be understood to be *analogies* based on the natural theology of quantum physics that have been extended and corrected through confidence in biblical revelation. Analogies suggest but never give proof. For instance, we can now understand that most miracles come about as God's will and power *cooperates* with humanity's mind, and its

12. Gribbin, *Schrodinger's Cat*, chapter 11.

13. For a Jewish interpretation of quantum physics see Bentley, "Uncertainty and Unity."

capacity to interact with matter through faith. This could be understood to mean that faith increases Planck's constant, $\hbar$, the energy available of mind to move matter.[14] Some miracles, however, as in the original creation, are purely the sovereign work of God.

Complementarity and Christian Doctrine

Complementarity was the first quantum principle discovered, and it serves well as another point of analogy to the spiritual life. Recall that complementarity deals with a reality that can have more than one manifestation, as with light being both a wave and a particle. Because complementarity is so alien to ordinary logic, it is almost impossible for the human intellect to understand complementarities. A complementarity is not so much *understood* as true as it is *accepted* as true.[15]

In biblical revelation there are many such fundamental complementarities, traditionally called "mysteries." For example, Jesus is *both* man and God, and human beings are free to choose their spiritual destiny, but God has predestined those who enter into the kingdom.[16] These mysteries might be understood as complementarities.

The English scientist-theologian John Polkinghorne has become the lead person in relating quantum physics to Christian theology.[17] Polkinghorne was for many years professor of particle physics at Cambridge University. There he played a major role in the discovery of the quark, an elusive subatomic particle. But in 1979 he resigned to become a priest in the Anglican Church. He is now a master Christian apologist to the scientific community in Great Britain. His books on the interface of science and religion have won wide recognition and respect. He gave the prestigious Gifford Lectures on science and religion in 1993, which

14. When I teach on this topic before a live audience I tell them to say to each other, "Planck's constant is not!"

15. Some of the complementarities of Christian doctrine have been noted in Polkinghorne's, *The Way*, 67–69. Karl Rahner, one of the preeminent theologians of the Catholic Church, has used the concept of complementarity in his theology of Christ. See Honner, "Unity-in-Difference."

16. Pointed out in Schaafs, *Physics and Miracles*," 81–83. This is one of the best works on quantum physics and Christian theology to date. See also the non-technical article in *Christianity Today* by Carolyn Arends, "Both/And."

17. Polkinghorne, *One World*, especially chapter 7.

became the book *The Faith of a Physicist*.[18] Fr. Polkinghorne's works deal with quantum physics as making the spiritual world understandable and plausible, and affirming the existence of God with the evidence of the anthropic principal. They unfortunately have little to say about answered prayer and healing.[19]

God as the Prime Observer

While the natural theology of quantum physics suggests that observation is necessary for the world to come into being, revelation tells us *who* that observer is. No less than seven times in the first chapter of Genesis a conjunction is made between God creating the universe and affirming it by observation. Genesis 1:31 is clearest on this: "And God saw all that He had made, and behold, it was very good." With this we can see that the ultimate source of stability and continuity in the universe is God and his continual observation of it, not humanity.[20]

The critical question in quantum theology is this: Why does ordinary matter not manifest the mystical properties of non-locality and responsiveness to the mind more easily? Paul addressed this problem nineteen hundred years before the scientific issue could even be defined. He saw that God masked the spiritual behavior of the ordinary world for the purposes of his overall plan, but in the fullness of time ordinary matter will be bestowed with its true spiritual functions.

> For the anxious longing of the creation waits eagerly for the revealing of the sons of God. For the creation was subjected to futility, not of its own will, but because of Him who subjected it, in hope that the creation itself also will be set free from its slavery to corruption into the freedom of the glory of the children of God. For we know that the whole creation groans and suffers the pains of childbirth together until now. (Rom 8:19–23)

In quantum terms, this passage means that God created the universe with a low h for our safety. He knew that before humankind came

18. He was also awarded the Templeton Prize in 2002 and was knighted by Queen Elizabeth as testimony to his great contributions.

19. This in no way diminishes the value of his work as a modern day apologist of the basic Christian faith. Polkinghorne sees his book *Quarks and Christianity* as his best general introduction to his writings. See also his autobiography, *Physicist to Priest*. A briefer autobiographical source is his article "The Life and Work."

20. On this see Yancey, "Insight on Eternity."

into the full conformity of his Son a higher $\hbar$ would lead to the chaos and mind wars of flying chairs and tables, etc., at every disagreement. As the elect become "in Christ" and have the "mind of Christ," such disharmony ceases to exist. Perhaps in the promised new heaven and new earth (2 Pet 3:13; Rev 21:1) $\hbar$ have a higher wattage and we will be able to create things just by thinking them.

The work done in the last decades by Christian scientist-theologians might well have been done in the 1920s or 1930s, as F.L. Rawson had pioneered. The reality of the spiritual world and the miraculous might have been proclaimed with renewed force to a generation of European and American intellectuals seeking answers to Fascism and Marxism, but it was not so.

Instead, mainline Christian theology from 1920 to 1980 went through its most apostate and heretical period. The mainline seminaries in the United States followed European fashions and adopted what is called "higher criticism" of the Bible (entailing that the miracles were myths), combined with various forms of Nietzschean or Marxian philosophy. These theologies assumed a materialist worldview and proclaimed that modern humanity cannot believe in miracles because miracles are incompatible with modern science. The awful marriage of eighteenth-century scientific/philosophical assumptions and materialist/cessationist theologies remained normative in the seminaries for a century after they were scientifically obsolete.

The Miracles and the Hermeneutics of Christian Idealism

Let us turn to several miracles described in the Bible to see how helpful the analogies of quantum physics and its idealist implications are in understanding them. The first miracle is an example of faith unsustained: Peter's aborted water walk (Matt 14:28–31). In this incident Peter initiated the miracle by asking Jesus to call him. Jesus called, and Peter did walk on the water, "But seeing the wind, he became afraid, and beginning to sink, he cried out . . ." After Jesus saved Peter, he rebuked him with the words, "O you of little faith, why did you doubt?"

This incident is especially instructive because it is fatal to the sovereignty-only theory of Christian materialism, most often cited by cessationists. Although God's sovereignty and power (through Jesus) were the basis of Peter's water walk, it was Peter's mind, acting in faith then fear, which determined the outcome. If the only factor in the miracle was that God sovereignly decided that Peter could walk on water, it should not have mattered that Peter feared, nor would Jesus' rebuke make sense.

Similar conclusions must be drawn from Jesus' failed ministry in his hometown of Nazareth (Matt 13:54–58; Mark 6:1–6; Luke 4:16–30). Matthew summarized: "And He did not do many miracles there because of their unbelief." Again the sovereignty-only theory fails. A miracle begins with a promise or covenant relationship with God, but must be completed through the mind operating in faith, which likely means that faith has increased the believer's $\hbar$.

Faith and the Resuscitation of Schrodinger's Cat

Quantum physics suggests that observation finalizes the structure of matter. The Bible demonstrates that faith, or anticipated observation, not only finalizes, but changes the course of events. Note the central New Testament definition of faith (Heb 11:1): "Now faith is the assurance of things hoped for, the conviction of things not seen." Two resuscitations, one in the Old Testament and another in the New, demonstrate this quite clearly. They also indicate that Mary Baker Eddy's method of negation and affirmation has biblical merit (she was partially right).

The first one is the resuscitation of the Shunamite woman's son (2 Kgs 4:8–37). The story began when Elisha and his servant Gehazi repeatedly passed in front of this unnamed woman's house. She discerned that Elisha was a prophet, and had a guest room built especially for him. Elisha reciprocated her kindness by praying for her to become pregnant, as she was childless and her husband old.

Within a year she gave birth to a son. Several years later the boy became feverish and died on her lap. Her immediate actions are most revealing. The woman told no one, quickly laid the dead boy on Elisha's guest cot, closed the door to the room and rushed to get the prophet. Her husband asked why she was leaving, and she replied, "It will be well" (v. 23). Before she arrived at Elisha's residence, the prophet sensed that something was wrong and that she was in distress. He sent Gehazi to inquire. When Gehazi asked as to her family, she replied, "It is well" (v. 26). At the feet of the prophet she did *not* blurt out, "The boy is dead!" With circumspection, she reminded the prophet that his prayers had been responsible for the lad's birth.

Elisha understood at once, but did not speak out the problem. He sent Gehazi ahead of him to place his own staff on the boy's body and followed with the mother. Before Elisha and the woman arrived, Gehazi returned with the news that the staff had not helped yet and that "the lad has not awakened" (v. 31). When Elisha got to his guest room he closed the door behind him, prayed to the Lord, and twice stretched himself out on the boy. The boy came to life and was restored to his mother.

From the perspective of Christian realism, the actions and dialogue of the incident are incomprehensible. The Shunamite woman was deluded or spoke a lie; things indeed were not "well." But with an idealist understanding of the spiritual power of *anticipated observation* (faith) to change events, both the dialogue and the actions make perfect sense. She affirmed a good, and negated the finality of the present negative situation.

Notice that no one in the incident ever proclaimed the death of the boy. The actions of the woman certainly took it into account, but she did not *say* it in spite of her anguish. Similarly, neither Elisha nor Gehazi used the words *death* or *dead*. When Gehazi had to report that his master's staff had not resuscitated the boy, he used the phrase "not awakened." He was reporting that the *energies* of God in the staff were not enough to accomplish the miracle. Elisha continued, and the miracle was completed by his prayers (the one element of the whole incident understandable in Christian materialism) and by stretching out on the boy so that even more of the *energies* of God in his garments and body would flow into the lad.[21] By revelation from the Scriptures (not by the natural theology of quantum physics) we can understand that *speaking* is a more powerful form of completing observation.

A similar sequence of events took place in Jesus' ministry in the resuscitation of Jairus' daughter (Matt 9:18–26; Mark 5:21–43; Luke 8:40–56). Matthew, Mark, and Luke give varying details about the incident, but the sequence is quite clear. Jairus meets Jesus and requests that he come to the bedside of his dying daughter. Jesus starts on the way, heals the woman with the issue of blood, and continues. News then comes that the girl had died. Jesus reassures Jairus: "Do not be afraid any longer; only believe, and she will be made well" (Luke 8:50).

At Jairus' house Jesus tells the crowd, "Stop weeping, for she has not died, but is asleep" (Luke 8:52). They howl in derision, but he puts them out and enters the girl's room with his disciples and the parents of the girl.

21. We will refer to this miracle later in chapter 18 in reference to the healing miracles facilitated by Agnes Sanford.

Jesus then takes the girl's hand and commands her to arise. Luke writes, "And her spirit returned, and she rose immediately" (8:55).

The sequence of events and statements are again unintelligible and contradictory from the perspective of Christian materialism. Jesus said the girl was sleeping. This could be interpreted to mean that with divine wisdom Jesus knew the girl was only in a coma. Also the crowd could have been mistaken because of the limited medical knowledge of the times. However, Luke makes it clear she was really dead by saying "her spirit returned." Thus, in the Christian realist interpretation Jesus was either mistaken or lying.

Obviously those alternatives were not intended by the Gospel writers. The crowd and messenger were right; the girl was observed as dead. By saying she was asleep, Jesus was affirming that the initial observation of death could be overruled by the power of God mobilized by the mind acting in faith, just as the Shunamite woman trusted that the power of God would overrule the death of her boy. Jesus was not misjudging the issue or lying, nor was the crowd mistaken. Rather Jesus used his words of faith as part and parcel of the miracle event.[22]

One can note the vast difference between our hermeneutic (moderate Christian idealism, which is buttressed with the analogies of quantum physics) and the hermeneutics of Christian materialism and cessationism. Whereas the understanding of the materialist forced a radical discontinuity between spiritual activities and the material order, those discontinuities have now evaporated. The spiritual order can now be understood to operate in harmony, not contradiction, with fundamental laws of the universe. The analogies between quantum physics and the spiritual life reveal a continuity of intention in the mind of the Creator. God intended the universe to be spiritual, from subatomic particles to archangels and galaxies. His laws for subatomic particles are the first level of a universe created for spiritual ends. We can reverse Bultmann's infamous quote and

---

22. In fairness we should note a contrary example, the resuscitation of Lazarus (John 11). In this miracle Jesus begins with the Old Testament pattern of declaring that Lazarus was "asleep" but not dead, but his disciples do not understand the point. Jesus then speaks plainly that Lazarus is dead, and then goes to resuscitate him. Why did Jesus break the earlier pattern? Probably because at this stage of his ministry the principal concern of the Father was that Jesus be glorified, and in this miracle teaching the disciples was no longer necessary. Note that Peter's resuscitation of Dorcas in Acts 9:36–43 and Paul's resuscitation of Eutycus in Acts 20:7–12 take a middle course between the older biblical model and Jesus' resuscitation of Lazarus.

boldly proclaim, "If you use an electronic device, you must believe in the biblical miracles!"

It should also be made clear that we are not implying that Christian spiritual life is a mechanical execution of the laws of quantum physics. Rather, what we have done is outline a *moderate idealist hermeneutic* which is useful in describing biblical spirituality. At the core of the Christian's life is the covenant relationship of creature to Creator, of dependent child to loving Father, which is intensely personal, not mechanical. Being a Christian involves the directing of the human mind and spirit to worship, repentance, praise, and love, all of which are activities of the will and, if my interpretation is correct, increase the value of h that a Christian can project. None of this has anything to do with mechanical applications of laws or principles.

In the hermeneutic we presented we used the vocabulary and imagery of modern physics, but the critical element is Christian idealism. Here we again must affirm that Mrs. Baker had it partially right. Negation and affirmation is a form of miracle-producing faith. Just as with the heretic Marcion, this does not mean her exaggerated doctrines that matter is unreal, etc., were valid. But she was *partially right* in precisely the area where orthodox Protestant Christianity was *disastrously wrong*.

We have also seen how New Thought writers already began to filter the extremism out of Christian Science. In the following chapters we will study the further corrections and biblical filtrations of Christian Science and New Thought, particularly those that came through pioneering Christian faith idealists such as Rufus Moseley, Glenn Clark, Agnes Sanford and others.

11

Visualization as Prayer

VISUALIZATION IS THE USE of the imagination to create images in the mind.[1] The use of visualization in Christian prayer and devotion has a long history, but its use as an instrument of faith, as in healing prayer, was discovered by New Thought leaders. This is not surprising, since *any* form of personal, effective healing prayer was rare prior to the nineteenth century.

The Roman Catholic Tradition of Pious Visualization[2]

The fire-and-brimstone sermons from Jonathan Edwards and many revivalists after him purposely stimulated the imaginations of their audiences for the sake of desiring heaven and dreading hell. In the broadest sense, they encouraged personal visualization as part of the conversion process. This is not to say that Jonathan Edwards was the first to introduce visualization into Christian practice. The Catholics had beaten him to it by hundreds of years.

As early as the thirteenth century, a popular book attributed to St. Bonaventura urged visualization as a form of prayer and Bible learning. The author of *Meditations on the Life of Christ* encouraged his brothers to read sections of the Bible, especially the Gospels, and then creatively enter into the scene with their imaginations (i.e. visualize). For example,

1. This chapter is a reduced and edited version of chapter 17 in *Quenching the Spirit*, "Visualization and the Christian."

2. Many of the insights of this chapter were suggested by Alexander's seminal article "Mind Power." Another key article is La Shell's "Imagination and Idol."

he urged his readers to become one of the shepherds that visited the new-
born Jesus in Bethlehem:

> Kiss the beautiful little feet of the infant Jesus who lies in the
> manger and beg his mother to offer to let you hold Him awhile.
> Pick Him up and hold Him in your arms. Gaze on His face with
> devotion and reverently kiss Him and delight in Him. You may
> freely do this, because He came to sinners to deliver them, and
> for their salvation humbly conversed with them and even left
> himself as food for them.[3]

This form of pious biblical visualization became a common form
of prayer for many Catholics. Those who practiced it—and many still
do—have always found it spiritually edifying. In the Middle Ages, before
the printing press, developing vivid Scripture memory was important as
few had private Bibles to consult. Unfortunately, this form of prayer was
mostly lost to Protestantism in the heat of the Reformation.

Another form of Catholic visualization exercises was developed by
St. Ignatius of Loyola (1491–1556), founder of the Jesuits.[4] The training exercises he developed for his priests as part of a month-long retreat
were aimed at strengthening their determination to lead sanctified
Christian lives.

At the heart of St. Ignatius' exercises was a series of individual visualizations wherein the person was given a general theme and encouraged
to allow his own imagination to create the specific details. In one, the
retreat master would suggest meditating on hell and suggest imagining
all the screams, smells, and sensations of the tormented souls. These visualizations were very similar to Jonathan Edwards' most famous revival
sermon, "Sinners in the Hands of an Angry God." In the subsequent session the participant would then spend time imagining the joys of heaven.
The trained retreat master would inquire as to the specific images developed by each participant and use that information for the purposes of
spiritual direction.

---

3. Bonaventure, *Life of Christ*, 38.

4. Rahner, *St. Ignatius Loyola*, and of course Ignatius of Loyola, *Spiritual
Exercises*.

The Reformation as Iconoclasm

The Reformation was in large part a new iconoclastic movement that re-volted against the Catholic use of statues in prayer and worship. Many in Catholic Europe were easily convinced by the reformers' arguments that the cult of statues was against the Second Commandment and a form of idolatry. Some of Calvin's most insightful writings critiqued Catholic statues and icons. With crisp logic he demolished this flawed theological edifice of the medieval church, exposing it as contrary to the plain understanding of Scripture and the practice of the early church. He warned:

> Therefore, when you prostrate yourself in veneration, represent-ing to yourself in an image either of God or a creature, you are already ensnared in some superstition. For this reason, the Lord forbade not only the erection of statues constructed to represent himself but also the consecration of any inscriptions and stones that would invite adoration.[5]

Calvin correctly saw that an act of homage, commonly termed *to bow down* in the Bible, is indistinguishable from worship, regardless of mental reservations with which Catholics distinguished worship from honor (Lev 26:1; Isa 44:12–17).

Although Calvin permitted paintings of historical and biblical scenes, he never really understood the need for religious art. This is indicated by his nervousness about the cherubim on the ark of the covenant, calling them "paltry little images."[6] Later, Reformed theologians went further and for all practical purposes closed down serious religious art within the Protestant nations, abandoning the fine arts to secular hands. This had unintended tragic consequences. Western art began to separate from its spiritual roots, which eventually led to art without meaning and ultimately to the godless fashions of modern art.

Shutting down Protestant religious art was one way of ensuring that the Catholic abuses would never recur. But later Reformed theologians also rejected the valid Catholic insight that the incarnation had modified the prohibition of representing God through Jesus. Thus, for rigorous Calvinists, not even a painting of Jesus in the setting of a Gospel incident was legitimate.[7]

---

5. Calvin, *Institutes*, I.ix.9

6. Ibid, I.viii.

7. La Shell, "Imagination and Idol," 311.

Yet another way to extend the biblical injunctions against idols was to prohibit images *in the imagination*. That step was hinted at in Calvin's writings but completed after him. Calvin had a low opinion of the imagination from the faculties psychology he inherited from St. Augustine and medieval theology. This way of understanding the mind stressed the primacy of reason and downplayed the importance of emotions and imagination.[8] In fact, Calvin declared that the mind "is the perpetual factory of idols."[9]

By the time the theologians of the famous Westminster Larger Catechism had written their proclamation of Protestant doctrine, the explicit step had been taken to extend the biblical prohibition against idols from sculpture and paintings to *images in the mind*. Question 109 of the Larger Catechism explains sin against the Second Commandment as "the making of any representation of God, of all or any of the three persons either inwardly in our mind, or outwardly in any kind of image . . ."[10]

This was simply and purely a religious "fence," i.e., an unwarranted exaggeration. The pious Protestant was thus prohibited from imagining Jesus during prayer. Of course, the theology of cessationism gave no consideration to the problem of Jesus' appearing in a vision, because in the post-biblical era that would simply not happen. Yet Calvinists and later Puritan theologians were not unreasonable. They understood that the imagination, which was created by God, had to have some positive functions. Thus the dilemma: How could the mental images of prayer, which often gravitated to Jesus, be idolatry? One of the favorite Puritan devotional books was *Looking unto Jesus: A View of the Everlasting Gospel, or, The Soul's Eyeing of Jesus*, by Isaac Ambrose, first published in the middle of the seventeenth century and continuously reprinted until the nineteenth. In spite of its Calvinist theology this book contained the following passage:

> O but my Jesus was crowned with thorns, and sceptred with a
> reed, and that reed was taken out of his hands to beat the crown
> of thorns into his head; and, besides, my Jesus was whipped with
> cords, and rods, *and little chains of iron*; that from his shoulders
> to the soles of his feet, there was no part free, and being now
> this plight, thou art called on to "Behold the man:" *Dost thou*

8. Calvin, *Institutes*, I.xv.6.

9. Ibid., I.xi.8.

10. Available online at http://www.epc.org/document.doc?id=106.

see him? Is thy imagination strong? Canst thou consider him at present, as if thou hadst a view of this very man![11]

Jonathan Edwards on Mental Images

Into the Protestant dilemma of attempting to avoid mental idolatry yet affirming the positive function of the imagination in the Christian's life entered Jonathan Edwards. Edwards was aware of the role of imagination in authentic revival. His experience as pastor in his church at Northampton had exposed him to experiences with the phenomenon of visions during revival and their relation to the imagination. He later explained the relationship between visions and the imagination in his famous work *Distinguishing Marks of a Work of the Spirit of God*:

> As God has given us such a faculty as the imagination and so made us that we cannot think of things spiritual and invisible, without some exercise of this faculty; so, it appears to me, that such is our state and nature, that this faculty is really subservient and helpful to the other faculties of the mind, when proper use is made of it...It appears to me manifest, in many instances with which I have been acquainted, that God has really made use of this faculty to truly divine purposes.
>
> Some are ready to interpret such things wrong, and to lay too much weight on them, as prophetical visions, divine revelations, and sometimes significations from heaven of what shall come to pass; which the issue, in some instances I have known, has shown to be otherwise. But yet it appears to me that such things are evidently sometimes from the Spirit of God, though indirectly; that is, their extraordinary frame of mind, and that strong and lively sense of divine things which is the occasion of them, is from his Spirit...though the imaginations that attend it are but accidental, and therefore there is commonly something or other in them that is confused, improper, and false.[12]

Edwards was saying something complex but important. In regard to mental images, visions, and spiritual experiences (such as a vision of Jesus), the details may vary according to the personality of the visionary, but this does not mean that the visions are merely fantasies. Rather they are *personal images empowered by the Holy Spirit* and thus valid in their

---

11. Cited in La Shell, "Imagination and Idol," 316.

12. Edwards, *Distinguishing Marks*, cited in La Shell, "Imagination and Idol," 317.

broadest meaning. (This understanding is especially important to our later discussion of inner healing and its use of visualizations.)

Edwards' *Distinguishing Marks* triggered a pamphlet war among Scottish Reformed clergymen. Scotland had been having its own revival during the years of the Great Awakening, and revival in the Colonies was watched carefully. The issue of images and visions of Jesus took central attention in Scotland, more so than in the Colonies. The Scottish opponents of the revival even went to the extreme of saying that Jesus' physical appearance on earth presented an impediment to true faith because of the danger it posed of idolatry to his disciples![13]

This obscure but heated Calvinist debate points to several important issues. The attempt of Reformed theologians to fence the real sin of idolatry with the imaginary sin of mental imagery was doomed to futility and confusion. The debate also resurfaced the original medieval position that the incarnation modified the prohibition against representing God, since Jesus was in the flesh and was God. It was a real issue that Calvinist theology could not adequately deal with.

Visualization and Healing

Prior to the nineteenth century there is no evidence of the use of visualization for healing in either Protestant or Catholic literature. Certainly the Protestants would not have thought of it because of their cessationism. Pious Catholics were used to the intercession of saints, relics, votive candles, etc., and would have thought it a presumption to use their own mind and faith for healing prayer (the Galatian Bewitchment). Thus visualization was reserved for devotional prayer only.

No one knows for certain when visualization was first used in healing.[14] Evidence indicates that it may have been an innovation of Phineas Quimby which was passed on to his disciples, among them Mary Baker Eddy. Certainly it was a part of Christian Science method of healing prayer by the time *Science and Health* was published in 1875.

It is probable that visualizations for healing were universally employed throughout the metaphysical and New Thought community well

13. La Shell, "Imagination and Idol," 325–26.

14. In the version of this chapter that first appeared in my *Quenching the Spirit*, I suggested that visualization as healing prayer may have been pioneered by an early Faith Cure itinerant preacher, Ethen O. Allen. Further research has shown there is no evidence that this is so.

before it spread to the orthodox Christian community. Those in the Bible-affirming wing of New Thought understood visualization as cooperating with God's love to bring healing. For example, Ralph Waldo Trine (1866–1958), in his immensely popular book *In Tune with the Infinite*, wrote:

> I now open my body, in which disease had gotten a foothold, I open it fully to the inflowing tide of the Infinite Life [God], and it now, even now, is pouring in and coursing through my body, and the healing process is going on. Realize this so fully that you begin to feel a quickening and a warming glow imparted by the life forces of the body. Believe the healing process is going on. Believe it and hold continually to it.[15]

For those in the universalist wing of the movement, visualization often functioned as a *substitute for prayer*. Those who desired money, a trip, or a fine house were told to imagine themselves in possession of it so that it would be theirs—by the law of attraction. For instance Fenwicke L. Holmes, who founded the Southern California Metaphysical Institute in 1926, urged visualizations that were completely independent of God, God's promises in the Bible or any sort of prayer: "If it is money you need, see yourself in possession of it. If it is a journey you wish to take, then venture out in a vision. Visualize the trip; go to Paris . . ."[16]

Note the difference between the New Thought Christian Trine and the universalist Fenwicke. Trine used visualization *as prayer*, as a mental petition to accompany our normal prayers. Fenwicke relied on the power of the mind disassociated with God's will or plans for our life. Most of New Thought followed the Fenwicke/universalist pattern.

The proof that they overestimated the power of the mind (divorced from God's will) is in the fact that in spite of millions of copies of New Thought books that were sold in the era, America did not become a paradise of wealth and health, but ultimately suffered the Great Depression of poverty and want. Many businessmen who bought into the New Thought visualization and prosperity ideology mostly wound up broke, with the rest of the country.

15. Trine, *In Tune*, 58.
16. Holmes, *Faith That Heals*, 34–35.

Visualization and Planck's Constant

In spite of the obvious limits of visualization, it seems that the visualization powers of the mind were designed by God for worship (as in the Catholic and Puritan pious visualizations) but also to be the instrument of extending the kingdom of God to the material realm of the earth, especially healing. The Lord's Prayer, "on earth as it is in heaven," gives a hint of this. The discovery of Planck's constant as the baseline ability of mind to influence matter should alert us that the human mind, made in the image of God, may have an inherent ability to increase the small wattage assigned to Planck's constant to a much greater value when faith is added.

Here, let me anticipate the thoughts on this issue of Mrs. Agnes Sanford, who is at the center of this study. She explained both faith and visualization in Trinitarian terms. That is, she understood that a person who believed in one God (Jew or Christian Scientist, etc.) and who had a positive outlook could use faith or visualizations to achieve a certain amount of healing effectiveness. This was enhanced by being a Christian and using the authority and name of Jesus. This was further augmented by being baptized in the Holy Spirit (see chapter 18).

PART III

The Rise of Christian New Perspective

A Creative Explosion in Theology and Practice

Introduction

In Part II we saw that the mainline churches did not incorporate, or rejected, the gains offered by the various revival movements. As a result they ultimately went on into ineffective and apostate forms of theology. In this section we will see how various graced individuals and parachurch organizations were able to escape the influences of Pharisaism and Sadducaism that had limited earlier revivals. These graced individuals made substantial gains in reorienting the church to its Spirit-empowered destiny. These persons and groups, which we term Christian New Perspective, showed immense creativity, and several morphed into a new form of Pentecostalism and became part of the Charismatic Renewal.

Those in Christian New Perspective (CNP) remained connected to their mainline Protestant or Anglican/Episcopal churches, but mostly operated in parachurch organizations. This enabled them to avoid the deadening oversight of Pharisaical or Sadducaic clergy. At the same time, their participation as individuals within traditional churches kept them in contact with the classical doctrines and creeds. This was different from Unity Christianity and other New Thought groups that formed independent churches. Because the CNP persons operated in their own parachurch organizations, they could experiment and innovate their way out of cessationism and into effective healing and prayer ministries without some Pharisee saying, "You shouldn't do that; its heresy!"

Their collective gains came from filtering through the Bible many of the partial truths of New Thought and Christian Science and representing these within the context of biblical orthodoxy. Those from the Anglican/Episcopal tradition made special efforts to incorporate insights and traditions from the non-cessationist elements of church history.

12

The Anglican Healing Revival

A Proactive Response to Christian Science

THE IMPACT OF EDDY'S Christian Science was not only momentous in America but also in England. And it was in England that a major denomination, the Church of England, first formulated a proactive response to Christian Science. The Church of England was the founding church of worldwide Anglicanism, which includes the Episcopal Church in the United States and its orthodox derivative, the Anglican Church of North America. Anglican churches, of which there are presently some thirty-seven independent national jurisdictions and about eighty million adherents, are the third largest grouping in Christendom, after Roman Catholicism and Eastern Orthodoxy.

Currently, however, the Church of England, the Anglican Church in Canada, and the Episcopal Church in America are all in the process of disintegration and loss of membership, similar to the other mainline denominations. This is the fruit of waves of the DOG theology and liberalism that overwhelmed the seminaries by the middle of the twentieth century. To the contrary, the Anglican churches in Africa and Asia, founded and guided by sacrificial and Bible-believing missionaries, remain solidly orthodox and are often Spirit-filled.[1] But in the period of

1. Full disclosure: I joined a Spirit-filled Episcopal church in 1980 and served as the chairperson for the local chapter of its healing group (the OSL, see below) from 1982 to 1984. I was invited to receive holy orders by the bishops of the CEEC (Communion of Evangelical Episcopal Churches), an independent Anglican "continuing" charismatic denomination in 2000. The leadership of the CEEC attempted to combine the sacramental worship of *The Book of Common Prayer* with the gifts of the Spirit, but wisely saw that the hierarchy of the Episcopal Church was largely heretical. After ordination I served as Hispanic pastor at St. Jude's Episcopal Church in Marietta,

this study, the beginning of the twentieth century, Anglicanism (including the Episcopal Church) was orthodox and Bible believing.

We noted earlier that the Anglican Church at its birth in the sixteenth century had a short-lived moment when healing prayer was reinstituted in the *Book of Common Prayer* as anointing with oil with the expectancy of physical healing (chapter 4). In fact, the healing ministry as a witness against cessationism was never entirely extinguished in the Anglican Church. Several of the factions that developed within Anglicanism attempted to reintroduce healing prayer and anointing of the sick, including a faction called the Non-Jurors of the eighteenth century.[2] Also, the Tractarians of the nineteenth century, a high-church group that attempted to restore Anglicanism to its early church and medieval roots, favored an active healing ministry.[3] Fr. Edward Pusey, a major leader of the Tractarians, wrote in his influential and widely circulated letter/essay *An Eirenicon* a section urging a Reformed rite of anointing of the sick that would avoid Roman Catholic abuses and restore a true healing intent to the sacrament.[4]

F. W. Puller (1843–1938): Recovering the Anointing of the Sick

A high point of this trend was a work produced by Anglican scholar and priest F. W. Puller.[5] Frederick W. Puller was born into a devout upper-class Anglican family and given the best education available—Eton and then Trinity College, Cambridge. He specialized in the literature of the church fathers and was ordained an Anglican priest in 1872.

Georgia. In January of 2003 I and about one third of the congregation at St. Jude's left that church in frustration over the heresy of the national church to form an "Anglican" (i.e., orthodox) congregation under the Anglican bishop of Bolivia. We are now part of the newly formed Anglican Church in North America.

2. Gusmer, "Anointing of the Sick," 265. The Non-Jurors were a group of devout clergymen who, out of conscience, would not renounce their loyalty to James II and affirm William of Orange as their new king.

3. Ibid., 267–68.

4. Pusey, *Eirenicon*, available online at http://www.ccel.org/ccel/pusey/eirenicon.

5. There is no published biography of Puller, due in part to the policy of the Society of St. John, which disdains publicity for its members. My section on Puller and his work, De Arteaga, "F. W. Fuller," 7–11, was assembled from his published works and several obituaries. Note the text of the article was mistakenly retyped, so that the title reads "Fuller" instead of 'Puller."

Puller joined a newly founded Anglican order for religious, the Society of Saint John, modeled after the Catholic Jesuits. He was sent to South Africa to labor among the colored's (Indians, North Africans, and those of mixed race) who were little served by the Anglican Church. Puller was also given charge of a congregation of Black African Christians who had earlier been converted to an enthusiastic and charismatic form of Methodism but now felt a leading to join the Anglican Church. Puller wisely discerned that although their worship was unusual, it echoed that of the early church, and the group was allowed to remain charismatic and Anglican.

After a decade Puller was recalled to England and made novice master to the Society of St. John. In that position he was able to continue his scholarly pursuits and wrote a series of high-quality and scholarly books.[6] Among these was the classic *The Anointing of the Sick in Scripture and Tradition*. We have cited this work for its excellent documentation and description of how the Catholic rite of anointing had degenerated from healing into the sacrament of extreme unction (chapter 3). Puller's command of the literature of the early church was put to good use as he demonstrated in text after text how the prayerful anointing with oil of the early church survived and effectively healed many until it morphed into extreme unction.

Puller's work was published in 1904, at the height of Christian Science's influence and growth. His work clarified and solidified the arguments for a restored, orthodox, and church-based healing ministry, but it did not produce an immediate rush to do so. The more practical work of establishing the healing ministry on a parish level was largely due to another Anglican churchman, one who formed the first Christian healing guild within Christendom.[7]

The Rev. Percy Dearmer (1867–1936): Pioneer of the Anglican Healing Ministry[8]

The Rev. Percy Dearmer was a person of seemingly endless energy and enthusiasm. Priest and vicar of St. Mary's of London and secretary of

6. Several of his works are available online; see http://openlibrary.org/a/ OL2609758A.

7. We saw in chapter 7 that the Faith Cure movement predates the healing movement of the Anglican Church by several decades, but the Anglican healing guilds are the first healing groups to stay within an established Christian church.

8. Percy Dearmer's first biography was written by his wife, Nan Dearmer, *Percy*

the Christian Socialist Union, he labored to bring social equality and compassion to the class-bound Victorian church. He was a historian of the medieval English church, and an expert and enthusiast of the spiritual value of art. He was also the editor and major contributor to the English hymnal. Before his death he was honored by a call to be dean of Westminster Cathedral, one of the most prestigious positions in the Church of England.

Like others of the period, the Rev. Dearmer was shocked into investigating the healing issue due to the sudden rise of the Christian Science Church. When he studied the Christian Science movement he immediately understood its heretical nature, yet he cautioned gentleness in dealing with believers of Christian Science.

> [T]his new movement which is so hopefully stirring around us, though it often speaks the language of heresy, is really a return to a forgotten orthodoxy with which we are much concerned, because it is a restoration of the original Christian idea [of healing prayer].[9]

The Rev. Dearmer understood that the New Thought and Christian Science groups were exaggerating the truth they had discovered by making divine healing into the central, almost sole aspect of their belief, whereas in true Christianity healing should be only one of many parts, of which worship is the principal duty.[10] But Dearmer also understood that the cause of so many defections by Christians to Christian Science was the traditional church's own absence of healing power. Unlike most of his contemporaries, Dearmer understood the concept of heresy as a Marcion Shove, and was anxious that the church learn what it needed to from these unorthodox groups.

> A religion that ignores the physical effects of the Spirit—health, that is to say—and the spiritual element of healing is clearly not commensurate with the Christianity of Christ. It is defective . . .

Dearmer (1941). Unfortunately, she gave little notice of his healing activities and research. A recent biography, which gives rich details of his education and family life, does the same thing, giving only one page to his work on healing prayer. See Gray, *A Parson's* (2000). On Dearmer's healing theology see Bates, "Extremely Beautiful." Most of the Rev. Dearmer's works are available online at http://www.anglicanhistory.org/dearmer/index.html.

9. Dearmer, *Body and Soul*, 343.

10. Ibid., 214, 343.

It is beyond controversy that our Lord devoted a great deal of his ministry to healing the sick, that he sent forth his first disciples to carry out the same two-fold mission of preaching and healing . . . Our duty is to take him as our pattern and to be imitators of him.[11]

Like the Rev. Puller, Dearmer made a careful study of both the early and medieval church records on the issue of healing, and presented his findings in his master work, *Body and Soul.* This work echoed Puller's finding that healing had continued all through church history. One of the most significant parts of *Body and Soul* is the appendix, which contains a selection of documents showing Christian healing from the Middle Ages to the present day. Among the accounts from the Catholic saints is one particularly charming story from the life of St. Bernard (1090–1153):

> At Toulouse . . . was a certain regular canon [Cathedral official] named John. John had kept his bed for seven months, and was so reduced that his death was expected daily. His legs were so shrunken that they were scarcely larger than a child's arms. . . . When the poor creature heard of Bernard's proximity, he implored to be taken to him. . . . The abbot [St. Bernard] heard him confess his sins, and listened to his entreaties to be restored to health. Bernard mentally prayed to God: "Behold, O Lord, they seek for a sign, and our words avail nothing unless they be confirmed with signs following." He then blessed him [John] and left the chamber . . . In that very hour the sick man arose from his couch, and running after Bernard kissed his feet. . . . One of the canons, meeting him, nearly fainted with fright, thinking he saw his ghost. John and the brethren then returned to the church and sang a Te Deum.[12]

Dearmer gave documentary coverage to the healings of George Fox (1624–1691), John Christopher Blumhardt (1805–1880), and others from more modern times. What all the documentary evidence of *Body and Soul* attempted to accomplish was to raise the reality of Christian healing from the realm of uncritical, and sometimes mythical, saints tales of Catholic hagiography to the level of classification and comparison found in of William James' classic *The Varieties of Religious Experience*, a work for which Dearmer had the greatest respect.

11. Ibid., 8.

12. Ibid., 360.

Many of the Rev. Percy Dearmer's writings are prophetic milestones of Christian theology. For instance, his work *The Power of the Spirit* (1919)[13] accepts the authenticity of Pentecostalism and gives an excellent account of the gifts of the Spirit. *Body and Soul* could easily be mistaken for a contemporary book on the healing ministry. Time after time, his insights were both biblically valid and a half century ahead of his contemporaries. In a sense, Dearmer's works were so far ahead of their time that the public could not fully understand or incorporate them into a real healing revival.

The Healing Guilds

Perhaps Dearmer's greater legacy in the struggle against the cessationist error was his part in the creation of the Guild of Health.[14] In the Anglican churches, guilds have been a form of in-house parachurch ministry which focus interest and activities on specific aspects of church life. For instance, Dearmer was also a member of the Guild of St. Michael's, which strove to encourage social justice and the rights of workers. The Rev. Dearmer was one of the three founders of the Guild of Health (1904) and served as its first chairman. The guild was formed so that its chapters would meet regularly, discuss books or issues of the healing ministry, and sponsor healing missions to churches. These missions would last several days and combine teachings on healing with services for the laying on of hands for healing prayer. The Guild of Health strove to make healing prayer normal in church life and give the healing ministry an "orthodox" setting in which to operate. In these matters it was at least partially successful. It is easy to miss the point that Anglicanism, part of the traditional, established churches, did have an active ministry of healing well before the other mainline churches.

13. Available online at online at http://www.anglicanhistory.org/dearmer/index. html.

14. The Guild of Health is active to this day in England. See http://www.gohealth. org.uk/index.html.

A Healing Guild for America:
The Order of St. Luke (OSL)[15]

In 1920 four Episcopal priests, among them the Revs. Henry B. Wilson and John Gaynor Banks, organized an American version of the Guild of Health called the Society of the Nazarene.[16] The Society's first Warden (director) was the Rev. Henry B. Wilson, rector of St. John's Church in Boonton, New Jersey. He published five books on healing and was the editor of *The Nazarene*, the society's healing journal.

The Rev. Wilson's books introduced the American public to the works of Dearmer and other Anglican healing pioneers.[17] He also produced an original contribution to the theology of healing in the book entitled *Ghosts or Gospels* (1923). In it he strongly distinguished Christian healing from spiritualist healings and spirit manifestations. This warning may seem obvious to readers today, but at the time it was a necessary reminder.

In the 1900s people who believed in healing were so few that it was not unheard of for Christians in the healing ministry to fellowship with spiritualists. Both groups held in common a belief in the present reality of spiritual phenomenon, unlike cessationist Christians. Much harm and confusion resulted in this, and it played right into the hands of the cessionists critics who believed that there was no distinction between Christian and spiritualist healing power.[18]

Wilson did not fully organize the Society of the Nazarene before his untimely death in 1929. The Rev. John Gayner Banks, another of the four founders of the Society in 1920, attempted to continue it, but could

15. Detailed information on the history of the International Order of St. Luke the Physician is difficult to obtain. When the headquarters of the order were moved to Texas in the 1960s the earliest editions of *Sharing*, its journal, were neatly bundled, and then thrown out (a cruel blow for the Christian historian indeed!). Several article-length surveys of the OSL have been published in *Sharing*, its monthly magazine. See Mead, "History," and Parke, "Reawakening." I did a later article in *Sharing* on the topic, "Making Respectable."

16. The other two were the Rev. Robert Russell, who later established a major church in Denver, and the Rev. Conover of New Jersey.

17. See especially Wilson, *Does Christ Still Heal?* (1917) and *God's Will* (1923).

18. It was not until the 1960s that most Christians accepted that the discernment that the spirits manifested in séances, automatic handwriting, pendulums, etc. are really *demonic entities* pretending to be spirits of the dead. This is known as the "demonic counterfeit" view of spiritualist manifestations. It was first put forth in modern times by Johann Blumhardt in the 1840s, then by Seventh Day Adventist writers in the 1850s, and definitively articulated in the Rev. John Nevius' classic *Demon Possession* (1896).

not get Wilson's widow's permission to continue it or even use its name. Banks simple continued the Society's work without an official name.

John Gayner Banks was an Englishman who had been active in the English healing guilds. He came to the United States after World War I to do graduate studies on the relationship between religion, psychology, and healing. He met with the Rev. Wilson and was encouraged by him to seek holy orders. Banks did so, receiving his theological training at the Episcopal seminary in Sewanee, Tennessee, while continuing in the healing ministry.

During a healing mission he led in La Jolla, California (1928), the Rev. Banks met Miss Ethel Tulloch, who had headed a local chapter of the Society of the Nazarene. They began a correspondence and subsequently were wed at Calvary Church in New York City by the Rev. Sam Shoemaker, later famous as the cofounder of Alcoholics Anonymous.

Fr. Banks accepted the call to be rector of St. Luke's Church in San Diego, and the church's parsonage became the headquarters of an unofficial Christian healing network (1930). A mimeographed newsletter was begun to spread healing information. This was named *Sharing*, which continues as a magazine to this day. The newsletter went out to the people in St. Luke's parish and others interested in healing throughout the United States. The subscribers came to be known as the Fellowship of St. Luke, and though most members were Episcopalian some were from other denominations. The Fellowship of St. Luke grew steadily and by 1936 was recognized as the official healing organization of the Episcopal Church.

Ethel Tulloch Banks: Healing Theologian (1885–1958)[19]

Interestingly, the principal writer and theologian of the Order of St. Luke the Physician was Ethel, who did most of the writing and editing of *Sharing*. She was the one who had the time and energy to read the latest publications on healing, while her husband was mostly engaged with his pastoral duties. Although she published some works under her name, she also ghost-wrote much of her husband's later writings. It was sacrificial to do so. She understood that his ordination and PhD gave him the authority to speak before a church audience. In an age where women had just gained

19. See a sketch of Mrs. Banks by her assistant, Powell, "Ethel Banks."

the right to vote, she would not have commanded similar authority or even a fair hearing had she put her name to her theological writings.[20]

In 1929 he was invited to preach a sermon on healing at the Washington Cathedral. He (and Ethel) expanded his remarks into his first major book, *The Redemption of the Body* (c. 1931). The theme of the work is that the human body is meant to be a sacrament of God, that is, a vehicle of God's goodness and means of bringing God's grace to others. Banks argued against the ascetical tradition of the desert fathers and the Middle Ages, which advocated lacerations on the body in continuous penances.

These ideas were most widely broadcast in the Rev. Bank's *Manual of Christian Healing*, which went through at least fourteen editions and was sent to every minister and priest who joined the OSL from the 1930 into the 1960s.[21] In it is contained a suggested liturgy for a church healing service and advice on the use of Holy Communion as a healing service. The desire to associate healing with the ritual and liturgy of the church was not just a theological issue. The other, unspoken agenda was to associate Christian healing prayer with the orthodox traditions of the church and away from its association with the Mind-Cure cults and Christian Science.

The Ministry of the Rev. Alfred W. Price (1899–1992)

The Rev. John Banks died in 1953 as he finished a lecture at a CFO camp (we will discuss this important parachurch group in chapter 13). For now, we should note that there was an interlocking membership and leadership between the CFO and OSL. By that time there were scores of OSL chapters established in Episcopal and Methodist churches throughout the country. The Rev. Alfred W. Price, also an Episcopal priest, took over as warden. Under Fr. Price the OSL spread to every state in the Union and to several foreign countries.

Alfred Price was born in Scranton, Pennsylvania, in 1899.[22] In his teen years Price became curious about Christian Science and witnessed several healings at the hand of their practitioners. Although he quickly

20. Taped interview by author of Rev. Alfred W. Price, March 30, 1985. The Rev. Price was the second warden of the Order of St. Luke and best friend of Banks.

21. See also also Banks, *Gospel of Power*.

22. The story of his studies at Harvard is described in his two part-pamphlet *God's Healing*, 78–83.

discerned that Christian Science theology was mumbo jumbo, he saw it also ministered valid healings.[23] After serving in the Marine Corps in World War I, Price entered the Episcopal seminary at Cambridge, Massachusetts, which was affiliated with Harvard University. In his last year of study he opted to do a master's thesis to complete his ordination degree. His topic: the gospel miracles. As his research developed he saw that the miracles described in the gospels were authentically recorded events. Certainly, if a Christian Science practitioner could heal the sick, it was only logical to assume the healing miracles attributed to Jesus were authentic. He presented his extensively researched thesis in 1929.

The dean of the school was aghast at the thesis and appointed a faculty committee to review what had gone wrong with Mr. Price's education. The committee interviewed him and gave him an ultimatum: if he did not retract his thesis he would not graduate or be ordained. He responded by refusing to rewrite a single line of the thesis, and told them:

> I understand this to be a liberal school with a great emphasis on intellectual integrity. I think it is my Bishop's responsibility to decide whether or not I have a vocation for the ministry, and I think it is your responsibility to evaluate this thesis and decide whether it meets the requirements and standards of the school.[24]

The faculty committee reconsidered its ultimatum and Mr. Price became the Rev. Price. The Rev. Price's first church was St. Philips' in Brooklyn. He spent twelve years there, all Depression years, which kept him active in coordinating church relief. He instituted a weekly healing service at that church, which was especially effective in praying for recovery from surgery or from infectious diseases, which, in the period before antibiotics, was a major anxiety for anyone who was ill.

Fr Price's major contributions to the healing ministry began in 1942 when he was transferred to St. Stephen's church in downtown Philadelphia. It was a dying parish. The congregation had been fleeing to the suburbs and the local population was mostly made up of transients, hobos, daytime business persons, and employees of the red-light district.

As the Rev. Price prayed over the situation he felt definite direction from the Lord to go out into the neighborhood and invite everyone to

---

23. Taped interview by author of Dr. Alfred Price at his home in St. Petersburg, Florida, March 30, 1985.

24. Price, *God's Healing*, 82.

church. He went to the bars, offices, restaurants, boarding houses, and brothels, and without condemnation invited all to come to the church services. To Price's surprise, both the business persons and the undesirables began coming to his church. After several months of ministering and seeing the needs of his parishioners he again felt the Lord's direction, this time to institute a healing service. He had a billboard posted, notices placed in the newspaper, and handed out fliers announcing the first weekday, noontime healing service. Twenty persons showed up and eight came to the altar to receive the laying on of hands.

From that first service there were dramatic healings of both mind and body. Soon the weekly services were filling the church. At the height of St. Stephen's healing ministry, in the 1950s, there were two Thursday healing services, one at noon and another in the evening. Price found that the down-and-outers of his district responded with great faith to his simple laying on of hands and prayer counseling. Alcoholics were dried out, and so many prostitutes were converted (including a woman who became his organist) that the madams moved their houses of business to another part of town. The healing services at St. Stephen's were simple services that followed the format of the Rev. Banks' *Manual of Christian Healing.* There was a reading of a Gospel account of one of Jesus' healing miracles, a brief sermon, and then people were invited to come forward for healing through the laying on of hands.[25]

Under the Rev. Price, St. Stephen's became the networking headquarters of non-Pentecostal Christian healing in the United States. In 1950 Price organized the first nationwide conference on the church's ministry of healing. In 1955 the meetings were renamed the International Conference on the Church's Ministry of Healing, reflecting the fact that they steadily attracted persons from Canada, the British Isles, and other parts of the world. The yearly conferences lasted into the 1980s, but it was in the 1950s and 1960s that they were most important. There many of the healing ministers of American Christian mainline churches, including some who were to become important in the charismatic renewal, met, networked, and had their yearly convention.

Many Episcopal priests, and some ministers from other denominations, were converted to and sustained in active healing ministries through the Order of St. Luke, and many of these became active in the Charismatic Renewal of the 1960s. Before the Charismatic Renewal made

25. See the account of St. Stephen's in the 1950s in High, "More Things."

healing acceptable and non-cultish, the OSL provided one of the few covers of respectability and theological orthodoxy available to the mainline clergy in the healing ministry. To this end, *Sharing* periodically published lists of its degreed professionals, physicians, ministers and priests, educators, etc. in an attempt to make Christian healing more respectable and lift it out of the public's associations with Christian Science and the Holy Rollers. In this it was only marginally successful, as OSL never made it into the seminaries, where cessationism and liberal forms of theology continued to hold sway.

All of this is to show that a mainline denomination did in fact make room for a healing ministry and opposed cessationism. Other denominations, like the Presbyterians, Church of Christ, and especially the Methodists, could have done the same but did not.

Christian New Perspective as Health Foods: The Life Abundant Movement

Another of the important CNP persons was an amazing Episcopal priest, the Rev. Robert B. H. Bell (1872–1956). He was rector of St. Thomas' Church in Denver, Colorado. The Rev. Bell learned of the healing ministry from both Anglican/Episcopal writers, such as the Revs. Percy Dearmer and Henry Wilson, and New Thought sources. By 1920 he had established a healing in his church with the weekly laying on of hands.

The Rev. Bell also developed a belief that natural, unprocessed foods are essential for sustained healing. He particularly feared the adulteration of foods by the food processing industry. He wrote a pioneer book on the interrelations between nutrition, positive thinking, prayer, and meditation, entitled *The Life Abundant: A Manual of Living*. His system was developed in cooperation with local physicians, and influenced by the literature of the food reformers of the 1840s, the precursors of the modern health food movement. The Rev. Bell also learned from New Thought writers that thoughts and attitudes affect the health of the body.

His system presented a three-tiered approach to gaining and maintaining good health. The first level is of proper nutrition. This includes eating large portions of fruits, especially citrus, and lightly cooked vegetables, and avoiding lard, fried foods, and refined white flour or sugar. Proper elimination (ideally three times daily) was also part of Bell's nutrition program. All of this is astounding for its modernity. The second level of good health dealt with the emotions. The Rev. Bell learned from New Thought writers and the Bible that the mind could pass on its negative or positive emotions to the body, and these would manifest as either poor or good health. He recognized that prolonged anger was especially destructive to the body's health, and he showed that the Christian had special resources in prayer and meditation for eliminating anger. For instance, a meditation he composed for temper control reads as follows:

> Lord Jesus, I am thine and Thou art mine. Teach me so to live that I shall not regret what I have said. May the peace of God dwell in my heart always to my credit.[26]

The last level of acquiring and maintaining good health was through prayer. The Rev. Bell urged his readers to an apostolic attitude to prayer, that is, a prayer life that was empowered by a faith that entertained no doubts. In this context, like the New Thought authors of his day, he believed that the best vehicle of faith was the imaginative powers of the mind, i.e., visualization. Therefore, the prayer of faith called for the supplicant to see in his or her mind's eye the thing desired as actually existing—the person in good health and looking happy.

The Life Abundant sold well enough to warrant a sequel in the form of a cookbook following the Rev. Bell's regimen, *The Life Abundant Cook Book*. By 1928 he was in much demand as a speaker, and resigned from his rector's position at St. Thomas to go into full-time ministry as a traveling healing minster and health teacher. He did many healing missions throughout the United States until his retirement in the 1950s.[27]

In 1937 he published his last work, *Intelligent Living*, which refocused on the emotional and spiritual/prayer aspects of good health rather than diet. He labored to establish a nationwide Life Abundant movement which developed active chapters throughout the United States, with a concentration in California. At the same time, he and his movement supported and cooperated with the OSL in healing missions. There was even some talk of merging the two groups, though that never happened.

The Rev. Bell's books and ministry had little influence upon the theological or nutritional establishments, which did not recognize the nutritional deficiencies of white flour and sugar until well after his death. The

---

26. Bell, *The Challenge*, 83.

27. He was sufficiently well known to be cited in *Time* magazine for his effective healing mission in St. Paul's Chapel in New York City, one of the most prestigious churches of New York. See "Hath Made."

Rev. Bell's followers, and others in what we would now call the health food movement, carried on at the fringes of American society until the 1960s. By that time his pioneer contributions were all but forgotten. His healing theology was, however, a major stepping stone in the development of the ministry of Mrs. Agnes Sanford, as we shall see later in chapter 14.

13

Glenn Clark

Recovering a Hebraic Perspective
on Effective Prayer

Introduction

IN THE 1960S, THOUSANDS of Christians met at special summer camps where they participated in prayer exercises, lectures on healing and deliverance prayer, the baptism of the Holy Spirit, and artistic activities. The latter, known as "creatives," encouraged people to participate in spontaneous drama skits, making up psalms to the Lord, drawing and music, all in the invited presence of the Holy Spirit. The purpose of these camps was to learn to become more effective Christians and at the same time to gain a sampling of what it would be to live all of one's everyday life in the kingdom of God.[1]

These camps attracted thousands of persons and became in the mid-1950s and 1960s the school house of the Charismatic Renewal. They were known as CFOs, or Camps Farthest Out. Meeting in many

---

1. Mrs. Sanford wrote about Glenn Clark and the CFO glowingly throughout her own autobiography, *Sealed Orders*. This sparked my interest in the CFO and I attended multiple CFOs camps during the 1980s and early 1990s. I made special efforts to talk to the "old-timers" who remembered the camps in their earlier days. The Rev. Tommy Tyson (1922–2002), a Methodist charismatic evangelist and frequent CFO speaker, was especially kind in sharing his CFO memories and insights. Now deceased, his website contains information on him and many of his recorded CFO messages: http://www.tommytyson.org/. During 1986–88 my wife and I served on the (Georgia) Golden Isles CFO "council ring," the local governing group. An early version of my work on Glenn Clark was published as "Glenn Clark" in *Sharing* (1992), then as more extensive and formal article in 2003, "Camps Farthest Out," in *PNEUMA*, (2003). *PNEUMA* is the academic journal of American Pentecostalism.

states, the CFOs were the place where the first generation of charismatic leaders presented their insights on faith, healing, deliverance prayer, and the new ministry of inner healing. Some camps, such as the one held at Kanuga, North Carolina, drew thousands of participants at a time. However, because of the CFOs original ties to New Thought, histories of the Charismatic Renewal have ignored the significant role of the CFOs in their movement.[2]

The founder of the CFOs, Glenn Clark, did not live to see the camps during the 1960s, when they were most influential. But decades before the Charismatic Renewal he had carefully and prayerfully established the CFO camps and led them to their final form and organization.[3] In addition to founding the camps, Prof. Clark wrote masterful books on the art of prayer which incorporated little-noticed or -used Hebraic models of prayer. He also wrote pioneer works on healing prayer. His camps and written works became an important part of the spiritual scene of American Protestantism from the 1920s to the 1960s, and an active witness and counter to cessationism.

In spite of his achievements, Glenn Clark remains relatively unknown among leaders of American religious life, and certainly not identified as a major contributor to the Charismatic Renewal. Much like Agnes Sanford, as well as E. W. Kenyon, father of the Word-Faith movement, Clark entered into, incorporated, then distanced himself from New Thought writings.[4] Like the others just mentioned, he filtered New Thought ideas through the mesh of the Bible and classic Christian literature, and represented them to the Christian public as a useful base upon which to spread empowered Christianity, including healing and deliverance ministries.

2. The exception is the excellent long article by Hocken, "Charismatic Movement."

3. Though much reduced in vitality and number from their peak in the 1970s, a few CFO camps are still active and can be contacted online at www.campsfarthestout.org.

4. That E. W. Kenyon borrowed from New Thought and Christian Science was brought to the attention of the Christian public by McConnell, *Different Gospel.* Although well researched as to the facts, McConnell had no broad historic understanding of Christian history, and thus missed the Marcion Shove that Kenyon experienced with Christian Science. For McConnell, associating Kenyon with Christian Science was equivalent of identifying him as a heretic, and thus calling fellow Pentecostals to repentance and renunciation of Kenyon's and Kennith Hagin's teachings. See my discussion of McConnell, Kenyon, and Hagin in *Quenching the Spirit,* chapters 18 and 20.

Clark brought his theology to the edge of the Charismatic Renewal by affirming the gift of tongues in the CFO camps a decade before the public renewal began. Although unheralded today, there is thankfully sufficient information on Clark to reconstruct the stages of his spiritual journey.[5]

Life

Glenn Clark's father was born in a rustic frontier cabin, and as a young man he joined the Union Army, where he rose from private to captain. After the Civil War he became a successful businessman and founded an insurance company that stressed Christian values, such as treating its employees with respect and courtesy. The Clark's were Presbyterian and the Bible was central to the family, but literature and science were also honored. As an adult, Glenn Clark remembered his household as "one of the most heavenly homes ever established on earth."[6] Born March 13, 1882, Glenn was the second son in a family of six children.

Glenn did well in school, attending high school and then Grinnell College in Iowa, where he majored in literature. He also loved sports, and played football and wrestled. In his college years he participated in many YMCA camps and activities. This was a time when the YMCA was an active evangelical organization and took seriously its mandate to form the youth of America as mature Christians.[7] Glenn also led a Sunday-evening Bible study during his years at Grinnell.

However, in his senior year he read a book by the German atheist philosopher Maurice Maeterlink, *Buried Temple*, which beguilingly argued that there was no evidence for either the immortality of the soul or the existence of God. Glenn recalled, "all my inherited religion, based

5. The principal biographical sources for Glenn Clark is his autobiography, *Man's Reach*, (1949), still in print. See also Miles Clark's biography of his father, *Glenn Clark* (1975), and Harding, *The Saga* (n.d.). So many editions of Glenn Clark's works were printed since the 1930s that copies of his works are found in many used book stores and online used book stores. My favorite is www.abebooks.com, and a recent search there turned up his principal works at reasonable prices.

6. Clark, *Man's Reach*, 319. It is difficult to imagine the wholesomeness and security of life in rural America at the end of the nineteenth century. The novels of William Keepers Maxwell Jr. describe this era and are a pleasure to read and a reminder of that lost past.

7. On how the YMCA lost its evangelical focus and became a sports activity organization, see Erdozain, *Problem of Pleasure*.

on authority, all my faith, built upon hearsay, were swept away."[8] His sojourn into agnosticism was an unhappy one but it did not last long. Glenn went Harvard for an master's in literature. There he had several private conversation with William James. It was through Professor James that Clark encountered New Thought writings. Here was a whole world of writings that believed in the reality of the spiritual world and had scientific confidence about it. A major stepping stone of Prof. Clark's spiritual recovery was his discovery of F. L. Rawson's, *Life Understood* (see chapter 7). Rawson's description of prayer as a form of energy made a strong impression on Clark, and *Life Understood* gave him a renewed belief in the reality of the spiritual world and brought him out of atheism.

After he completed his master's (1906), he accepted a call to be teacher and athletic coach at a tiny (thirty-eight-student) college in Illinois. After several years there he went to Macalester College in St. Paul, Minnesota, where he remained for the rest of his life, heading the English and athletic departments, serving as football coach—and raising his family. In 1919, Clark was called to his father's death bed.

> I sat at his bedside and held his hand as his spirit took flight, even as I had foreseen I was going to do. And the sensation of release I had was the same sensation I had experienced while witnessing the birth of my child. Then I realized with a deep, incontrovertible realization that only as I gave myself to the Spirit of God and was reborn as a Son of God could I bring into birth the Truth of God. So I stopped my little brain from thinking and let the Holy Spirit rise within me, overshadowing me.[9]

As he went back to his teaching he found new delight in reading Scripture. He discovered that for the first time Paul's epistles made sense, a sign that the Spirit had answered his prayer. He also began reading the classics of Western spirituality. This included modern Protestant devotional writers such as Rufus Jones, the Catholic mystics, and "all of the Evelyn Underhill's books that I could lay my hands on."[10] Underhill was the great expositor of Christian mysticism, whose tremendously successful work *Mysticism* (1911) became a classic in its field.

---

8. Clark *Man's Reach*, 101.

9. Ibid., 154–55.

10. Ibid.,158. Underhill still stands as one of the great expositors of Christian mysticism. See especially her *Mysticism* (1911), many editions after.

But within Christian mysticism his single favorite book was Brother Lawrence's *Practicing the Presence of God*. Brother Lawrence's ability to live in the joy of God's kingdom while working in the monastery kitchen gave Glenn a model that deeply resonated within him. He also continued reading New Thought literature.[11] He had special delight in following the scientific discoveries that were unfolding ever more quickly as the century progressed. This was one reason why Rawson's work so impressed him.

> I felt especially drawn to F. L Rawson's *Life Understood*, whose abstract principles balanced the concrete simplicity of Brother Lawrence . . .
>
> Using Christ as my center, and putting my hand in my Savior's as my guide and my friend, letting whole being become released and expanded in this new dimension of heaven on earth, I trained myself in Rawson's denials and affirmations, and things began to happen.[12]

Prof. Clark had a chance to meet with Rawson when he came to the Twin Cities on a lecture tour.

> [I] discovered that he had never read a novel or a poem in his life, was purely scientific and used his imagination hardly at all. . . . He was a foundation-layer but he lacked the imagination for converting the science of prayer into an art. I determined then and there not to be a mere follower of his, but to begin where he left off.[13]

Discoveries in Prayer

At the same time, Clark remained as an active layperson in mainline Protestant Christianity. Clark worshiped regularly at the Macalester Presbyterian Church of Minneapolis, where he became a deacon. He also taught a Sunday school class at the Plymouth Congregational Church of the same city. His Sunday school studied Rawson's *Life Understood*, and it became a prayer laboratory where Clark and his class probed for the secrets of effective prayer.

---

11. Clark, *Man's Reach*, 158–59, for a description of his readings in these formative years.

12. Ibid., 159.

13. Ibid.

They began by disciplining themselves in Rawson's denial and affirmation method. This was done in a Quaker-like setting of silence, and with supplicants' names lifted up to God. When Prof. Clark had been absent for several week a member came up to him and asked:

> "Why is it that when you are present our prayers are answered so much more effectively than when you are away? Tell us what it is you do." . . .
> "I just love them," I replied.
> If I had dropped a bombshell into their midst I couldn't have startled them more.
> "I never thought of that!" exclaimed one.
> "I just do some mental work," said another.
> We had already discovered that the first ingredient necessary for all true prayer was a Faith that mounted to an absolute Knowing, . . . and now we were led to our second great discovery, and that was that Love is the most powerful of all ingredients in all true prayer."[14]

A third element came when Prof. Clark discerned that when a certain young lady was absent from the group there also seemed to be a decline in prayer power. She was almost annoying in her light heartedness and joy, making it difficult for the group to enter into silence.

Clark asked her what she did when she prayed for the supplicants.

> Instantly she replied, "I put a lot of Joy into it."
> "Do you mean you put joy into it when we prayed for the one-legged popcorn man and for the old lady who had cancer?'
> "Sure, it thrilled me to think how happy they would be when they got cured."[15]

Sadducee vs. Christian in The Atlantic Monthly

Tales of Clark's effective prayer power circulated at Macalester College, and a student asked him to put in writing his manner of praying. The result so impressed his students that they urged him to submit it for publication. He sent the manuscript to the *Atlantic Monthly*. Providentially, the magazine was planning to publish an article on prayer. They had

14. Ibid.,161.

15. Ibid., 161–62.

already contacted the celebrated Harvard biblical scholar Rev. Kirsopp Lake to present the modern (liberal) view.

The Rev. Lake began his religious career as an Anglican clergyman in England where he was told by his vicar that prayers for the seriously ill were useless, and served mainly to alert the congregation of the person's impending death. On the side, Lake developed considerable skills in sleuthing early church manuscripts, and turned this talent to an academic career. In 1913 he was invited to Harvard. There he demonstrated the perfect Sadducaic life of teaching church history and biblical scholarship without belief in the supernatural or trust in the truthfulness of biblical record.[16]

Lake's article for the *Atlantic Monthly* was simply called "Prayer." He began by pointing out that prayers of petition were still said in public worship, but "few educated men believe in its efficacy. The laws of life—which is the Will of God—are not changed in their working by prayer."[17] He conceded that prayer placed a person in spiritual communion with God—though it did no earthly good. This truly reflected the nadir of liberal theology and its destructiveness to spiritual life.[18]

Prof. Clark's article was entitled "The Soul's Sincere Desire," a phrase much used in Ralph Waldo Trine's New Thought work *In Tune with the Infinite*. Clark's article appeared in the same issue with Lake's so that the readers had both sides of the prayer issue at hand.

Clark affirmed his own experiences in answered prayer, and outlined a fifteen-minute-a-day program of prayer based on the Lord's Prayer and the Twenty-Third Psalm. In describing his prayer life and methods we can see a seamless weaving of New Thought faith idealism, Christian piety, and biblical grounding. He compared his program to the daily-dozen exercises then in fashion, and promised that following his program would revolutionize a person's life.[19] Clark's specific method of praying uses analogies from athletic training. Just as an athlete practices deep breathing, the first stage for the praying Christian must be to "pray out the bad and pray in the good; dismiss from our mind the trouble which seems imminent and restate emphatically the great promises of

16. See Lake's biographical sketch in Casey, *Quantulacumque Studies*, vii–viii.

17. Lake, "Prayer," 163–66.

18. This is not an isolated or extreme view of early twentieth-century liberal belief on prayer. The great saint of liberal Protestantism, Florence Nightingale, believed similarly, See Larsen's, "St. Flo."

19. Clark, "Sincere Desire," 167–72.

God: forgive the sinner and accept forgiveness for the sin."[20] The second stage is the use of the affirmation/negation technique, but it is specifically related to the Bible:

> ... denial and affirmation, is suggested figuratively in the Psalm by "Thy rod and They staff," and the actual denials are given in very clear cut form: "I shall not want," and " I shall fear no evil." Each of these are followed by a series of affirmations ...

The third phase, keeping the prayer thought as a continuing force throughout the day, is suggested very beautifully in both the examples we are using: "Surely goodness and mercy shall follow me all the days of my life, and I will dwell in the house of the Lord forever"; and "Thy kingdom come, Thy will be done in earth as it is in heaven." You can see in these statements a realization of the kingdom here and now, about us, in whatever activity we may be engaged.[21]

Hebraic Breakthrough, Improvised Psalms

What Clark next suggested was original in the history of Christian prayer literature, and he was aware that to many of his readers it seemed strange.

> The only new and revolutionary idea that I am introducing into this discussion of prayer, in fact, is a plea for reinstating the psalm, the little brother of prayer, in our private and public worship ... What I wish to see is the bringing of the psalm back in the form and manner that the old Psalmists themselves made use of as a frank and spontaneous improvisation in the presence of a real need, an immanent calamity, a present sorrow upon the outstretched arms of God, and the breathing of His healing peace, comfort and love.[22]

Although Paul mandated that Christians bring psalms to their prayer meetings, this was discontinued and even forbidden by later church decree at the Council of Laodicea in 364. Certainly all Christian denominations continued to use the biblical psalms in liturgy and private prayer. And starting with the Brethren, and then Lutheranism, non-biblical hymns (psalms) were added to church services. But Prof. Clark's

20. Ibid., 169.
21. Ibid., 169.
22. Ibid., 170–71.

suggestion that *every* Christian write his or her own psalm is right out of
1 Corinthians 14:26, and to my knowledge original.

Clark's article created a sensation and unexpectedly sold out the edition. The editors asked Clark to expand his article into a book. The result
was *The Soul's Sincere Desire* (1928). Clark's book, like his article, presented an approach to Christian prayer that incorporated New Thought
idealism and optimism, classic Christian piety, and his own tested insights. Besides psalm praying, he gave the reader another Hebraic tool:
praying in parables.[23]

Clark's study of the Gospels led him to understand what he believed
to be Jesus' way of thinking and prayer. For Prof. Clark, Jesus' attitude
toward life was one of converting what he saw and touched into parables,
symbols of a greater world. This insight came at the cost of overstatement—a common fault among pioneers. Clark wrote that Jesus always
taught, thought, and prayed in parables. Certainly Jesus did not always
speak in parables. However, when we understand the Hebrew word that
is translated as "parable," his overstatement fades. The Hebrew word
is *mashal* and means "comparison" or "to become like." A *mashal* is a
comparison with or without a story elaboration, as in Luke 13:20–21. A
mashal was a common Hebraic manner of making a point.

As part of prayer, Clark defined parable thinking as the ability to
look at "reality through the lens of divine imagination."[24] In terms of
mashal, it is comparing the present situation with God's perfect will for
the situation. For example, if a person is ill, an effective way to pray for
that person is to believe the person well and active and lift that thought
to God as a *mashal*. Clark's *mashal* theology was clearly a biblically orthodox idealist theology which enabled the Christian to affirm an anticipated outcome without stumbling into the fallacy of Christian Science,
which denied the reality of evil or illness.

Prof. Clark's assumption in his prayer technique was that the same
Holy Spirit that inspired David and the other psalm writers was available to every believer. From his own prayer experiences, Clark assured the

23. Clark's insight on the importance of parables in the spiritual life of the believer
preceded by almost half a century the expansion in parable studies that currently en-
gages many linguistic and biblical scholars. The publication of Jeremais' *The Parables
of Jesus* (1955) ushered in this new era of understanding of parables in the ministry
of Jesus, which continues in such scholars as John Dominic Crossan. However the
academic literature on parables does not address the issue that Clark raised, the use of
parables and parable thinking in the Christian's prayer life.

24. Clark, *Soul Sincere*, 24.

reader of *The Soul's Sincere Desire* that the act of parable prayers and psalm writing gave prayers a power and energy not found in mental prayer alone. Significantly, Clark believed that the current age is the one in which Jesus commissions Christians to do greater works than himself (John 14:12).[25] From New Thought writers he had learned the biblical truth that the kingdom of God was as much in the here and now as in the hereafter. The accountability of the Christian life lay not in supposed sound doctrine, which included cessationism, but in the Christian's ability to pray the kingdom of God into existence on earth. This placed Clark in a position of radical anti-cessationism, which was closer to both New Thought and Pentecostalism than to the Protestant orthodoxy of the times.

The Soul's Sincere Desire sold well, and Clark became a popular speaker at Christian conferences, especially YMCA events. He continued his writings, first focusing on the spiritual aspects of athletics and business. Clark's reflections on the spiritual potential of athletics was a unique adaptation of Brother Lawrence's basic attitude that all activities can come under the kingdom of God. In *The Power of the Spirit in the Athletic Field*, Clark encouraged the godly athlete to surrender the obsession to win, a surrender that allows the release of God's power and joy while playing sports. Clark believed that with this attitude new abilities often developed and victory came as a byproduct.[26]

Clark's writings on business were based on his earlier observations of his father's successful insurance businesses. The elder Clark's policy was to discuss business actions and goals with his employees until a consensus was reached, and then pray for success. He gave meticulous attention to the welfare of both employee and customer.[27] Though the only business Glenn Clark would manage himself was his religious publishing house, Macalester Park, he became a spiritual counselor to many businessmen. Tom Watson, the founder of IBM, attended Clark's Sunday school classes and accepted his teacher's business principles, making them part of IBM policy.[28]

25. Ibid., 18–20.

26. Clark, *Athletic Field* (1929) and *Power in Athletics* (1935). Perhaps the most readily available document of Clark's athletics-as-spiritual-activity genre is found in his pamphlet *Thought Farthest Out* (1930).

27. For a summary of Glenn Clark's views on business see his *Power in Business* (1945) and *Senior Partner* (1945).

28. Compare Clark's views on business with the description of the IBM founding ethic in Peters, *Search of Excellence*.

In the same period Clark went on to write a series of novels and pamphlets on prayer, including another major book on prayer entitled *I Will Lift Up Mine Eyes* (1937). The central point of this work was Clark's discovery of yet another principle of effective prayer, which he called "hind's feet on high places." That is, the seeker must order his or her mind into a harmonious whole so that the conscious and subconscious parts desire the same thing. This was the way to implement Jesus' admonition to move mountains by faith, with no doubt in the heart (Mark 11:23).[29]

Founding the CFO

Prof. Clark's books on prayer made him a much sought out speaker, and he favored the YMCA venues. But during these speaking engagements he discerned an unevenness in the spiritual atmosphere. Some were truly blessings to the participants, but others were decidedly arid. He observed that to the extent the camps dwelt on contentious or controversial issues, they lost their spiritual power.[30] He yearned for a Christian camp in which harmony would rule, and the principal concern would be prayer.

In the summer of 1929, Clark vacationed with his family on an island off the coast of Maine that the locals called the "island farthest out." Here, he tentatively planned a summer camp to be called the Camp Farthest Out. The objective would be to promote a place of Christian fellowship in which the art of prayer would be exercised, and ideas and prayer techniques he had learned could be tried without contention. Later that year, despite the fact that the nation was into the Great Depression, the members of his Sunday school class agreed to finance the camp. Many of its members were among the professional and business elite of the Twin City region.

The first Camp Farthest Out (CFO) was held in August 1930 at Minnesota's Lake Koronis.[31] Seventy participants attended, with Prof. Clark as coach, for he modeled the camp after football camps. There Christians were exercised as athletes of the spirit in the way that imitated Brother Lawrence's life. For three weeks, Clark gave two talks a day on prayer, and

29. See also the apostle James' admonition not to be "double-minded" in James 1:7–8.

30. See Prof. Clark's description of a particularly contentious YMCA in *Man's Reach*, 191–92.

31. Described in Harding, *The Saga*. See also a description of the early Lake Koronis camps in Osburn, "Koronis."

like football camps there was drill and practice as campers prayed for and with one another in small groups.

Glenn Harding, a young man who attended the first camp and in subsequent years became a major speaker and leader at CFOs, recalled:

> We knew it was to be a training camp—a place of action. We were not there just to sit down and listen to lectures—but for a new adventure! And adventure it was! Glenn was not only a teacher, but a coach—and there is a vast difference between the two. We were there not to pass examinations but to learn by doing. . . . As a coach, Glenn knew how deadly criticism and self-consciousness can be to an athlete in restricting his true ability and performance. . . . He made sure that in all our sharing, we were to find and see only the good in ourselves and others—never the negative—and the effect was like magic in releasing power and freedom from fear . . . He was a layman. With very few exceptions, we were all laymen together. This meant that we didn't have to be "churchy". . . . We could try anything we wanted to, provided only that it was an expression of Christ's spirit of love and harmony.[32]

Other activities included devotional singing, classes in art appreciation and creative writing, and rhythmic exercises where the campers prayed as they exercised to music.[33] Some campers put on dramatic skits to emphasize a prayer lesson—or just for fun.[34] A midday period was left for recreation and rest. The underlying tenet of the camp was that God's Spirit could and would inspire the wholesome creative activities of lay Christians, whether in work, writing, exercising, or dramatic skits. This was the assumption of Brother Lawrence's classic *Practicing the Presence of God*, which had such a profound impact on Glenn Clark's life.

The first camp was an unqualified success. It continued at Lake Koronis yearly, and soon other camps were started in several states. In the beginning years the only speaker was Clark himself. He was fearful that

---

32. Harding, *The Saga*, 10.

33. This now popular form of prayer is described in Robie, *Devotion in Motion*.

34. The combination of serious creative purpose and fun with others seems to work well in both religious and secular activities. Niels Bohr's physics center and retreat camp outside of Copenhagen, where the theory of quantum mechanics was hammered out, was similar to the CFO settings. The younger physicists delighted in producing dramatic skits that spoofed the serious business at hand. See Segrè's *Faust in Copenhagen*. For a summary of scientific studies that show the good that results when adults engage in playful activities, see Neyfakh's "What Playfulness."

other speakers might not share his beliefs in the power of prayer or might bring in theological contention.

Healing Prayer

To backtrack, after the astonishing success of the *Atlantic Monthly* article "The Souls Sincere Desire", Prof. Clark was deluged with prayer requests from all over the country. Many were for physical healing. This troubled Clark, for although he believed in modern-day miracles, he was still influenced by cessationism and did not associate healing prayer with the present-day kingdom of God. Clark's wife, Louise, was especially fearful that he not pray for healing, as that was a cult activity of Christian Science. In spite of this, Prof. Clark felt that he was duty bound by the plain testimony of the Gospels to pray for healing. He did so, and was astounded by the effectiveness of his prayers. He collected data on his own healing prayers and began systematic readings from New Thought and Unity writers on the topic. Healing prayer became a major teaching topic of the CFO camps.

In 1940 Prof. Clark published his first book on healing prayer, *How to Find Health Through Prayer*. In this work are combined the idealist perspective of New Thought with biblical accountability and his own original discoveries. Prof. Clark divided healing prayer into four categories or types.[35] The first was the denial method, which is most purely idealist in the method of Christian Science. Clark cited the incident in Luke 8:49–56 as a biblical warrant for this method. He wrote:

> My first experiment in the field of effective prayer was with this method. I based it upon Jesus' statement that the Kingdom of Heaven is within us. Using that as my starting point I would say emphatically and aloud, "There is no sickness in heaven. All is harmony, wholeness and health."[36]

Note the subtle but profound difference between Clark's position and that of pure Christian Science. He is not denying that evil and sickness exist on earth; rather he is affirming that by activating the kingdom of God on earth its heavenly qualities can be brought to bear on the negative earthly situation.

35. Ibid., 86.
36. Ibid.

The opposite of the denial method of prayer is what Clark calls "knowing prayer." In the Pentecostal tradition, of which he was unaware at the time, this is called the "prayer of faith." In Clark's understanding, the knowing method happens when prayers are spoken with full assurance of success. This takes much spiritual discipline and an ability to unite the desires of the conscious and unconscious with faith (as in his earlier *The Soul's Sincere Desire*).

The most traditional method of healing prayer that Prof. Clark described is what he called "relinquishing prayer." Relinquishing prayer lifts the patient up to the throne of God for his or her highest good, which in the case of serious illness might even be death. Clark encouraged this type of prayer in cases where the patient and prayer petitioner are close, as in parent and child. This method seems to release the petitioner from the fear and anxiety associate with the situation and allows for a greater flow of God's healing love.[37]

Prof. Clark had intimate experience with this type of prayer. In spite of his athletic prowess, he always had a heart murmur, and by middle age it had become a serious problem. He had made it a habit not to travel to high elevations, as that would trigger dangerous heart palpitations. However, he was invited to a national YMCA conference as the main speaker and prayer leader that was scheduled in Estes Park, Colorado, at eigth thousand feet elevation. He declined the invitation, but felt uneasy about it until he reversed himself and accepted. He said goodbye to his family knowing he was in God's will but not knowing if he would see them again this side of heaven. The first night at the conference center facility he felt his heart racing and pounding itself to death. He prayed as he looked out at the beautiful mountains:

> You made me, Father. I am more wonderfully made than the mountains. If you want to take me—take me. If you want to preserve me You can easily preserve me. I leave it entirely to You, O Lord, for I am your man.[38]

By the time the weeklong conference was over, his heart was completely healed.

Another method of healing prayer suggested by Clark was most unusual and curiously prophetic: laughing at illness. Clark experimented

37. Ibid., 21. Cf. Catharine Marshall's experience of her prayers for her granddaughter in Marshall, *Something More*, 13–14.

38. Clark, *Man's Reach*, 191.

with this method when his three-year-old daughter's ear infection lingered and did not respond to other forms of prayer. His daughter was surprised by Clark's laughter, but in fact she was healed.[39] Unfortunately this unusual method of healing prayer was not followed up by other Christians, and an elaboration of the relationship between laughter and healing had to await for forty years when the physician Norman Cousins discovered the effectiveness of laughter in his own serious illness.[40]

How to Find Health Through Prayer was quite successful. By 1940 Clark had a wide reputation as prayer teacher and his writings were sought after by major publishers. Harper published *How to Find Health Through Prayer* and it remained in print for years. Clark reworked its materials in the early 1950s into a correspondence course format which was managed through CFO headquarters.[41]

In the fall of 1945 Prof. Clark called a special meeting of established Christian healers to share with each other their witnesses, what they had learned, and what needed to be learned. The meeting took place on the shores of Lake Idi Hopi, near Minneapolis. The keynote speakers were Louise Eggleston, Ruth Robison, and Agnes Sanford, all of whom might accurately be designated as Christian New Perspective. Prof. Clark referred to them as the "wonderful triumvirate." Persons from Unity and Divine Science (a form of Christian Science) were also invited. Dr. Rebecca Beard, who later established an important healing center in Vermont, and who would become a fixture at CFOs, wrote:

> The spirit of the people whom I met at the first Healing Advance was beyond anything I had ever experienced. I had attended many medical conventions where everyone was stampeding . . . to be heard. Here were thirty-five or forty consecrated people with the light of God shining in their faces, every one of whom said, "I would rather not talk. I want so much to hear what you have discovered"—eager and willing they were to step aside.[42]

In the next five years Prof. Clark called three similar leadership conferences. These meetings solidified a network of CNP ministers who kept in communication with each other. By the 1950s Prof. Clark no longer

39. Clark, *Health Through*, 89. For a similar case see Kenneth Hagin's description of the healing of his son's illness in Hagin, "Life of Faith."

40. Cousins, *Anatomy of an Illness* (1979).

41. Clark, *Correspondence Course* (1953).

42. Beard, *Everyman's Search*, 6.

found it necessary to call such meeting, as the yearly Order of St. Luke conferences at St. Stephen's functioned as the networking vehicle for the Christian healing movement (chapter 12), and many in CFO leadership positions were also in the OSL.

The CFOs Metaphysical Period

From the beginning the CFO camps manifested a blend of classical Christian piety and New Thought idealism. In a pamphlet advertising the upcoming 1932 camp, Mrs. Ruth Kennell, the director of rhythmic exercises, wrote in typical New Thought gobbledygook:

> The art of rhythmic movement is one of the most potent means of achieving a completely harmonized mental, physical, and spiritual balance in an at-one-ment with God . . . we convert our bodies into luminous fluidity, surrendered to the inspiration, joy and harmony of the human soul, "flowing with the tide of eternity," and becoming a part of the eternal rhythms of the spheres manifest in Divinity.[43]

The decade from 1930 to 1940 was Professor Clark's metaphysical period, a time when he almost slipped into the Gnostic entrapments so common in the universalist wing of New Thought. The same factors that made him a confident pioneer almost brought him and the new CFO to ruin. His home life had given him a deep belief in the goodness of God and his own secure place as a child of God. This secure faith base allowed him to experiment and to flourish as one of the most successful prayer pioneers of modern times. But it also caused a certain blindness toward the deceptiveness of Gnosticism. William James, in his classic *Varieties of Religious Experience*, calls the happy, optimistic religious type of person that Prof. Clark exemplified as "once born." This is in distinction to what he termed "twice born." The latter type is the person who has experienced tremendous evil and injustice, and yet is able to see God in the world in spite of its evil. The great Christian writer Alexander Solzhenitsyn, who suffered greatly under Stalinism, is an example of a twice-born Christian. Prof. Clark was most definitely not twice born.

In this period Prof. Clark accepted the metaphysical myth that evil is principally a question of ignorance, not spiritual/moral choice. He assumed that evil, as in the form of sin and disease, could be completely

43. Kennell, "Camp Farthest Out" (1931), 6.

overcome by prayer and positive thinking. In 1940 he asserted that disease could be eliminated from the face of the earth within fifty years with a combination of healing prayer and medical innovations.[44] He would have been surprised that in the twenty-first century, seventy years later, the world would be fighting the most deadly epidemics, such as the Ebola virus and AIDS. In fairness, it should be pointed out that Clark's spiritual optimism was common to many mainline Protestants of his era. For instance, Dr. Shailer Mathews, dean of the prestigious University of Chicago Divinity School from 1907 to 1933, wrote a widely read and influential work entitled *The Spiritual Interpretation of History*. In this work Dr. Mathews claimed that humanity had evolved in ethics and morals, and that even the shock of World War I would produce a nobler social order. He had no inkling that fomenting in Germany's defeat in World War I were the evils of Nazism.

Clark's most metaphysical work was his 1931 novel, *Water of Life*. It grew out of a course he taught at Macalester College in which he integrated the themes of Homer's *Odyssey*, the Hindu *Bhagavad Gita*, Dante's *Divine Comedy*, and the biblical Book of Job. His thesis was that all great religions and the great masters of literature had a share of divine revelation—the key concept of the universalist branch of New Thought. *Water of Life* also attempted to reconcile Eastern and Western religion with each other, and all with modern science. Prof. Clark described heaven as the place where all religions meet and blend. In one scene of the novel, Dale, the protagonist, is given a vision of heaven and hears the voice of God:

> Then there came a voice from the cloud which spoke even to Dale, Heaven is that place where distinctions remain, but separation ends. . . . Where ALL are ONE and One is ALL. I am where all religions that ever have been and ever will be meet and blend.[45]

In another revelation to Dale, a Hindu sage reveals that India's past spiritual masters are now reincarnating in America.

> Even as Columbus stamped the name Indians upon your humble native inhabitants, thinking they had discovered us, so the spiritual credentials of prophethood, which God is today stamping on the inner souls of spiritual leaders in America, are the same as in ancient days he stamped upon the souls of humble native

44. Clark, *Health Through*, chapter 1.
45. Ibid., *Water of Life*, 88.

masters in India. For as the great masters of ancient wisdom once inhabited our land, now in these last incarnations, they are appearing in America.[46]

Jesus is described as one of many world masters or teachers who have come into the world. Although Jesus has primacy as sin bearer, it is not at all clear if Jesus is the Son of God in the unique manner that is the core of Christian revelation.[47] All of this could have been penned by any New Thought universalist. At this stage, 1935–1940, Prof. Clark and his CFO could have easily descended into the pit of metaphysical/Gnostic thought and perhaps spiritualism, as many New Thought groups did. The CFO could have become nothing more than a summer camp cult.

But by the grace of God that did not happen.

46. Ibid., 90–91.

47. Ibid., 257.

14

Glenn Clark's CFO

From Christian New Perspective
to Pentecostalism

SEVERAL IDENTIFIABLE FACTORS STEERED Professor Clark and the CFO away from becoming just another New Thought group, and towards evangelical and then Pentecostal Christianity. Unlike Unity Christianity, reincarnation, with all its Gnostic temptations to vanity, never became an official CFO doctrine. There is no record that Clark ever declared himself to be the reincarnation of anyone, important or not. Reincarnation was entertained as a possibility and openly discussed in the CFOs well into the 1960s, but it faded after that. In this context, West Coast CFOs, particularly the California CFOs, tended to have lingering metaphysical elements, and the Southern and Midwest CFOs much less.

Most importantly, biblical accountability was central to CFO worship, teaching, and practice. CFO members were from every denomination of Protestant Christianity, and their common ground was the Bible. Even in Clark's *Water of Life*, the primacy of biblical revelation was affirmed, and Jesus was identified as Lord and sin bearer, a role that no other master had. This Christology was definitely suborthodox and irregular, but it met the Bible's minimal criterion for Prof. Clark to continue in the grace of the Body of Christ (Rom 10:9). Prof. Clark's prayer time with the Father was the focus of his spiritual life, and he prayed for humility. God answered this request, as he was known for humility and good humor, and he was quick to praise his colleagues in the Lord.[1] This short-circuited any drift towards forming a Glenn Clark cult.

---

1. See for example Clark, *The Way* (1946), 16.

Glenn Clark's fear that different speakers might spawn a spirit of contention could well have been exaggerated and demonized into a belief that only he had the wisdom to teach on prayer. This fear was put aside as the CFO attracted faith-filled evangelical Christians leaders who reintroduced Clark to the depths of Christian revelation about the unique, divine nature of Jesus.

Evangelical Leaders Renew the CFO

The first to join Clark as a CFO speaker was Starr Daily. He had been a hardened criminal who had learned a demonic, yoga-like discipline for efficiency in crime. At the time the police were apt to use enhanced interrogation techniques on crime suspects to elicit confessions. His yoga discipline was aimed to resist this. Daily met Jesus in a powerful visionary experience while in solitary confinement, and the Lord's grace transformed his criminal disciplines into a systematic life of prayer and helpfulness toward others in prison. He was miraculously and unexpectedly paroled. He became a gentle, anointed teacher of prayer. The CFO audiences loved to hear Daily's witness of conversion and miraculous release, and for decades he served as a principal CFO speaker.[2]

In 1942 the Rev. Frank Laubach (1884–1970) came to the U.S. from the war-ravaged Philippines and joined the CFO leadership. He was one of the most important and influential Christian missionaries of the twentieth century.[3] As a young man he received a classic Protestant education at Princeton University and Union Theological Seminary. His first overseas assignment was to the Philippines, then as seminary instructor in Manila. But he had an arid spiritual life until he surrendered his ambitions for academic fame. He followed the Lord's guidance and became a humble Christian witness to the Moros, a Muslim group in the southern islands.

Among the Moros, he devised a brilliant literacy campaign called "each one, teach one." He established an international agency to carry on this method of literacy instruction. Eventually it functioned in over one hundred nations and brought literacy to over sixty million persons.[4]

2. See Glenn Clark' biography of Daily, *Crime to Christ* (1948), and Starr Daily's autobiography, *Release* (1942).

3. Gowing, "Frank Charles Laubach," and a book-length study of his life and ministry, Mason's *Apostle to Illiterates* (1966).

4. See the website for Pro Literacy Worldwide, http://www.proliteracy.org.

The Rev. Laubach was especially sensitive to the poverty of Third World nations and warned the American people about the dire consequences of the global imbalance in wealth. He also attempted to remold his "each one, teach one" method of literacy education into a method of personal Christian witness[5]—alas, with less success, perhaps because evangelization is a gift that cannot be presumed as universal (Eph 4:11).

Besides all of this, the Rev. Laubach was, like Prof. Clark, a master of prayer, and a person who experienced many miracles through prayer. In his work *Channels of Spiritual Power* (1954), Laubach described going through life, like Brother Lawrence, using mundane or routine activities for prayer: "It is a wonderful thing to shoot silent flash prayers at people whom we meet. If we are sitting in a church or railroad station, it is good to pray for the people around us."[6]

The Rev. Laubach loved experimenting with prayer's power to bless others. He also understood that accountability in spiritual experiments is difficult:

> In the realm of the spirit it is not easy to determine what is truth and what is superstition, because spiritual facts are more difficult to count and hold steady than most physical phenomenon. . . . Each of us must go into the laboratory of his own soul, try most of his experiments alone, and exchange notes with other men who are trying similar experiments.[7]

Here the Rev. Laubach was noting a principal reason why religion and Christianity could not quite become a science (as Mrs. Baker Eddy believed), and we shall say more of this in chapter 22. Now, it is important to note that he did have a love and joy about prayer experiments. Unlike mixing chemicals, such prayer experiments can do no harm; at worst, spot prayers might be ineffective on the intended person, but no harm would result. Laubach recounted his own experiments:

> Some time ago, I was looking at a man sitting by an open window half a block away. I shot a rapid fire of prayer at him, saying three or four times a second "Jesus, friend—Jesus is coming to you." In thirty seconds that man put his head in his hands and bent down over his desk, as though in prayer.[8]

5. Laubach, *Win One* (1964).

6. Laubach, *Spiritual Power* (1954), 95.

7. Laubach, *Prayer* (1946).

8. Ibid., 74.

The Rev. Laubach loved how the CFO camps encouraged and conducted its prayer experiments and exercises, as in its hand-holding and united broadcast of prayers at the end of a camp week. In one such broadcast prayer Laubach saw Prof. Clark form the campers in a circle, and in faith they visualized the President of the United Stated at the center of the circle. They then prayed for God's goodness and wisdom to come into him.[9] The Rev. Laubach's love of prayer and willingness to experiment in prayer made him a natural CFO speaker and leader. His Christ-centeredness and biblical orthodoxy, as well as his experience with the poverty and suffering of the world, was a restraint on Prof. Clark's naïve optimism and irregular ideas.

Another prominent Christian leader, Dr. John Gaynor Banks, founder of the Episcopal Order of St. Luke (see chapter 12), also became a CFO speaker and leader. Banks spoke at CFO camps of the power of the Christian sacraments to heal the sick. There were also women like Louise Eggleston, Agnes Sanford, and Marcia Brown who had established independent ministries and were mature, Jesus-centered Christians.

It was Marcia Brown's husband, the Rev. Roland Brown, who gave Prof. Clark an important lesson on exorcism and the demonic. This was important for Clark, who tended to be naively optimistic in spiritual matters, as were most New Thought writers. This happened when Pastor Brown visited at the Clark home in St. Paul. For two years Prof. Clark had weekly visited the home of a World War I veteran named Frank to pray for his healing from schizophrenia. The man had been diagnosed as insane for twenty years and was declared incurable. A fear had gripped him that confined him to his bedroom, and then to his bed. Pastor Brown, who had experience in exorcism within his own church in Chicago, shared his views on the demonic and exorcism with Clark as they went together to pray over the veteran. Starr Daily recorded what happened as both Clark and Brown were praying at Frank's bedside:

> Dr. Clark suddenly asked the patient a rather peculiar but apt question, "What would you say a demon is?"
>
> "Well, if a lion were caught in a butterfly net and thought he was a butterfly, he would be possessed by a demon."
>
> That gave Dr. Clark the leverage he had been waiting for two years. The prayers of Pastor Brown, sitting silently in the room, had helped to bring it to a focus. Now Dr. Clark prayed silently, "Heavenly Father, Frank has at last perfectly defined the

9. Ibid., 70.

demon that possessed him. He is a man who thinks he is caught
in a cage. . . . In the name of Jesus Christ I command this demon
to leave him now and never return."[10]

Frank was healed at that moment, and although physically weak, he arose
from his bed. In just a few days he arrived at a nearby CFO camp where
he was loved on and prayed over by Prof. Clark and others. Frank went
on to become a healthy and active church member.

That incident, which took place in August of 1939, convinced Clark
of the need for the ministry of exorcism. This biblically orthodox and
non-metaphysical point of view was included in his 1940 book, *How to
Find Health Through Prayer*.[11] This was decades before most evangelical
Christians would awaken to the necessity of an exorcism ministry, and of
course theological liberals still negate the need for this ministry.

The Pentecostal Ministry of Rufus Moseley

However, the most important figure that turned Glenn Clark and the
CFO away from metaphysics and toward biblical orthodoxy and Pente-
costalism was Rufus Moseley, a humble, Spirit-filled pecan farmer from
Macon, Georgia.[12] Moseley was born on August 29, 1870, to a devoutly
Christian farming family in the mountain town of Elkin, North Carolina.
His father had a reputation for absolute integrity and kindness in all his
dealings. Rufus recounted:

> When he offered for sale, or in trade, a horse or a mule, he first
> told its faults to the full. When he took a load of watermelons
> to sell, he sought to have the larger ones at the bottom instead
> of the top.[13]

10. Daily, *Recovery* (1948), 42–43.

11. Clark, *Health Through*, 50.

12. Moseley's major work, which is an autobiographical narrative of his spiritual pilgrimage, is *Manifest Victory* (1941). He attempted to put the same insights in
simpler language in a later work, *Perfect Everything* (1949). Moseley's monumental
influence on the CFO and other parachurch groups was first pointed out to me by the
late Rev. Tommy Tyson, a Methodist charismatic evangelist, in an interview of him
on November 18, 1984. Wayne McLain, a disciple of Moseley, published two works
on Moseley, *A Heavenly View* (1993) and a biography, *Resurrection Encounter* (1997).

13. Moseley, *Manifest Victory*, 22

Rufus was a good student, but his family could not afford to send him to secondary school, so he read his way through the secondary school curriculum. Through great sacrifice by his parents Rufus was able to attend the first year of college; he missed a scholarship for that first year because his hand writing was *terrible*. Thereafter, his own brilliance allowed him to gain one scholarship after another. At Peabody College in Nashville he fell in love with the idealist philosophers. "Plato so gripped me that I completely forgot my body. For the first time in my life I was lost in pure intellectual delight."[14]

But at Peabody he also became a born-again believer. In his second year a visiting evangelist from Texas came to preach at a nearby church.

> When the evangelist made the altar call it seemed that I stood in jeopardy if I did not respond. Some of my college teachers and many of my student friends were present. Their presence made it all the more difficult to take on the cross by acknowledging my need to yield to the Spirit and follow Jesus.[15]

The following night he returned and went to the altar again, this time for a prayer of total dedication to the Lord.

After graduating from Peabody, Moseley went on to graduate studies at the University of Chicago, at Heidelburg in Germany, and finally to Harvard University. At Harvard he studied under William James while the renowned philosopher-psychologist was preparing the *Varieties of Religious Experience*. As with Glenn Clark, James introduced Moseley to New Thought and Christian Science. After his formal studies he accepted a teaching position at the Baptist Mercer College in Macon, Georgia (1894). There he became a much-loved teacher.

But as Mosley read the literature of Christian Science and New Though his beliefs about spiritual healing came into conflict with the solidly cessationist Baptist doctrine at Mercer. He came to a crisis of conscience. Moseley felt, just as his father could not hide the smaller watermelons, that he could not hide his attraction to Christian Science. He felt especially drawn to it because it was the first form of Christianity he had seen that offered demonstration for its doctrine in the form of real healings, and because it was an idealist-based system. He felt he had to resign. In a talk he gave years later, Moseley recounted:

14. Ibid., 31-32.

15. Ibid., 32

One of the most difficult ordeals that I ever faced was to go before the Board of Trustees of a Southern Baptist college [Mercer] and let them know that I was a big enough fool, in their estimation, to feel there might be something in Christian Science, and to resign my position and go see if there was. For I felt I can't afford to bring this thing into the college until I know about it and I can't know about it unless I find out (that is, enter into the movement and experiment with it). And if there is a ray of hope here (in Christian Science), what is conventional success in comparison with finding out the truth.[16]

Moseley resigned from Mercer and formally joined Christian Science. He quickly learned its affirmation/denial method, and through it he was healed of a digestive disorder that had tormented him for years. He continued in the Christian Science movement as one of its practioners and as an apologist for the movement. His articles explaining the Christian Science position and biblical commentaries appeared frequently in the *Christian Science Journal* and *Christian Science Sentinel* from 1901 to 1909. His articles show a philosopher's understanding of the Christian Science idealist position and interpretation, but also a very strict adherence to the biblical record. He was attempting to bring Christian Science into biblical accountability.

But by 1908 he was uneasy about the cult that arose around Mary Baker Eddy and, prompted of the Holy Spirit, resigned from Christian Science. Moseley continued his healing prayers among Christian Scientists and independent Christian churches, including Pentecostal congregations, where he learned about the gifts of the Holy Spirit.

He earned a living by tending a ten-acre Pecan grove. After World War I he also received a small income from his columns in the *Macon Daily Telegraph*. He focused his ministry on the poor, sick, and imprisoned, especially on condemned prisoners. Moseley became an activist against capital punishment and had some successes in having death sentences commuted. He also preached racial tolerance and reconciliation. On one occasion in the 1920s he personally confronted a lynch mob and stopped their intended murder.[17]

The year after he cut all ties to Christian Science, he felt the presence of the Holy Spirit increasing in his life. By then there were several Pentecostal churches in Macon. Visiting one, he was told by its minister,

16. McLain, *Resurrection Encounter*, 58.
17. Manis, *Black and White*, 127.

"You will have to become more orthodox before God will baptize you [in the Spirit]." I replied, "The promise is not to the orthodox, but those who hunger and thirst and ask."[18]

In March of 1910 he was seeking for the baptism of the Spirit with single-mindedness. One night, alone in a house he was staying, he was awakened early in the morning by the Lord. This began a profound experience of Jesus in his ascended glory. His experience with Christ resembled that which the famous nineteenth-century revivalist Charles Finney had with Jesus at the beginning of his Christian life.[19] Moseley recalled:

> I became aware of a glorious Presence standing immediately before me in the tangible form of a man, imparting the sense of barely concealed powers and immense sanctity. He made Himself known as Jesus and infused Himself within me.... I fell upon my face at His feet, as one dead and yet more alive than I dreamed it possible ever to be. I knew at once that He was in me and I in Him, and the Father was in Him and He in the Father.[20]

This experience was so profound, and resulted in such unalloyed joy and exuberance, that his family committed him to the local mental hospital to have him checked out. It took him a week to convince the staff he was not crazy, or at least not dangerous. He began manifesting the gifts of the Holy Spirit, including a much-strengthened ability to witness to others, to heal, and to proclaim the gospel. He knew of tongues, but resisted that gift for eight months.

Though never an ordained minister, Moseley was teacher and spiritual director to many. Most importantly, he was an itinerant witness to the power of the Holy Spirit. Moseley particularly influenced parachurch organizations such as E. Stanley Jones' Christian Ashram movement, Dr. Albert E. Day's Disciplined Order of Christ, and especially the CFO.[21] He and Prof. Clark became close friends, and Moseley regularly spoke at CFO camps. He was known at the camps for his rumpled suits and absolutely wonderful talks and ministry. Prof. Clark called Moseley's

18. Moseley, *Manifest Victory* 69.

19. Compare Moseley's experience in *Manifest Victory*, chapter 5, with the experience of the great evangelist Charles Finney as described in his *Memoirs*, chapter 2.

20. Moseley, *Manifest Victory*, 80

21. The Disciplined Order of Christ was, like the CFO, a non-cessationist parachurch organization. It was founded by Albert E. Day, an influential Methodist minister. See McKinley, *Disciplined Order.*

Perfect Everything "the greatest book on the Holy Spirit ever written."[22] Wherever Moseley witnessed or taught, some in his audience received the gifts of the Spirit. Many others were prepared for the *idea* of a personal Pentecostal experience, and when the Charismatic Renewal began in the 1960s they were able to accept it. We will note his influence on Agnes Sanford below.

Glenn Clark's Mature Theology

The biblically orthodox and graced individuals discussed above (Moseley, Laubach, Daily, the Browns, and others) inspired a decisive shift in Clark's theology and prayer life from the 1940s.[23] Whereas his prayer consciousness had been centered on the Father, he now became acutely aware of the role of Jesus and arrived at a greater appreciation for the work of the Holy Spirit. In 1942 Clark published a forty-five-page booklet and then a full-length book that demonstrated the direction of his mature works. The pamphlet was entitled *The Three Mysteries of Jesus: The Cross, the Blood, the Name* (1942), and the book that expanded the pamphlet was entitled *The Way, the Truth, and the Life*. These works have a viewpoint unlike anything found in traditional Christian theology. They are deeply Trinitarian, having a renewed appreciation of Jesus and the Spirit. The pamphlet sought to explain the atoning work of Jesus and the Christian's call to participate in the experience of the cross. In Clark's view, the true disciple had to share a multitude of crosses in order to be empowered and useful in the kingdom. These crosses, or sufferings, are to be expected and welcomed by the Christian as preparation for his or her effective role in the kingdom of God. This follows traditional Christian spirituality, for instance, the crosses of humbling, of discipline, and of persecution. But he also included the insight that for effectiveness in prayer one has to

---

22. Quoted from the back cover to the paperback edition of *Perfect Everything* (1968).

23. I believe that the *ultimate* reason for this shift to biblical orthodoxy was that there was an "evangelical cabal" of devout old ladies in tennis shoes ever present at CFO camps who prayed for Prof. Clark and the CFO. But we will never know who the intercessors were this side of heaven. My *suspicion* is that Mrs. Phyllis Learmont, who went by the pen name of Mary Light, was one of the ringleaders. Tommy Tyson and his gang are also among the "usual suspects."

accept the cross of secretiveness. "That is, one had to keep one's major prayer projects secret lest they be muddied by desire for notoriety."[24]

Clark's understanding of the role of the blood of Jesus was biblical, but unusually literal and earthy—perhaps best described as Hebraic. Clark utilized the New Thought concept of vibration as being a carrier of values and personality. He also understood the Hebrew idea that the blood contains the *nephesh* (soul, mind, and life) of its host (Gen 9:4; Lev 17:14; Deut 12:23–25). Therefore, the blood of Jesus carries his life and vibration. Clark speculated that after Jesus' blood fell to the ground from his flogging and crucifixion, it dried and pulverized, remained on the earth, and continuously sanctifies those who call on the name of Jesus.

> The blood shed by Jesus on Calvary may even now in the form of powdered dust, still remain upon the earth, and we, if we vibrate into it properly, might know what Jesus thinks and wishes for us today. Since he shed it for us, since he offers it to us, then if we believe in him, we shall have access to the power of that blood whenever we wish it.[25]

However speculative this theory may be, it constitutes an example of using New Thought vocabulary to explain the biblical truth that we have access to the mind of Christ and the blood of Jesus (1 Cor 2:16). Interestingly, St. Paul used the Gnostic vocabulary of his day to convey the gospel—this was an issue that prevented his letters from gaining rapid acceptance in the universal church. Prof. Clark's speculation on this may be false, or it may be closer to the truth than more conventional orthodox theology, especially if the new string theory turns out to be correct. The significant thing is that Prof. Clark's view of Christ was the diametrical opposite of Mary Baker Eddy's and other New Thought writers who denied the importance of matter, the importance of Jesus' blood, and the unique sin atonement of Jesus.

Most significantly, one of Clark's last completed works was entitled *The Holy Spirit* (1954). The story of its writing reveals much about the CFO in the 1950s. At the time, due largely to Rufus Moseley's influence, many members were praying in tongues before and after their sessions. This distressed Starr Daily, who did not understand the phenomenon,

24. Ibid., 110–12.

25. Clark, *The Way*, 139. The whole train of thought, of vibration carried by blood, was triggered by a book by the artist and mystic Vera Stanly Alder, *Fifth Dimension* (1940).

and he threatened to quit the CFO unless it stopped. On the other hand, Frank Laubach recognized tongues as a legitimate expression of the Holy Spirit and encouraged its practice.[26] Clark, always the diplomat, mediated the problem. He soothed Daily by promising to write on the gifts and to explain their rightful use to CFO members.[27]

Though influenced by Rufus Moseley, Clark's *The Holy Spirit* contained much that was based on Clark's own experience, and revealed his command of the classics of Christian spirituality. He shared with the reader that he received the gift of tongues decades before, prior to beginning his classic work on prayer, *The Soul's Sincere Desire*. Examining the gifts of the Holy Spirit as defined in 1 Corinthians 12, he also considered the gifts enumerated in Romans 12:6–8 as equally important. Two aspects of Clark's theology placed him closer to the traditional Catholic understanding of the gifts than to that of more modern Spirit-filled Christians. First, he believed that the gifts are received by the believer only after much seeking after God—the classic Galatian Bewitchment. Second, like much of Catholic mystical theology, Clark stressed subordinating the gifts of the Spirit to the fruits of the Spirit. Clark believed that using the gifts draws spiritual energy from the fruits, much like an old-fashioned steamboat slows down after it blows its huge whistle, its steam wasted.[28]

From the perspective of Pentecostal/charismatic theology, we can see that Prof. Clark was mistaken in both of these assumptions. The fruits of the Spirit are indeed more important than the gifts, but they do not compete. Indeed, the gifts empower the working of the fruits of the Spirit. In spite of this, the most significant thing is that Clark's *The Holy Spirit* allowed for the continued manifestations of the gifts within the CFO, bridging classical Christian spirituality and the newer, more accurate Pentecostal/charismatic understanding of the gifts.

The High Tide of the CFO

By the 1950s, the CFO headquarters in Minneapolis included a coordinating committee, publishing house, bookstore, library, and a headquarters prayer group called the United Prayer Tower. The prayer group handled prayer requests from all over the country. CFO camps existed in

26. Laubach, *Mightiest Force*, 42, 44–45, 47–48.

27. Clark, "Holy Spirit," talk from a New Mexico CFO in 1954.

28. Clark, *Holy Spirit*, 15.

most states, and several had more than one camp per year. The publishing house, Macalester Park, owned by Prof. Clark, was technically independent from the CFO and run as a business. It was destined to play a key role in publishing the works of Agnes Sanford and the earliest books on inner healing.

Until his last days, Prof. Clark believed in the relatedness of science and Christian spirituality, and this he passed on to his CFOers. For example, in *The Way, the Truth, and the Life* he advised believers to develop their spirituality:

> . . . begin by reading a book by a great scientist dealing with the laws of this world. As one reads he should mark passages that reveal laws that could be made equally applicable to the spiritual world. After one has laid the foundation of bones and sinews, he can clothe them with flesh and blood by turning to the poetry of Wordsworth, Browning, or better still, the poems of David and the poetic prophecies of Isaiah.[29]

Concerned about the continuity of the CFO after his death, Prof. Clark decentralized authority within the CFO. Each camp became independent, governed by its council ring of experienced members. Speakers, topics, and camp directors were chosen by local council rings. However, in order to be called a CFO camp the council ring had to adhere to a standard daily schedule, which remains unchanged. By the time that Prof. Clark succumbed to his weakened heart, on August 26, 1956, CFOs had become self-perpetuating institutions.

By the mid-1950s, the CFOs had become a potent semi-Pentecostal parachurch organization, blending traditional Catholic and Protestant spirituality, Pentecostal use of the gifts, and Christian New Perspective concepts and vocabulary. Their experience with the Holy Spirit led members to pray to and praise Jesus openly, something not common at the time among mainline Christians.[30] Those of us who are now senior citizens can remember a period when Protestants almost universally directed their prayers to the Father, not to Jesus. The influence of the Holy Spirit made CFOers more Pentecostal than evangelical in this regard.

The special training in prayer, and experience with healing and deliverance and the gifts of the Spirit, made CFOers both a leaven and

29. Clark, *The Way*, 62.

30. From an interview of Mrs. Ruth Brown, wife of Pastor James Brown, pioneer of Presbyterian Charismatics, October 8, 1985. She was founder of the Eastern Carolina CFO.

gadfly to mainstream churches. Very often, members returning to their home churches with tales of healing and miraculous answers to prayer were ostracized or labeled as fanatics. Clark warned CFO members to act as a silent leaven for their home congregations. Many did, and became leaders of countless small prayer and healing groups nationwide. No one ever kept an account of how many participated in CFO camps through-out their history, but from 1930 to 1970 tens of thousands attended.

Not only did CFO camps train much of the charismatic leadership during the 1950s and 1960s, but in the 1960s and 1970s the camps be-came a major institutional expression of the Charismatic Renewal. Some friction arose between the old guard—the 1930–40s generation, who had been taught by Prof. Clark, the Rev. Frank Laubach, etc.—and the new charismatic element streaming into the camps. The old guard distrusted the heavy emphasis the charismatics placed on the gifts of the Spirit, and preferred the traditional CFO spirituality which stressed the camp as an experience in kingdom living (the Brother Lawrence model). On the other hand, the new charismatic element was leery of the New Thought heritage of the old guard, and was more interested in using CFOs as char-ismatic training grounds for the church as a whole.

The speakers mix at the CFO camps of the 1970s is an interesting reflection of old guard and new charismatic. For example, in1973, at the height of the Charismatic Renewal, speakers from both elements often shared the same camps. The old guard was represented by such persons as Norman Elliot, Roland and Marcia Brown, Glenn Harding, Ruth Rob-inson, Louise Eggleston, and Genevieve Parkhurst. Charismatic speakers included Robert Hall, Ruth Carter Stapleton, Fr. Francis MacNutt, Merlin Carothers, and Howard Hill.[31]

The CFOs at their peak, in the 1960s, were really a unique place of mature Christian spirituality. It was a place where Paul's injunction to test all things (1 Thess 5:21) had been taken seriously and bore great fruit in discoveries in prayer and healing prayer. It was a place where the war between science and religion, which afflicted so much of evangeli-cal Christianity, was *not* fought. It was a refuge for mainline Christians to live a Christian life without cessationism and to practice effective prayer. Unlike liberal Christianity, the Bible was understood as the Word of God, and there was nothing mythical about Jesus' miracles. Unlike evangelical brethren, and like the Pentecostals, they believed that all of

31. 1973 CFO directory.

the miraculous stories of the Bible were not only true in the past but repeatable in the present. It was a curious mix that honored the classic Christian piety of Brother Lawrence, trying to model the practicing of the presence, but incorporated into that presence the power of effective prayer and Pentecost.

The CFOs have suffered a period of steady decline since the 1970s and are now a mere shadow of their peak days. Like Demos Shakarian's Full Gospel Business Men's Fellowship International, which has also declined in recent decades, the CFOs' decline was mostly due to their success. What was radical and unique to the CFO camps in the 1950s and 1960s, such as instruction in healing prayer, deliverance, and the gifts of the Spirit, has now become the norm in charismatic churches. One no longer has to go to a special summer camp to learn these things.

Unfortunately, the other unique aspect of the CFO program, allowing the Spirit to interact with a person's practice of art, exercise, drama, and music (the creatives), has not been widely adopted by many churches.[32] In spite of this, the legacy of the CFO as a place where effective prayer was taught, Pentecostalism was spread to the mainline churches, and deliverance ministry and inner healing was propagated, makes the CFOs and their achievements one of the great unheralded institutions of twentieth-century Christian history.

32. This is perhaps putting it too strongly, as in fact art in all its forms is steadily gaining its place among evangelical and Spirit-filled congregations as a function of general Christian maturity and self-confidence, and led by such persons Gregory Wolf and his Christian magazine *Image*. See Winner, "God's Sake."

Prof. Glenn Clark

The Rev. Frank Laubach

Rufus Moseley

PART IV

Agnes Sanford: Apostle of Healing

15

Discerning the Path of Christian Healing

BY FAR, THE MOST influential and original of the persons we have termed
Christian New Perspective (CNP) was Mrs. Agnes Sanford.[1] She was
born Agnes White in 1897 and came from a household that had been
in Christian ministry for generations. Her grandfather was an ordained
Presbyterian minister and during the Civil War was the chaplain to
Stonewall Jackson, the famous Confederate general. Agnes Sanford's father, the Rev. Hugh W. White, felt a call to the ministry as a young man
and attended Union Theological Seminary in Richmond, Virginia. After
his graduation (1894) he volunteered as a missionary to China, where he
married, raised his family, and, except for home leaves, stayed until his
retirement in 1940.

In China the Rev. Hugh White was forced to confront the inadequa-
cies of orthodox and cessationist theologies during two crises in his ministry.[2] The first was one of those cultural problems that every missionary
dreads. He believed in giving his Chinese assistants a maximum of authority. In this context, one of his trusted elders baptized an entire family
that had recently been converted. Wonderful! However, in this family
the husband had *two* wives, as was the custom among the merchant class

1. I sent a first draft of the chapters on Agnes Sanford found in this work to Mrs.
Sanford's daughter, Virginia ("Tookie") Sanford-Clark. She graciously corrected and
annotated the manuscript. I also had several lengthy telephone conversations with her
about her mother, and her insights enabled me to enrich the text in many ways.

2. The Rev. Hugh White's trials with Presbyterian orthodoxy in China are mentioned in Agnes Sanford's *Sealed Orders*, chapters 1 and 2, but more fully described
in her autobiographical novel, *Second Mrs. Wu*, which is a detailed description of her
years at the family mission station in Hsuchoufu, China.

in China. For the Chinese elder there was little choice in the matter. To have suggested to the husband to renounce one of his wives would have condemned the rejected wife to disgrace and either starvation or a life of prostitution.

The elder, who read his Bible literarily, recognized that there was no biblical conflict about the two wives. First Timothy 3:2 clearly takes into account the situation. A Christian overseer may have only one wife, thus the Jewish convert to Christianity who had several wives could not be an overseer. The presence of polygamy in the Jewish communities at the time of Paul corresponded to the situation in China.[3] Unfortunately, as clear as this was *biblically*, Presbyterian mission policy forbade such baptisms.

The Rev. White saw the biblical point and backed his elder, but the mission board ruled against the Rev. White.[4] As a result he and his family were forced to leave their comfortable mission compound and establish a new mission territory in the hinterland. White was so beloved by his congregation that thirty of them left their own homes to follow him to a new rural station.[5]

The second issue had more profound theological implication. We should remember that Presbyterian theology (cessationist) at the time held that exorcism was a papist myth and superstition, and that demons were no longer active on the earth. Reality impinged on the Rev. White when another one of his trusted evangelical aides, the elderly Mr. Tai Shi Rung, gave his weekly report.

> "And in the village of Ta-Tsanf," murmured the old man placidly, combing his long gray beard with serene satisfaction, "I baptized two babies, I received three inquirers into the Jesus church and I cast a demon out of old Mrs. Tsu."[6]

3. Satlow, *Jewish Marriage*. On the Old Testament license for polygamy note Deut 21:15-17 and Exod 21:10.

4. As early as 1834 missionaries in Calcutta, India, held a conference on polygamy and decided that multiple wives could be baptized but that the husband could not then have any church office. See W. B. Sloan, "China Inland Mission," 277–79. Most, but not all, mission boards that have dealt with polygamy in Africa in contemporary times have taken the Rev. White's approach. Polygamy will continue to be an issue as the church deals with converts from Islam in the coming decades. An excellent contemporary work on polygamy has been done by the Roman Catholic theologian Hillman, *Polygamy Reconsidered*.

5. Sanford, *Sealed Orders*, 21.

6. The description of this incident is found in Sanford, *Second Mrs. Wu*, 209. See

The Rev. White was astonished by the reported exorcism and decided to investigate. He accompanied Mr. Tai on his next rounds, and sure enough the faith-filled aide ministered another exorcism.[7] This was a shock to his theology. But from that time the Rev. White began collecting evidence on possessions and exorcisms, eventually participating in many exorcisms himself. By the time he was ready to publish his conclusions he had collected firsthand information on 368 cases. He also had become well versed in the findings of the then emerging literature of psychoanalysis, made possible by the extensive Presbyterian Church presence in China and its web of hospitals and missionary libraries.

He presented his views in a book called *Demonism Verified and Analyzed*, published in 1922. The Rev. White believed that possession was a mental problem, a form of violent disassociation, yet held that exorcism itself was real in the sense that it was a form of instant psychotherapy. His theory may not be entirely satisfactory,[8] however, it was an attempt to integrate biblical revelation with contemporary psychology, and was a great step beyond the reality-denying cessationism of his peers.[9]

The Rev. White's ministry taught his daughter, Agnes, that certain elements of orthodox theology could be both totally wrong and stubbornly unscriptural. It also showed her that perfectly sincere Christians, such as the fellow missionaries who opposed her father, could be all too ready to confuse conventional doctrine with biblical truth. Her father's difficulties with orthodoxy and its cessationism, and his steadfastness for the biblical evidence rather than conventional doctrine, gave Agnes an example that would help her in her own struggles with cessationism later on.[10]

---

also Sanford, "Prayer of Healing."

7. Sanford, *Second Mrs. Wu*, 213–16.

8. In fact, the Rev. White's book was inferior to a work produced (and forgotten) a generation earlier by yet another Presbyterian missionary, the Rev. John Nevius, *Demon Possession*, which is now considered a classic in the literature of exorcism. On the amazing and important ministry of the Rev. Nevius see my article "John Nevius."

9. The reduction of the demonically oppressed to a psychological disorder is popular but very unsatisfactory. Unfortunately, it persists to this day among well-meaning and often well-educated Christians. Note the similarities between White's view of exorcism in the 1920s and that of M. Scott Peck, whose books on evil have deservedly become bestsellers. See especially Peck, *People of the Lie*. chapter 5, "Of Possession and Exorcism."

10. See Sanford's, *Sealed Order*, 156, for the influence that Mrs. Sanford's China years had on her belief on the demonic and exorcism.

Childhood, Education, and Marriage

Agnes White came into the world in the Chinese city of Hsuchooufu on November 4, 1897. She was the eldest child of six, one of whom died as a baby of dysentery.[11] Life in the mission compound was difficult and lonely. With only one friend in her age group in the missionary compound, Agnes learned to rely most of the time on her own resources for her entertainment. Agnes was home-schooled by her mother, Augusta Graves, who turned out to be an excellent teacher. She was not only given the basics of Bible memorization and catechism, but also a program of reading, history, Latin, French, and mathematics. Agnes developed her own interests in writing to the point that at age ten she sold her first piece of writing to the *Shanghai Mercury*.

At age nine, during one of her father's periodic home leaves, she attended a revival in a rural Virginia church and committed her life to Jesus.[12] Although only a child, this initial spiritual experience with Jesus as her Lord was a profound one, and Agnes began to experience an unusual closeness to God. By eleven she was wondering why modern Christians no longer did miracles. Agnes was entirely dissatisfied with the conventional arguments that miracles were for the apostolic age alone. Later, as a teenager, she was deeply disturbed over denominational disputes over doctrines that often broke out when missionaries got together, under the rubric of securing sound doctrine. But her commitments to Jesus and the Bible were unshaken.[13]

In 1914, at age seventeen, Agnes was sent to the United States to finish her education. She enrolled in Peace Institute, now William Peace University, but then a Presbyterian finishing school for girls in Raleigh, North Carolina. There she received a teaching certificate for the state. Already her spiritual discernment was acute. On summer break she helped the local Presbyterian Church do revivals among the poor in the Appalachian Mountains. In that capacity she prayed for the salvation of her Sunday school students, and to her surprise they were all saved. However,

11. There are fascinating similarities, and deep differences, between Agnes Sanford and another child of Presbyterian missionaries in China, Mrs. Pearl Buck. Mrs. Buck's novels won her a Nobel Prize in literature, but she took a turn to theological liberalism and spent much of her life in humanitarian causes. See Spurling, *Burying the Bones*. Mrs. Buck's sister was one of Agnes' dearest childhood friends.

12. Sanford, *Sealed Orders*, 11.

13. Ibid, 23, 27.

she felt an unease that they would soon backslide, because something was missing. She later understood that something to be the empowering Holy Spirit which was needed to keep them from the clan fights and alcoholism, and in holiness. [14]

After her graduation and certification she enrolled in Atlanta's Agnes Scott College. She attended for two years (1917–1918), preferring to take courses to her liking, particularly in literature, astronomy, and psychology, rather than follow a degree program. She particularly loved a course in astronomy that was very demanding mathematically, but in it she found a reassurance of God's creation as revealed in Genesis.

This was the period when America entered World War I. From its inception Agnes felt an unease about the war. She wrote a poem that appeared in the 1918 edition of *The Silhouette*, her school's yearbook. It showed prophetic discernment. Part of it reads:

> Oh, think, the waste of it—the hopeless, heartless waste of it!
> The flower of our manhood gone, and who knows why?
> In their massing and their passing and the silent, solemn haste of it,
> We only can remember they are going forth to die.
>
> Ah no, we feel it not—thoughtlessly we felt it not,
> Wrapped in our own selfishness, like thick, hard shells.
> The future-hiding veiled rending, yet we cry: "Reveal it not!"
> And cowering, will not hark to what our own heart tells. [15]

When World War I ended (November 1918) there was tremendous rejoicing and celebration at the college, for the world had been "made safe for democracy." Agnes participated initially in the celebration, but:

> I knew that there was nothing to rejoice about. The world had not been made safe for democracy. Evil had not been banished from among men that righteousness might prevail . . .
> My conscious mind told me to rejoice and give thanks and wave banners and shout around the campus. But the spirit within me must have known that real peace could not be made upon the earth save by the peacemakers—those who are called children of God—and they make peace by no power save by the power of the Holy Spirit of God. [16]

14. Ibid, 42.

15. White, "Waste of It."

16. Sanford, *Sealed Orders*, 45.

Agnes returned to China to a teaching position in Shanghai at a secondary school for missionary children, and there taught English literature and French.[17] In that city she met and fell in love with Edgar (Ted) Sanford, who was an Episcopal priest (ordained in 1920) and principal of another missionary children's school, Proctor's School for Boys. They were married in April of 1923, and Agnes soon was confirmed into the Episcopal Church—not so much out of conviction, but to assist Ted in his career. The first of three children arrived the next year, and soon after Ted accepted a post in the interior of China.

It was a harrowing time for them. The family was caught in one of the many local wars between the warlords of pre–World War II China. One incident was particularly touching. Agnes and her baby were away for a brief holiday in a Chinese mountain city of Mokansan to escape the summer heat for a few weeks. At that point a warlord rivalry broke out into a shooting war. Mokansan was in the midst of the action and under the threat of being captured and sacked. Ted determined to get his family out. From his post it was over thirty miles by canal boat. Unfortunately, the warlords had roving press gangs to kidnap any unarmed males seen. Those impressed would serve as forced labor to carry supplies, dig entrenchments, etc., and rarely returned home alive.

Ted needed an eight-man crew to row the available boat on the overnight trip to Mokansan. He asked the servants and staff of the missionary compound for volunteers. At first none came forward, but then a sixteen-year-old servant boy spoke to the staff:

> Every day I hear you say "the Sien-sang [Ted] is a wonderful employer, fair and kind." Every day I hear you praise Sihs-mo [Agnes] and say there is no one as good as she. . . . Now they are in trouble. Now they need you . . . I will row the boat.[18]

One by one the men of the staff joined the young boy until Ted had a full crew. They rescued Mrs. Sanford and the baby without meeting any of the press gangs—a miracle in itself.

---

17. Agnes Sanford's novel *Rising River* contains autobiographical details of this period of her life.

18. Sanford, *God's Healing*, 157.

Trinity Church, Moorestown, New Jersey

After this close call the Sanfords decided to take a temporary leave from China so that Ted could get an advanced degree. The year was 1925, and while in graduate school Ted felt a calling to go into the pastorate in America. He also believed, quite correctly, that China was entering a period of warfare more serious than the local conflicts among warlords. In fact, Proctor's School for Boys was overrun and burned by Communist guerillas while the family was in the United States. He was then called as rector to a small church in Moorestown, New Jersey, Trinity Episcopal Church.[19] Providentially, the church and parsonage were less than half an hour's drive from downtown Philadelphia and St. Stephen's Church, which was to become an OSL healing and teaching center.

When Agnes and Ted arrived in Moorestown in the spring of 1926, it was to a parish that was well established, with its ministries in place. The church building was a solid brownstone structure graced with ivy and beautiful stained glass windows. One of the windows was of "Christ the Healer," which showed Jesus laying hands on a sick person. Six months after their arrival a noted local architect showed up at the parish and spread before Ted the plans for a beautiful complex comprising the church, parish hall, parsonage, and garage, all done in exquisite English Gothic style. The most astonishing thing was that this beautiful complex was already *paid for* by an anonymous donor, and all that was needed was the vestry's approval for the various documents and the details of temporary relocation, demolition, etc.[20]

All of that was quickly done, with a local Methodist church providing the Sunday worship space during the year of demolition and construction. The old stained glass windows were saved and placed in a side chapel where the garage had been planned. The completed building was consecrated in May of 1929. It was not understood by anyone at the time

19. Dr. Howard Rhys, New Testament professor at the University of the South, and friend of the Sanfords for decades, informed me that the *more important* reason Ted stayed in America was that, unlike Agnes, who spoke Mandarin Chinese perfectly, Ted had a terrible time learning the language and was embarrassed about the situation.

20. The story is told in the history of the parish, Joan Rogers McKeon's *Trinity Church*, 23-29. Eventually the anonymous donor was identified as Eldridge R. Johnson, who founded the Victor Talking Machine Co. (Camden, NJ), a leading manufacturer of phonographs and phonographic records of the era. The company was sold to a banking concern and became one of the major components of RCA. Trinity Episcopal Church is listed in the National Register of Historic Places.

that that year would be the beginning of the Great Depression. For the parishioners of Trinity Church, they would begin the 1930s in an exquisitely beautiful, debt-free church.

Ted quickly became a loving, efficient, and creative rector. He was meticulous in his visitation schedule. When I visited the parish in 2003, several of the senior citizens recounted how loved he was and what an effective a pastor he had been. He helped form an alliance of seven Moorestown churches to help one another and establish an ecumenical spirit in the town. Under Ted's leadership, Trinity hosted Good Friday services for the whole town, and various ministers were invited to lead those services—a thing highly unusual then and now. As the Great Depression worsened, Ted and the seven churches organized local relief services and attempted to stimulate new work and spread part-time work among as many persons as possible. Ted also organized the Trinity's Boy Scout troop and served as its first scoutmaster.

During this period the Sanford's had their last child, John, who was to become a noted psychologist and writer. But at this period in her life Mrs. Sanford went into deep depression. Ted came from a New England family where the women developed into impeccable housewives. They were frugal, efficient, and wonderful cooks. Consciously, Agnes wished to emulate that tradition because she loved Ted and wanted him to have a happy home. But because she was raised in China, where all domestic work was done by servants, she had no skills in the domestic arts. The harder she tried to be a perfect housewife, the more depressed she became.[21]

When John was a year and a half old he developed a severe ear infection. He had a high fever that made him weaker and weaker, becoming a serious situation. The rector of a nearby Episcopal church, the Rev. Hollis Colwell, dropped by the Sanford residence to see Ted on church business. The Rev. Colwell was a person of deep faith like the Sanfords, but he also believed in healing. He had read New Thought works on healing, including the work of Fr. Robert Bell, *The Life Abundant* (see chapter 12 above). By the time he visited the Sanford's he had developed into a practiced and faith-filled healer. He asked about the family. Agnes, writing decades later, vividly recalled what happened next:

"Oh, the baby's sick," I replied, "He's been sick for six weeks."

---

21. Described with great candor in Sanford, *Sealed Orders*, 92-100.

"Well," said he in a pleasant voice, quite casually, "I'll go up and say a little prayer for him."

This surprised me greatly. . . . "Oh, the baby wouldn't understand. He's too little." . . .

At this point with supreme wisdom, the minister Hollis Colwell, simply went on about his business. He did not argue, preach, or in any way try to convince me of the reality of spiritual healing. If he had done so, I would have stiffened in my refusal, for I was not prepared to hear this iconoclastic "new thought."

"Now, shut your eyes and go to sleep," he said to the baby. "I'm going to ask God to come into your ears and make them well. And when you wake up, you'll be all right." . . .

He laid his hands on the baby's ears and kept them there for several minutes. "Please Lord Jesus," he said, "send your power right now into this baby's ears and take away all germs or infection, and make them well. Thank you Lord, for I believe that You are doing this, and I see these ears well as you made them to be."

The child shut his eyes, grew very pale as the fever died out of his face, and went to sleep. And when he woke up, his temperature was normal and his ears were well.[22]

This perplexed Agnes. Why did God answer the Rev. Colwell's prayer for healing and not her own desperate cries? But it did not occur to Agnes to ask Colwell for prayers for the healing of her depression. That inspiration came weeks later when the depression had reached a crisis point. As she received the Eucharist she heard an interior voice tell her to go to the Rev. Colwell. Agnes went for a series of healing sessions. In the first session he simply laid hands on her and prayed for her release from depression. The prayer worked wonderfully, although within a week the darkness had begun to slip back in. Colwell also taught Agnes to combine the prayer of affirmation and thanksgiving with visualization, similar to the ones taught by the Rev. Bell. Every day Agnes would

> . . . imagine my body strong and well, relieved of its accumulated pain and stress, and would say, "Thank you, God. Your power is working through me and I am doing this work in Your strength."[23]

At the fourth session, Colwell discerned that the root cause of her depression was at a spiritual level. Specifically, Mrs. Sanford was violating

22. Ibid., 97.

23. Ibid, 102.

her God-given nature by attempting to be the perfect housewife, not the writer he created her to be. Colwell prescribed as her therapy two hours of creative writing every day. She followed this advice, and also spontaneously developed the habit of saying a modified form of the Jesus Prayer so well known in the Eastern Orthodox Church. For a year, whenever her mind was not occupied with something that needed full attention she would repeat silently, "Lord Jesus Christ, Son of God, fill me with Thy life."[24] As she wrote her first major piece, a blank verse play about King Solomon, "The House of Saul," her depression evaporated away.[25]

The Quest for Healing Knowledge

The Rev. Colwell also encouraged Mrs. Sanford to pray for the healing of others. In spite of her father's work in China as an exorcist, Agnes was reluctant to do any sort of healing prayer. However, she began to investigate, and at the very beginning made a critical decision. She determined to compare whatever she read or heard by the standard set up by Jesus in the four Gospels. This was her discernment anchor. Writing decades later, she described how she traversed from cessationism into a more accurate understanding of the healing ministry.

> There are many books today that try to explain this matter [healing prayer]. But at the time I knew none of them. Therefore, I decided to find the answer in two ways: first, by studying the words of Jesus Christ, and second, by trying what He said and seeing whether it worked or not.
>
> This sounds very simple, but it did not prove to be so. First of all, I found that what He said went directly contrary to many of the explanations concerning religion that I had been taught since my youth. For instance, I had been told that the age of miracles was past—yet I had seen a miracle. . . . I also knew that there was no use in trying to understand what I had not

---

24. Ibid, 107. For a masterful description of the Jesus Prayer and its adoption to modern times, see the many works of Fr. George Maloney, especially *Inward Stillness*.

25. It is actually a good play, but nothing that would do well on Broadway in our current era. It was written in blank verse, and at a time when audiences still accepted Shakespeare-like formality of language in dramatic dialogue. It was produced back in the 1980s in a regional theater, The Globe, in Odessa, Texas. It has been occasionally produced by amateur groups, such as CFO camps, who especially revere the memory of Mrs. Sanford. The original typed manuscript now resides at the Wheaton College library. I have a copy in my possession.

experienced. Therefore I set myself to find an *experience* of God's power.

In order to do this, I laid aside temporarily all that I had been taught concerning Christianity. I did not disbelieve it, I merely laid it on the table to be considered later. And that is what all of us must do if we are to learn.[26]

Agnes read the Gospels closely and attempted to follow closely Jesus' instruction on healing. At first she experimented by praying for herself, for instance, when she was coming down with a cold. She was delighted to find that God could spare her the days of illness and inconvenience that a cold would bring to a busy mother.[27]

The Rev. Colwell, following Bell's *The Life Abundant*, believed that the key ingredient of the healing ministry was adherence to a strict health food regimen. He advised Mrs. Sanford to do likewise. Agnes looked into this and read Bell's works and some of the health-food literature available at the time (1931–1932). In fact, for the rest of her life she adopted what would now be recognized as a moderate health-food diet for herself and her family which avoided processed foods and stressed fresh fruits and vegetables. These things have become normal in recent times, but it is another example of Agnes' ability to be decades ahead of her own time. More to the point, she quickly discerned that although health foods were *good*, they could not be the *foundation* of the Rev. Colwell's or anybody else's healing power.[28]

Then Agnes sought books on healing. "I did not know that there were any other books upon the subject of the prayer of faith, except possibly *Science and Health*. I tried to read it, but to me it did not make sense."[29] She laid that aside quickly. Much more useful was the New Thought writer Emmet Fox. With his *Sermon On the Mount* Agnes found profound resonance. Here was a person who believed in the power of God and of Scripture for the here and now, including healing. She continued to look into the available literature of healing, including the literature of the Unity school of Christianity. She also made contact with a small church in Philadelphia run by a female minister who had been expelled from her Baptist congregation for practicing Christian healing.[30]

26. Sanford, *Your God*, 1–2.

27. Sanford, *Sealed Orders*, 102.

28. Ibid., 107.

29. Ibid., 103.

30. Ibid., 103–5, for a description of the sources in her first years in the healing ministry.

The Rev. Colwell continued to urge her to pray for the sick, but she was reluctant to do so. Then she learned of a young child dying of severe infection at a nearby hospital.

> I was terrified. I would as soon have walked up to the mouth of a cannon, or so I thought. But the urge of compassion was strong, for I knew the child would die unless *something* intervened. So I drove to the hospital. . . . I spoke to the mother, who promptly dissolved in tears and would have let me do anything I wanted to do. She took me to the room of the little three-year-old and there left me alone. Strange to say, as soon as I sat down beside the bed and began to talk to the child, I had no fear at all! The venture seemed as simple and as natural as if I had been doing it all my life. . . . I laid hands on the region of the heart and simply asked Jesus to make him well, and then thanked Jesus because I knew he was doing it. The next day the child's blood stream and heart were free of infection. The kidneys took one more day.[31]

Her second case was of a young man with severe mental illness, but it ended in failure and discouragement. Such cases are difficult, as she later learned, and take repeated prayer and much faith. It was three months after that that Agnes had the courage to pray for another person, this time someone with shingles, but this prayer was successful and the person recovered completely.[32]

Experiments in Healing Prayer

This period, from 1933 until the end of World War II (1945), was a time when Agnes Sanford experimented, probed, and did everything she could to learn about Christian healing prayer. She did not keep a diary, and so the sequence and dates in which she tried various procedures or learned different ways of praying cannot be precisely recovered. Mrs. Sanford, like many persons of deep spirituality, had a fine memory for significant spiritual events and relationships in her life, but little concern for precise dates and location details.[33]

31. Ibid., 110–11.

32. Ibid., 112.

33. I had a conversation on this with the Rev. Jamie Buckingham, prolific writer and former editor of *Charisma* and *Ministries Today*, and ghostwriter of several charismatic classics. He related how he had the same problem with Corrie Ten Boom as he was helping her write *Tramp for the Lord*. She could remember the spiritual issues

It is known that soon after her first healings she formed a lady's Bible study and prayer group which met in the chapel once a week. Providentially, when the chapel of Trinity Episcopal Church was constructed earlier, the beautiful stained glass window of Jesus healing the sick from the earlier brownstone church was set in it. This group developed great power in intercessory prayer and healing. It played the same role as Glenn Clarks' Sunday school: a spiritual laboratory where different modes of prayer could be tried and faith developed.

It needs to be said that at the beginning of her search Agnes drifted into the universalistic New Thought view of Jesus as one of the many spiritual masters.

> But a sadness would come upon me as I thought thus, and at times I would feel like Mary at the tomb: "They have taken away the Lord and we know not where they have laid Him (John 20:2)." And though I told myself that I must grow up in understanding and must not cling to childish and medieval concepts, nevertheless this sense of loss remained and dimmed the power of healing prayers.[34]

She then came to another critical discernment. She firmly rejected this universalistic, anti-Christian idea, and affirmed Jesus as "only begotten son of God, born of a virgin."[35] Her depression lifted and her healing energies were fully restored.

In this early period Agnes made another serious, and thankfully short-lived, error. She investigated a group that claimed they were Christian spiritualists. Their séance proved to be banal and boring (as with most mediumistic sessions—the demons have little creativity). Agnes went a second time, "carefully keeping an open mind, for I sincerely desired to understand this matter and to rid myself of any from any prejudice concerning it."[36] This time she got to know the medium better. He was called Sylvester and complained of constant headaches, and he added

---

and relationships of persons she met, but little of the times and specific places. The Rev. Buckingham had to constantly probe for physical and historical details of Corrie's story. In mock vengeance, Corrie sent the Rev. Buckingham a letter from Paris in which she minutely detailed the furnishings of her hotel room, and nothing else!

34. Agnes Sanford, *Your God*, 72.

35. Sanford *Sealed Orders*, 148.

36. Ibid., 151.

that the spirits "bother me all the time."[37] She noticed that his breath was horrible. At that séance she was asked to pray for Sylvester's mother, who had a minor heart ailment and who was present at the séance. Agnes gladly prayed for the lady.

> The next day I felt terrible. I was so drained of life that I could hardly move. I was in deep depression, and most freighting of all, I could taste in my own mouth that odor that had been on Sylvester's breath.
>
> "Oh Lord," I said out loud, "if you will get me out of this, I promise You I will never go near a séance again."[38]

She kept her promise, but she also heard that Sylvester's mother died suddenly. In the coming months she noticed that whenever she prayed with anyone who was involved in spiritualism something terrible would happen—an accident, illness, or death. Agnes consulted on this with a Christian woman who was expert on the occult. This woman verified that praying with a spiritualist as in the laying on of hands was extremely dangerous, for it mixed God's energies, going through Agnes, with the spiritualist's demonic energies. This created a spiritual short circuit of sorts. Agnes understood, and from that point on she scrupulously avoided all contact with spiritualism. Years later, when she and Ted founded the School of Pastoral Care, all applicants had to affirm that they had not been in (or had repented from) occult involvements, especially spiritism.[39]

On another issue, Agnes noticed that when she or her Bible study group prayed for long-distance healing the effects were meager. She complained about this to the ex-Baptist minister in Philadelphia who initially encouraged her.

> "Oh my dear, you're seeing them sick," cried the beautiful old minister.

37. Ibid., 152

38. Ibid.

39. Ibid, 153. See also the description of Mrs. Sanford warning occultists not to come forward for the laying on of hands in one of her services in the 1970s in Payne, *Heaven's Calling*, 152. Disgustingly, one of Mrs. Sanford's most ignorant critics cites this period of Agnes's life as "Flirting with Spiritism," chapter 7 in Gumprecht, *Abusing Memory*. The distinction should be noted in praying *for* a spiritist, as in for salvation and repentance, which is good, and praying *with* a spiritist, which is dangerous.

"What do you mean?' I asked puzzled. "I'm not seeing them at all, I'm just thinking of them. And of course, they're sick, or I wouldn't be praying for them."

"Yes, you are seeing them," she replied patiently. "When you think of someone, you always see the person in your mind. If you really believe he's going to be well, you see him well. . . . When you pray for someone, dearie, you must learn to see him *well*."

And a voice within me said, "That's right."

We pray not only with the conscious mind. Nine-tenths of the thinking is in the sub-conscious, and the spirit uses the path of the subconscious in sending forth the power of prayer. Therefore if the sub-consciousness retains the picture of the person sick, the spirit can send at best only a divided message, suggesting life and death, health and illness at the same time.[40]

Agnes had stumbled on the application in healing of what Glenn Clark wrote in *I Will Lift Up Mine Eyes*: that for effective prayer the conscious and subconscious must be in harmony (see chapter 13).

But not everything her minister friend suggested was correct. She also suggested that to increase one's ability to be a vehicle for God's healing power one should be celibate. This was the doctrine of Unity Christianity and probably the source of this minister's idea. Agnes unwisely agreed to accept her mentor's prayer for this, and for a time abstained from sexual relations with Ted. Needless to say, this was a disaster. Ted was very unhappy and soon Agnes realized that celibacy after making the wedding covenant could not be God's will for her. She commented on this Unity celibacy theory in *The Healing Light*.

But if they [healing ministers] are married and endeavor to express love "only upon the spiritual plane" they are bound for trouble. At first, true, their spiritual power is increased through this sublimation, because they are forcing all their creative energy into one channel. But after a while it begins to dwindle because they have shriveled up the very channel through which love flows.[41]

Somewhat later (c. 1938) Agnes discovered some of the works of the Anglican/Episcopal healing tradition and the newly formed Order of St. Luke. She and was able to regularly access Philadelphia's Saint Stephen's Church, with its wonderful healing resources. She and Ted became

40. Sanford, *Healing Light*, 145.
41. Ibid., 119–20.

friends with the director of the OSL, John Gaynor, and began speaking at OSL functions by the late 1940s. Mrs. Sanford verified the Anglo-Episcopal sacramental tradition of healing by observing her husband's ministry. She noticed, for instance, that baptism sometimes produced physical healing for infants, even when ministered without conscious intent of healing. In a case cited in *The Healing Light*, a six-month-old baby who had been dead for half an hour was miraculously resuscitated by the administration of that sacrament.[42]

World War II

By the outset of World War II she was well read and well practiced in healing, and reflective of her mistakes. She had gone through multiple crises in discernment—healing though health food as a panacea, spiritualism, healing enhanced with celibacy, Jesus as merely one of the many masters, etc.—and had *chosen the biblical path in each case.*

During World War II, which started for America in December of 1941, her Bible study/prayer group honed its skills in intercessory prayer. Like most churches in America, Trinity Episcopal Church prayed constantly for the safety and protection of their sons and husbands serving in the armed forces. Her group discovered that their prayers were most effective not in praying directly for victory, but for protection of their own soldiers. Miraculously, none of the men from the immediate families of the prayer group were killed in the course of the war (130 men). During the war most of the young men in the parish were inexplicably assigned non-combat duties. But even those in combat had miraculous protection. A buddy of one of the soldiers whose mother was in the prayer group wrote the mother:

> What is it with George? I've seen him wading out of a landing barge with his gun held over his head and men falling on every side of him and nothing can touch him! I swear bullets are deflected.[43]

Mrs. Sanford volunteered for service at Tilton Army Hospital in Fort Dix as a Gray Lady. The hospital was less than thirty-five miles from

42. Ibid., 92–93. The same baptismal healing miracles occurred *regularly* in the ministry of Fr. Richard Winkler, an Episcopal priest and unsung pioneer of the Charismatic Renewal. See Payne, *Heaven's Calling*, 148.

43. Sanford, *Sealed Orders*, 176–77.

her home. Every week she would spend a full day there, sometimes two. Her duty was to pass out candies, comics, and magazines to the wounded soldiers. It was strictly and absolutely forbidden to pray for the men. Soon, however, her compassion overcame her respect for the lawfulness of authority (Acts 4:18–22). This was not an easy choice, as she was scrupulous all of her life in obeying civil authorities. She began praying for the more seriously wounded, always being careful to explain in simple terms to the soldiers what she was doing as she laid her hands on their injured bodies.

Agnes later came to see this period in her life as the most fruitful in her healing ministry. God's healing power flowed through her and her Bible study/prayer group to an unusual degree, partly because there was no publicity associated with her healings, and partly because war wounds were not associated with the personal sin of the soldiers. Thus the healing power of God could flow without impediment from unresolved sin or unforgiveness.

Mrs. Sanford had to proceed delicately, not only to keep out of view from any supervisor, but also because the faith and religious levels of the soldiers varied, from atheist to deeply religious and Christian. One soldier named Sammy had been in traction for months waiting for his bone to heal from a wound. The healing was slow and the doctors were considering an additional bone graft. Agnes suggested that he ask for a speed up in nature's healing. Sammy was skeptical, but Agnes suggested he ask God to help in the natural processes of healing his bone.

"But I don't know anything bout God."

"You know there is *something* outside of yourself, don't you? After all, you didn't make this world. There's some kind of life outside of you."

"Oh sure. When you're scared enough, you feel like there must be something."

"Well then, ask that *Something* to come into you. Just say "Whoever you are or whatever you are, come into me now and help nature in my body to mend this bone, and do it quick. Thanks. I believe you're doing it. Then make a picture in your mind of the leg well. Shut your eye and see it that way."

"I get you."

"Good! Then after you see the leg well, give a pep talk to all the healing forces of your body, Say, "look here, I'm boss inside of me . . . now get busy and mend that leg . . . and say "Thank You God. I believe it's going to be O.K."[44]

Note how Agnes moved Sammy from agnosticism to belief in God. Agnes would repeat this pattern many times. Another case was of an officer who had his stomach shot out. He was slowly dying, for back then intravenous feeding could only slow starvation, it could not maintain a person. When Agnes first saw him he was at the point of death, with hideous blood clots where his stomach should have been. Agnes laid hands on him and prayed the prayer of faith, and when she went home she called up every faith-filled prayer group she knew, her Christian underground, to intercede for the officer. Two weeks after her first prayer for him he was up and about and eating. The Lord had given this soldier a new stomach. Several weeks after that he was discharged as completely well. Not unnaturally, his miraculous recovery led to his conversion, and he left the hospital dedicated to Jesus.[45]

Just after the war ended Agnes was caught in the *very act of praying* for a soldier. She was brought to her nurse supervisor, who happened to be a dedicated Christian woman. This woman tongue-lashed Agnes as a dangerous heretic and witch and dismissed her from the Gray Ladies. Agnes went home in anger and sadness, knowing that there were still many soldiers to heal. But she also understood that retained anger and unforgiveness would ruin her ministry. She went into the chapel and asked forgiveness for her anger and also forgave her supervisor. Agnes' teenage daughter, Virginia (Tookie), was home when her mother came in early. Virginia wrote decades later:

> The memory of that moment has never left me. I was incensed. Mother said if she couldn't forgive the authorities, she might as well hang it up. She wouldn't be able to pray with power again. And, she added, "I would have to do it fast, because someone was coming to see her in two hours for prayer."
>
> The lesson bit deeply into my consciousness, and made possible for me, many years later to do an equally difficult act of forgiveness.[46]

---

44. Sanford, *Healing Light*, 35.

45. Sanford, *Sealed Orders*, 186–88.

46. From an annotation by Virginia Sanford-Clark, dated Feburary17, 1986 in the margins of the first draft of this chapter.

The Lord turned evil into good, however. Agnes then had more time to continue her ever-increasing speaking circuit and ministry, and to go back to her writing. She wrote a successful novel based on her experiences at Tilton Army Hospital, entitled *Oh, Watchman!* (1951).

16

The Healing Light

A Theology of the Energies of God

IT WAS DURING HER volunteer work at Tilton Army Hospital that Agnes Sanford wrote her first book, *The Healing Light*. It was a pioneering masterwork on the energies of God. It would not be an exaggeration to call *The Healing Light* the most influential book of the twentieth-century Christian healing revival. Not only did it become the standard work for many Christians who were into the healing ministry before the 1960s, but it served as the initial teaching text for many charismatics in the 1960s and early 1970s. First appearing in 1947, it is still in print to this day. Many readers notice a special power and anointing about the book.[1]

The Healing Light was based on the notes Mrs. Sanford prepared for a church adult education class that she gave in Philadelphia during World War II. Though the manuscript was finished in 1945, it was not published until two years later. Agnes sent it to the major publishers but it was rejected by all. However, the Rev. John Gaynor Banks saw the manuscript and serialized several chapters in the OSL's *Sharing* magazine. Prof. Clark noticed them in *Sharing* and recognized that they were superior to any he had seen on healing prayer. He offered to publish it through Macalester Park Press and Agnes accepted.

Macalester Park Press was then a small religious publisher whose offerings were not listed in *Books in Print*, the standard wholesaling catalogue. This normally would have severely limited sales of *The Healing Light*. But because of the word-of-mouth networking through the OSL

---

1. When I give a workshop on Mrs. Sanford someone, usually an elderly charismatic, will come up and say something to the effect of, "I'm glad I reread *The Healing Light* again; it's so anointed."

and CFOs, etc., it overcame this and had to be reprinted in its first year of publication. It was reprinted twice in 1948 and five times in 1950, and went on to sell over a million copies.[2] Part of this success was due to the simplicity of its language. In fact, Mrs. Sanford read the manuscript to her nine-year-old niece and was not satisfied with the text until the girl could understand it.[3]

The Healing Light incorporated much of the theology of CNP that was circulating at CFOs and OLS events. Her debt to Prof. Glenn Clark is particularly clear. For example, she repeated his assertion that the blood of Jesus remained on earth and its vibrations enabled the Christian to receive both healing and forgiveness of sins.[4]

The Energies of God as Healing Light

The title, *The Healing Light*, points to the main thesis, that the healing power of God is a light energy, and that it is accessible to all who understand its lawful application, especially in regards to compassion and love. Thus healing is a natural and normal event within the kingdom of God, not a "supernatural" or rare event.

> God works immutably and inexorably by law. Until humankind learns and keeps the laws of life, God's will cannot be fully manifest. He has never from the beginning until now healed anyone by the interposition of an arbitrary or capricious force. But He heals continually *by the addition of higher spiritual energy to a lower physical energy.*[5]

Mrs. Sanford speculated that the healing light is the primal light that originated at the beginning of creation, and that this light cannot be perceived by ordinary eyes, but is everywhere as a form of background radiation. It is analogous to the scientific theory that microwave radiation, which is constant in the universe, is part of the residue of the Big Bang.[6] On the practical level, Agnes taught the reader how to use the

---

2. *The Healing Light* was translated and published in Portuguese, but sadly not into Spanish or other languages.

3. From a taped interview by the author of Dr. Harry Goldsmith in April 1983.

4. Sanford, *Healing Light*, 127, and also see p. 167 for her use of Prof. Clark's concept of "prayer levers."

5. Ibid., 40.

6. Mrs. Sanford's speculations on the primal nature of the healing light are further

free gift of God's healing light as a tool to achieve physical and emotional healing. This is done by visualizing God's light flooding the afflicted area of hurt. In a simple prayer meditation she suggested:

> When we ask for the indwelling of God's Holy Spirit in the body, let us think of that part of the body that most needs His life. Let us imagine His light and life glowing like a fire, shining there like a light. Then through the rest of the day let us continuously give thanks that his life is at work . . .[7]

In another section Mrs. Sanford describes how she ministered healing prayer to a young girl crippled in her knees by polio:

> I placed my hands above the rigid knee in that instinctive laying on of hands that every mother knows . . .
> And I asked that the light of god might shine through me into the small, stiff knee and make it well.
> "Oh, take your hands away!" cried the little girl" "It's hot."
> "That's god power working in your knee, Sally," I replied. "It's like electricity working in a lamp. I guess it has to be hot, so as to make your knee come back to life. So you just stand it for a few minutes, while I tell you about Peter Rabbit."[8]

When she finished the story the girl's knee was flexible and healed. Agnes explained that sensations of heat and vibration are not the energy of God themselves, but its effect on our bodies.[9]

This type of prayer meditation and healing prayer is strange to Christians and suspicious to many evangelicals. There is simply no precedent for it in Western Christian theology and devotional works. We have discussed the philosophical prejudice of the early church to slight the biblical accounts of energy in favor of the permanent categories of form and essence, and how this hamstrung the healing ministry (chapter 3). Thus, when Mrs. Sanford discussed the energies of God as light she stepped into the lamentable theological vacuum of Western Christian theology about the energies of God.

We need to point out that the New Testament uses of the word "light" as synonymous to the energies of God, or as a specific form of the energies of God. For instance, in Ephesians 5:9 Paul wrote, "For you

---

elaborated in her later work *Healing Power*, chapter 1.

7. Sanford, *Healing Light*, 28.

8. Ibid., 31

9. Ibid., 32-33.

were once darkness, but now you are light in the Lord. Live as children of light (for the fruit of the light consists in all goodness, righteousness and truth) and find out what pleases the Lord." Notice that "light" in this passage describes an energy that results in virtues.

Significantly, the Eastern Orthodox Church developed a theology of light dating from the Middle Ages, due in part to one of its greatest theologians, St. Gregory of Palamas (1296–1359). St Gregory called God's light "uncreated energies." His light theology and that of others in Eastern Orthodoxy concerned themselves with prayer and sanctification, which in Eastern Orthodoxy is called "deification." [10] The use of God's light and energy was not considered for the purposes of healing prayer. An article in the premier Orthodox journal in America, St. Vladamir's Theological Quarterly, points to the biblical issues that Mrs. Sanford dealt with when she advocated the use of God's light and energies for healing prayer. The author of the article, David Bradshaw, shows that St. Gregory's belief in the light and energies of God is entirely consistent with the New Testament, especially the writings of Paul. [11] All of this indicates that when Agnes Sanford wrote about the presence and use of God's light/energy she was on firm biblical ground.

How Mrs. Sanford came to such a forceful and practical appreciation of the light of God is not detailed in her writings. Certainly the hints from Glenn Clark and his appreciation of prayer as energy and vibration were important. But more likely it was also a matter of personal experience in prayer. On this we have a hint from the text of The Healing Light, where she describes some of her own prayers with the light of Christ. It is a passage that seems strange and mystical to many evangelicals, but right at home among the monks at Mount Athnos of Eastern Orthodoxy. She wrote:

> Some of us feel an actual current of life entering into the center of the body and rising through the spine. So forceful is this vibration or stream of life that we are forced to keep the spine erect and the breathing light and even. For a little time we cannot speak. We are so filled with the fullness of Christ that there is within no room for words. [12]

10. On the Eastern Orthodox theology of light see Maloney, *Mystic of Fire*, especially chapter 3, "Mysticism of Jesus." Also see Zimany, "Divine Energies," 281–85.

11. Bradshaw, "Divine Energies."

12. Sanford, *Healing Light*, 144.

Here we should recall that Agnes was aware that not all spiritual light is from God, and that spiritualists can generate demonic light and energies, as she learned from her encounter with spiritualism. In *The Healing Light* she did not bring in such complications; it was after all a basic textbook on Christian healing prayer.[13] Further, Agnes saw that God's energies to heal had infinite potential, but real limitations for us. The problems with healing prayer are not due to weakness in God's healing energies/light, but rather in our inability to channel, through faith and love, sufficient amounts of it to achieve healing in difficult cases. She urged the reader to first choose small prayer projects, such as headaches, and to build up faith from there to more difficult healing tasks.

Agnes' use of visualizations also had the effect of avoiding double-mindedness (Jas 1:8). This she had learned from Prof. Clark. Nowhere is this harmonization more difficult than in forgiving someone who has hurt or wronged us. We may wish to do so, but part of our mind rebels. For such cases she suggested:

> . . . hold this person before the mind, surrounding him with the light of God's love. Some of us see in our minds the picture of Jesus Christ and then see the other person, placing the picture of the one we would forgive upon the picture of Christ. Having done this, we say to the one whom we would learn to like, "I forgive you in the name of Jesus Christ, and I give thanks to God because you are now forgiven. Amen."[14]

New Thought Plus Christian Sacramental Healing

Prof. Clark wrote in the preface to *The Healing Light*:

> [Agnes Sanford] has studied and tried every form of healing that has ever been known. Never have I met one who combined the metaphysical and the sacramental approach as she does. I have never met anyone more Christ-centered nor anyone more

---

13. To the modern reader who may be concerned about the origins of the light of his or her prayers, the answer is that to channel demonic light it is necessary to be a spiritualist, occultist, or polytheist of some description. In those groups, as Mrs. Sanford found out, the Spirit of Jesus is actively rejected, and the healing light of God, which is the normal light of the universe, is replaced by its demonic counterfeit.

14. Sanford, *Healing Light*, 64.

church-centered and yet more utterly unconcerned about the creed or lack of creed of those that she ministers to.[15]

This jars the contemporary Christian reader, as the term "metaphysical" now connotes New Age, tarot cards, crystals, etc. We must understand that what Agnes meant as "metaphysical" was New Thought, Unity Christianity, and Prof. Clark's Christian New Perspective. Clearly, Agnes defined metaphysical as "an open mind and the visioning faculty."[16] That she would consider an open mind and testing as the realm of New Thought and not normal Christianity is a sad testimony to the doctrinaire attitude of most Christian theology, which normally sees no need to test things beyond logical consistency. I will comment further on the relationship of testing, science, and Christianity in chapter 22. Mrs. Sanford knew that her New Thought techniques of prayer (meditation and visualization) were strange to traditional Christians. She was also aware that, like many others in CNP, she was in two *apparently* incompatible camps at the same time.[17]

Mrs. Sanford used both New Thought and traditional sacramental traditions for healing prayer as appropriate. For example, Agnes was able to coax a devout Roman Catholic soldier into accepting healing prayer by identifying herself as a friend of the local nuns (which she was), and by suggesting to the soldier that he accept the healing power of the Lord through Holy Communion. Another Jewish soldier, who would have nothing to do with Christian healing, was healed by meditating on God's healing light coming into his body.[18]

As participant in both New Thought and traditional Christianity, she could see advantages and disadvantages of the two. She understood that even the most powerful form of personal prayer in the orthodox Christian traditions, contemplative prayer, had no power to heal the sick. It was a prayer tradition that was effective in bringing a person to a state of great love for God, but was too detached from concerns for the body.[19]

15. Ibid.,10.

16. Ibid., 167.

17. Ibid., 131. Significantly, the ability to bring into harmony apparently contradictory systems of thought has been recognized by experimental psychologists as one of the characteristics of creative genius. This ability is often the key that enables major breakthroughs in science. See Briggs, "Genius Mind."

18. For Mrs. Sanford's explanation of her different approaches to healing, sacramental and "metaphysical," see *Sealed Orders*, 179–83.

19. Mrs. Sanford's point has been underscored in the past few years as several

On the other hand, she was aware of the dangers of New Thought. She recognized that many in that movement tended to be self-exalting and stressed one's role as child of God without going through the stage of repentance of sins (i.e., Gnosticism).[20]

The Healing Light was written well after Mrs. Sanford rejected the universalist wing of New Thought, and it is *biblically orthodox* and unambiguously Christian where it counts: in asserting who and what Jesus is. In practical terms, this means that the "name of Jesus adds power to all prayer."[21] Though God loves all humankind, it is through Jesus that God's loving and healing power can be concentrated to do the great healing works described in the Bible.[22]

Mrs. Sanford's participation in her husband's life as an Episcopal priest had given her an appreciation of the healing effectiveness of the Christian sacraments she could not have gained either in her Presbyterian upbringing or from New Thought circles. In her husband's ministry she noticed that the sacrament of baptism, even ministered without conscious intent of healing, very often resulted in physical healing. She came to discern that "Every minister is consecrated for God's service, and only ignorance, fear or prejudice can prevent his being used for healing."[23] She had also learned from John Gayner Banks and the OSL missions the value of formal, liturgical healing services to supplement individual and group healing prayers.

Another indicator of the biblical orthodoxy of *The Healing Light* is Mrs. Sanford's belief that God is *both* immanent and transcendent. "God's light shines both within us and without us, and by learning to

---

studies have attempted to document the ability of long-distance healing prayer. The investigators almost invariably chose Catholic nuns, who have a great reputation for prayer, and in fact are trained at contemplative prayer, but normally know little of healing prayer. The results showed little or no patient improvements. See Cary, "Long-Awaited." More recent studies, choosing more experienced healing prayer intercessors, have shown much better results. See Brown, *Testing Prayer*.

20. Sanford, *Healing Light*, 147.

21. Ibid., 64.

22. Ibid., 128.

23. Ibid., 93. It is interesting to note that the most famous of the Word-Faith ministers, Kenneth Hagin, came to the same conclusion. In Hagin's view an ordination that involves laying on of hands in faith bestows an extraordinary amount of spiritual power. Hagin, much like Mrs. Sanford, came to this view experientially, even though he came from a theological background that is distinctly non-sacramental. See Hagin, *Laying on of Hands*, 7.

receive Him within we begin to perceive Him without."[24] This is the traditional view common to Catholicism and Eastern Orthodoxy, though some evangelicals value the transcendence of God to the suspicion of his imminence.

Mrs. Sanford's Christian New Perspective had important practical consequences. She discovered that a balanced prayer life of Christian meditation and silence in the presence of God, visualization of good outcomes, and active mental prayer of praise, thanksgiving, and petition are all ways of optimizing one's ability to mediate God's healing power. This is in distinction to the metaphysical movement, which so stressed meditation and visualization that it often neglected the importance of worshiping the transcendent God. It was also different from traditional Protestantism, where prayer life did not include either meditation (contemplative prayer) or visualization of any sort.

Healing by Command in Christ

The Healing Light also pioneered an aspect of healing that was little noticed at the time: command healing. That is, healing is often accomplished by a command rather than a prayer of petition. Actually, there are no petitionary prayers for healing in the New Testament. All healing is done by command, either by Jesus or his disciples (check it out). This was vaguely understood by Christians of all ages in the fact that exorcism has always been done by command, but the command approach was not applied to healing in spite of the clear scriptural model.

Command healing has been sporadically recorded in the Christian healing literature through the ages. For example, healing commands were common in the ministry of the famous faith teacher and healing evangelist Smith Wigglesworth. In one of his resuscitations from the dead, he came into a sick room as the woman died:

> . . . I reached over into the bed and pulled her out. I carried her across the room, stood her against the wall and held her up, as she was absolutely dead. I looked into her face and said, "In the name of Jesus I rebuke this death." . . . her whole body began to tremble. "In the name of Jesus, I command you to walk," I said. I repeated, "In the name of Jesus, walk!" and she walked.[25]

24. Sanford, *Healing Light*, 77.
25. Frodsham, *Smith Wigglesworth*, 59.

It appears that the first focused theology of command prayer as normal and repeatable came in the 1950s. It was through one of the secondary figures of the post–World War II healing revival, Otis L. Jaggers, and is found in his book *Everlasting Spiritual and Physical Health* (1949). Jaggers believed that command healing was a key to effective healing and rightly cited the Scriptures to that effect. However, he also affirmed that command healing is something that only ministers could do.[26]

Mrs. Sanford discovered this aspect of the Christian healing ministry sometime in the 1940s. She wrote about it, without making it a major issue, at several places in *The Healing Light*. In one case she badly burned her finger and used it as an instant response.

> "It is unnecessary to stop frying potatoes and pray. We have already prayed for the indwelling of God's Holy Spirit. Let us then act upon it, assuming the dominion that is ours as children of light and assuming it in simple words that come to mind. . . . "I'm boss inside of me," I'm apt to think, "And what says goes. I say that my skin shall not be affected by the boiling oil, and that's all there is to it. I see my skin well, perfect and whole, and I say it's to be so."[27]

Decades later a Pentecostal couple, Charles and Frances Hunter, made command prayer much more widely known and practiced among Spirit-filled believers in their now classic book *How to Heal the Sick*. They toured many cities in the United States and abroad, and taught the command method of healing at large healing rallies they called "healing explosions." Command healing has since become common among Pentecostal and charismatic churches.[28]

The Scientific Attitude

The Healing Light was prophetic in many ways, small and large. This is especially clear in Mrs. Sanford's understanding of science and its relationship to healing prayer. In this she continued the agenda of Mary Baker Eddy and New Thought writers, who believed that there was an intimate relationship between science and the Christian faith, but she did

26. Jaggers, *Everlasting Spiritual.*

27. Sanford, *Healing Light*, 75.

28. See my description of the Hunter's extraordinary ministry in my blog post "The Hunters' Revolution."

not fall into their extremism that Christianity was science. *The Healing Light* was written well before Karl R. Popper's seminal understanding of science had spread into the English-speaking world (see chapter 6). Yet Agnes, like Popper, understood that the heart of science is a methodology of knowledge that is related to exploration and testing. Chapter 2 of *The Healing Light* is entitled "The Scientific Attitude," and in it she suggests that the reader conduct several *experiments* to see if healing prayer works. As with any scientific endeavor, she warned that failures would occur and to not be discouraged by them.[29] And again like Popper, Mrs. Sanford understood that *humility* is an essential ingredient in the scientific process.

> "Blessed are the meek, for they shall inherit the earth." The scientific attitude is the attitude of perfect meekness. It consists in an unshakable faith in the laws of nature combined with perfect humility toward those laws and a patient determination to learn them at whatever cost. . . . Through the same meekness those who seek God can produce results by learning to conform to his laws of faith and love.[30]

In this last point Mrs. Sanford was radically different from both Mary Baker Eddy and Karl Marx, who appropriated the term "scientific" in order to authenticate their systems without a real understanding of the scientific method as testing and experimentation.

Healing as a Practical and Everyday Occurrence

One of the most practical and usable insights of *The Healing Light* is Mrs. Sanford's five-step process for receiving the healing power of God. The first step is to relax (or in biblical vocabulary "be still") and make contact with God. Relaxation dampens the emotion of fear, which allows the healing energies of prayer to flow more effectively. The second step is to specifically ask God to send his heavenly power into your body. The third step is to believe that God's healing power and light is in fact coming into your body and to *give thanks* for it. The forth step is to observe the healing action take effect, seeing how God works in each specific case. (Note here the analogy with our understanding of quantum physics: observation solidifies outcome.) Again, as in any scientific experiment

29. Sanford, *Healing Light*, 23.
30. Ibid., 21.

there must be a tangible, observable goal, such as a specific healing. Mrs. Sanford was aware that people fear holding their prayer effectiveness to any form of accountability:

> How strange it is that people who fear to do this [testing] do not hesitate to pray for the most difficult objectives of all, such as the peace of the world... If they have so little confidence in prayer that they do not dare to test their powers of contacting God by praying for an easy thing, it is probable that their cosmic intercessions are of little force.[31]

In *The Healing Light* Mrs. Sanford gave us a wonderful example of her healing method as a combination of visualization, the laying on of hands, authoritative command, and mental prayer. Mr. Williams, her next-door neighbor, who was a cessationist and did not believe in healing prayer, suffered from rheumatic fever and had a damaged and weak heart. One night he returned from work at the point of death, and his children rushed over and begged Agnes to come and pray. She found Mr. Williams slumped on a chair in the living room, his heart beating furiously and erratically.

> As soon as my hands were firmly on his heart, I felt quiet, serene, in control. Forgetting the heart, I fixed my mind on the presence of Our Lord and invited Him to enter and use me. Then, Mr. Williams being quite unconscious, I talked informally to his heart, assuring it quietly that the power of God was at this moment re-creating it and it need labor no longer. Finally, I pictured the heart perfect, blessing it continuously in the name of the Lord and giving thanks that it was being recreated in perfection. Soon I could feel the heart beats becoming more quiet and regular. I could even feel that strange inner shifting that reports the rebuilding of flesh and tissue.[32]

When the doctors next examined him they were astounded that his heart changed from grossly swollen to normal in size and rhythm.

Another major contribution to the Christian theology of healing found within *The Healing Light* is Mrs. Sanford's use of healing as *evangelization*. Recall that it was written in 1945, when evangelicals were cessationist and did no healing prayer. Thus, to orthodox Protestants the combination of healing with evangelization was ridiculous or cultic in

31. Ibid., 23.
32. Ibid., 96.

spite of the evidence of Scripture (Luke 10:9). Mrs. Sanford's method in this was biblically correct. She would pray unconditionally for all those who wanted healing, regardless of their spiritual state. During or after their recovery she would nudge them to a Christian understanding of their healing experience. Defending her method, she explained:

> Some may wonder whether it is right to pray in the name of Christ and by the power of Christ for one who might not be willing to accept Christ. But after all, was it not that way when He was on earth? Did the nine lepers accept Him as Savior? Did the lame . . . and blind who came to Him understand the theology of redemptive work yet to be accomplished? Indeed no! They saw a light through the darkness of this world—that is all.[33]

In the present era, when John Wimber's Vineyard churches have popularized the concept of power evangelism, Mrs. Sanford's observation is no longer controversial. But even at the beginnings of the charismatic movement in the 1970s many of its leaders taught that the healing ministry is only *from* Christians *for* Christians. We have already noted in chapter 15 how her most dramatic healing, that of the officer with his stomach blown out, was accomplished in this manner: physical healing first, followed by specific Christian evangelization.

We should note here that *The Healing Light* was particularly influential in the first decade of the Charismatic Renewal (1960s), when few works on healing were in print and the classic books of the Faith Cure movement were largely unavailable. It was issued as a Logos International paperback and edited to fit the new audience. Glenn Clark's introduction, which called her book metaphysical and sacramental, was eliminated to avoid misunderstanding. Also downgraded was the New Thought agenda to try to make Christianity scientific. For instance, in the original Macalester Park edition chapter 2 is entitled "The Scientific Attitude: Choosing a Healing Prayer Objective." This is changed in the Logos edition to "Experiments in Prayer."

On the Edge of the Healing of Memories

In retrospect, it is clear that another major advance to the practice of Christian healing found in *The Healing Light* was in the area of healing the mind and spirit. In chapters 11, "The Healing of the Emotions," and

---

33. Ibid., 139.

12, "The Healing Power of Forgiveness," were found many of the insights and prayer techniques that subsequently helped establish the ministry of the healing of memories or inner healing. Basic to that ministry is both an ability to empathize with the sufferer and a belief that emotional distress has a spiritual root cause. Mrs. Sanford described her original and effective counseling method:

> Often as I sit and listen with keen and loving attention to a tale of woe I pray, "Oh God, please make her say the thing that will lead me into her mind." And the patient goes directly, though often unintentionally, to the inward grief or disharmony that has caused the outer trouble. So the door is open before me. And I go into that door and make myself a part of that problem, no matter how trivial or sordid it may be.[34]

Mrs. Sanford discovered a secret of ministering to the depressed in the process of being healed from her own severe depression. It was to enter into the sorrow and pain of the counselee, but protected by the love of God, so that the person ministering does not become depressed. The counselor should agree with the depressed person that the situation is indeed dark, and has had similar dark episodes in his or her own life. Once the counselor and sufferer are on the same level the healer can begin bringing the counselee up with prayer and the love of God, for in depression it is love and prayer that heals.[35]

In her ministry to the depressed Mrs. Sanford discovered that much emotional pain and often physical illness is caused by unforgiveness. In *The Healing Light* Mrs. Sanford described the fruits of her experiences with the traditional pattern of Roman and Anglican/Episcopal confession. Brought up as a Presbyterian, Mrs. Sanford was taught that one only confesses one's sins to God, yet she felt a definite leading from the Lord to make a sacramental confession. True to her belief in testing all things spiritual, she decided to give confession a try. She sought out advice from some Anglo-Catholic nuns in Philadelphia who explained to her the methods of examination of conscience and other aspects of the Anglo-Roman tradition. They recommended to her an Episcopal confessor, Fr. Weed of St. James Episcopal Church in Philadelphia, who met her needs precisely.

She found that the actual experience of confession was embarrassing and distressful. However, after it was over she found herself flooded by a

34. Ibid., 108.
35. Ibid., 108–9. See also Sanford's talk "Power to Become."

wave of God's healing power that not only healed her at a deep emotional level but gave her renewed physical energy as well. She realized that in the confessional she could not use alibis, or the vocabulary of New Thought, such as negative thought habits, etc. Sin was sin. It had to be confessed. Her experience brought her to a deeper understanding of the distinction between the metaphysical belief of evil as ignorance and mistake and the Christian view of sin as moral trespass against the laws of God.

In *The Healing Light* Agnes also suggested to the reader a specific exercise of examining one's conscience from the present to childhood, invoking the help of the Holy Spirit to recall sins buried and long forgotten. Again, the key was relaxing and allowing the Holy Spirit to move within the subconscious mind and bring up long-suppressed memories. At this time (1945) Agnes believed that the confessional was all that was needed to heal subconscious hurts and many deep-seated emotional problems.[36] It took her awhile to realize that this was not quite true, that some forms of emotional/spiritual hurts do not respond to the traditional confessional.[37]

The first hint that some of her own emotional hurts were not completely healed by the confessional came on a train trip back from one of her healing missions. She sat next to a physician who had heard her lecture and asked her, "What makes you so nervous? You spoke very well, but you grew more and more nervous until you were keyed as high as a kite. What is it?" Mrs. Sanford could not answer, and the physician suggested, "There is something in your memories that makes you that way."[38] The doctor had four sessions with Mrs. Sanford. Each time he lay hands on her head and prayed for her memories to be healed. He also suggested that she use the confessional in a new manner, attempting to associate every wrong thought or misdeed that she confessed with some hurtful memory of the past. That process of associating sin with past emotional hurt worked marvelously, and she soon found complete freedom in speaking before others. How she combined her personal experiences with sacramental confession, and that unidentified doctor's healing prayers into the healing of memories, is the subject of the next chapter.

---

36. Sanford, *Healing Light*, 124–30.
37. Sanford, "How to Receive."
38. Sanford, *Sealed Orders*, 191.

17

Harry and the Healing of Memories

Healing a Wounded Jewish Soldier

DURING THE TIME THAT Agnes was writing *The Healing Light* she began ministering to a soldier named Harry Goldsmith at Tilton Army Hospital.[1] While his physical healing was not quite as dramatic as that of the infantry officer who lost his stomach, Harry's case pushed Mrs. Sanford beyond her confidence in the sacrament of confession to heal all emotional and spiritual injuries. By the time she had finished ministering to Harry she had not only made a convert, but had stumbled (or more properly, been guided by the Holy Spirit) into a new ministry—the ministry of healing of the memories, later renamed inner healing.[2]

1. This account is based on an interview the author had with Harry Goldsmith, PhD, at his home in Tampa, Florida, in April of 1983, as well as Mrs. Sanford's descriptions of Dr. Goldsmith's healing and evangelization, found in her *Sealed Orders*, 193–96; *Behold Your God*, 74-76; and her taped talks "The Real Meaning" and "Healing of Memories." Goldsmith's written description of his healing under Agnes' ministry was given in his "Anatomy of a Healing." Harry served as the model for the hero in Mrs. Sanford's first novel, *Oh, Watchman!* Note that many of these tapes are being transcribed into the MP3 format and can be downloaded at the CFO audio library, online at http://www.cfoclassicslibrary.org.

2. It has been understood among persons who are informed on the issue that Mrs. Sanford was the first person to do inner healing prayer. She certainly was the first person to bring this to a *repeatable* ministry with a concurrent theology. However, as I was doing the final editing of this text my friend and colleague in the healing ministry Fr. Mark Pearson, of the Institute for Christian Renewal in New Hampshire, informed me that she was not the first to pray for inner healing. Two decades ago at Oxford University he was doing an advanced class on the Cappadocian fathers, a group of influential fourth-century theologians. He noticed that one of the fathers

Harry Goldsmith was born in Czechoslovakia of Jewish parents, but his mother was also an American citizen. In Czechoslovakia Harry suffered from considerable anti-Semitism at the hands of his Czech neighbors (common in all of Eastern Europe at the time). When the Nazis took over that unfortunate country at the beginning of World War II, Harry's family suffered intensified humiliations and persecutions. After Pearl Harbor and American's entry into the war, they and other American citizens were gathered up and exchanged for German nationals who were in the United States.

In America, Harry finished high school and then enlisted in the army (1944). Since he spoke perfect German he was sent to Europe, where he served as an infantryman and translator in an armored reconnaissance unit. He was badly wounded by a German "screaming mimi" (rocket artillery) a week before the war ended. The shrapnel from the rocket caused severe wounding in his thigh that not only shattered his femur and cut the nerves, but carried fragments of his uniform and earth into the wound and caused a severe infection. The doctors in England packed the wound with maggots and shipped him to the United States. Maggots may be disgusting to us, but they are effective in preventing gangrene, and currently being reintroduced into medical practice for this reason.[3] For Harry, his shipboard trip back to the United States was filled with maddening itching from the maggots.

By the time he arrived at Tilton Army Hospital in Fort Dix, New Jersey, he had developed severe osteomyelitis. Harry was placed in the "wet ward" for draining wounds, where, in spite of the newly developed penicillin, many patients died from infections. When Mrs. Sanford first saw Harry on her rounds as a Gray Lady he was running a high fever and deeply depressed. The doctors were trying to reduce his infection with massive doses of penicillin in preparation for surgery and amputation of his leg up to the pelvic bone.

Agnes began talking to him about the healing powers of the body and how they could be increased. Agnes offered to lay hands on his wound to increase the healing power. Harry recounted later that he was at point where he would try anything, "including burning chicken feathers under

wrote about something identical to inner healing. Everyone in the class read the passage and agreed. However, he does not remember which of the fathers it was or what specific work they were reading. I leave this project of rediscovery to someone with a good command of Greek.

3. Arnold, "Maggots Heal Wounds."

my bed."[4] He allowed Agnes to lay hands on his leg. He was astonished by the warmth he felt—the first feeling his leg experienced since his wound. His fever quickly subsided. Mrs. Sanford prayed for him twice a week for several weeks, with the usual *Life* magazine over her hands to disguise what she was doing. Both the draining of the wound and the infection cleared up quickly.

Although not religious, Harry was gifted with spiritual sensitivity and at times saw a light and felt a presence around Mrs. Sanford when she prayed for him.[5] He was also naturally inquisitive and Agnes slowly began to reveal to him just what she was doing. She first taught him to visualize the light of God making his leg perfect, and gave him a copy of Emmet Fox's *The Sermon on the Mount.* Soon Harry was not only praying for his own healing but organizing the men in the wet ward into a prayer group whose members prayed for one another. Before Mrs. Sanford was dismissed from Tilton Hospital the wet ward had closed after everyone in it had been healed.

Within six weeks Harry's leg was completely healed. A three-inch segment of smashed and missing femur bone had been restored. The surgeon responsible for Harry ordered three different sets of x-rays, as he could not believe what the plates revealed. Harry walked out of Tilton Hospital with a cane and returned to civilian life, entering City College of New York City via the GI Bill. However, his muscles were not as strong as he thought, and in a game of soccer he fractured a bone in his injured leg and was back in Tilton. He discerned that the accident was providential, and asked Agnes, who came to visit him (not as a Gray Lady this time), what else she had not taught him. Agnes admitted that there was something *very* important:

> I have not dared to tell you, because when I try to tell Jewish people they usually get upset, and I can understand why. It is embarrassing to me to say "I am a Christian" to a Jew, for a Christian means someone filled with the love of Christ and we have not acted toward Jews as though we were filled with the love of Christ. . . . I still don't know how to tell you the rest, so

---

4. Taped interview by author of Dr. Harry Goldsmith in April 1983

5. The experience of sensing a physical light during healing is reported in other accounts in the literature of Christian healing. See for example Kerin, *The Living Touch*, 28.

I will give you the story of His life and maybe you will see it for yourself.[6]

Agnes brought Harry a Bible and told him to read the Gospel of John. He read it three times, and then, on his own, read the other Gospels. He discerned that the healing presence he had felt next to Mrs. Sanford was indeed Jesus. After he left the hospital, Ted Sanford baptized him and prepared him for confirmation into the Episcopal Church.

Hurts from the Past

As Harry returned to college and part-time jobs, he found himself in alternating fits of depression or irrational outbursts of temper. On one occasion he threw a typewriter across the room over a minor annoyance. Harry shared his problem with Mrs. Sanford and she prayed every way she knew how for Harry's mental state. She prayed against his depression, his temper, etc., but nothing seemed to work. She described how she proceeded after her prayers failed:

> Therefore I prayed for guidance: "Well then, Lord—How *shall* I pray?" It came to me first that the trouble was not in the conscious young man but in the little boy within him who had lived in the Gestapo regime.
>
> "Yes, Lord," said I, "but how can I pray for that little boy who lived ten years ago?"[7]

Agnes was led into a process of intercessory prayer for Harry, or rather for the little Harry who had been so badly taunted, abused, and psychologically scarred in Nazi Europe. The manner in which she prayed for Harry's healing of the memories was unusual and important in understanding how the healing of memories ministry arose. At this period

6. Sanford, *Behold Your God*, 74–75.

7. Sanford, *Sealed Orders*, 195–95. Contemporary readers often compare the insight she received from the Lord about the origins of Harry's problems with the work of W. Hugh Missildine. His book *Your Inner Child* is now considered a classic of modern psychology. In it Dr. Missildine asserted that the inner child coexists in the adult not as a chaotic "id" of Freudian psychoanalysis but as an unfinished entity that remains until adequately recognized and dealt with. This is essentially what the Lord revealed to Mrs. Sanford about Harry. He had an injured child self within his soul that needed ministry and comfort. Lest someone believe that the healing of memories was an *imitation* of psychological theory, let us remember Harry's case happened in 1946 and Dr. Missildine wrote his work decades later.

of her life Mrs. Sanford was influenced by an understanding of the Body of Christ and prayer intercession which was part of the heritage of Anglo-Catholic theology, that branch of the Anglican and Episcopal churches which draws heavily on Roman Catholic sources. This understanding was deeply sacramental and had its roots in the theology of classical Christian mysticism. Already in *The Healing Light* Mrs. Sanford had advocated a form of intercession for others, termed reparation, which she cites as ancient form of Christian prayer. She had learned of this from Episcopal nuns she befriended in a nearby convent. [8]

This prayer intercession process which Mrs. Sanford used for Harry is described in detail in her novel *Lost Shepherd* (1953). For our purposes let us call it travail prayer. The intercessor determines that he or she is willing to take on the hurts of a specific person. At the same time, the intercessor covenants with God about a time of prayer and fasting on behalf of this person's sins. This establishes a special spiritual relationship between the intercessor and the supplicant. A sign of this is when the intercessor begins to experience thoughts and emotions not his or her own, but reflecting the hurts, confusion, and distress of the supplicant. To reach this stage of spirit melding and empathy usually takes days, and at times weeks, of intercession in prayer and fasting. The intercessor then takes the sin burden and hurts of the person to the Communion table and asks God to forgive his or hers sins, and be reconciled with that person through Jesus' blood and body.

In the case of Harry, when Agnes went into the travail prayer she in fact experienced the boy Harry's emotions of hurt, insult, and anger. When she completed her travail prayer week and went to the Lord's Supper, Harry was *immediately* healed of his mood changes and irrational behavior. He sensed that Mrs. Sanford was behind it. He wrote her to find out what she did. Agnes explained that she had been interceding for him. Harry went on to earn a PhD in psychology, and became a Spirit-filled teacher at Mrs. Sanford's pastoral teaching institute, the School of Pastoral Care (see chapter 18). For many years he practiced his own very effective mix of counseling and Christian healing prayer.

The theology of travail and burden bearing was given its modern articulation decades before by several Anglican lay theologians, of whom C. S. Lewis was the most famous. A friend of Lewis, Charles Williams, brought this theology to its fullest expression. Mr. Williams' theology

8. Sanford, *Healing Light*, 136–37.

centered on the apostle Paul's little-noticed understanding that as members of the Body of Christ we are called to bear one another's burdens and suffering. This is especially clear in a passage in the letter to the Colossians (1:24): "Now I rejoice in my suffering for your sake, and in my flesh I complete what is lacking in Christ's afflictions for the sake of the body, that is the church . . ." Williams believed, as John Sandford rediscovered later and wrote about in his work *The Transformation of the Inner Man*, that the essential spiritual duty of every Christian is to accept some form of suffering and inconvenience for the sake of others. This is the central moral choice which was indicated if one wanted to accept fully being a Christian. Williams called this "the way of exchange."[9]

It is not known at what date Mrs. Sanford read Charles Williams' works, but at the time of her death her library study contained several of his books.[10] It can be definitely established that from the beginning of her writing career she read many of the works of C. S. Lewis.[11] Lewis believed in his friend's theology of the "way of exchange." In fact, when Lewis' beloved wife was dying of bone cancer he prayed that he might accept some of her disease and pain. She was relieved of suffering and Lewis mysteriously underwent a calcium loss in his leg.

Some evangelical readers may be thinking that all this is scripturally unwarranted. After all, Jesus said on the cross, "It is finished" (John 19:30), and this has come to be understood that the entire work of redemption was done by Christ on that day and no further additions can be made. However, Scripture itself points to the validity of travail prayer. Paul states it very clearly and succinctly in Colossians 1:24: "Now I rejoice in my suffering for your sake, and in my flesh I complete what is lacking in Christ's afflictions for the sake of the body, that is the church . . ."

It would be enlightening to compare Mrs. Sanford's experiences in travail prayer with the experiences of Mr. Rees Howells, the great Christian intercessor of the Welsh Revival. His was also based on the understanding of the Christian's call to burden bearing and co-suffering with

---

9. Williams' theology was written as fiction, much like C. S. Lewis. Unlike Lewis, whose novels can be read by children, Williams' are sophisticated and nuanced. It may be best to first encounter Williams' theology by way of McDermott, *Romantic Love*, especially chapter 8, "The Way of Exchange."

10. From a note on Virginia Sanford's annotations to the first draft of this chapter.

11. Sanford, *Behold God*, 88

Christ. Howells spent decades in fasting and prayer for the women of India, for whom he felt a special burden.[12]

Mrs. Sanford came to understand that this classical form of travail prayer was dangerous, as it could lead to serious confusion, and in later years discouraged it. She considered it imperative that this prayer *not* be done on a non-Christian, whose spirit may contain occult or idolatrous elements. More importantly, she discovered that although this travail prayer is powerful and possible, it is *not necessary*. The same effect can be achieved with much less heroic effort.

Again, it was in a process of intercession for a Jewish woman that she learned this lesson.[13] Like Harry, the woman had been persecuted under the Nazis and had seen most of her family murdered. She had become a Christian and had, at least consciously, forgiven her oppressors. Like Harry, she also suffered severe bouts of depression and anger. Mrs. Sanford went into the travail prayer cycle for the woman. But well before Agnes believed it was complete—in fact, only after *asking* that little Jewish girl within be comforted with Jesus' love—a complete healing was brought about. It was the Lord's way of educating Mrs. Sanford that his forgiveness is not dependent on specific and prolonged techniques of prayer and fasting.

In the last years of her life, Mrs. Sanford declared that her original technique of travail prayer should never be used.[14] This is probably to protect the technique from being used by immature Christians who wish to do heroic things as part of their spiritual life. The milder form of travail prayer, taking the emotional hurts of a supplicant to the Communion

---

12. See Grubbs, *Rees Howells*. Leanne Payne, Agnes' disciple in inner healing, found in her ministry that she had to do healing prayer on several persons who did this form of travail prayer, as they were often seriously confused and troubled. See Payne, *Heaven's Calling*, 194.

13. See Sanford, *Behold God*, 110–14, for a description of this second case of the healing of memories. Mrs. Sanford, like Carrie Ten Boom, had a special love for Jews and ministered to them often. On this see also Sanford's taped talk "Redemption of Our."

14. From the author's interview of Mrs. Barbara Shlemon on May 20, 1984, at St. Phillip's Cathedral in Atlanta. Mrs. Shlemon, a frequent CFO and OSL speaker and disciple of Mrs. Sanford, was among the first Catholic laypersons to come into the Charismatic Renewal, and ministered often with Mrs. Sanford. She published several works on inner healing; see her *Healing Prayer* and *Hidden Self*.

table, but without going into travail, was picked up and practiced especially among Catholic charismatics since the 1970s.[15]

In 1948, just after her initial travail prayer intercessions, Agnes came to a new understanding of the relationship of the healing of memories to Christ's atoning work. Emmet Fox (see chapter 9) came to give a public lecture in Camden, New Jersey. His topic was Jesus' work as intercessor before the Father. The Rev. Fox believed that the reason Jesus shed bloody sweat at Gethsemane (an occasionally observed natural phenomenon) was not that Jesus was frightened of his coming crucifixion, but rather that as he prayed in the garden he looked into the "collective unconscious" (a Jungian term meaning "total memory") of all of humankind and saw there all the sins of hatred, selfishness, rejection, and evil that humankind had committed or would commit. It was the horror of that vision-experience that caused the bloody sweating. As Jesus continued to pray, he accepted the bitter cup of the grief and sorrows (Isaiah 53:4) that those sins had or would produce onto himself.[16]

Agnes meditated on Dr. Fox's lecture and searched the Scriptures. She came to the conclusion that Fox was correct. Jesus' activity in the garden made the healing of memories possible, just as his flogging and physical blows made our physical healing possible (Isaiah 53:5). She incorporated this understanding into her talks and writings on the healing of memories, and the Fox theory was passed on to many of the early writers and ministers of inner healing.

Some may object to this division in the passion of our Lord, which is not explicit in Scripture. Certainly it is normative for a Christian to believe in the forgiveness of sins through the blood of Jesus without this particular understanding. We can only note that theology must be the servant of Scripture, and if the Fox theory of Jesus' travail at Gethsemane helps us understand, or adds to, our faith expectancy about the reality of the ministry of forgiveness of sins, so much the better. In support of the Fox theory we would cite the ninth chapter of the letter of Hebrews. There the writer makes an equation statement: "without the shedding of blood there is no forgiveness." We may safely assume that the bloody

15. Powell, "Holy Communion." Powell shows that this form of prayer intercession is effective for patients with schizophrenia. My wife and I have used this Communion intercession often for the more normal pastoral needs that arise in our church and counseling.

16. Sanford, *Sealed Orders*, 189. Explained fully in Sanford, *Behold God*, chapter 8, "The Current of God's Love on Calvary."

sweat shed by Jesus at Gethsemane was not an accident, but part of God's providential provision for the forgiveness of sins. It certainly makes sense to associate Jesus' *mental* anguish at the garden with humankind's *mental* suffering. It was also in the context of Jesus' redemptive work at Gethsemane that Mrs. Sanford came to her final correction of her belief about travail prayer. She understood that one did not have to suffer the confusion and pain of the other person, but rather only serve as a connector between the person and Jesus.[17]

Other Methods for the Healing of Memories

The change in the healing of memories ministry from that of intercession through the Lord's Supper to other ways of prayer came in several stages. It happened at CFO camps and at the OSL and other healing missions, which she did with increasing frequency after the release of *The Healing Light*. In these settings she had to deal with dozens of persons at a time. The first was the use of the laying on of hands on the head of the supplicant, just as that unnamed doctor had laid hands on Agnes about her nervousness at speaking engagements.

> I simply pray, usually with the laying on of hands, for the love of Christ to come into this one and forgive the sins and heal the sorrows of the past as well as the present- the little child who used to be, as well as the grown person who is now. I begin at the present and go back through the memories, mentioning every sin and every grievous incident that has been told me. Indeed, I go further back than this, and pray for the healing of those impressions of fear or anger that came upon the infant far beyond the reach of memory. I carry this prayer back to the time of birth and even before birth and pray for the restoration of the soul, for the healing of the soul—the psyche—of the real, original person.[18]

At times, as when people came to the parsonage specifically for healing prayer, she could do more than just lay hands and pray briefly. She described this healing of memories/counseling methodology as: listening, questioning, and praying. She would arrange for a period of time in which the person talked about his or her problem. While the counselee

17. Sanford, *Sealed Orders*, 95.
18. Sanford, *Healing Gifts*, 133–34.

talked, Agnes prayed that God would lead the person to mention the root problem of their distress, which he or she often did immediately. If the counselee reported that they had a happy childhood, Agnes then asked, "When did you first become unhappy?" This was usually all that was needed to get to the root of the problem. If the person reported an unhappy childhood, she asked *why* they believe their childhood was unhappy. The answer to that question would again point to an unhealed spiritual root. Once the root problem was identified, a prayer would be prayed that was concise and to the point of the sin or hurt of the past.[19]

It seems that from the very beginning Agnes integrated the use of visualization with prayers for the healing of memories. She had used this technique to bring persons to forgive others in *The Healing Light*. In her healing of memories/counseling session she would ask the counselee to imagine and invite Jesus into the hurtful memories. Sometimes, when the imaginative powers of the counselee were weak, she visualized Jesus healing the incident in her mind. In this way, like the original form of long-distance intercessory prayer that Agnes learned long before, she used her imagination to add to her mental or oral prayers. Mrs. Sanford did her own healing of memories on the little child within herself. As an eight-year-old her father was ill and little Agnes greatly feared for her father's life. Mrs. Sanford invited Jesus into her memory to comfort the little girl, which he did. To be doubly sure the trauma of the memory was banished, she received Communion for the "little" Agnes.[20]

A Prayer Mashal for the Healing of Memories

For those occasions when Agnes was teaching at large CFO camps or healing missions and could do little individual counseling, she developed a group meditation/visualization which she would pray over her audience. It was a parable prayer, or as Prof. Glenn Clark had taught her, a *mashal* (chapter 13). In this case it was for the cleansing and healing of memories of the audience.

---

19. Ibid.,131–34.

20. Ibid., 117–18. Some time ago my wife and I counseled and did repeated inner healing on a woman who had been severely sexually abused by her father. She improved greatly, yet, the clouds of depression and insecurity were not completely dispersed until we took her to church one Sunday and all three of us received communion for the abused little girl within her.

Lord Jesus, I ask you to enter into this person who has need of
your healing in the depths of the mind. I ask You to come, Lord
as a careful housekeeper might come into a house that has long
been closed and neglected. Open all the windows and let in the
fresh wind of Your Spirit. Raise all the shades, that the sunlight
of Your love may fill this house of the soul. Where there is sunlight there cannot be darkness. Therefore I rejoice that as the
light of Your love now fills this mansion of the soul, all darkness
shall flee away. . . .

Go back, O Lord, through all the rooms of this memory-
house. Open every closed door and look into every closet and
bureau drawer and see if there be any dirty and broken things
that are no longer needed in one's present life, and if so, o Lord,
take them completely away. I give thanks, for this is the promise
of the Scriptures: As far as the east is from the west, so far hath
he removed our transgressions from us. . . .

Follow the soul of this Your child all the way back to the
hour of birth and heal the soul even of the pain and fear of being
born into this darksome world. Restore in the soul that bright
memory of your eternal being that is not exactly a memory, but
which is rather an emanation, an unconscious infilling of the
eternal radiance from which this one was born. And if even
before birth the soul was shadowed by this human life and was
darkened by fears or sorrows of the human parents, then I pray
that even those memories or impressions may be healed, so that
this one may be restored to Your original pattern . . . so that
whatever Your purpose may be for its human pilgrimage, that
purpose may be filled.[21]

Mrs. Sanford was also careful to explain that the healing of memories is not a form of induced amnesia, but rather a prayer of forgiveness
and transformation

The memories will not be lost . . . but the emotional tone that
surrounds them will be changed. Memories of old grief will no
longer cause you grief. They will bring joy, for you will think,
"How thankful I am that that is all gone away!" Memories of
guilt will bring exceeding joy, for you will think, "Oh, how wonderful to be entirely free of that, so that it has nothing to do
with me anymore!" Memories of resentment will be changed to
tenderness, because the love of Christ will so fill and flood the

21. Ibid.,120–23.

heart that there will no longer be any cause of resentment, for even old bitter things have been changed to joy."[22]

A Major Name Change

In the 1970s Fr. Francis MacNutt, who would later become the lead healing theologian of the Catholic Charismatic Renewal, was ministering at a CFO camp with Mrs. Sanford. He began using the term "inner healing" for the healing of memories. It seems elderly persons were coming up to the healing lines believing that their failing memories and onsetting dementia would be restored with the "healing of memory" prayer.[23] Inner healing became the name that stuck, though Mrs. Sanford never liked it.

The healing of memories/inner healing is turning out to be, in view of its use throughout the world of Spirit-filled churches, one of the major healing prayer innovations of all time. It is the bringing into biblical fullness the church's ministry of the forgiveness of sins. It completes the rite/sacrament of confession. That is, the sacrament of confession brings to the cross of Christ the sin that a person commits (or omits). The healing of memories brings the forgiveness of sins to the other dimension of sin, the sins that are focused on us, the sinful acts we receive at the hands (and tongues) of others. These sins cannot be "confessed" because we are not responsible for them, yet they are sin structures that deeply affect us. As Agnes described in her book *The Healing Gifts of the Spirit*:

> The truth is that any wound to the soul so deep that it is not healed by our own self-searching and prayers is inevitably connected with a subconscious awareness of sin, either our own sins or grievous reactions to the sins of others. The therapy that heals these deep wounds could be called the forgiveness of sins or it could be called the healing of memories.[24]

Before the healing of memories was birthed, Christians knew that they had to forgive and pray for their enemies—a most basic and difficult commandment of Christianity (Matt 5:44). Knowing that, however, never developed into a systematic, repeatable ministry of how "sins upon us" poison our emotions and reactions, and can be healed. The ministry

22. Sanford, *Behold Your God*, 69.

23. Conversation with Dr. Francis MacNutt at a North Carolina "Disciplined Order of Christ" conference in 1982.

24. Sanford, *Healing Gifts*, 126.

of healing of memories/inner healing is the product of Mrs. Sanford's willingness to listen to the Lord and experiment with forms of prayer to achieve what was given to her as a revelation.

Inner Healing and the CFO Women

By the late 1960s inner healing was being taught at the Schools of Pastor Care (see chapter 18 below), at Agnes' many healing missions, but principally and consistently at CFOs. It was at the CFOs, with their week-to-ten-day summer programs, where Agnes discipled several men and woman to do inner healing ministry. Most prominent among the first inner healing ministers were Ann White and Genevieve Parkhurst.[25] Mrs. Parkhurst was a particularly beautiful and dignified woman who held the attention of her audiences just by her presence. Her works on inner healing were particularly insightful, and among the best of the early works on inner healing, marred only by her use of Jungian vocabulary to explain the ministry.

This error was mostly Mrs. Sanford's fault, as she did the same in several of her earlier writings. Mrs. Sanford was not a devotee of Prof. Carl Jung's writings. Rather, she absorbed Jungian vocabulary from the table talk of the many guests that came to her home to discuss spiritual healing with her. Jung's writing were all the rage among academicians in the 1950s and 1960s, as it was the only branch of the psychoanalytic movement that recognized spiritual phenomenon. Only later were the dangers of Jungian psychology understood, especially in its confusion of archetypes for demonic influences and possession. Her son John went deeply into Jung and received a degree as a Jungian psychologist. In her later years Mrs. Sanford came to greatly regret that. She shared this to her *spiritual* son and disciple John Sandford (note the *d* in his name). She asked him to pray that her two boys, Fr. Morton Kelsey, her pastor in her later Californian home and a writer and Episcopal priest, and her son John Sanford be separated from Jungian influences.[26]

But the major CFO woman who put the inner healing ministry on the map of national and international consciousness was Mrs. Ruth Carter Stapleton (1929–1983). Raised a devout Southern Baptist, she

25. White, *Healing Adventure*, and Parkhurst, *Glorious Victory*.

26. From conversations with John Sandford at the CFO camp in Leesburg, Florida, January 18, 1986.

came to a CFO in the mid-1960s.[27] Mrs. Stapleton met Agnes Sanford several times, and read her works, but was more directly mentored by the Rev. Tommy Tyson, a disciple of Rufus Moseley. Tyson was a Methodist evangelist and frequent CFO speaker. Mrs. Stapleton's first work was a devotional pamphlet which elaborated an earlier work by A. W. Tozer. The pamphlet, *Power Through Release*, was published by Glenn Clark's Macalester Park Press.[28]

In 1971 Mrs. Stapleton's brother, Jimmy Carter, became governor of Georgia and, after his term expired in 1974, began a presidential quest. By the time Mrs. Stapleton finished writing her first work on inner healing, governor Carter was in the midst of his election campaign. She chose to garner some publicity for the inner healing ministry by changing her name to "Carter Stapleton," which she used for the rest of her life. Her work *The Gift of Inner Healing* became a sensational best seller.

Her books on inner healing were totally dependent on the works of Agnes Sanford, but Mrs. Sanford, who was already somewhat controversial, was never mentioned in them. Mrs. Carter Stapleton briefly mentioned using a *mashal* prayer within a prayer group, but Mrs. Sanford's rich theology of forgiveness of sins was not discussed.[29] Rather, the inner healing ministry was presented in a series of stories of personal distress and healings through *visualizations* in which Jesus intervened in memories of the supplicants. It was all told simply and thankfully without Jungian vocabulary.

The Gift of Inner Healing was soon followed by Mrs. Carter Stapleton's second major book, *The Experience of Inner Healing*. The book did have extensive notes citing multiple Bible passages in order to counter the mounting evangelical critique that the ministry was "unbiblical." That accusation continued to haunt the ministry, and John Sandford, in his *Transformation of the Inner Man*, specifically addressed this lack.[30] The highly critical work of Dave Hunt and other self-appointed anti-cult ministers understood inner healing as merely a ministry of visualization, not understanding the subtleties of Mrs. Sanford's ministry and theology.[31]

27. Stapleton, "First CFO."

28. Stapleton, *Power Through Release*. On p. 6 she clearly credits Tozer's work as her inspiration.

29. Ibid., 24.

30. Sandford, *Transformation*.

31. Hunt, *Seduction of Christianity*.

In any case, by the late 1970s Ruth Carter Stapleton was perhaps the most well known and photographed of the new charismatic leadership. *Newsweek* did a cover story on her, authored by Kenneth Woodward and entitled "Sister Ruth," comparing her to the famous 1930s Pentecostal healing evangelist Aimee Semple MacPherson.[32] Inner healing had become the signature ministry of the new charismatic movement.

32. July 17, 1978.

18

Theologian to the Charismatic Renewal

By the time Mrs. Sanford had written *The Healing Light*, she had developed as practical an understanding of the Holy Spirit as one could without being an outright Pentecostal. She assumed, for instance, that the Spirit speaks to every Christian, and that all Christians need to do to hear his voice is to practice listening quietly without anger in their hearts. In *The Healing Light* she related the charming story about a little boy in her children's Bible class who wanted to go swimming even though he still had a cold. When he asked the Holy Spirit in prayer, the child distinctly heard, "Not yet."[1] Mrs. Sanford also shared with her readers how she often asked the Holy Spirit to enter into people to accomplish certain specific spiritual tasks. For instance, if her own children came from school cross or unhappy she would pray that the Spirit enter into them and give them peace and happiness.[2]

But none of this was a prayer for the baptism of the Holy Spirit, nor did she have an understanding of the gifts of the Holy Spirit other than healing. This was in spite of the fact that she had a long conversation with Rufus Moseley in the 1940s and was tremendously impressed by him.[3] Like many of us, new information was not incorporated on the first time hearing. After Mrs. Sanford received the baptism of the Holy Spirit much of what Rufus Moseley had told her made sense, and her later theology of the Holy Spirit was greatly indebted to him.[4]

1. Sanford, *Healing Light*, 77–78.
2. Ibid.,66.
3. See the description of her first meeting with Moseley in *Sealed Orders*, 173–75.
4. Sanford, "Forgiveness of Sins."

How she came into an understanding of both the baptism of the Spirit and the other gifts of the Spirit is another example of the Lord teaching her just as she was ready to learn.[5] It happened during an especially hectic period of her life, 1952–1953. Agnes was writing, praying for many individual healings, touring the U.S. and Canada in CFO camps and OSL missions, and answering independent church invitations—besides raising a family. She was exhausted yet felt an inner compulsion to preach the good news that Jesus heals today and counter the deadly effects of cessationism on the church.

Mrs. Sanford was scheduled for a healing mission in Tucson, Arizona. Providentially, when she arrived in Tucson the mission was canceled, and she had time to rest and pray with two local women who were also in the healing ministry. All three felt an exhaustion from their constant ministry and cried out to God for healing from that and other ailments. But nothing happened. Then they prayed for guidance, and all three received a word from the Lord to pray for the Holy Ghost. Agnes was sure this was from God, not her own mind, as she always referred to the Holy Spirit.

As they were praying a Spirit-filled medical doctor (and brain specialist) dropped by. He was a friend of one of the women. He entered into the prayers and conversation and shared his belief that the health of the pineal and pituitary glands is related to a person's spiritual life. In his view, these glands were the physical vehicle for channeling God's spiritual energies into the person. When a person came into the fullness of the Holy Spirit both glands would expand and reach their intended fullness and health.

This sounds strange and materialistic, partly because we are not used to the idea that spiritual energies affect the body (Jonathan Edwards would not have been surprised by this theory), but similar theories have had a long history. The great French mathematician, and Christian apologist, and philosopher Blaise Pascal (1623–1662) believed that the pineal gland is the conduit for God's grace into the mind and body. Charles Fillmore, founder of Unity, also believed that the pineal is the organ by which faith enters the mind. Perhaps either of these sources inspired this unnamed physician's theory. The theory might be true, and with modern imaging techniques might even be subject to testing.

Whether this doctor's theory was accurate, partly true, or completely bogus was not as important as the fact that just at that moment in time

5. Sanford, *Sealed Orders*, 216–18. See also Sanford, "Power in the Body."

the pineal/pituitary theory produced in these three women a great sense of *expectancy and faith* to receive more of the Holy Ghost. Like the vibration of blood theory of Prof. Clark (chapter 13), it was not as important whether the theory was precisely correct as much as that it served as a vehicle to increase faith in a valid biblical concept.[6]

At this point there is no way of knowing if the pineal theories of Pascal and that unnamed doctor are correct. There is no indication that Agnes ever discarded either of them.[7] In any case the three women then prayed for one another, two on one, and each received the baptism of the Holy Spirit. All three experienced a burning sensation on the top of their heads, and waves of energy flowed through their bodies. They also received several of the gifts and fruits of the Holy Spirit, especially joy and peace. The three were instantly healed of their exhaustion and other maladies.

Mrs. Sanford discovered quickly that she received the gift of "illumination." She noticed that many of the theological problems she had been mulling over were resolved by a deeper understanding of the Bible. This is the same gift that is often manifested when a person becomes born again, and suddenly the Bible changes from a confusing anthology of writings into an exciting picture of spiritual truth. The gift of illumination takes a person from a given stage of spiritual understanding to a higher level. It was a spiritual gift much esteemed in the Middle Ages and was considered an important step in the life of a devoted believer. In fact, in traditional Catholic literature the three major steps for the perfected Christian are: purification, illumination, and union.[8] One finds this gift cited in contemporary Pentecostal or charismatic writings also under the name "revelation knowledge."[9]

6. Theology has often sprung out of unprovable ideas. An example from church history that comes to mind is the Catholic concept of transubstantiation, which attempted to define the real presence of Jesus in the Eucharist, and depended on the philosophy of Aristotle via St. Thomas. The Protestant reformers, no longer impressed with Aristotle's philosophy, rightly insisted that the word *transubstantiation* is not biblical. This disagreement was one of the hot-button issues that led to the Jesus Wars II (the horrible Thirty Years War, 1616–1648). What had been a faith encouragement for the medieval mind sadly became a source of warfare, and has remained an obstacle to reconciliation among Christians.

7. Sanford, *Behold Your God*, 154. The pineal/pituitary theory especially could be tested today. For instance, CAT scans could measure the size of the pineal glands of two groups, Spirit-filled Christians vs. atheists and agnostics.

8. For a sympathetic description of the theology of illumination as revelation, from a modern Pentecostal viewpoint, see King, "Thomas Aquinas."

9. Note the dramatic gift of illumination/revelation of persons who are illiterate

Neither Agnes nor the other two women received the gift of tongues, since they neither expected it nor understood it. Later the two Arizona women attended a local Pentecostal group and received tongues. They wrote Agnes about it, but she wrote back saying that tongues was a ridiculous notion. One of the women, Mrs. Marion Lovekin, wrote back showing Agnes the biblical basis for tongues and challenging her to meditate on the issue. On the next occasion that Mrs. Sanford passed by Tucson the two women again prayed with Agnes. Mrs. Sanford had agreed to accept any gifts God wanted for her, though she still did not *want* tongues. As soon as the prayer session began Mrs. Sanford reported:

> . . . immediately I desired the gift of tongues with a great long-ing! And in another moment I spoke as they had spoken, in words that the conscious mind did not understand. . . . I felt as though the love of Christ, already in me, now moved down, down to a deeper level.[10]

She spent several days in deep prayer and praise. When she returned home she did not share her experience with anyone, partly because she did not understand it herself. Again, Agnes was given the right guidance at the right time. She went on a healing mission in Florida, where she stayed with a Christian woman who had had the gift of tongues for twenty years. The woman was able to resolve her theological and biblical reservations about speaking in tongues. After that meeting Agnes utilized tongues daily in her private prayer life. As soon as Agnes returned home she canvassed her husband's theological library to find out what traditional theologians had to say about the Holy Spirit and began piecing together a better understanding of the Holy Spirit.

Move to Westborough

A few years earlier (1948), after the children had left for college, Ted resigned as rector of Trinity Church. He and Agnes moved to a country cottage in Westborough, Massachusetts, about thirty-five miles west of Boston. There Ted accepted charge of two small churches while Agnes concentrated on her writing and speaking program. By the time they left

---

but enabled to read and understand the Bible cited in Hagin, *Laying On*, 22. See also mention of the same gift in the anonymous nineteenth-century Russian Orthodox classic *The Way of the Pilgrim*.

10. Sanford, *Sealed Orders*, 221.

Moorestown Ted was a full partner in Agnes' ministry. He had some initial reservations about healing, and disliked his wife's countless speaking engagements and never-ending writing. Agnes never pushed her views on her husband, and at the same time she supported him and appreciated his talents as pastor.

Once Ted became convinced of the authenticity of Agnes' work, he joined her ministry enthusiastically. A touchable example of this is Agnes' book for children, *Let's Believe* (1954), which was illustrated with charming pen and ink drawings by Ted. Ted's sound command of theology acted as a restraint on Agnes' speculative flights, and his sense of liturgy and gift of pastoring complimented Agnes' special gifts of speaking and writing. After their move to Westborough Ted accompanied Agnes on her healing missions, sharing speaking assignments as well as the individual prayer ministry that surrounded them wherever they went. He developed a gift for physical healing that was in its way as powerful in mediating God's healing light as Agnes'.

The Fruits of Illumination

In the years following her baptism with the Holy Spirit, Mrs. Sanford wrote books which were truly Holy Ghost in outlook. They combined her illumination and new knowledge of the Holy Spirit with reflections upon her experiences as a healing minister and Bible teacher. The first one, *Behold Your God* (1958), was specifically theological in nature. After that came *The Healing Gifts of the Spirit* (1966), which described the gifts of the Holy Spirit in the practical aspects of the healing ministry, and gave her definitive description of her ministry of healing of memories. The last work of this series, *The Healing Power of the Bible* (1969), was based on her Bible study lesson to her woman's prayer group.

These works played a major role in the spiritual education of the men and women who were coming into spiritual maturity in the 1960s and took part in, or became the leaders of, the Charismatic Renewal. These works have not been widely recognized as the major works of theology that they are because they do not fit the Western-Hellenistic pattern of theology, that is, combining gospel and academic philosophy. Rather, like her contemporary Pentecostal theologians, hers were writings that correlated the biblical narrative with her rich and varied spiritual experiences in a relationship of analogies.[11]

An example is her treatment of the incident described in 2 Kings 4:11–37, the resurrection from the dead of the Shunammite woman's son, explained in her work *The Healing Power of the Bible*. Mrs. Sanford believed that incident was true and a miracle, but not therefore inscrutable. Rather, since it was a miracle, it had identifiable and discrete elements of spiritual laws, and was understandable as the power of God at work. By analogy from her life, she was able to explain why the prophet prayed over the child, but stopped and walked about.

> Prayer is work. It demands a tremendous amount of spiritual energy. Elisha felt his body becoming stretched and strained with weariness. Therefore he ceased praying for a while, and walked to and fro in the house. . . . In the old days [before her baptism in the Spirit] when I prayed for the sick with tremendous insistence, I found that if I ceased praying for a while and walked to and fro in the house, probably making beds and picking up children's clothes, and putting them in the closet, then I could return to my prayer with increased energy.[12]

Mrs. Sanford ended her commentary on the biblical incident by citing a resurrection that took place in her parish of a baby born dead and laid aside for two hours. Mrs. Sanford had prayed for the mother but was not present at the birth. When the mother awakened from the opiates given her because of the critical labor process, she insisted on baptizing the infant. The child revived as the water was poured over it by Ted.[13]

Note Mrs. Sanford's method of biblical interpretation. She compared the biblical incident with the experiences from her own healing ministry and that of other believers, and brought into the discussion her understanding of spiritual laws and the energies of God as constantly available, Old Testament and New. It all combined to give the reader greater faith in the reality of biblical revelation and encouragement of his or her healing ministry.

In contrast, liberal theologians would find this passage inscrutable. In the liberal demythologizing interpretation, then standard in mainline seminaries, it would be assumed that the biblical narrative was an

---

11. Smith, "Thinking in Tongues."

12. Sanford, *Healing Power*, 96–98.

13. Ibid., 98.

exaggerated folktale or myth. No healing miracle took place in the past and none can take place in the present. The cessationist evangelical would believe the incident as described, but would not understand its dynamics, as in stopping and resting before resuming intense prayer.

One reason why Mrs. Sanford's books from this period were so original and powerful was her freedom from denominational commitments. She had no obligations or ties with any university or seminary, and thus could not be brow beaten by what was presently politically or theologically correct at the time. She had many pharisaical critics, but she paid no attention to them, nor were they a threat to her standing as she had no seminary or church post. She had in fact created her own audience from her books, CFO and OSL events, and her many independent healing missions.

An example of her independence of mind was her speculation on extraterrestrial life. Mrs. Sanford had once seen UFOs from her home in Westborough, and felt that it was highly unlikely that God had made the immense cosmos without other spiritual-physical beings similar to ourselves. She speculated that the parable of the one lost sheep and the ninety-nine could be interpreted to mean that our planet was one lost planet out of a hundred that had to be rescued by the Good Shepherd.[14] Before recent discoveries that have proven that there are perhaps millions of Earth-like planets in our universe, such speculations were considered by most evangelicals as impious and somehow detracting of the centrality of Jesus in the created order.

Similarly, C.S. Lewis, the great Christian fiction writer and apologist, who also had an independent audience, felt the freedom to speculate in his novels on the characteristics and possibilities of extraterrestrial spiritual beings.[15] Back in 1945, when he was already well respected, Lewis addressed a group of Anglican priests and youth leaders and suggested the same interpretation as Agnes for the parable of the one lost sheep among the ninety-nine. That address, "Christian Apologetics," was not published until 1970.[16]

14. Sanford, "There Is Now," and also Sanford, *Healing Power*, 88, 99, 120, 135.

15. Lewis, *Space Trilogy*, (1975).

16. Lewis, *God in the Dock* (1970). The problem of coming to any conclusions about UFOs and extraterrestrial life is a difficult one. Here again the masterful methodology of James' *Religious Experiences* is most valuable. One lines up the data from as many observations as possible, from the least credible to the most reliable, and comes to limited conclusions based on what is most reliable. On this see Hynek, "UFO

Behold Your God: The Capstone of Mrs. Sanford's Charismatic Theology

The most important work of this period, *Behold Your God*, came after two novels, which Mrs. Sanford termed teaching parables, and several children's works. The first novel was written immediately after she was fired as a Gray Lady, called *Oh Watchman!* It will not rank among the great works of Christian literature. In fact, most of her novels would probably not have been published had it not been for her success with *The Healing Light* and the ready-made audience that produced. Her second novel, *Lost Shepherd*, was strengthened by the fact that it contains a fictionalized account of the travail prayer and Eucharist technique used to heal Harry Goldsmith of his destructive memories. Of her novels, the best one is *The Second Mrs. Wu*, but it is really an autobiography of her childhood experiences in China. The story line, which includes her father's real journey out of cessationism, is more interesting than the fictional plots of her other novels.

Perhaps of more lasting value are the two children's works she wrote in this period, *Let's Believe* and *A Pasture for Peterkin*. Both are also teaching parables that weave instructions on prayer and faith into the story line. Both were effective and entertaining for children. Agnes was a great children's storyteller by nature. When her grandchildren visited she would hold them enthralled with her ad-lib stories of local animals such as "Mr. Raccoon."[17]

Mrs. Sanford's brother, Edgar, liked her novels well enough but wanted something more theologically meaty and asked her to write a commentary on the creeds. This struck Agnes as a word from the Lord and she began her work *Behold Your God*. It ended up more as a Spirit-filled commentary to *The Healing Light*, with references to the creeds appearing almost by accident.

Behold Your God is not recognizable as a work of formal theology because it has none of the scholarly paraphernalia of academic scholarship such as an index or bibliography. It did not concur with the *agenda* of contemporary theology, such as higher criticism, or the importance of social action. Further, like all her writings, it is simple in its language and extremely humble. Mrs. Sanford admits, for example, to be totally

Phenomenon," which essentially executes James' methodology.

17. Related to this author in a telephone conversation with Mrs. Sanford's son, Ted Sanford, on May 12, 2014.

befuddled by the theological discussions of the Holy Spirit that deal with the *filioque* debate that separated Christendom in the eleventh century.[18] Yet her understanding of the Holy Spirit's role in human life, as well as her understanding of the spirit of humankind, were both pioneering and profound.

By the time Mrs. Sanford wrote *Behold Your God* she had been in contact with many forms of spiritual healing, from spiritualist, metaphysical, and Christian Science, to the healing power experienced by her woman's Bible study/healing group during the war, to the renewed powers given her in the baptism of the Holy Spirit. She was, therefore, in a position to evaluate these forms of healing, both biblically and experientially.

In her understanding, spiritual healing can come at any one of three levels, which she related to the doctrine of the Trinity.[19] At the first level of God's healing power, any person who believes in God and who prays to God for healing (and believed that healing was possible) can mediate some healing energy. This is true whether a person is a Christian or not. This position, which some Christians currently deny as impious, is in fact the biblical position. The healings in the Old Testament all took place not because of faith in Jesus Christ but because of faith in *God* as healer (Exod 15:26; Ps 103:3; 147:3). Agnes saw the contemporary equivalent of Old Testament healing in her acquaintances in Christian Science and the metaphysical movement. Often these persons had a strong faith in God, though often they saw nothing uniquely divine in the person of Jesus, and thus were not Christians.

However, once a person believes in the divinity of Jesus, the person is elevated into a position of potential healing power that is double that of the Old Testament position. The third and highest level of healing is reached when a believing Christian accepts the person and baptism of the Holy Spirit and receives the gift of healing. Mrs. Sanford's insight makes clear the sad situation of the contemporary world: that metaphysical

18. The debate on the *filioque* centered on whether the Holy Spirit proceeds *only* from the Father or from the Father *and* the Son. John 15:26 indicates that the procession out of Father and Son is correct, as insisted by the Western Church. However, the Roman Catholic Church, without consulting the Eastern Orthodox churches, added to the Nicene Creed the phrase that the Spirit proceeds out of the Father *and* the Son. This deeply offended Eastern Orthodox churchmen, who had other grievances against the Roman Church. This dispute resulted only in mutual rancor and excommunications, which culminated in the final separation between Roman Catholicism and Eastern Orthodoxy.

19. Sanford, *Behold Your God*, 136–37.

believers can be powerful spiritual healers, while born-again Christians are under the beguilement of cessationism and cannot be channels of God's healing power because they have a *negative faith* about healing. Thus, for instance, Harry Goldsmith, as a Jew, was able to pray effectively for the healing of himself and others in his hospital ward well before he became a Christian, but the pious Christian nurse who dismissed Agnes for the witchcraft of healing had no spiritual healing power whatever because she did not believe in it. This understanding is more biblically accurate than what is often taught in many Pentecostal or charismatic churches today, where all spiritual healing is either Christian or demonic (as in spiritualists) in origin, and there is no possibility of valid spiritual healing from a non-Christian.

This concept of levels of healing power was broadened by Mrs. Sanford to explain the relationship between the powers of the soul, the psychic powers, and the powers of the human spirit. Like the traditional Catholic doctrine that grace perfects nature, Mrs. Sanford believed that the powers of the soul were God-created and therefore good. These psychic powers can legitimately be studied in the science of parapsychology, although Agnes was aware of the dangers of studying in this area without spiritual protection or discernment.[20] Again, a born-again believer who is open to spiritual phenomenon will find his natural psychic powers increased to a gift of spiritual perception. Agnes had seen this in the life of Harry Goldsmith as he transitioned from an agnostic Jew to a fully Spirit-empowered Christian.

> The Holy Spirit does not do violence to our natures, but only increases and develops in us gifts that are already potential to our natures. Some people have natural-born spiritual sensitivity, and if they use them only in the realm of meditation and spiritual living, avoiding séances, Ouija boards and automatic writing, this gift can be greatly used in God's service.[21]

This is basically a Roman Catholic understanding of psychic abilities that Catholics call the preternatural abilities of the soul. This is in opposition to the normative evangelical understanding that anyone who is psychic is practicing witchcraft. Again, biblically this is nonsense. Note for instance the God inspired precognitive (prophetic) dreams all through the story of Joseph and his brothers in Genesis 37–41. Again,

20. Ibid., 143–44.
21. Ibid., 146.

take for example the story in 1 Samuel 9:5–9, where the young man Saul went out to look for his father's donkeys.

> When they reached the district of Zuph Saul said to the servant who was with him, "Come, let's go back, or my father will stop thinking about the donkeys and start worrying about us." But the servant replied, "Look, in this town there is a man of God, he is highly respected, and everything he says comes true. Let's go there now. Perhaps he will tell us what way to take." Saul said to his servant, "If we go, what can we give the man? The food in our sacks is gone. We have no gift to take to the man of God. What do we have?" The servant answered him again. "Look," he said, "I have a quarter of a shekel of silver. I will give it to the man of God so that he will tell us what way to take." (Formerly in Israel, if someone went to inquire of God, they would say, "Come, let us go to the seer," because the prophet of today used to be called a seer.)

The "man of God" was the prophet Samuel. But notice the expectancy of the servant that Samuel could divine where the donkeys were, which Samuel did in fact. The man of God seemed to have a reputation for this sort of thing, and also a tradition to be paid for it. Today it would be called a psychic reading by evangelicals, and categorized as witchcraft. But to our main point: Agnes' siding with the traditional Catholic understanding on this issue was biblically correct but theologically contentious, as most evangelicals and Pentecostal/charismatic believers held to the evangelical (Calvinist) view.[22]

Similarly, Mrs. Sanford understood the practice of positive thinking and visualization as a first level of prayer power. It is God-given and good, and available to any believer in God, however nebulous his or her understanding of God (as in the confusion of Christian Science). The powers of visualization and positive thinking are increased when a person becomes a believer and adds the name of Jesus to his or her prayer visualizations (as in her experience in CNP). Agnes looked at the biblical

22. One of the standard works for missionaries to read is Richardson's *Eternity* (1981). Richardson was a missionary with much experience, and this work includes accounts of various shamans who see into the psychic realm and practice appeasement of demons as part of their work. When they convert to Christianity they do not lose their ability to see into the spirit realms, i.e., being "psychic," but rather use this gift to become excellent exorcists and prayer intercessors. In this work Richardson, an evangelical, unintentionally affirms the Catholic view of the preternatural gifts (and Agnes Sanford's) and verifies it as more accurate than the anti-supernaturalism of Calvinist-based theologies.

evidence and saw a pattern that explains this. Jesus first taught *faith*, i.e., positive thinking, to his disciples and later in his ministry revealed his divine nature.[23] Again, this takes into account the sad reality that she had experienced: positive-thinking non-Christians often had more prayer power than pious Christians afflicted with cessationism.

This brings us to the most controversial points of *Behold Your God*, and indeed of all of Mrs. Sanford's theology: her belief in the pre-exis-tence of the human spirit, that is, the belief that the spirit of a person exists before it is called into specific incarnation on earth. This is *not* reincarnation, which states that the spirit has multiple incarnations on earth. In fact the idea of the pre-existent spirit is strongly hinted at in the Bible in both the Old and New Testaments, for example Jeremiah 1:4–5:

> The word of the LORD came to me, saying,
> "Before I formed you in the womb I knew you,
> before you were born I set you apart;
> I appointed you as a prophet to the nations."

Ephesians 1:3-4 echoes this:

> Praise be to the God and Father of our Lord Jesus Christ, who has blessed us in the heavenly realms with every spiritual bless-ing in Christ. For he chose us in him before the creation of the world to be holy and blameless in his sight.[24]

The idea seemed far out principally because it had been ruled off the theological agenda as heresy in the fifth century. At that time the Byz-antine Emperor Justinian I, who fancied himself as a great theologian, pushed through a condemnation of the concept of pre-existence in a council of dubious validity.[25] His prejudice became part of the accepted theological agenda of the medieval church and went unchallenged even during the Reformation period.

---

23. Sanford, *Behold Your God*, 35–36.

24. We should also note 2 Thess 2:13, as well as Wisdom of Solomon 8:19-20, in the Catholic canon of Scripture. One commentator I saw years ago explained all this to mean we existed as a dream in God's mind before incarnating.

25. On the falsity of the accusations against Origen, a brilliant early theologian who believed in the pre-existence of the spirit, and on the duplicity of the Fifth Coun-cil, see Farrar, *Mercy and Judgment*, chapter 12. See also Gerostergios, "Religious Policy." Philip Jenkins also takes a dim view of this council in his masterful study *Jesus Wars*, 251.

Mrs. Sanford believed that the human spirit, because it was in some form of communication with God before its earthly incarnation, has an inherent knowledge of the moral law and can tell good from evil. According to Agnes, the spirit is the seat of humanity's conscience, and communicates with the conscious mind through feelings of joy or sadness according to the moral situation. It is also the job of the spirit to remind the conscious mind of its spiritual obligations (recall that when Mrs. Sanford was attempting to be a good housewife she fell into depression). Thus, monitoring one's sense of joy or sorrow is an important part of the spiritual life. Mrs. Sanford believed that it is only when a person is baptized in the Holy Spirit that the human spirit is given the power to carry out its instinctive judgments.[26]

In spite of the book's theological originality and importance, it did not sell well. Like *The Healing Light* it was published by Clark's Macalester Press, which automatically limited its distribution. The fact that *Behold Your God* was not primarily a how-to book but rather a "why" book also limited its sales. Thankfully, it was republished in a paperback and has since sold steadily, if slowly. Its influence has always been constant, even among the charismatic leaders who do not like some of the more unconventional elements of Mrs. Sanford's theology.[27]

The Schools of Pastoral Care[28]

One of the most important achievements of the Sanfords in their joint ministry was the founding of the School of Pastoral Care. Both Ted and Agnes were burdened by the faith-destroying way in which biblical studies and pastoral direction were presented in the major seminaries. Then, just as now, this often resulted in pastors who knew little of effective prayer and nothing of healing or exorcism. Agnes was especially

26. Sanford, *Behold Your God*, 63–66.

27. For example, one can spot her influence in Dennis and Rita Bennett's *Trinity of Man* (1979), which elaborates Mrs. Sanford's attempt to define the separation of soul and spirit. See also Agnes Sanford's taped talk from the 1960s, "Trinity of Man."

28. The chief sources for this section are: the MA thesis by Rev. Francis B. Baltz, "Agnes Sanford," chapter 3, "The School of Pastoral Care"; the author's taped interview of Dr. J. Howard Rhys, seminary professor at the University of the South, Sewanee, Tennessee, and formerly national director of the School of Pastoral Care, on August 13, 1983; and Dr. Rhys' brief article "School of Pastoral Care." See also Sanford's "How to Receive."

saddened by the demoralized state of seminarians that her son John frequently brought home for a few days' holiday.[29] Her special prayer for the
redemption of the mainline seminaries was published in her devotional
book *Twice Seven Words*:

> May your light enter anew into the church, awakening therein
> faith, hope, joy, and love. We lift up before you the seminaries
> where young ministers are trained to do your work. Drive out of
> them, oh Lord, the spirit of materialism and false teaching, even
> as you drove the money changers out of the temple of Jerusalem.
> Let these modern money changers be shaken and awakened by
> a rush of your active power, Lord Jesus...Let your ministers go
> forth in joy and power to save and to heal, proclaiming to all the
> kingdom of heaven has indeed come nigh![30]

The Sanfords wanted a place where pastors, medical professionals,
and seminarians could be taught the spiritual dimensions of healing and
integrate these skills in their ministries. Although Mrs. Sanford loved
ministering at the CFO, OSL, and church healing missions, she knew
that these were inadequate for training ministers. The CFO camps, which
were generally led by laypersons, attracted only a small percentage of
ministers or medical professionals. In none of these missions was there a
screening process, so that attendees sometimes included those who were
neurotic or severely disturbed and incapable of any real learning. Also,
the size of these missions tended to be too large to allow for individual
ministry, instruction, and counseling.

To address these shortcomings the Sanfords founded the School of
Pastoral Care. It was based out of their home in Westborough, with Ted
as its first director and chief administrator. The physical facilities were
provided by the Episcopal diocese of Western Massachusetts, and the first
sessions met at Laselle House, the diocesan retreat center. The inaugural
school took place October 10–14, 1955. The audience was limited in
number and screened to include only pastors, medical professionals, and
seminarians. The program stressed the basics of effective prayer, praying for physical healing, healing of memories, and deliverance/exorcism.
One of the instructors would be a physician or nurse, the other a priest

---

29. John Sanford had a successful career as Jungian psychologist and published
many books from a Jungian-Christian viewpoint, including several on healing. I do
not agree that his Jungian viewpoint was a positive development in Christian theology.
Among John's major works see his *Healing and Wholeness* and *Dreams and Healing*.

30. Sanford, *Twice Seven Words* (1971), 93.

or pastor, and the third a lay Bible teacher (Agnes). The ideal program of the schools was to have a week-long session, with three instructors and no more than forty participants.

The heart of the program was *practice in prayer*. To this end, midday was reserved for a prayer clinic in which all participants would group around one person and pray for that person's needs. There would also be time for the participants to be individually ministered to by the instructors. In the first years Ted and Agnes always ministered together at the schools, with different physicians serving as the third instructor. Instruction on the baptism and gifts of the Holy Spirit was also part of the overall teachings. Many of the participants first experienced the Holy Spirit through the schools. In the years before the Charismatic Renewal broke out (1960), several hundred pastors and religious leaders were prepared for it by their experiences at the schools.

By the early 1970s the schools were at their peak, with many persons who were touched by the Charismatic Renewal wishing to be further trained into the healing ministry clamoring to gain entrance. The presence of the Holy Spirit was especially strong in many of these schools. Dr. Harry Goldsmith, who often co-taught at the schools with Mrs. Sanford in the 1970s, recalls that there was not only a multitude of physical and inner healings at these events, but even highly unusual miracles. In one school the Communion wafers were instantly multiplied when they were about to run out, and in another, when the Holy Spirit was invoked, the whole building shook and a wind was heard, just as in Acts 2.[31]

Mrs. Sanford was forced to prioritize and insisted that pastors be given priority even over the most earnest laypersons. In the following letter to Dr. Howard Rhys, professor of New Testament studies at the University of the South, who was then acting as administrator to the schools, she referred to the upcoming school at the Kanuga Episcopal retreat center in North Carolina.

> Dear Howard,
>
> Thank you for the cheques toward travel. That "does it" very nicely. As to Kanuga Nov. 13–17 in 1972—I'll relent and let you have sixty people if you do not have more women than men. The ministers just can't stand that. "I thought this was a clergy conference!" one of them said to me in a Northern Calif. SPC,

---

31. Interview of Harry Goldsmith in April 1983.

"Here are all these women! I see them at CFOs—every time I turn around I see them and here they are again!"[32]

With the success of the SPC Mrs. Sanford was forced to decrease her appearances at CFO and other church missions. We get a glimpse of her hectic schedule in another letter she wrote to Dr. Rhys:

Dear Howard,

My last trip was badly planned (by me.) I thought I could rest by visiting between missions but I found that was impossible. And I guess you saw that by the time the SPC came I was over-tired. Anyway, I went to work and got shingles when I got home. And that is rather bad. Brought on my high blood pressure and over-work etc. . . . I am planning to take the year 1973 as a sabbatical year. As one of my minister friends said it is more customary to have a sabbatical every seven years than every seventy. At least I'll do no lecturing from January to September 1. In the fall I may go to England and Sweden.

I'd also like to lighten my schedule some next year. How would it be to ask Harry [Goldsmith] to come with me to Florida and [have him] skip Mississippi or get someone else to take my place? I'd really like to do this. I feel it would be well to work in some more women to take my place for the thing needs a woman to lighten it and sort of relieve the professional burden. Edith [Drury] is one but she would not be accepted everywhere—perhaps not anywhere except in the South which she adores! Very odd! A friend yesterday suggested my daughter Mrs. Miles Clark. She would be ideal. She began doing this work at fourteen and though interrupted by a difficult marriage and four adopted children, still is wonderful at healing both physical and mental and also at lecturing.

. . . How is Peggy? Give her my love and tell her I do want to be in Florida in February especially to see her. But I want to work with Harry. That's of major importance for the Lord still has things for him to do that he hasn't done yet, His wife has just given birth to a defective baby who died so Harry still needs a bit of lift too.

If you could get Harry for Florida this winter we could work out all the rest when I come.

Affectionately,

Agnes[33]

32. Letter from Agnes Sanford to Howard Rhys, dated August 6, 1971. Copy in author's possession.

33. Letter from Agnes Sanford to D. Howard Rhys, dated November 8, 1971. Copy

Not everything went well in the schools. Jungian influence was brought in by Agnes' friend and pastor Fr. Morton Kelsey. He unfortunately turned heavily towards Jung after his seminal and excellent works on healing and dreams.[34] Fr. Kelsey began introducing Jungian concepts into the schools, which inadvertently camouflaged the reality of the demonic under the heading of Jungian archetypes. Leanne Payne, whom Agnes invited as an instructor in the schools as the lay participant and Bible teacher, immediately sensed the danger in Kelsey's Jungian-Christian mix. She had a joint School of Pastoral Care with Kelsey in 1977, which was filled with contention. She warned Agnes, and Agnes was ultimately persuaded by her and the Rev. John Sandford to stop the Jungian influence.[35] In fact, two years before her death Mrs. Sanford and Dr. Howard Rhys reorganized the schools and eliminated the pro-Jungian instructors.[36] Mrs. Payne, whose inner healing ministry focused on healing homosexuals out of their lifestyles, went on to found her own version of the Schools of Pastoral Care, called Pastoral Care Ministries.[37]

Agnes' Schools of Pastoral Care were important in the spiritual formation of the first generation of charismatic clergymen, and especially influential among Canadian ministers, as the Schools had a heavy presence in that country. However, after both Ted and Agnes died the schools declined in vitality and impact. Like so many renewal movements, they accomplished their tasks and then faded. It is no longer scandalous or unusual for Christian doctors and nurses to incorporate healing prayer into their practices, such as praying before an operation, or conducting a prayer huddle before the nursing shift begins. But that was unheard of in the 1950s. In 2007 the Schools of Pastoral Care were enfolded into the OSL in Canada and ceased being an independent entity.

in author's possession.

34. Fr. Morton T. Kelsey (1917–2001), an Episcopal priest, served as rector at St. Luke's in Monrovia, California, from 1959 to 1969. This was the parish where Agnes worshiped in her later years. He then served as professor of theology at Notre Dame University. He was a prolific writer and pioneer of the healing ministry. Among his most important works are *Dreams* and *Healing and Christianity*. His work was pioneering and original, and of much value for today's discerning reader. Unfortunately, he was beguiled by Jungian psychology, which was fashionable in the 1960s and 1970s. Had he not taken this tract he might have been the most important charismatic theologian of his generation.

35. See Leanne Payne's excellent critique of Jungian thought in two of her books: the appendix in *Real Presence* and chapter 14 in *Healing Presence*.

36. Payne, *Heaven's Calling*, 243–47.

37. Leann Payne's classics on healing homosexuality are *Broken Image* and *Healing the Homosexual*.

19

First Theologian of Nature Miracles

THE REV. TED SANFORD died on November 6, 1960. He had been ill for some time, but the prayers of his congregation upheld his life to the point that both he and Agnes discerned that he was overdue to leave the earth. A week before he died he had the following dream, which was written down by his son John.

> In the dream he awakened in his Westboro [sic] living room. But then the room changed and he was back in his room in the old house in Bellows Falls where he was a child. Again the room changed: to Hardwick, Conn., then to Changshu. China, then to Concordville, then to Moorestown, N.J, and finally back to Westboro [sic]. In each scene Mother was present. In China she was there as a young woman. She changed with each room in accordance with her years, but always appeared somehow "the same." . . . Finally back in Westboro [sic], he sees himself lying on the couch. Dr. Reiman is in the room and Mother is descending the stairway. Dr. Reiman says, "Oh, he's gone." Then (the others fade in the dream) my Father's attention is drawn to the clock on the mantelpiece: the hands are moving, then they stop! As the hands stop a window of light opens behind the clock and a bright light shines in the room. He walks out on the path of light and disappears.[1]

Agnes suppressed her grief though her travels for a while, but it erupted two years later at a School of Pastoral Care. Thankfully, the Rev. John Sandford, her disciple and spiritual son, was able to minister to her

---

1. From an undated account of the incident by the Rev. John Sanford. Copy in author's possession.

in prayer a healing for her deep grief. In a letter to her old congregation in Moorestown, Agnes explained how she dealt with Ted's death:

> Ted and I knew that he would not be here long and our plans were made. I was to go ahead with the work and did so, indeed I added to those missions planned quite a few others, thinking it would be good to be occupied. There was a trip to New Zealand and Australia which I was going to cancel if Ted had lived, but which instead I lengthened. It proved to be a life-saver. . . . In New Zealand, the most beautiful and fascinating country I ever saw, I had one mission in Christ Church in the South island. In the North Island I had two missions, also a week of rest and sight-seeing.
>
> In Sydney, the first thing was the School of Pastoral Care, so-called but very different from ours here. It was held in the Cathedral and included eighty ministers and only me for a leader. And the need for personal interviews was terrific so that I worked from 8:30 A.M until 11 P.M, except for a break at noon. By the end of the week I was exhausted.[2]

In 1965, at age sixty-eight, Agnes moved to California in response to the Lord's prompting. She chose Monrovia (just north of LA) to be close to her children and another one of her disciples, the Rev. Morton Kelsey, all of whom had settled near there. Her house gave her a beautiful view of the mountains and was surrounded by well-planted and carefully tended beds of flower. In her new home she continued her writing, teaching, and speaking career and wrote some of her most important books, including her autobiography, *Sealed Orders*.

In Monrovia she fully developed what might be called her nature ministry, which involved praying for the created order such as plants and the earth itself. The dominion that humankind should have over nature was demonstrated in Jesus' stilling of the storm on the Sea of Galilee and his pronouncement on the fig tree (Matt 21:19–20). This aspect of Jesus' ministry was not recorded in the Book of Acts and was found only occasionally in Christian literature. For instance, Gregory of Pontus (213–270), the "Wonder-Worker," had a major healing gift and miracle ministry. Witnesses reported that he commanded by prayer a large boulder to be removed from an inconvenient spot as workmen were digging

---

2. Letter printed in *Trinity Church Chimes* (newsletter of Trinity Episcopal Church, Moorestown), January 21, 1962.

a foundation for a new church.[3] Nature miracles were also recorded in accounts of several Celtic missionaries who calmed storms and changed the direction of the winds to confound their Druid opposition.[4] Most Christians, influenced by cessationism and its assumptions, simple write off nature miracles as once-only events by Jesus, in spite of the fact that Jesus proclaimed a future of greater works than his own for his disciples (John 14:12).

That nature participates in worship of its Creator is an obvious theme of Scripture, but it is rarely understood or preached by contemporary Christians. The prophet Isaiah gave us a glimpse of nature and man worshiping together:

> You will go out in joy
> and be led forth in peace;
> the mountains and hills
> will burst into song before you,
> and all the trees of the field
> will clap their hands. (55:12)

A few notable Christians (and most certainly countless unknown ones) have entered into cooperation and ministry with nature, such as St. Francis of Assisi. George Washington Carver, the famous African-American botanist, prayed over and talked to his plants. This was considered eccentric, mystical, and unscientific, in spite of the fact that he accomplished tremendous discoveries with limited and improvised scientific equipment.[5] Like so many things, this biblical insight of communication between plants and humans, perhaps better termed our God-given dominion over the plant kingdom, was brought to popular attention with Peter Tompkins' bestselling *secular* book *The Secret Life of Plants* (1973). When this work came out many Christians promptly concluded that such unusual activity must be occultism—another sad misunderstanding.

In any case, Mrs. Sanford had a Washington Carver-like understanding of and communications with plants. A story related by Mrs. Barbara Schlemon, a CFO speaker and noted inner healing minister, tells of an incident in Agnes' Monrovia home. Agnes was scheduled to give

---

3. Telfer, "Cultus of St. Gregory." The article is written from a liberal and unbelieving perspective, but the original sources are cited.

4. Adamnan. *Life of Columba*, 2.11.

5. Glenn Clark had the insight and discernment to see there was a great spiritual truth in Carver's interaction with plants; see Clark, *Man Who Talks*.

a healing mission in a nearby town, and when Barbara came to drive her there she found Agnes amidst a circle of her house plants with arms upraised and deeply in prayer. She asked Agnes what she was doing, and Agnes said, "I'm praising the Lord with my prayer group, and they are doing a better job!"[6] Agnes also has great spiritual rapport with animals. She would gently command wasps away from her home, and they would leave. At her home in Monrovia she had a special friend in "Jimmy," a blue jay who would come to her hand every day.[7]

Agnes' prophetic work on the topic of nature ministry was *Creation Waits* (1978), her last book. The title comes from the passage in Romans in which Paul exclaims:

> The creation waits in eager expectation for the sons of God to be revealed. For the creation was subjected to frustration, not by its own choice, but by the will of the one who subjected it, in hope that the creation itself will be liberated from its bondage to decay and brought into the glorious freedom of the children of God. (8:19–21)

In Agnes' view, the secret to prayer power in regards to plants and the lower created order is standing in the authority of the Christian:

> It is far more effective to talk directly to sea or sky, wind or storm, than simply to ask God to do this or that. We are God's agents upon this earth. When praying for people we ask in His name and by His power, because we so often lack the necessary understanding of the people for whom we pray. In praying for nature, however, it is more effective to speak directly to wind or storm or tempest. That, after all is the way Jesus stilled the storm. "Peace, be still!"[8]

Agnes developed a confidence and authority in this nature ministry not seen even among the famous saints of the Lord. She recounts a bout she had with a threatening wildfire near her home in Monrovia:

> One night I awoke after midnight and went out to my upper balcony where I could smell the smoke, and already knew from the papers that the winds were blowing directly towards me. So I called aloud to the wind, muting my voice just a little lest I wake my neighbors: "Hear me, wind!" I said, holding out my hand in

---

6. Interview of Mrs. Barbara Schlemon on May 20, 1984.

7. San, *Prayers of Faith*, 110.

8. Ibid., 16.

its general direction. "You are to swing around now and blow from the west, bring in mist and rain from the sea. Come now! It may take you a little while to do so, but by morning let it be accomplished! . . . In the name of the Lord Jesus Christ I give you this order, and I rejoice, believing it will be so!"[9]

A day later the wind unexpectedly changed direction, and rain came in from the Pacific Ocean.

But in fact Agnes was called by the Lord to pray against something more far-reaching than wildfires. It began while she was still living in Westborough, Massachusetts. She felt a strong leading that she had to pray for *some* part of the earth.

> "Lord, where is it?" I asked, and listened. There came to my mind the northwestern part of the United States, and it seemed that some calamity threatened that region.
>
> "May I pray that whatever is to happen may be averted?" I asked, and listening heard a negative response . . .
>
> "May I pray for it to be minimized?" I asked and quite distinctly I heard, "Yes."
>
> So for three days I prayed for the Northwest, for the land and area itself, and when not in active prayer I held it as an undercurrent to other thoughts. And then there came the earthquake in the state of Washington which just missed being a really destructive one. And my burden was lifted . . .[10]

The Lord called her to pray for the same intention in California. Agnes' home in Monrovia was right along the San Andreas Fault

> I began to pray, with particular emphasis on the section of this fault in southern California, that it might accomplish its work by relieving the tension in the earth's crust quietly, with sufficient small tremors, but without destructive earthquakes.[11]

In fact, in the years that she lived in Californian there were no serious earthquakes on that fault line.

This nature ministry has been slowly coming into acceptance with charismatic and Pentecostal groups. Pat Robinson, the famous televangelist, received much publicity for praying against a hurricane that was

9. Ibid., 17.

10. Ibid., 3. The earthquake she cites occurred on April 29, 1965, and had a magnitude of 6.5. It killed several persons and caused over $12 million in damage.

11. Ibid., 2.

threatening the Christian Broadcasting Network complex at Virginia Beach—and he was much ridiculed for it in spite of the fact that the hurricane veered off and did not hit Virginia Beach.

After Hurricanes Katrina and Rita devastated New Orleans and other parts of the Gulf Coast in 2005, several Pentecostal/charismatic churches in Florida began praying consistently against incoming hurricanes for the next season. Significantly, in spite of dire predictions for the 2006 season, not a single hurricane has touched the Southern seaboard since. As I write these words, the national news has reported a new series of devastating tornadoes in the Midwest. It happens every year. This cries out for the churches in that area to learn the prayer of command over nature and direct the tornadoes to non-populated areas. Losing a hundred acres of corn is certainly less costly than losing a hundred homes. This may be among the last prayer frontiers that the church in the twenty-first century needs to recover, and again it was Agnes who led the way.[12]

Mrs. Sanford and the Charismatic Renewal

Mrs. Sanford had been baptized in the Holy Spirit almost a decade before the Charismatic Renewal broke out. Her experience with the gifts of the Holy Spirit had shown her that Prof. Glenn Clark was mistaken and the Pentecostals were right. The gifts, especially tongues, do not *take* energy away from the workings of the fruits of the Spirit; rather they re-energize the person and enable a greater manifestation of the fruits. However, like Prof. Clark, she cautioned those who received the baptism to be prudent in both public manifestations of the gifts and in talking about them. Certainly, before the Charismatic Renewal became well established, practicing the gifts publicly often brought nothing but ridicule and ostracism from other Christians. Agnes also felt that public manifestations of the gifts of the Spirit would make a person especially susceptible to demonic attack. She believed this is why Jesus counseled many of those he healed to silence.

Mrs. Sanford was suspicious of the Charismatic Renewal during its early years. She was particularly leery of the value that the new charismatics placed on the gifts of tongues, especially the doctrine, derived from traditional Pentecostals, that this gift is an *indispensable* sign of

---

12. I discuss this ministry with special applications to tornadoes in my blog post "Calming Tornadoes?"

having the baptism of the Holy Spirit.[13] She saw that forcing the gift of tongues in order to prove that one had the Holy Spirit often produced nothing more than subconscious babble, an opinion often mentioned among charismatics but rarely written about.[14]

Her book on the gifts of the Spirit, *The Healing Gifts of the Spirit*, was written in the early years of the Charismatic Renewal, and in it she warned her readers that receiving the baptism of the Holy Spirit is strong medicine, and that a person who has a weak ego or a poorly disciplined Christian life may have serious problems handling the energies of the Spirit.[15] Just like Prof. Clark, she exhorted newly Spirit-filled charismatics to have prudence and patience, and to infiltrate their old churches with the power of the Holy Spirit rather than confront the congregation. She cited her church in Moorestown as an example of how the gifts of the Holy Spirit were introduced into common usage through the patience and prayers of her Bible study/healing group.[16]

Mrs. Sanford was particularly concerned about the damage to the charismatic movement caused by inexperienced and imprudent ministries of exorcism. For a period in the 1960s there circulated a teaching among charismatics that any personality fault or sin is due to a demonic spirit. Thus people were being delivered from "spirits" of smoking, overeating, and whatnot. Agnes was insistent that exorcism is the ministry of last recourse, not for immediate use as was the fashion. She had personally witnessed much damage done to persons who were put through charismatic exorcism rituals when in fact they needed counseling or inner healing.[17]

13. Sanford, "Illumination."

14. Sanford, *Creation Waits*, 63-64. In this issue Mrs. Sanford was again prophetic and went against the theological stream. Recent studies have indicated that both traditional Pentecostals and charismatics practice the gift of tongues much less than their official doctrines suggest, and that healing and deliverance is really the prime gift manifested in Spirit-filled churches. See Crosby, "New Kind." One of my Catholic friends from the first charismatic prayer group I belonged to, back in the 1970s, related to me how in his first visit to a FGBMFI meeting he asked for the baptism of the Spirit. The encircling brothers laid hands on him and he felt a surge of the Spirit, but did not speak in tongues. They insisted that *something* come out of his mouth. He accommodated them by saying a few words in Greek that he had learned in college, and everybody was happy.

15. Sanford, *Healing Gifts*, 14.

16. Ibid., 70–79.

17. Ibid., 144. See also the very excellent teaching done in the 1980s examining the early charismatic fashion of healing-by-exorcism by Agnes' disciple, John Sandford,

Her suspicion of the new charismatics faded with time. From the vantage point of her home in Monrovia, California, she learned to appreciate the "Jesus People," those most exuberant hippy children of the Charismatic Renewal.[18] Through the mid-1960s and 1970s, when the charismatic movement exploded in the American scene, Agnes continued her ministry engagements at the CFOs, OSLs, church healing missions, and the Schools of Pastoral Care.

Just how much Agnes' ministry and writings helped bring about the Charismatic Renewal is impossible to quantify. She personally spoke to thousands about the baptism of the Holy Spirit in the decade before the renewal broke out. She informed and touched many more through her books. Her books were especially influential in the Episcopal and Roman Catholic wings of the renewal.

None of this should be taken to mean that Mrs. Sanford was the only person of the Charismatic Renewal that had a mature theology of the Holy Spirit and gifts of the Spirit. In fact the Charismatic Renewal was blessed from the very beginning with many outstanding leaders who had excellent theological training and insight. Such persons as Dr. Howard Ervin, who received his degree from Princeton Theological Seminary and became a professor at Oral Roberts University, brought much wisdom and maturity to the renewal. So did Oxford-trained Derek Prince, who did so much to teach the charismatic community about deliverance and exorcism.[19] When the Charismatic Renewal broke out among the Catholics in 1967 there immediately arose a group of outstanding lay and clergy Catholic theologians, such as Fr. Francis MacNutt and Dr. Killian McDonnell and others, who did impressive work in establishing a solid theology of renewal.

Into the Glory

Agnes slid into full retirement by the mid-1970s. In a circular letter she described her activities in what was to be the last year of her life.

"Sensible View."

18. See her portrayal of the Jesus People in her last novel, *Route 1*.

19. Mansfield, *Derek Prince*.

Dear Friends,

As many of you know, I am comfortably retired, living in my own home in the San Gabrial [sic] foothills, enjoying my family and friends, doing an occasional pastel (and selling one now and then), and feeling restful and relaxed after a fairly energetic life. When a plane flies overhead, or we start on a pleasure drive, I exclaim with delight that I no longer have to travel here and there, sleep in strange beds, and make the tremendous effort of lecturing and holding missions. I will never forget the hospitality and kindness of countless people during those years, but now I am luxuriously at home, with no backward looks. I thank the Lord that He fills me with expectancy of the future, in this life and the next.

Physically I am extremely well, and take a strenuous walk downhill and up most days. In September, 1980 a cataract was removed from my left eye, with lens implanted at the same time, which so improved my sight that I no longer wear glasses except for reading. I can see better to do my pictures and to enjoy the glories around me. We go frequently to the desert, mountains, and seashore. At the beach I go wading, and revel in my favorite outdoor lunch of hot dogs, onion rings, corn on the cob, and root bear. Flowers bloom in my garden the year round, in contrast to my childhood in China where one tiny violet blooming on a grave would send me into ecstasy, so barren was the landscape. My memory isn't much good these days, but my friends understand, and some see to it that any important message is received for me by someone else! My friend Edith Drury is still with me, and is a wonderful help . . .

With prayers and best wishes for all of you.[20]

Mrs. Sanford went to be with the Lord in February of 1982. She was full of vitality and curiosity to the very end. The night before she died she was given a revelation by the Lord that she was about to come to her heavenly home. She directed her secretary of many years, Edith Drury, to cancel a scheduled trip on a glider, and told her the reason. Edith expressed her joy that Agnes would be face to face with the Lord soon. Agnes responded, "Well, I really wanted you to say, I'll miss you, Agnes!"[21] She did not wake up the following morning. She was spared of living through the savage attacks on her person and ministry that broke out in 1985, but we will tell that story in a later chapter.

20. Circular letter to her friends, dated November 24, 1981. My copy is from the signed letter to Dr. Howard Rhys.

21. Interview of Barbara Shlemon on May 20. 1984.

20

Two Ministries Carry On

John and Paula Sandford: Spiritual Law Clarified and Inner Healing Explained Biblically

THE DEFINITIVE APOLOGETIC FOR inner healing and the description of biblical spiritual laws was done through the counseling and writing ministry of a husband-and-wife team, John and Paula Sandford.[1] Both were children of the Depression and learned habits of thrift and resilience from that traumatic period. John was born in 1929 and is still living; Paula was born in 1931 and died in 2012. John's mother, an Osage Indian, had been raised in the old exuberant tradition of Methodism which believed in the Bible and affirmed the absolute reality of its moral laws. During her first month of pregnancy with John, she had a dream in which she felt a thousand volts of electricity run through her body and heard God's voice announce, "Do not be afraid, for I am God. You are to have a son who will be my servant."[2] Unfortunately, by the time of his birth she had drifted into liberal Protestantism, and John was raised in that weakened

1. No biographical book has appeared on John and Paula Sandford, certainly one of the most influential couples of the Charismatic Renewal. A brief biographical article by Julia Loren, "Healers of Wounded Soul," was done for *Charisma*. John and Paula's writings give details of their lives with disarming candor. Some of the biographical information in this section is based on conversations the author had with the Sandfords at various CFOs in the 1980s, especially a long interview during the North Florida CFO in Leesburg, Florida, on January 18, 1986. Note that all of the Sandford's books are still in print and may be ordered from the Elijah House website, http://www.elijahhouse.org.

2. Loren, "Wounded Soul."

form of Christianity. Paula's household, on the other hand, was richly and devoutly evangelical.[3]

From his Indian heritage John inherited a special sensitivity towards both people and nature which is often given the pejorative term psychic. As a young man he was especially sensitive to the meaning of dreams, and on several occasions received prophetic, or precognitive, dreams of dreadful events. At the time he did not know that the function of prophetic dreams is to trigger intercessory prayers to lessen or cancel the impending event. Only after his baptism of the Holy Spirit and his encounter with Mrs. Sanford was he able to fully understand, interpret, and pray through these prophetic dreams. In fact, his later insights on the role of dreams in the Christian's life are among the best in Christian literature.[4]

John attended Drury College in Springfield, Missouri, where he met Paula. They fell in love and eloped. They both felt that the Lord had placed them together for his service. John did well at Drury and earned a scholarship to the renowned, and liberal, Chicago Theological Seminary. There he worked towards a Master of Divinity degree as he pastored a small church in Streator, Illinois. He also drove a taxi in Chicago to provide for his growing family. At seminary he accepted the predominant liberal theology and higher criticism perspective of his teachers and was well on his way to becoming yet another liberal pastor preaching social activism, situational morality, and very little gospel.

But the grace of God intervened.

During his practice preaching he attended a minister's breakfast meeting in Streator where he met Fr. Wilber Fogg, rector of the local Episcopal church. Fogg had attended a School of Pastoral Care and been baptized by the Holy Spirit, and was moving his congregation towards what became the Charismatic Renewal. He felt called to activate his Spirit-filled prayer group to pray for John, especially that he be shown the glory and the fullness of the Holy Spirit.

Within a few months of his ordination, John Sanford consciously and deliberately decided to reject liberal theology and to affirm the literal truth of the Bible. That decision was quickly blessed by God as John experienced the baptism of the Holy Spirit during prayer. He was confused by the experience and went to Fr. Fogg for advice. Fogg laughed and rejoiced

---

3. Sandford, *Wounded Spirit*, 19, 21.

4. Sandford, *Elijah Task*, chapter 12, "Dreams, the Sleep Language of God."

at this and was able to explain the biblical basis for his experience. John then quickly led Paula into the baptism of the Holy Spirit.

At the urging of Fr. Fogg, John attended one of Agnes Sanford's Schools of Pastoral Care in the summer of 1959. John was suffering from severe back pain and asked for prayer. Mrs. Sanford discerned that the root cause was a spiritual problem, specifically, his dysfunctional relationship with his mother. Although John had reconciled with his mother, deep hurts remained. Agnes ministered inner healing prayer and then laid hands on his back, and he was completely delivered of all pain and back problems.[5] This was John's first experience of inner healing, a topic that would occupy much of his ministry and writings. In a later session of that same SPC Agnes prayed for his anointing in ministry and prophesied over him. She sensed John's deep thirst for the things of the Lord and his keen intellect, and a close friendship developed between them.

John rapidly read through the Agnes Sanford's books and the charismatic books that were beginning to appear. Paula began ministering with John at his parish charge, putting into practice what they had learned from Agnes Sanford. They also were particularly influenced by Derek Prince's writings, whom they personally met, and by the writings of Watchman Nee. John was led in a prophetic dream to move to Council Grove, Kansas. There he and Paula pastored the Wallace United Church of Christ until 1973. They practiced and further developed what they had learned from Agnes Sanford on inner healing and deliverance, and the gifts of the Spirit. [6]

John was Mrs. Sanford's assistant as often as he could get away from his pastoral duties. He accompanied her at healing missions, CFO engagements, and as many as six Schools of Pastoral Care per year. At the beginning John's principal duty was as intercessor for her. While Agnes was speaking he would pray in tongues for her anointing. Within a short time John began to share some of the actual teaching tasks. His academic training and pastoral experiences as a Spirit-filled minister made him wonderfully qualified to assist Mrs. Sanford. By 1961, when he finished his MA in theology, he had become the lead minister of the schools.[7]

After Ted died in 1962, John also doubled as Agnes' chauffer, as she disliked driving and often got lost. He was careful to drive conservatively

5. Sandford, *Inner Man*, 4-5.

6. Sandford, *Elijah Task*, 177–78.

7. Interview of John and Paula Sandford on January 18, 1986.

and quite unlike a cab driver in order to please her.[8] On one occasion Mrs. Sanford had received several criticisms that the schools were run too loosely. Actually, they were structured to allow the Spirit maximum reign. But Agnes was determined that the next one would be more carefully managed, and instructed John and the other staff to be meticulously prepared and to keep to schedule.

John picked up Agnes at her home, but for the first time he got lost. When it was apparent that they were going to be late Agnes cried out, "The Devil take to one who first calls hold!" and John drove on like a crazed Chicago cab driver. In spite of that, they got there late, with Agnes' hair a mess, only to find that the venue had been changed because of a flash flood. Everything had to be improvised, and everything was off schedule. It turned out to be one of the most powerful schools ever held, as the Lord showed Agnes that he could move in the midst of chaos.[9]

In December of 1973, in response to the Lord's leading, John resigned from his very successful pastorate in Council Grove. He and Paula received direction to move to Coeur d'Alene, Idaho. There they did not seek a church, but set about writing a series on the inner healing ministry, starting with *The Transformation of the Inner Man*. They also began a counseling ministry that served the local churches and ultimately became Elijah House Ministries. There inner healing and deliverance and ministering under the anointing of the Holy Spirit were taught to ministers and laypersons alike. It became something like a residential School of Pastoral Care. Thousands of students and ministers have taken its courses, either at Elijah House or via its videos, and it continues to this day as an effective school of Spirit-filled ministry.[10]

Refining the Theology of Inner Healing

It was during his years with Agnes that John was forced to examine the biblical basis of inner healing, as he was constantly challenged on this. John carefully combed and elaborated what had been described by Mrs. Sanford. Recall that Agnes had originally cast the ministry of the healing

8. Others who regularly assisted Agnes at CFOs and other healing missions this decade included Tommy Tyson, a Methodist charismatic evangelist, and Fr. Francis MacNutt, a healing evangelist and theologian for the Catholic Church.

9. Sandford, "Blessedness of Brokenness," and an interview by the author on January, 18, 1986.

10. The website of Elijah House Ministries is http://www.elijahhouse.org.

of memories as a form of Eucharist intercession and burden bearing. John quickly found verification for this form of ministry in the New Testament, specifically Galatians 6:2; John 15:13–16; and Colossians 1:24.

At the same time, he recognized that the evangelical critique of intercession and burden bearing had some merit. Truly, one person cannot repent for the sins of another individual. John came to the understanding that the intercessor and burden bearer did not repent for the other person, but rather served as a channel for God's grace of repentance to come to the other. Similarly, as we pray for salvation of a friend or relative, that does not imply we are saving that person, but rather we are serving as vehicles for God's saving graces. Ultimately every person must receive his or her own salvation, and repent of his or her own sins. But intercessors are called by the Spirit to stand in the gap while the person is weak and not even aware of their spiritual needs.[11]

The Sandfords' understanding of Jesus' burden bearing accepted Emmet Fox's theory of Jesus' suffering at Gethsemane (see chapter 17). But the Lord showed John another section of Scripture that was especially important in burden bearing:

> Therefore, there is now no condemnation for those who are in Christ Jesus, because through Christ Jesus the law of the Spirit who gives life has set you free from the law of sin and death. For what the law was powerless to do because it was weakened by the flesh, God did by sending his own Son in the likeness of sinful flesh to be a sin offering. And so he condemned sin in the flesh, in order that the righteous requirement of the law might be fully met in us, who do not live according to the flesh but according to the Spirit. (Rom 8:1–4)

Under the Lord's prodding John realized that the law of the Spirit which replaces the law of death in the heart of the Christian is the commandment to imitate Jesus' burden bearing and self-sacrificing love for others. Then Sanford also came to understand that inner healing is a gift to the church that assists the life of sanctification. That is, it is not just a ministry of the forgiveness of sins, but also is a ministry that breaks the obstacles to sanctification and allows a person to proceed from glory to glory in the grace of God.[12]

---

11. The Sandford's theory of burden bearing in relation to inner healing is covered fully in chapter 14 of their *Wounded Spirit*.

12. Sandford, *Inner Man*, 4–5.

John was especially concerned with Ruth Carter Stapleton's books on inner healing, as he saw her books as a dangerous oversimplification of this ministry.[13] Mrs. Carter Stapleton had been on the CFO circuit, but not an instructor at the Schools of Pastoral Care, which were more demanding theologically, nor was she theologically trained. John also saw that the coupling of inner healing with Jungian vocabulary, as in some of the CFO women and in Agnes' own talks, would lead to trouble. He prophesied to Mrs. Sanford that her ministry would suffer from this. John set about writing his work on inner healing, *The Transformation of the Inner Man*, to remedy these issues. The very title indicates that he would use no vocabulary other than biblical vocabulary to express the profound truths of this ministry. John hoped his work would be finished and published to dampen what he foresaw as a wave of anti–inner healing literature. Sadly, that did not happen (see chapter 21 below on Dave Hunt's work). John is now retired from active ministry, and his son Lauren carries on the leadership of Elijah House.

Dr. Francis MacNutt: Christian Healing Ministries

Christian Healing Ministries in Jacksonville, Florida, is arguably the premier Christian healing ministry center in North America. Founded by Dr. Francis MacNutt and his wife, Judith, it has instructed thousands of ministers and lay leaders on healing, inner healing, and deliverance prayer, effectively continuing the work of the Schools of Pastoral Care. The books the MacNutts have authored are among the most influential and effective in the contemporary Christian healing movement.[14] Several of their works have also branched out into other areas of Christian spirituality. For instance, Judith produced a fine work on angels and Francis did a book on the phenomenon of being slain in the spirit, which is now a standard on the topic.[15]

13. Correspondence from John Sandford to the author, dated February 13, 1985.

14. When I teach a workshop on healing prayer, I tell the audience that the best general introduction to healing prayer is Francis MacNutt's *Healing*, and that the best introduction to exorcism and deliverance is his *Deliverance from Evil Spirits*. A bit of trivia: Francis MacNutt is the only modern healing evangelist whom I know of that has had a poem about his ministry published in a mainline Christian journal. See R. Siegal, "Straight at the Blue."

15. MacNutt, *Angels Are Real* and *Overcome by the Spirit*.

Francis MacNutt was born in 1925 to a well-to-do Catholic family. His father was especially devout and passed his spirituality on to his children. Francis went to Catholic prep school and then attended Harvard as a pre-med student. This was interrupted by World War II. Drafted in 1944, he served as a Navy medic and surgeon's assistant. He later returned to Harvard, where he graduated with honors, but changed career goals to speech therapy and got a master's in speech from the Catholic University of America.

While there he read Thomas Merton's *The Seven Storey Mountain*, a book on modern monasticism that was deeply influential among Catholics in the postwar era. MacNutt decided to become a Dominican monk (famed for their preaching) and entered that order in 1950. He was ordained as a priest six years later. His speech training served him well, and he developed as an excellent and anointed preacher. The Dominicans sent MacNutt to the Aquinas Institute, where he earned a PhD. He then taught homiletics at the Dominican seminary and wrote a homiletics textbook for Catholic priests.[16] During this period he founded the Catholic Homiletic Society. He was a rising star among Dominican priests.

The 1960s was the decade when Pope John XXIII opened up Catholic scholarship to outside influences and allowed priests to attend conferences and services of other denominations. In 1960, at the Presbyterian Seminary in Dubuque, MacNutt heard a presentation on the Christian healing ministry by Dr. Alfred Price, then the OSL national director.[17] But it was not until he met a CFO workshop leader, and a person gifted in healing prayer, Mrs. Jo Kimmel, that his curiosity about Christian healing was really kindled. After a lengthy conversation, Mrs. Kimmel not only invited Francis to attend a CFO but even paid his expenses there.[18]

It was the 1967 CFO in Maryville, Tennessee, led by Agnes Sanford, Derek Prince, and Tommy Tyson. Agnes later recounted her meeting with this handsome, white-robed Dominican priest. He immediately told her that he wanted the baptism of the Holy Spirit. Agnes directed him to go to a group that was doing that type of prayer at the end of the day. MacNutt did so, but was disappointed. Agnes recalled his response:

16. MacNutt, *Sermon Effectiveness*.

17. Rae, "Extraordinary Becomes Ordinary," 23.

18. Kimmel, *Prayer Power* (1972). The work could aptly be entitled "Praying the CFO Way," as it is based on the work of Glenn Clark, Frank Laubach, Agnes Sanford, and the other leaders of the 1950s CFOs.

"Oh, I spoke in tongues, that was no trouble. But nothing really happened inside."

Well, then, I had better pray for you," said I. We went with two others into my room, and there with the laying on of hands, I prayed for the real entering of the Spirit of God—into the heart, into the soul, into the unconscious. And it happened! He was so overwhelmed with holy joy that he laughed aloud, not in any hysterical fashion, but in a deep outpouring from his heart.

"Oh, this is the way I thought it would be!" he cried again and again. . . . He has since led countless others into this experience.[19]

Agnes also prophesied over Fr. MacNutt that he would be used by the Lord to bring healing prayer back to the Catholic Church.[20] The next year he attended a School of Pastoral Care in Wadesville, Massachusetts, for further instructions in healing ministry. This was led by Agnes and the Rev. Tommy Tyson. Agnes recognized MacNutt's theological learning as well as his anointing in healing, and from then on had him assist in her SPCs and missions. Francis learned all he could from Agnes and has repeatedly declared his indebtedness to her teaching and writings.[21]

As Mrs. Sanford prophesied, MacNutt became one of the key leaders of the new Catholic Charismatic Renewal, and a teacher of healing prayer to that movement. He was a frequent speaker at its early conventions and meetings, and a keynote speaker at the famous Kansas City conference of 1977, which gathered together classical Pentecostals and the new charismatics for the first time. MacNutt's keynote address, delivered in his flowing Dominican robes, made a profound impression on those attending. Two years later, Fr. MacNutt was the lead figure in spreading the Catholic Charismatic Renewal to Latin America in a series of missions to Central and South America.[22]

When not on the road, his home base was the Dominican Merton House in St. Louis, which was the center of the Catholic Charismatic Renewal for the area. Francis was also the founder of the Association of Christian Therapists, which aimed at integrating healing prayer into the

19. Sanford, *Sealed Orders*, 225–26.

20. Foster, "Conversation with MacNutt."

21. MacNutt, *Healing*, 12–13, and also, MacNutt, "Sharing God's Love."

22. Sadly, after the 1980s the Catholic Charismatic Renewal fizzled in the United States. However, it has flowered in Latin American and especially in Africa, where it is a major component of Catholicism's growth.

medical profession. The group continues its work to this day and produces the excellent *Journal of Christian Healing*.[23]

The year 1974 saw the publication of Francis' first work on healing prayer, *Healing*. It became a bestseller, as it explains in simple terms the varied aspects of healing prayer, as in physical healing, inner healing, and deliverance. It supplemented Mrs. Sanford's *The Healing Light* as the preferred book to introduce new charismatics to healing prayer. *Healing* includes a very wise chapter on why some persons are not healed, a problem that has bedeviled the healing ministry since its beginnings.[24]

In those years Francis labored constantly to interpret Pentecostalism and its understanding of the Holy Spirit to his Catholic audience. For instance, he tackled the thorny problem that some Catholics were asking about being rebaptized. Pentecostal brethren often suggested rebaptism to newly Spirit-filled Catholics, but ancient doctrine and tradition forbade repeated baptisms. Fr. MacNutt cut the Gordian knot on this issue by suggesting that infant baptism is good, as it often results in unexpected healing and protection from demonic influences, but every Christian needs to make an adult recommitment to Jesus. Francis rebaptized those Catholics who requested it with the words, "I *renew* your baptism in the name of the Father, Son and Holy Spirit."[25]

MacNutt's Influence on Catholicism

It is difficult to overestimate the positive influence that Fr. MacNutt had on the healing ministry of the Catholic Church. He was not the only Catholic priest of the early Catholic Charismatic Movement, nor the only one who promoted the new inner healing ministry. But he was undoubtedly the most prominent among them. It is safe to say that, with his writings and ministry in the lead, the Galatian Bewitchment was largely weakened in the Catholic Church. It lingers in the more traditional sectors of the Church. It is also safe to label present-day Catholic charismatic healing theology as second-generation Agnes Sanford. This is so partly because so much of Mrs. Sanford's original work was sacramental and came out of the deepest streams of Catholic theology and practice.

---

23. Their website is at http://www.actheals.org.
24. MacNutt, *Healing*, chapter 18, "Eleven Reasons Why People Are Not Healed."
25. MacNutt, "A Proposed Solution."

This has not been adequately noted since the Galatian Bewitchment was never an official doctrine backed by encyclicals or catechism statements, etc., but only a strong tradition. Thus its passing was not fought against once it began to dissolve. I know of no Catholic clerical Pharisee who made an argument that healing prayer must be restricted to monks or designated holy persons. The obvious biblical basis for the laying on of hands and the immediate effectiveness that this ministry brought to countless Catholic charismatic prayer groups simply made the Galatian Bewitchment a ghost of a doctrine. This is in contrast to what has happened in Protestantism, where Calvin's elaborated doctrine of cessationism (chapter 4) continues to be defended by many evangelicals.

Perhaps only persons old enough to remember the healing practices of 1950s Catholicism can appreciate the sea change that has occurred. When I was a boy, healing prayer practiced in our parish in New York City ranged from lighting a votive candle to Mary or some saint to saying a rosary for a healing intention. No one laid hands on the sick with the intention and expectancy of real healing to be accomplished. Priests ministered the sacrament of extreme unction for those dying with no expectancy that they would experience physical healing.

Fr. MacNutt's Catholic ministry came to an end when he married Miss Judith Sewell in February of 1980. He was not given the usual dispensation of vows from his superiors, and this closed his ministry to Catholic churches and conferences. This saddened the MacNutts, but it unexpectedly opened new doors of ministry for them with Protestant and Pentecostal churches. Many conservative Protestants and Pentecostals would not invite "Father" MacNutt to speak at their functions, but would certainly welcome "Dr." MacNutt. The MacNutt's joint ministry grew to become today's preeminent charismatic prayer and teaching institution. Ultimately, in 1993, the Catholic hierarchy relented and officially laicized Francis. That is, he and Judith were received as Catholics in good standing. Catholic invitations resumed. In 2008 Francis, then eighty-three, handed over the reins of Christian Healing Ministries to Judith, who now does most of the speaking and teaching at CHM, as it continues its work in carrying on the legacy of Mrs. Sanford.

The Rev. Ted Sanford, 1942

Agnes and Ted with their car, cir. 1958

Agnes Sanford in Arizona, 1953

Agnes Sanford at her home in Monrovia with Judith MacNutt, cir. 1980

Paula and John Sandford with author (center) at a Florida CFO in 1984

Trinity Church Today

The Healing Christ stained glass window at Trinity

PART V

Reflections

21

Agnes Sanford as
Controversial Theologian

WELL BEFORE HER DEATH, Agnes Sanford was controversial and shunned in many Pentecostal/charismatic circles. Significantly, she was *not* a keynote speaker at the great Kansas City 1977 conference. That was the first of several large conferences where classical Pentecostals and the newer charismatics met together, taught together, and fellowshipped together.[1] Ironically, two of her disciples, Mrs. Ruth Carter Stapleton and Fr. Francis MacNutt, were keynote speakers, while Mrs. Sanford had only a workshop.

Indeed, by then Mrs. Sanford was the subject of various rumors and innuendoes centering on her ties to New Thought and Christian Science. As I have labored to explain, the ties were real, but providential. However, in the 1970s even the most astute pastors and leaders of Pentecostalism or the newer charismatic groups were unaware of the Marcion Shove and how it related to church history. Dr. Harold Brown had not yet published his masterful work on the topic, *Heresies*, and even when it came out years later it circulated mostly in academic and seminary circles. Thus, for many in the 1970s the mere association of New Thought and Agnes Sanford was enough to seriously soil her reputation.

Similarly, many Pentecostals and more traditional charismatics were suspicious of inner healing and its supposedly weak scriptural base. Again, the remedy, in John Sanford's *Transformation of the Inner*

---

1. See Manuel, *Mighty River.* A glimpse on the planning and dynamics of the conference is given by Dr. Vinson Synan in his *Eyewitness Remembers*, 84–94.

Man, did not come till several years after. Along the same lines, Mrs. Sanford's theology of the gifts as related to natural powers of the soul, though biblically accurate, was unacceptable to most Christian leaders. It went counter to the widely accepted assumption that psychic manifestations of any sort are occult and have no relation to the gifts of the Spirit. Many charismatics and Pentecostals were then reading the works of the Chinese pastor Watchman Nee, and he strongly reaffirmed the Calvinist faculty psychology position that psychic powers are intrinsically evil and used *only* for occult purposes.[2]

There was a further element of Mrs. Sanford's teaching that was suspicious to Pentecostals and charismatics of the 1970s. She talked about and boosted the theology of the Jesuit theologian and paleontologist Fr. Pierre Teilhard de Chardin.[3] Fr. Teilhard pioneered the first Christian theology of intelligent design as an alternative to Darwinian evolution. He accepted evolution as fact, but saw God's hand in and through evolution, providentially shaping its course to bring about humankind as worshiping beings. His theology was, and continues to be, controversial, and had an array of strange new words such as the "noosphere." For a time it was suppressed by the Catholic Church, although now Catholics honor him as a pioneer and insightful theologian. Now, forty years later, most evangelicals and Pentecostals would be thrilled to have any intelligent design (ID) theory presented in public schools as an alternative to Darwinian mechanical evolution. But back in the 1970s any form of evolutionary thought was viewed as heresy by most Christians. Again, Mrs. Sanford was ahead of her times, and paid a price.

Later, when she published *Sealed Orders* and explained her theory of the pre-existence of the human spirit, further suspicion was cast on her writings. On this issue, even Fr. Dennis Bennett, the Episcopal rector who triggered the Charismatic Renewal, and later became a major player in the inner healing movement with his wife, Rita, distanced himself from Mrs. Sanford's writings. He felt she was sometimes far out.[4] When he and his

2. Nee, *Spiritual Man*. Nee took this position, I believe, because the only examples he ever saw in China of psychic powers were related to traditional Chinese shamanism.

3. Sanford, *Healing Gifts*, 29. She often talked about Fr. Teilhard in her CFO talks, where controversial topics were not scandalous. Teilhard's pioneer work on evolution as intelligent design (the term had not been invented yet) was his *Phenomenon of Man*. The original French text was written in the 1930s but did not see print until after Fr. Teilhard's death in 1955.

4. Conversation with Fr. Dennis Bennett at his inner healing conference in Seattle,

wife did their popular workshops on inner healing, they conspicuously did not have any of Mrs. Sanford's books on the book table.

Pharisaism Resurgent: Dave Hunt

The mid-1980s saw major assaults on the Charismatic Renewal. Several authors produced works that frightened and dismayed many Spirit-filled Believers. The most significant was the work by Dave Hunt (1926–2013), *The Seduction of Christianity*, which appeared in 1985 and became a massively popular bestseller. Hunt published a further broadside on the Charismatic Renewal in his book *Beyond Seduction*, which appeared in 1986.

Unlike the assaults of Charles Chauncy on the Great Awakening and of James Buckley against the Faith Cure movement, the attacks by Hunt and others, though severe, were not fatal.[5] But the Charismatic Renewal was shaken and stalled, and a case could be made that the glory days of the Charismatic Renewal came to an end with Hunt's books.

Dave Hunt was a self-educated anti-cult investigator who did excellent work in his first books.[6] With Ed Decker he wrote an exposé of Mormon doctrines, *The God Makers*, and with Rabi R. Matharaj he produced an exciting book on the conversion of a Hindu priest.[7] Hunt did an excellent job in ferreting out facts, influences and connections, etc., but

---

Washington, 1983. The Bennetts wrote some of the best books of the Charismatic Renewal, including some fine works on inner healing. See Rita Bennett, *How to Pray*.

5. My work *Quenching the Spirit* (1st ed. 1992) played a significant role in limiting the damage done by the Dave Hunt's books. Although *Quenching the Spirit* sold only a fraction of the Hunt books, it was bought by Spirit-filled pastors and church leaders, on whom it was especially influential. For a time it was issued free to graduates of Kenneth Hagin's Rhema Bible school. Mr. Steven Strang, owner of Strang Communications, the parent company of *Charisma* magazine, Creation House, and Charisma House Books, worked hard to have *Quenching the Spirit* endorsed by many leaders of the Charismatic Renewal. Note the front pages of *Quenching the Spirit*. Mr. Strang then arranged for my appearances in Paul Crouch's PTL TV program, which was the most widely viewed of the charismatic TV programs. Thus many in the Charismatic Renewal leadership quickly comprehended the Hunt attacks as Pharisaism. *Quenching the Spirit* has continued selling, mainly to Pentecostal and charismatic seminaries, and is still in print.

6. I give a detailed review of his life and journey from cessationist to Spirit-filled believer, and then to cessationist again, in *Quenching the Spirit*, chapter 21.

7. Decker and Hunt, *God Makers*, and Matharaj and Hunt, *Death of a Guru* (1977).

his work was basically the research of a reporter, with no broad historical knowledge.

Thus, when Hunt critiqued the Charismatic Renewal it was on the Pharisees' origins argument, that is, that the Charismatic Renewal, and especially Mrs. Agnes Sanford's work, were contaminated with occult and metaphysical elements through its influence by New Thought and Christian Science. Therefore, the Charismatic Renewal should be cleansed of these elements and returned to a pure evangelicalism or Pentecostalism. For Hunt, merely demonstrating that Mrs. Sanford had New Thought influences was equivalent to saying her writings were heretical. Hunt's origins arguments had profound resonance among the Christian public. One could not expect the normal pew Christian who learns church history at Sunday school to know about the subtleties of the heresy-to-truth process of church history (the Marcion Shove). For most Christian readers Hunt's origins argument was self-evidently true.[8]

Classic Pharisaism: The Seduction of Christianity

We need to examine Hunt's work, as his books remain in circulation and his arguments are often repeated by cessationists to defame the legacy of Agnes Sanford or attack inner healing. Hunt calls Mrs. Sanford a "shaman" and pantheist. He cites her with cut-and-paste quotations:

> [S]he calls God "the very life-force existing in the radiation of an energy . . . from which all things evolved," and declares that "God is actually in the flowers and all the little chirping, singing things. He made everything out of Himself and somehow He put a part of himself into everything."[9]

In this particular assault Hunt is both confused and ignorant. Of course, he does not understand Mrs. Sanford's breakthroughs in talking about the energies of God, and thus cannot understand the original context of her statement. His definition of pantheism, as God in nature, is biblically ignorant. Pantheism is the theory that God is diffused throughout nature only, but not also a being separate from nature, as is biblically revealed. Note what Paul says in Ephesians 4:4–6:

8. The fact that people seek the easy way to understand truth rather than it's more accurate and complex forms is common to all humankind; psychologists call it "cognitive fluency." See Bennett, "Easy = True."

9. Hunt, *Seduction of Christianity*, 78.

> There is one body and one Spirit—just as you were called to
> one hope when you were called—one Lord, one faith, one bap-
> tism; one God and Father of all, who is over all and through all
> and in all.

Mrs. Sanford was definitely not a pantheist and knew God as both in
nature and above nature as a person. She made this clear from her first
book, *The Healing Light*:

> God is both within us and without us. He is the Source of all
> life; the Creator of the universe; and of unimaginable depths of
> inter-steller space and of light-years without end. But he is also
> the indwelling life of our own little selves.[10]

Associated with the charge of pantheism is the accusation that Mrs.
Sanford was a shaman. Chapter 9 of *The Seduction of Christianity* is in fact
titled "Shamanism Revisited." The accusations boiled down to the fact that
traditional Western theology gave little attention to the many instances in
Scripture where nature is addressed, or shares in worship of God.

All this is covered in chapter 19 above, and I concluded that although
Mrs. Sanford's beliefs in this area are original, especially in her under-
standing of our authority in Christ to command nature, it is all biblical.
But to a cessationist it all seems bizarre, and thus must be shamanistic.

Hunt claims that, "Consistent with her shamanistic beliefs, Mrs.
Sanford tells of her baptism of the Holy Ghost that came "through the
sun and the waters in the lake and the wind in the pine trees."[11] Again
Hunt is both mistaken and ignorant. The original quotation comes from
Mrs. Sanford's *The Healing Gifts of the Spirit* and refers to a period in her
life before her baptism of the Holy Spirit by the two women in Tucson
(covered in chapter 18). It was a period of ministry that was stressful and
she needed God's grace and help. Mrs. Sanford recalled:

> On a cold October morning I rowed across a small lake and
> found an isolated rock overhung with pine trees. There I lay
> upon the pine needles with the warmth of the sun soaking into
> me. The wind breathed through the pine trees and a few late
> birds fluttered silently among them, their songs laid away for the
> winter. I prayed for God's life to reach me through the rays of the
> sun. And even though I did not know the Holy Spirit, the Spirit
> of God entered in a way so defying understanding that I have

10. Sanford, *Healing Light*, 19.
11. Hunt, *Seduction of Christianity*, 129.

never before tried to explain it . . . I can only say that for a split second I lived consciously and aware in the bliss of eternity.[12]

Mrs. Sanford had a moment of the special touch of God's grace and presence, but she did not confuse that with the baptism of the Holy Spirit, as Hunt did. Many Christians have had similar experiences. Mrs. Sanford's experience on the lake should be compared with what Jonathan Edwards experienced as a young man after he was touched by God's grace through reading 1 Timothy 1:17:

> After this my sense of divine things gradually increased, and became more and more lively, and had more of that inward sweetness. The appearance of everything was altered; there seemed to be, as it were, a calm sweet cast, or appearance of divine glory, in almost everything. God's excellency, his wisdom, his purity and love, seemed to appear in everything; in the sun, moon, and stars; in the clouds, and blue sky; in the grass, flowers, trees; in the water, and all nature; which used greatly to fix my mind. I often used to sit and view the moon for continuance; and in the day, spent much time in viewing the clouds and sky, to behold the sweet glory of God in these things; in the meantime, singing forth, with a low voice my contemplations of the Creator and Redeemer.[13]

Hunt on Visualization

In *The Seduction of Christianity* Hunt asserted that any use of prayer visualization by Christians is sorcery.[14] He affirms that before Agnes Sanford prayer visualization was unknown among Christians. Naturally, he does not mention, and was probably unaware of, the long-standing Catholic practice of Bible visualization.

Following the old Scottish Calvinists that Jonathan Edwards had to contend with (see chapter 11) and their faculty psychology, Hunt asserts that persons who form an image of Jesus in prayer are committing an act of idolatry and sorcery, and possibly opening themselves to a demonic spirit guide.[15] Hunt's arguments were principally concerned with

---

12. Sanford, *Healing Gifts*, 25-26.

13. Faust, *Jonathan Edwards*, 7.

14. Hunt, *Seduction of Christianity*, chapter 10,

15. Ibid., 160, 170–72.

visualization in inner healing, but were applied to all forms of visualization. His argument is that of guilt by association: the technique of visualization is not found in the Bible and not found in Christian literature before Agnes Sanford (wrong of course), but it is found in shamanism and metaphysical writings; therefore, it is an occult practice and sorcery.

Hunt tried to distinguish between the normal and good use of visualization in creative work, such as an architect planning his building, and its sorcery aspects. A sure sign of this impossibility and contradiction came in his book *Beyond Seduction*, where he attempted to define an acceptable form of visualization prayer—something he did not permit just a few years previously.

> It is not wrong for a pastor on his knees, because this is the passion of his heart, sees in his mind his church filled to the overflowing and people going forward to repent, and cries out to God in prayer for this to become a reality. It is wrong, however, if he thinks that by concentrating on this imaginary scene until it becomes vivid in his mind he will thereby help it to occur . . . Mental imagery is a normal function of the human mind . . . But to attempt to visualize God or Jesus, or to change or create reality by visualization, is to step into the occult.[16]

Even a cursory evaluation of Hunt's thinking here shows all sorts of contradictions. Aside from the pious language of the pastor being on his knees, Hunt's evangelical pastor did exactly the same thing that Agnes Sanford did when she imagined a sick person well. Yet, according to Hunt, Agnes committed sorcery, but his evangelical pastor made a prayer!

An Evangelical Discernment

Hunt's accusations on visualization as sorcery stirred a huge controversy, and frightened many Christians from this form of prayer and away from inner healing. Among the literature produced during the controversy was a masterful article by Brooks Alexander. Mr. Alexander was the founder of the prestigious evangelical anti-cult institute called the Spiritual Counterfeits Project. The SCP, as it is known for short, was founded in Berkeley, California, during the 1970s at the height of the occult revival. Alexander and others got together to provide an informed evangelical perspective on cults and the occult. Their publications, especially the

16. Hunt, *Beyond Seduction*, 223

SCP Journal, reached the highest standards of evangelical apologetics and discernment.[17]

In 1990 an entire issue of the *SCP Journal* was dedicated to visualization. Alexander provided the lead article.[18] He carefully demonstrated the occult uses of visualization and cited various sociological works that show that visualization is the central practice of shamanism. Mr. Alexander cites evidence that visualization was used by the highest levels of Hitler's Nazi party to plan world conquest. More common in present-day America is the use of visualization in New Age circles as spiritualism to contact spirit guides.

Mr. Alexander's article could have closed there and claimed, as Dave Hunt, that visualization is always evil and only an occult practice. But Mr. Alexander is a scholar, and his article takes a turn worthy of Jonathan Edwards. As Edwards, he sees the imagination as God-created; therefore, visualization has its good and proper functions. Alexander repeatedly compared the imagination and its capacity for visualization to humanity's sexual function: it can easily be misused, but it is a wonderful gift from God.[19]

Surprising for a convinced evangelical, Alexander credits the Catholic practice of Bible story visualization as a legitimate practice and even admires the Ignatius exercises. His summary is worth quoting:

> There is nothing wrong with inner imagery *per se*. Our imagination is a gift of God, and it was given to be used. But there is a simple rule of thumb for exercising that gift in religious and spiritual life.
>
> Use images in prayer as a means of communication *to* God. Do not use your own created images as a source of communication *from* God. Use images as you use words—to express your worship and your petition. Do not use images as instruments of control, having power in themselves because of their nature.
>
> *And remember who you are praying to.* God almighty, the creator of heaven and earth, knows the heart of the atom and the heart of man. He certainly knows what you want before you ask for it. And He knows what you need better than you do. Visual detail is no more important to God's hearing of prayer than is

17. Stafford, "Cult Watchers," 18–23.

18. Alexander, "Mind Power," 8–20.

19. Ibid., 11.

verbal detail. What *is* important is the inclination of your heart—
your real reasons for wanting this moment alone with God.[20]

Unfortunately, Alexander's masterful article did little in combating
the anti-visualization hysteria that Hunt caused among the evangelical
and Charismatic churches. Many pastors and counselors who were experimenting with inner healing simply shut the ministry down.

Several inner healing ministers quickly wrote works presenting
their ministries as biblically sound, and that visualization was not at its
core, etc.[21] But the damage had been done. Inner healing became a rare
ministry among charismatic and Pentecostal churches. The exception
was Wimber's Vineyard churches, where it continued to be taught and
utilized. The other exception is that Hunt's critique had little or no impact among Catholic charismatics and their use of inner healing. Hunt's
blatant and constant anti-Catholicism made his counsel unacceptable in
Catholic circles.[22]

After almost a quarter of a century we can see that Hunt's asser-
tions still linger in many evangelical circles, but have also much dissipated. Many of the present generation of Spirit-filled believers simply
do not know who Hunt was or what he wrote. Inner healing is slowly
recovering as a ministry among Spirit-filled churches, but with several
restraints. Principally, inner healing has become a ministry of trained
volunteers and church counselors. This has been facilitated by important
parachurch organizations such as Dr. Francis MacNutt's Christian Healing Ministries in Jacksonville, Florida, and the Sandford's Elijah House
Ministry in Idaho. These parachurch ministries give extensive training
to aspirant ministers, and they incorporate inner healing with physical
healing and deliverance/exorcism.[23] Inner healing with a name change,
called theophoistic healing, has also had an impact. Far gone are the days
when someone would pick up a copy of Ruth Carter Stapleton's *The Gift
of Inner Healing* and begin doing inner healing prayer on their neighbors.

There is a further grievous injury that has been done to the Body
of Christ by Dave Hunt's pharisaical works. They damaged the church's

---

20. Ibid., 20. For a recent article by an evangelical author on how visualization
prayer is helpful in the Christian life, see Boyd "Imaginative Prayer."

21. For instance Tapscott, *Biblically Ministered* (1987).

22. On Dave Hunt's anti-Catholicism see his *Woman Rides* (1994).

23. For information on these parachurch ministries and their programs see their
websites, christianhealingmin.org, elijahhouse.org, and theophostic.com.

ability to heal and confront homosexuality. Agnes Sanford successfully prayed over homosexual persons with the laying on of hands and inner healing prayer for them to leave their practices and realign their attractions according to God's plan. That aspect of her ministry was taken up by several of her disciples, and was the special concern of Mrs. Leanne Payne, who served with Mrs. Sanford in the Schools of Pastoral Care. It was Mrs. Payne who led the fight to rid the schools of Jungian influences (chapter 18). Mrs. Payne's now classic work on healing homosexuality is *The Broken Image*.[24] Dr. Francis MacNutt also did a book on the issue.[25]

By frightening evangelical and Pentecostal/charismatic pastors away from the inner healing ministry, the healing of the homosexual attraction became a rare and specialized ministry. Had it become a normal and common event in the 1980s, the church as a whole would have been in much better position to resist the onslaught of pan-sexual theologies, which have overwhelmed the mainline denominations and which make homosexuality equivalent to heterosexuality.

Pharisaism as Ignorance

Brief notice must also be taken of another book, one that specifically targets Agnes Sanford and the inner healing ministry. It is an uninformed and poorly researched work, and I mention it only because it pops up in Google and Amazon searches when either Agnes Sanford or inner healing are queried. It is the work of Jane Gumprecht, MD, entitled *Abusing Memory* (1997). It was written like a hurried college term paper. A hypothesis was formed, a few quotes gathered, and conclusions drawn. In Gumprecht's case, she affirms that inner healing is a concoction of Jungian psychology and New Thought doctrines.[26] There is no discussion of Harry Goldsmith, travail intercession, or the laying on of hands in regards to this ministry. Dr. Gumprecht is deceased, so we cannot interview her, but I suppose she had in mind the popular version of inner healing

---

24. See also her *Healing Homosexuality*. One of Mrs. Payne's disciples in this ministry has written an excellent account of his own journey from homosexuality to being a joyfully married man and father: Bergner, *Love in Order*.

25. MacNutt, *Homosexuality*. Note that Dr. MacNutt normally published his works through a major publisher, but this work was issued from his organization. Were the major publishers afraid of such a controversial topic?

26. Grumprecht, *Abusing Memory*, 6.

in Ruth Carter Stapleton's books, but her accusations are still inaccurate, as Mrs. Carter Stapleton did not use Jungian concepts.

Equally uninformed is Dr. Gumprecht's attempt to categorize Mrs. Sanford as a New Ager who had no sin consciousness.[27] What! What about her writings, such as *The Healing Light*, where she described how she learned and appreciated the Anglo-Catholic tradition of oral confession? Mrs. Sanford found great healing in confessing *her own sins* and urged others to do the same. Or how about chapter 5 of *Behold Your God*, which is all about how we can appropriate God's forgiveness of our sins through the cross?[28] Enough said on this ill-informed and amateurish book.[29]

27. Ibid., 16.

28. Sanford, *Behold Your God*, chapter 5, "Forgiveness of Sins."

29. Dr. Gumprecht wrote an earlier nonsense and amateurish book, *Holistic Health*. In this book she affirmed that all forms of alternate medicine, such as acupuncture, iridology, etc., are occult and demonic, and that nutritional supplements are a waste. The book has gleanings of truth, as some forms of alternative medicine do have occult origins. But so does one of the central disciplines of the medical profession—chemistry, which morphed out of alchemy. On alternative medical practices, there seems to have been the equivalent of a Marcion shove. That is, Western medicine has been shocked into examining other ways of healing. Some alternate disciplines have been scientifically proven to be effective, such as acupuncture for pain relief. When I first entered the Charismatic Renewal in 1974 I was exposed to similar teachings, i.e., that herbal medication and supplements are occult. The use and steady growth of herbal and nutritional supplements by Christians, and their obviously good benefits, exposes such teachings as exaggerations to the point of falsehood.

22

The Christian Healing Pioneers
and the Wisdom of God

It is clear that Mary Baker Eddy's attempt to make Christianity scientific was a futile illusion. Christianity can never be, nor should it be, a science in the full sense of the word. Its fundamental doctrines cannot be tested, nor can they be accountable through falsifiability, as Karl Popper taught us. For instance, one cannot devise a present-day experiment to prove or disprove the second coming of Christ.

Yet, Christian Science and the various New Thought groups simulated good fruit, if indirectly. For one, they reintroduced the factor of the demonstration of Christianity by the power of God (Heb 2:1–4), the very thing mostly missing for over a millennium within the Christian tradition. The persons involved in the Faith Cure understood the relationship between faith and demonstration also. Through the Faith Cure pioneers this demonstration viewpoint was passed on to Pentecostalism—but ignored or treated with contempt by mainline Christianity. This demonstration awareness was redeveloped by the pioneers in CNP.

If we step back, we can see that because of the influence of Christian Science, and especially CNP, a new attitude was introduced into Christian life. It may have begun as the mistaken quest to make Christianity scientific, but it quickly broadened to an idea akin to the scientific method: *that discovery and testing are part of Christian spirituality.* After centuries of doctrinal Christianity where only the *transmission of established doctrines* was valued, this testing was new and revolutionary. We saw this in Fr. Robert Bell, with his mix of Christian healing and health food, in Prof.

Glenn Clark and his CFO healing camps, and again, especially and most self-consciously, in Mrs. Agnes Sanford's quest for healing effectiveness.

Sadly, even today most Christians do not understand that testing is a biblical mandate. Paul wrote to the Thessalonians, "Do not put out the Spirit's fire; do not treat prophecies with contempt. Test everything. Hold on to the good. Avoid every kind of evil" (1 Thess 5:19–21). Paul wrote with the assumption of the continuous presence and activity of the Holy Spirit in the church, and also the continuous presence of harassing and confusion-causing demonic spirits.[1] The cessationist error was far into the future, and probably unimaginable to him. But Paul made it clear that Christians need the tool of discernment/testing to separate what is good and from the Holy Spirit from what is false and destructive, be it either flesh or demonic. Although the context of Paul's directions in 1 Thessalonians 5 is the prophetic ministry, it is plain that what Paul meant by "test everything" was precisely that: to test every kind of spiritual activity, phenomenon, or manner of spirituality (see also in this context, 1 Tim 3:10 and Gal 6:4).

With the arrival of doctrinal Christianity, and later with cessationism, the mandate to test was rendered incomprehensible, and Paul's injunction to test became a historical passage like 1 Corinthians 12–14. Or more precisely, Christians have most often confused testing with comparing. That is, anything new in spirituality, theological development, or religious practice is compared with church doctrine (Calvinist, Catholic, Greek Orthodox, Methodist, etc.) and declared good or heretical on that comparison.

Paul, however, asked Christians to test everything and "Hold on to the good." This implies a possibility of things that are new, and that Christians may make some initial mistaken discernment and errors. Hold on to the good, but let pass the evil or the false after it has been tested and discerned. Remember that Mrs. Sanford immediately dropped séances after she discerned they were demonic. This concurs with Jesus' teaching that spiritual things are to be judged by their fruit (Matt 7:15–18) and that sometimes spiritual fruit takes time to mature.[2]

In fairness, doctrinal comparison has its place in Christian discernment, as it avoids reinventing the doctrinal wheel and repeating gross errors. For instance, groups heavily impacted by the Holy Spirit sometimes

1. Kallas, *Satanward View* (1956).

2. This point was brought up by Fr. Poulain in his classic on Christian discernment, *Interior Prayer*, 380–82. Modern editions are available.

are so enamored by the fresh insight that the Spirit gives that they disdain church history and traditional creeds. This happened to the Christian church formed out of the Second Great Awakening, which soon lost its orthodox bearings. This also happened in the early Pentecostal movement, which lost one third of its adherents to the Jesus-only theology that rejected the Trinity.

The method of comparison discernment can also be used creatively to reestablish something lost in church history. We saw this in the works of Fr. Puller and Fr. Percy Dearmer, whose magnificent scholarship helped recover the church's healing ministry by comparing the situation in Victorian England to the evidence of the early church. But comparison discernment by itself can also lead to disaster, as when cessationism became established and then became the point of orthodox comparison to denounce healing prayer. Thus, comparison discernment is part of Christian discernment, but it is not the fullness of Paul's testing for something that may come to the church's attention.

Let me mention one personal example of Paul's injunction to test all things in reference to inner healing. In the 1980s, when the great inner healing controversy was raging, one of the issues brought up was that inner healing is nothing more than pious suggestion; no real grace is present. This argument was put forth by sincere Christians who pointed out that inner healing as visualization is carried out by secular therapists using a friend, such as an uncle or grandfather, as the visualized healing agent. The result is that some emotional healing often takes place. Thus, these critics argued, inner healing ministry is mental suggestion, not a grace.

I had noticed in reading Agnes Sanford's writings that there were several stories where she ministered inner healing to neurotic or traumatized animals.[3] This was significant because an animal's mind cannot receive a verbal or imaging suggestion.[4] My wife, Carolyn, and I had an opportunity to test this when our own dog experienced a close lightning strike. The concussion of the strike threw her across the yard. Tuppan, a Boston Terrier, was so traumatized by the event that from that time any explosive sound would send her into a panic. Our sleeping during

---

3. Sanford, *Pasture for Peterkin*, 36–37, and, *Creation Waits*, 113.

4. Just how much animals can understand is the topic of much ongoing investigation. Some higher animals can understand certain symbolic commands such as "place ball in basket," but a suggestion such as "visualize a peaceful scene with a ball" is beyond any animal's capacity.

summer thunderstorms was impossible, as the dog would jump on our bed and whine and pant in panic behavior.

Carolyn, who has special compassion for animals, prayed over Tuppan. She asked Jesus to "enter the memory of the lightning strike" and heal that memory. After that prayer, Tuppan never again demonstrated panic behavior or panting excesses during thunderstorms or explosive noises. This prayer experiment demonstrated that inner healing prayer was more than mere suggestion, and indicated that it was a grace. We reported this in the prestigious *Journal of Christian Healing*.[5] We had wished that this would trigger a multi-animal experiment with veterinarians and psychologists involved, etc. But alas, we received no queries, and have never had an opportunity to help work a protocol for a larger experiment. This was a lesson to us that Christians on the whole make weak connections between spiritual phenomenon and testing possibilities.[6]

Lady Wisdom as the Wisdom of God[7]

Here we need to stop and describe the biblical wisdom of God and its relationship to science. The wisdom of God operating in human beings is an idea that occurs throughout Scripture, in both Old and New Testaments. We find it mentioned in the historical books in, for instance, the wise woman of 2 Samuel 20:16, who gave sage political advice.[8] The most famous wise man of the Bible was King Solomon, who was given a special gift of wisdom when he asked God for it in a dream at the beginning of his reign (1 Kings 3). Solomon was full of both wisdom and knowledge, which extended into, among other things, what we would call biology, as he studied the plants and animals of the earth (1 Kings 4:32).

But the wisdom of God is central in the book of Proverbs. How Proverbs came about is yet another example of how the Spirit used unusual sources to stimulate the formation of Holy Scripture—the Marcion Shove before Marcion! It started in earnest during King Solomon's reign, when

5. De Arteaga, "Fido Factor," 11–13. Yes, dear reader, at last an example of good and godly DOG theology!

6. Thankfully, this decade has seen the growth of scholarly books that demonstrate the power of prayer. See especially Brown, *Testing Prayer*.

7. On the wisdom of God and wisdom literature in Israel see the magisterial work by von Rad, *Wisdom in Israel*. On the history of "Lady Wisdom" (Sophia) see the excellent articles by Lefebure, "Sofia and Christian Theology" and "Dialogue Theology."

8. See Camp, "Wise Women."

cultural intercourse between Israel and Egypt were continuous. Recall
that Solomon married one of Pharaoh's daughters to ensure peace on his
eastern border. Centuries before in Egypt there had accumulated a court
wisdom literature that gave moral advice and counsel for everyday life.[9]
This body of literature included the "Instructions of Amenomope," written sometime between 1300 and 1075 BC. Section 4 (out of thirty) reads:

> The hot-headed man in the temple
>
> is like a tree grown indoors;
>
> Only for a moment does it put forth roots.
>
> It reaches its end in the carpentry shop,
>
> It is floated away far from its place,
>
> Or fire is its funeral pyre.
>
> The truly temperate man sets himself apart,
>
> He is like a tree grown in a sunlit field,
>
> But it flourishes, it doubles its yield,
>
> It stands before its owner;
>
> Its fruit is something sweet, its shade is pleasant,
>
> And it reaches its end as a statue.[10]

Note the similarity to Psalm 1. Under the anointing of the Holy Spirit,
Egyptian wisdom literature stimulated Solomon, and the unnamed
scribes of the First Temple Era, to begin forging similar pieces of wisdom
literature in Hebrew. Unlike the persons we have studied in Christian
New Perspective, the creators of Proverbs had perhaps only the first few
books of the Bible as Scripture to guide and correct them. It was God's
Spirit that inspired them to separate out occultic, negative, and nihilistic
elements that were predominant in Egyptian (and Mesopotamian) wisdom writings as they composed the book of Proverbs.

Out of this First Temple environment came the inspiration about
Lady Wisdom, the central figure of the book of Proverbs. The word "wisdom" in Hebrew is a feminine form, and thus the wisdom of God is per-
sonified in Proverbs as Lady Wisdom. She teaches on the ways of being
wise, and the things to avoid to not become a fool. Proverbs pictures Lady

---

9. Biblical scholars have known for a long time of the influence of Egyptian and
Babylonian wisdom literature on the formation of Proverbs and other Hebrew wisdom
books. See Clifford, *Wisdom Literature* (1998).

10. The *Instructions* are found at various websites, and this quote is taken from
http://www.maat.sofiatopia.org/amen_em_apt.htm#3a.

Wisdom as a personification that was with God before the creation of the world and doing the work of creation with God:

> The Lord begot me, the firstborn of his ways,
>> The forerunner of his prodigies of long ago.
> From of old I was poured forth
>> At the first, before the earth . . .
> Then I was beside him as his craftsman,
>> And I was his delight day by day. (Prov 8:22–23, 30, NAB)

This seems to be a picture of the preincarnate Christ, and this is buttressed by the fact that Paul calls Jesus the Wisdom of God (1 Cor 1:24, 30). However, there are difficulties with this interpretation, as Lady Wisdom in the above passage could be interpreted as created before the rest of the universe, and thus not coeternal with God. We will not try to solve this difficult issue, but only wish to point to the importance that Lady Wisdom and the wisdom of God has in Scripture. In Eastern Orthodoxy the role of Lady Wisdom (Sofia) has a much greater part in devotion and theology than in Western Christendom. For instance, the great patriarchal church of the Byzantine Empire was the Hagia Sofia, now a museum in Istanbul, Turkey.[11]

What is important for our study is the methodology that Lady Wisdom advocates to achieve wisdom and avoid foolishness. First, to be wise a person must desire to be wise and to acquire wisdom. Fools, on the other hand, despise both (Prov 1:7–8). She cries out to all an invitation to gain wisdom and knowledge, and a warning to avoid foolishness and folly:

> "How long will you simple ones love your simple ways? How long will mockers delight in mockery and fools hate knowledge? If you had responded to my rebuke, I would have poured out my heart to you and made my thoughts known to you." (1:22–23)

Second: the wise person must have a fear of the Lord. "The fear of the LORD is the beginning of wisdom, and knowledge of the Holy One is understanding" (9:10). This fear of the Lord is understood as awe mixed with real fear of God's wrath on the disobedient. It is specifically defined in Proverbs:

> To fear the LORD is to hate evil;
> I [Lady Wisdom] hate pride and arrogance,
> evil behavior and perverse speech. (8:13)

11. See for example Pentiuc, "Self-Offering God."

Third: the response to reproof and correction is central to acquiring the wisdom of God.

> He who ignores discipline comes to poverty and shame,
> but whoever heeds correction is honored. (13:18)
> He who ignores discipline despises himself,
> but whoever heeds correction gains understanding. (15:32)

The fool hates gathering knowledge or accepting reproof:

> Since they hated knowledge
> and did not choose to fear the LORD,
> since they would not accept my advice
> and spurned my rebuke,
> they will eat the fruit of their ways
> and be filled with the fruit of their schemes.
> For the waywardness of the simple will kill them,
> and the complacency of fools will destroy them . . . (1:29–32)

On the other hand, those who labor for wisdom will be rewarded:

> and if you call out for insight
> and cry aloud for understanding,
> and if you look for it as for silver
> and search for it as for hidden treasure,
> then you will understand the fear of the LORD
> and find the knowledge of God.
> For the LORD gives wisdom,
> and from his mouth come knowledge and understanding.
> (2:3–6)

Later in Proverbs the rebuke process is described in terms of human accountability and refinement:

> As iron sharpens iron,
> so one man sharpens another. (27:17)

Pious Jews took these scriptures most seriously. By the time of Jesus they had molded this into the Pharisees' system of education and theological debate. The Pharisees attempted to use the wisdom of God to hone more accurate ideas about the law of Moses and how to please God. But their methodology had fallen into legalism, partly because it was mostly authority based, quoting chains of rabbinical opinions, not Spirit led.[12]

But the debate and reproof form of the wisdom of God is part of the New Testament heritage too. Many have called the Letter of James the Proverbs of the New Testament. In it we see the rabbinical discourse as it should be, without exaggeration, and filled with both seeking the wisdom of God and humility:

> But the wisdom from above is first of all pure. It is also peace loving, gentle at all times, and willing to yield to others. It is full of mercy and good deeds. It shows no favoritism and is always sincere. (Jas 3:17, NLT)

The Wisdom of God as Proto-Science

We should recall that Karl Popper's work clarified that science was a methodology of discovering truth by hypothesis generation, testing, and reproof. All of this is to be done in humility and with the expectation that errors will be part of the process. Because errors can teach too, if we accept their reproof, as in Proverbs.[13] Thus in its simplest definition, the wisdom of God is a form of proto-science. It is not science, but it is certainly *like* science.[14] Mary Baker Eddy and other New Thought

12. Historians have noted that there was an explosion of Jewish thought in the sciences and medicine in the nineteenth century, as the restrictive laws against the Jews were revoked in Europe. This bore fruit in the large number of Nobel Prizes given to Jewish scientists in the twentieth century. Part of the answer is of course that Jews cherished an imbibed tradition of the wisdom of God and had only to experience legal freedom to apply it to such formerly forbidden professions as medicine and science for the great flowering of Jewish thinkers to emerge. Similarly today, the nation of Israel has developed, in spite of its poor natural resources and small population, into a scientific superpower. See Senor and Singer, *Start-Up Nation* (2009).

13. Popper, *Conjectures and Refutation.*

14. There has been much scholarly discussion on why and how science as a self-sustaining methodology arose in the Christian West at the end of the Middle Ages. Why not in ancient Greece or China? Both had scientific elements in their cultures, such as high technology, superb craftsmanship, and excellent mathematics and engineering, but in these countries they never combined and converted into the self-sustaining discipline of true science. The great Catholic scholar Stanley L. Jaki, working out of Fordham University, studied the problem extensively and came to the conclusion that the biblical base of Christianity gave the impetus for the final formation of science through such persons as the Franciscan friar Roger Bacon (1214–1294). See Jaki, *Road of Science*. He did not note the methodology of the wisdom of God in Proverbs.

advocates thought Christianity could become scientific, and that was an illusion, but they were *partially right* in so far as the real wisdom of God is similar to science.

The healing pioneers we have studied, especially Glenn Clark and Agnes Sanford, accepted the Christian Science/New Thought goal that Christianity could be made more scientific. Because of that goal, they wound up doing theology with the wisdom of God. We should remember especially Glenn Clark's use of his Sunday school class to test various approaches to prayer, and his call in 1946 to gather experienced Christian leaders to share their knowledge and wisdom on the healing ministry. Agnes Sanford's understanding of testing as a spiritual methodology in *The Healing Light* manifested most fully the wisdom of God on this issue.

The OSL, and especially the amazing CFO camps of the 1950s and 1960s, used the wisdom of God to discover truths about prayer and healing that had been lost, and pioneered new ways in both areas. Acquiring knowledge, testing and being sensitive to truth and error, and trying to be wise on these issues all seemed dangerous and scandalous to cessationist Christians who felt there was no role for experimentation in Christianity. It was however, all within the wisdom of God.[15]

One reason why CNP thinkers were able to function in the wisdom of God was that they were mostly detached from sectarian creeds and demands. Their interdenominational focus ensured that they stayed away from the unsolvable traditional debates, such as free-will vs. predestination, etc. They were left free to gather information and investigate how to recover the church's healing ministry and the power of prayer.

We can now understand why the Holy Spirit burst upon the CFO and found a home there from the 1950s, and not on some Southern Baptist summer retreat or annual Lutheran or Presbyterian minister's conferences. The CFO was functioning in the wisdom of God from the very beginning, even in its irregular metaphysical period. The irregular ideas that some CFO persons held was less important to the Holy Spirit than their openness to the things the Spirit wanted to teach. We should recall that Rufus Moseley, who had been deep into Christian Science, was able to receive the fullness of Holy Spirit baptism. Similarly, it was Glenn Clark, who had also been baptized in the Spirit early in his Christian life, who helped the CFO

---

15. The wisdom of God should be the methodology of all disciplines, whether they are properly scientific or not, such as gardening; see Lane-Gay, "Direction for Gardiner."

to come into Pentecost. Nothing similar happened in mainline seminaries, fundamentalist Bible colleges, or mainline summer programs.

It is important to note also that there are examples of spiritual exploration and testing that were not within the wisdom of God, and bore only the fruit of occultism and confusion. For example, Spiritual Frontiers Fellowship (SFF) was founded in 1955 to investigate psychic and spiritual phenomenon. In spite the fact that most of its members were from Christian mainline churches (a demographic identical to OSL and CFO membership) it was doomed to failure and confusion from the start. Its founder, Arthur Ford, was a medium. Because mediumship is disobedience to the clear word of God, the SFF lacked the fear of the Lord necessary for the wisdom of God.

Another example of not fully understanding the wisdom of God, this time in a Spirit-filled context, is the early Pentecostal movement. Because many Holiness believers at the turn of the twentieth century had an understanding that the Bible pointed to a baptism in the Spirit, they experienced Pentecost at the famous Azusa Street Revival. But they were little influenced by Christian Science or New Thought, and did not have the model of reproof and testing that Christian New Perspective leaders had. Not having the reproof model of the wisdom of God led to long-lasting problems with the theology of tongues, specifically the confusion of tongues with xenolalia, as in Acts 2:5–12, where a speaker is understood in multiple languages. This was confused with tongues as a prayer language, as in 1 Corinthians 12 and 14. The latter is now understood as the normal gift of tongues, and xenolalia as a rare gift. Several Pentecostal pioneers sent missionaries without foreign language training to foreign lands believing that the missionaries would communicate the gospel in tongues. That failed, and it did much to discredit early Pentecostalism. The Pentecostals also affirmed that without tongues one did not really have the baptism of in the Spirit. For the early Pentecostals these things were presented as *doctrines*, not as hypotheses that were close to the truth but might need be corrected or refined.

All this is not to diminish the Pentecostal movement, which needs to be recognized as the most important development in Christianity since the Reformation. Rather, two points should be made. First, the spiritual phenomenon and gifts of the kingdom did not need to be perfectly understood in order to be active blessings to the church. An approximately true hypothesis is much better than no hypothesis at all (a point made by Karl Popper about the progress of scientific truth). The core truth that the early Pentecostals discovered was that the gift of tongues is important in the life of the Christian community. An exaggerated belief about tongues is certainly better than the cessationist belief that tongues occurred only in New Testament times.

Second, had the Pentecostal leaders possessed as good an understanding of reproof and testing the wisdom of God as the leaders of CNP, their pioneering theories would have been more quickly corrected to greater biblical accuracy. Perhaps Pentecostalism might have spread more rapidly and with less resistance in its first decades.

Lastly, in reflecting about the achievements of the pioneers we have studied—Percy Dearmer, Frank Laubach, Glenn Clark, Rufus Moseley, etc.—it seems that Agnes Sanford was the giant of employing the wisdom of God. She began with the fear of the Lord (which is why she immediately rejected occultism), but went on to gather information and advice, and proceeded to test everything, as Paul commanded. She held on to what is good. She was not flawless, but her errors, such as her acceptance of Jungian vocabulary, pale in comparison to her achievements.

23

The Villains of the Story

The Seminaries as Sanhedrin

You stiff-necked people, with uncircumcised hearts and ears! You are
just like your fathers: You always resist the Holy Spirit! (Acts 7:51)

IT IS USEFUL TO examine the contributions from the mainline seminaries
towards the re-establishment of the healing ministry and the spiritual
re-empowerment of the church. Specifically, what did mainline seminary
theologians make in the way of original contributions to the cause of
Spirit-empowered prayer and ministry?

The answer is not complex: nothing, *nada*, zip.

This is not an exaggeration. It is true that a few mainline theologians
and scholars in recent decades have revisited the miraculous and Pentecostalism favorably, as did Harvey Cox. Some theologians, like Thomas
Oden, known famously for his paleo-orthodoxy, have been instrumental
in recovering the faith-filled legacy of the early church. Certainly this
study has some citations to books and articles from Christian scholars
who have been helpful in telling the story of the church's slow recovery
from its cessationism.

But truly, I do not know of a single *original* contribution by a mainline theologian to the restoration of the gifts of healing or the ministry of
deliverance, or of anything as original as inner healing. Seminary writers have done nothing for the church to compare to the spiritual and
practical utility of Glenn Clark's *Soul's Sincere Desire*, Agnes Sanford's
The Healing Light, or John and Paula Sanford's *Transformation of the
Inner Man*. All of these works gave Christendom original insights into

285

the Bible, useful, accountable tools for prayer effectiveness, and revelations about the nature of spiritual reality. Those things have been alien to mainline seminary literature.

To the contrary, the mainline seminaries have been a tremendous drag upon the church's re-empowerment and its healing ministry. Like the Sanhedrin of New Testament times, they have been institutions of opposition to the renewing work of the Holy Spirit.[1] We should note that the seminaries in colonial New England took a strong anti-revival position towards the Great Awakening. Thus, although Jonathan Edwards left a great revival heritage in his writings, the interest in and cultivation of revival was not continued in the seminaries, the exception being the Presbyterian log seminaries on the frontier. They honored Edwards' writings and encouraged the revivals of the Second Great Awakening.

But the mainline Protestant seminaries seemed to have been predestined to slip into Sadducaism and Pharisaism of one sort or another. Most formed their theology from the writings of the reformers, where cessationism was embedded. As we have shown, core orthodox doctrines, as for instance the divinity of Jesus, are difficult to sustain without the witness of the power of God in miracles and the gifts of the Spirit. Thus, a drift into Sadducaism and deism in one form or another, as ultimately in DOG theology, was almost inevitable.

Harvard was founded in 1636 to ensure an educated and orthodox clergy for New England by faithful and orthodox Puritans, but it soon veered to deism/Sadducaism. By 1700 many Christians in New England were dissatisfied with the deist turn at Harvard and founded Yale. But that did not last a century as it too began slipping into deism and liberalism.[2] Next, Andover was then established as a bastion of Protestant orthodoxy. The faculty at Andover was required to subscribe to a statement of orthodoxy as a way of ensuring that deism and Unitarianism would

1. There is much literature on the problem of faithlessness in the mainline seminaries, which of course has been ignored by the seminary community. Among the best pieces is Montgomery's *Suicide of Christian Theology*. An especially insightful article by noted Pentecostal theologian and scholar Ruthven is "Pentecostal Seminaries?" Evangelicals are represented in the discussion by Jones, "Sabotaged from Within?," and Jewell, *Long Way Home*. Even liberal scholars have seen the problem; see Nielson, "Loneliness of Protestantism," and especially Fareley, *Theologia*. The latter is an excellent work, somewhat marred by an unclear writing style.

2. That Yale also became Sadducaic, and eventually a predominantly anti-Christian institution, is documented by the seminal book of the modern American conservative movement, William Buckley's *God and Man*.

not sneak in as it had at Harvard and Yale. After the 1860s, however, the statement of orthodoxy became less and less effective in stemming the logic of liberal theology and German higher biblical criticism (the myth hermeneutic). Eventually Andover became the most liberal of northern seminaries and was absorbed into its old enemy Harvard.[3]

The Rev. Dennis Bennett, the Episcopal priest who triggered the public charismatic renewal in 1960, went to a prestigious Presbyterian seminary in the early 1950s. On his first day of classes a senior seminarian told him:

> "Of course, we no longer believe in the miracles of the Bible. The divinity of Jesus, or the virgin birth," he stated . . . "Science has shown those to be impossible, also life after death, and other such things. We can no longer accept the supernatural. We must develop a natural, scientifically respectable religion that will be accepted by modern intellectuals!"[4]

Later Bennett discovered that many of his teachers were atheists. "One of our most respected professors, and a distinguished scholar, began his semester classes in the psychology of religion with: 'I want you to understand that I am an atheist.'[5] Bennett had experienced a powerful personal revelation of Jesus before he entered seminary and survived with his faith intact, though not as lively as when he arrived. But many of his fellow seminarians were not so fortunate and spread the distemper of religious atheism and DOG theology where ever they went.

During the same period Don H. Gross, a trained physicist, went to an Episcopal seminary. He later reflected on how the teaching staff there stubbornly resisted the good news that the new quantum physics gives analogous evidence and validation of the biblical worldview (as indicated in chapter 10). His book *The Case for Spiritual Healing* contained a pioneering section on the relationship between quantum physics and healing.[6]

Gross received a graduate degree in physics just after World War II. He then felt a call to the Episcopal priesthood and was ordained in 1949. His interest in healing was flamed through a lecture given by the Rev. Alfred Price, warden of the OSL. Subsequently, Gross investigated several of Katherine Kuhlman's rallies and witnessed many healings.

3. Meyerhoff, "Andover Seminary."
4. Bennett, *Nine O'Clock*, 12–13.
5. Ibid., 13.
6. See especially the appendix, "On the Creation and Annihilation of Matter."

While at seminary Gross noticed a radical distinction between the methodologies he learned as a scientist and those of his theology professors. As a scientist he knew that progress in scientific investigations depended in discovering facts and phenomenon that was not understood in terms of current theory (anomalies). Such anomalous facts forced a scientist to revise or reject current theory and seek better theories to cover the newly discovered phenomenon. Gross saw, on the contrary, that his seminary professors operated with an opposite, premodern methodology. When he presented his seminary professors with evidence for spiritual healing, they would not pursue investigation, no matter how well documented the evidence, nor would they modify their cessationist or liberal theories and philosophical materialism. No data contrary to their assumptions was recognized. While his professors listened politely to his enthusiastic presentation of why the miraculous was possible in terms of quantum physics, it made no impression on their beliefs. They continued in their belief that the world is a materialist/realist universe where the miraculous cannot happen.[7]

Most Christians in the pews were unaware of the apostate poisons spreading from the seminaries. Things continued to get only worse. In the 1960s and 1970s there was a period of further radicalization of the seminaries, due in part to a flood of many new seminarians who felt no particular call to the ministry, but found seminaries a safe place to avoid the draft and service in the Vietnam War. In the 1980s I had many conversations with some still faithful clergy of the Episcopal Church, and urged them to prepare to leave and to warn their congregations of what was happening in the seminaries. One told me, "The situation is hopeless; but why trouble the flock?" Another said, "They won't believe how bad things are, or if they do they will leave the church."

Also in the 1980s I attended one of the most distinguished mainline seminaries in the United States. The resistance to the reality of the miraculous that Gross had documented decades earlier was still present among the professors. I recall one incident in a class on pastoral counseling that was especially telling. Actually, it was one of the better courses I took, and the professor was an evangelical, although cessationist. For our first reading assignment we studied William James' classic *Varieties of Religious Experience*, one of the most read works in religious studies courses even to this day. We had noted carefully James' methodology. James insisted

---

7. Gross, *Case for Spiritual Healing*, chapter 4, "The Well-Springs of Reason."

that when examining spiritual phenomenon of any sort it is important to search out as many examples as possible, and to categorize them from the bizarre and destructive to the useful and creative.

For example, James noted that the doctrine of celibacy as practiced by the desert fathers could lead to destructive exaggerations such as monks fleeing in panic from the view of their own mothers. But James also noted that if you search well, you can also find good and non-neurotic persons who used celibacy to focus their service on others. This was Paul's point in 1 Corinthians 7:8–9. Thus, one has to collect much information from observations, and look carefully at the entire range of the occurrence of the phenomenon to avoid false judgments.[8] Everyone in the class understood this.

A few weeks after we had finished James' work, one of the seminarians began ridiculing the healing evangelist Ernest Angley, claiming he and other healing evangelists were all frauds. In fact, Angley's mannerisms have always been a bit odd, but he is a sincere and effective minister of God's healing graces.[9] I said to him, "Why don't you do the William James thing on this? Instead of bad-mouthing Angley, why don't you go out to places where people say healing is taking place, and to an Angley service, and line them up according to false, or deluded—or maybe real and effective? And then judge."

The professor looked at me with a surprised, "Ah-ha" look, as if saying, "Yes, of course!," *but he said nothing.* The critical seminarian gave me a look of disgust and said, "Why don't we just go on with today's class." The moment of grace disappeared into the Sadducaic normality of the seminary.

Few other professions would get away with this sort of data avoidance.[10] In that wonderful movie *The Bucket List*, Jack Nicholson plays cancer-stricken businessman Mr. Cole. His daughter had married an abusive man who repeatedly beat her. As a remedy, Mr. Cole got mob goons to kidnap and beat up his son-in-law as an encouragement never

8. James, *Varieties of Religious Experience.*

9. My wife, who was educated in childhood development, saw his effective ministry with children and with her professional eye concluded his ministry and healings of young children could not be faked.

10. Coming in second and third for avoidance of unwelcomed facts are the politically correct sociology and political science departments of many universities. On this I have space only to cite two classics, Bloom, *Closing of the American Mind*, and Genovese, "Question."

to abuse his daughter again. It worked. Now, the point is that Mr. Cole, as a law-abiding but greedy businessman, had no business card for "Mob Goons & Associates" in his Rolodex file. He didn't know how to contact them. But he "Asked someone, who knew someone, who knew someone, who got back to me."

Any seminary professor or DOG theologian who wanted to sniff out the truth about the miraculous or healing ministry could have "Asked someone, who knew someone . . ." Even back in the 1950s, before the Charismatic Renewal, they would have been referred to some Pentecostal healing revival, a CFO Camp, or an OSL mission, etc. They could then have investigated the miraculous and healing claims in the manner outlined in *The Varieties of Religious Experience*, which was first published in 1903.

The Guild Methodology vs. the Wisdom of God

All of this is to say that mainline professors have seldom, if ever, functioned in the wisdom of God, as was done by the healing pioneers such as Dr. Cullis, Prof. Glenn Clark, Mrs. Agnes Sanford, etc. Rather, as St. Paul warned, they were "blown here and there by every wind of teaching and by the cunning and craftiness of men in their deceitful scheming" (Eph 4:14).

In fact, the methodology of the mainline seminaries is premodern and rightly termed guild methodology.[11] It is a methodology based on authority, and stresses the established opinions. Fundamental critiques and questions are dismissed. Ever more radical secular opinions are welcomed and entertained, but orthodox views are shut off as reactionary.[12] The premodern approach and destructiveness of the guild methodology is disguised with the secondary aspects of scholarship, as in sophisticated vocabulary, multiple sources that repeat the same assumptions, accurate footnoting, and impressive-looking bibliographies.

One of my professors in seminary was an atheist and Marxist. He made repeated claims that he was practicing theology in a scientific manner because he did not believe in the myths of the miraculous, and used

---

11. The term "seminary guild" is often used in the literature on the seminaries; see for example Fareley, *Theologia*.

12. This is common to many aspects of academic life in the Western world today; see Goldberg, *Liberal Fascism*.

Marxist analysis in his research. He had heard of Karl Popper's work on science, but of course had no time to read it. His career was one of delusion, pretention, and destruction. I saw several seminarians wither into faithlessness under his teachings.[13]

The Sadducaic seminary guild of the mainline seminaries has been, and continues to be, a fellowship of self-esteem. That is, they think themselves to be in the vanguard of progress, while disdaining the peasants in the pews who take part in revivals and still believe in the miracles of the Bible, the reliability of the Scriptures, healing prayer, and the divinity of Jesus, etc. Their position is superior to all of this and verified because other seminary professors whom they respect believed similarly.

With this poisonous combination of guild methodology, data avoidance, and misplaced self-esteem, the mainline seminary guild has never produced original contributions on the miraculous, or healing, or deliverance ministries in the church. There have been a few works that suggest that the healing ministry is valid and should be incorporated into mainline Protestant life. But in comparison to the heroes of faith I have written about in this work, the guild seminary contributions have been *weak and entirely unoriginal.*[14]

An Invitation-by Paul Tillich

Not that the guild professors were not invited to something better.

For instance, in 1945 one of the most prestigious and beloved of mainline theologians, Paul Tillich, presented a paper on religion and health at Columbia University. In that address he urged the acceptance of healing prayer as real and urged a scholarly effort to discern true healing prayer from psychic suggestion and magical procedures.[15] His suggestion was, in effect, the William James approach. A decade later he repeated the theme in a sermon given to ministers at Union Theological Seminary in New York City.

---

13. His writings are obscure and deserve to remain so, and I will not mention his name. For an equivalent Sadducaic romp into spiritual destructiveness and apostasy, see (if you can hold your spiritual nose) the works of Episcopal Bishop John Shelby Spong, especially his *Christianity Must Change.*

14. See for instance Hiltner, *Religion and Health.*

15. Tillich, "Religion and Health."

> You are not supposed to become physicians; you are not sup-
> posed to become psychotherapists; you are not supposed to
> become political reformers. But you are supposed to pronounce
> and to represent the healing and demon-conquering power im-
> plied in the message of the Christ . . .[16]

Strangely enough, there was no rush by mainline seminarians or professors to follow Tillich's advice. In 1958 Tillich's views on healing were published in an anthology on healing and the church. The editor, Simon Doniger, expressed his frustration at the lack of progress on this issue. In the preface he dedicated the book, tongue-in-cheek, "to the modern Pharisaic mind that seeks to disprove all things and hold fast to that which is traditional."[17]

Caveat to All This

In truth, a few mainline seminaries have become more evangelical in the last decades. This happened to the one I attended. Other mainline evangelical seminaries of the more traditional sort have avoided Saddu-caism, but at the cost of less than satisfactory fundamentalism, with ces-sationism, as in Bob Jones University. A very few, like Fuller Seminary in Pasadena, have maintained their evangelical witness with great integrity and effectiveness, and with a nod towards the charismatic movement.[18]

There have also been the Pentecostal seminaries, established by the Pentecostal denominations, which naturally teach the reality of the mirac-ulous. Many of these belong to the smaller Pentecostal denomination, and do not have high academic records, and some restrict their teaching to only what their denomination believes. On the other hand, several Spirit-filled seminaries, such as the School of Theology and Missions at Oral Roberts University in Tulsa and Regent University School of Ministry at Virginia Beach, have grown to academic excellence and international renown. Their graduates are making a major impact on many denominations in

16. Tillich, "Heal the Sick," 7.

17. Doniger, *Religion and Health*, 5. Note that Doninger is using the concept of the Pharisee as a religious person who holds firm to tradition and is ultimately in opposition to the true work of the church. This is an early understanding of what I subsequently elaborated in *Quenching the Spirit*.

18. Fuller Seminary hosted the famous "Signs and Wonders" classes by John Wimber, the leader of the very charismatic Vineyard Fellowship.

destroying the cessationist delusion.[19] The Anglican seminary, Trinity School of Ministry in Ambridge, Pennsylvania, is now mostly Spirit-filled and teaches the healing ministry effectively to its students.

The Presence of the Demonic as a Spiritual Issue in the Seminaries

The absurdities of data avoidance of the DOG and other guild theologians could be attributed to a psychological drive to be comfortable, undisturbed, and in power. That is, if academic achievement is the criteria of prestige, position, and promotion in the seminaries, why endanger, enlarge, or confuse the criteria by acknowledging a church with the disciples' authority and gifts of the Spirit? That an unlearned layperson who has read Agnes Sanford or had been raised in a Pentecostal/charismatic church might be more effective in ministry and more knowledgeable about real spiritual issues than a guild professor is very threatening.

This is a psychological understanding of the issue. But I believe that what has really happened is that the seminaries became infested by demonic "principalities and powers" that clouded the minds of the staff to biblical truths. As Paul warned:

> For our struggle is not against flesh and blood, but against the rulers, against the authorities, against the powers of this dark world and against the spiritual forces of evil in the heavenly realms. (Eph 6:12)

The stubbornness and the illogical argumentation of the guild professors indicates this. In a conversation with the atheist/Marxist professor I mentioned above, I described a miraculous healing at a revival I had attended. He responded, "But that is witchcraft, sheer witchcraft!" Here was a man who was a Marxist/materialist and consistently denied the possibility of any spiritual phenomenon, but believed that there is a spiritual realm of witchcraft! I was astounded to silence.[20]

19. On this see Ruthven's "Pentecostal Seminaries." In my own Anglican/Episcopal tradition only two seminaries, out of eleven in the United States, managed to remain biblically orthodox and non-Sadducaic: Nashota House in Wisconsin, and Trinity Episcopal School of Ministry in Pennsylvania. The rest have fallen into the spiritual black holes of Sadducaism and political correctness.

20. The combination of belief in atheism, Marxism, and negative spirituality (spiritualism or Satanism) is illogical and contradictory, but it is also widespread. See this in reference to Cuba in Espiritu Santo's "Powers of the Dead."

Recently, direct evidence of demonic entry and involvement in DOG theology has emerged. In 2006 Thomas J. J. Altizer's released his autobiography, *Living the Death of God*. Recall that Altizer was one of the leading figures of the DOG movement.

Thomas J. J. Altizer was born in 1927 into a seriously dysfunctional and nominal Episcopalian home. His father was an alcoholic and his uncle murdered his own son. Thomas went to St. John's College in Annapolis, where he majored in philosophy, and then went on to the University of Chicago for graduate studies in religion. There, while studying an article on Nietzsche, he had a conversion experience—to the Death of God theology![21] During his studies at Chicago he already showed signs of severe emotional instability and depression. He was counseled for a time by the dean of the law school, who was a psychiatrist.

Altizer felt a call to the Episcopal priesthood (What else is a philosophy major to do for a living?) and began seminary studies. In the last year of that process he took the psychological examination required of candidates for the priesthood. This showed that he was deeply troubled and unacceptable as a minister. One of his professors rejoiced at this and said it was providential, as his real gift was in theology![22] Altizer proceeded, and received a doctorate in religious studies and theology. In his studies he found Rudolph Bultmann's theology to his liking, but that of Karl Barth distasteful and much too orthodox. His dissertation was on Carl Jung. Altizer recounted what happened to him just before his fateful psychological examination.

> Shortly before this examination, I was in a turbulent condition. . . . I was visited by a deep depression, one which occurred again and again throughout my life, but now with particular intensity. During this period I had perhaps the most ultimate experience of my life, and one that I believe profoundly affected my vocation as a theologian, and even my theological work itself. This occurred late at night, while I was in my room. I suddenly awoke and became truly possessed, and experienced an epiphany of Satan which I have never been able fully to deny, an experience in which I could actually feel Satan consuming me, absorbing me into his very being, as though this was the deepest possible initiation and bonding, the deepest and yet most horrible union. Few who read me know of this experience, but it is not accidental that

21. Altizer, *Living the Death*, 9.

22. Ibid., 4.

> I am perhaps the only theologian who now writes of Satan, and
> can jokingly refer to myself as the world's leading Satanologist:
> indeed, Satan and Christ soon became my primary theological
> motifs, and my deepest theological goal eventually became one
> of discovering a *coincidentia oppositorum* between them.[23]

That he considers himself the only theologian who writes about
Satan is but an indicator of the restricted vision and reading range of
liberal and DOG theologians. More importantly, we need to parse what
he meant by *coincidentia oppositorum*, which is a pillar of his satani-
cally inspired theology.[24] It is merely the old Gnostic lie that Satan and
Jesus are brothers doing God's work, and that really there is no evil, only
ignorance? A further Satanic motif of Altizer's is his understanding of
Jesus' death on the cross. For Altizer, Jesus was indeed God, but when he
died God transited from a transcendent God to imminence in the world,
which negated his transcendence and personhood (pantheism). Thus,
the satanic payoff: God is not a being that one prays too, nor expects to
perform the miraculous, etc.

Altizer taught this demonic mix at Emory's Candler Seminary
for over twenty years as a controversial but admired professor. He was
broadly instrumental in radicalizing much of the faculty there, and was
the subject of much publicity, including several major articles in *Time*
magazine.[25] Many alumni and other Methodists were deeply outraged
over the theological atrocities he advocated, and tried to have him removed from his teaching position. They were rebuffed under the rubric
of academic freedom. In the 1980s I interviewed a professor who remembered him well and considered him a personable and good professor.
That speaks volumes about academic lack of discernment. Sadly, a 2012
Public Broadcasting Atlanta documentary on Emory University perpetu-
ates the myth of Altizer as a good professor. In this documentary, which
supposedly covered the history of Emory University, scant coverage was
given to its founders, or their intention to found a pious Methodist College. The focus is on the modern secular period, and much attention is

---

23. Ibid., 4–5.

24. I read much DOG theology back in my college days, but for my renewed
understanding of Altizer I am relying on the extensive article by Winquest, "Altizer
in Retrospect." Winquest is a fellow DOG theologian who admires Altizer's writings.

25. See "God Is Dead" (1965).

given to the academic freedom issue raised by Altizer, the hero of the piece.[26] Sadducaism triumphed in the media again.

We must stop our comments on the seminary issue here, only noting that some denominations are now avoiding seminaries altogether. That is, a person who feels called to the ministry begins ministering at an entry level, as in a youth ministry volunteer, music assistant, home fellowship leader, etc. As the person progresses in ministry he or she is directed to read books on liturgy, denominational history and doctrine, etc., and attached to a minister/mentor. Greek and Hebrew can now be learned on a computer. This takes longer than the three-year seminary cycle but produces spiritually tested and mature ministers. Some of the successful evangelical megachurches have discovered they can run effective seminaries on their own campuses, and thus avoid the Sadducaic influences that poison so many seminary graduates.[27]

26. "Wise Heart."

27. Ross, "Workers Are Few."

The Final Word

Jonathan Edwards on Agnes Sanford
and Her Companions

THE THEOLOGY AND MINISTRY of Agnes Sanford and her companions in Christian New Perspective may seem as strange to traditional Christians as the Holy Rollers were to mainline Christians a generation ago. However, when you apply a biblical perspective on what is truly a work of God and what is not, as codified by Jonathan Edwards, strangeness is no longer a major concern.

Let us revisit from chapter 7 what Edwards said about identifying a true work of God. I wish to make clear that practically everything I say about Mrs. Sanford and her Christian New Perspective companions would apply to many Pentecostal leaders and healing ministers of the era, but were not the subject of this study.

Jonathan Edwards' first point:

> When the operation is such as to raise their esteem of that Jesus who was born of the Virgin, and was crucified without the gates of Jerusalem; and seems more to confirm and establish their minds in the truth of what the gospel declares to us of his being the Son of God, and the Saviour of men; is a sure sign that it is from the Spirit of God.[1]

We must first recall the period we are discussing. The beginning of the twentieth century to the 1960s was the period of liberal theological ascendency. Liberal theology was Arian and even sub-Arian. This means

---

1. Edwards, *Distinguishing Marks*, 266. This book is available online at http://www.ccel.org/ccel/edwards/works2.vii.html.

that Jesus was relegated to being a nice teacher of ethics, but certainly not a miracle worker, nor really Son of God. Evangelicals kept hold of a traditional view of Jesus as Son of God, but also tended to center their prayer life on God the Father (not entirely universal, but common). With the coming of the Holy Spirit at the CFOs, the Schools of Pastoral Care, and later in the OSL, Jesus became the focus of worship in these groups, just as in Pentecostalism. We saw this progression in the writings of Glenn Clark and Agnes Sanford. *The Healing Light* was focused on God the Father, but *Behold Your God* was focused on Jesus, as for instance Jesus' role in the forgiveness of sins. Glenn Clark's later works, such as *The Way, The Truth, and the Life*, were similarly Jesus-focused.

Further, with the rise of the sustained healing ministries inspired by Mrs. Sanford, the OSL and CFO camps, the healing missions, etc., doubts about Jesus as a miracle worker and healer dissolved under the weight of observed miracles done in the name of Jesus. Persons who came to these camps or missions with a weakened, liberal attitude of a demythologized Jesus were sure to have left with a greater appreciation of him as Son of God. Also, inner healing prayer increased the esteem of Jesus, as persons subject to such prayer would often have a grace experience with Jesus that they would not likely forget.

Second:

> When the spirit that is at work operates against the interests of Satan's kingdom, which lies in encouraging and establishing sin, and cherishing men's worldly lusts; this is a sure sign that it is a true, and not a false spirit.[2]

In this category the persons of Christian New Perspective were splendidly fruitful, especially in destroying Satan's strongholds via the practice of exorcism and deliverance. The CFO camps and the OSL conferences were places where healing and deliverance prayer was *normal*, in contrast to the destructive ignorance of most mainline churches and practically all seminaries.

Recall that Prof. Clark included exorcism prayer as part of healing in his 1940 book, *How to Find Health Through Prayer*. This was decades ahead of most Protestant writers and ministers, both evangelical and liberal. Even to this day many Christian leaders remain reluctant to recognize the legitimacy of that ministry. Mrs. Sanford taught deliverance prayer from the very first School of Pastoral Prayer to thousands of

2. Ibid., 267.

ministers and lay leaders over its years of operation. Thus her deliverance ministry became multiplied throughout time. Further, both John Sandford's Elijah House Ministries and Francis MacNutt's Christian Healing Ministry contain extensive teachings on deliverance and exorcism prayer, and continue to spread that knowledge throughout the world. That is a legacy from Christian New Perspective.

Presently, Francis MacNutt's book *Deliverance from Evil Spirits* has become a standard on the topic, and it encourages both laypersons and ministers to do deliverance prayer. MacNutt was a traditional Catholic priest in the 1960s, and before his encounter with Mrs. Sanford and the CFO camps he could not have written such a book.

We should observe that in the writings of Christian New Perspective there was never a drift into the extremes of the prosperity doctrine that fouled some of the Pentecostal Word of Faith teachers. For instance, Glenn Clark wrote about managing a business as a Christian ministry that would result in prosperity, but not as a source of all the riches one could desire or imagine.

Next:

> The spirit that operates in such a manner, as to cause in men a greater regard to the Holy Scriptures, and establishes them more in their truth and divinity, is certainly the Spirit of God.[3]

Again, in reference to the period of our study, the persons of the Christian New Perspective all came to a high view of Scripture as true and reliable. The miracles of healing and answered prayer they mediated verified by analogy the Gospel narratives. We find no trace of demythologizing in their works. Indeed, as we noted in Mrs. Sanford's analysis of the resuscitation done by Elijah, her understanding of that biblical passage authenticated the biblical narrative as true in a way that even the best evangelical commentators could not understand. Glenn Clark's understanding of Jesus' use of parables was another step forward in biblical understanding not yet fully appreciated.

This carries out to this day if one goes to a CFO or OSL event or conference, or the sessions run by Christian Healing Ministries or Elijah House. Those who attend these events come from a variety of Christian denominations, some of which are weak in affirming the truthfulness of the Scriptures, or from churches with theologically liberal pastors. But

3. Ibid.

their experience strengthens their belief in the truthfulness of the Bible, at times to the discomfort or embarrassment of their home pastors.

> Another rule to judge of spirits may be drawn from those com-
> pellations given to the opposite spirits. . . . "The spirit of truth
> and the spirit of error." These words exhibit the two opposite
> characters of the Spirit of God, and other spirits that counterfeit
> his operations. And therefore, if by observing the manner of the
> operation of a spirit that is at work among a people, we see that it
> operates as a spirit of truth, leading persons to truth, convincing
> them of those things that are true, we may safely determine that
> it is a right and true spirit.[4]

The most obvious and central demonstration of this criteria was that the leaders of Christian New Perspective hammered at, confronted, and, in conjunction with their Pentecostal brethren, largely overthrew the error of cessationism and its cousin, the Galatian Bewitchment. The struggle was long and continuous, as those errors had been long stand-ing and were woven into the very fabric of orthodox theologies. But the errors were challenged and dissipated at CFO camps, the Schools of Pastoral Care, and healing missions, etc., and in the splendid literature produced by the leaders of Christian New Perspective. Recall the meeting in which Jo Kimmel persuaded Fr. Francis MacNutt to go to a CFO. What enormous consequences a single providential conversation can have!

The overthrow of cessationism is not complete. Recently there was a furious counterattack and reaffirmation of cessationism in the boldest of terms in a new wave of Pharisaism. This latest incident was spearheaded by the popular radio and television Bible teacher John MacArthur, with his book *Strange Fire* (2013) and the related conference. In spite of that, cessationism and the Galatian Bewitchment are fast becoming a minority opinion in Christendom, and are practically extinct in the Global South, where Christianity is expanding rapidly.

It is also clear that Agnes Sanford in particular made startling con-tributions to theology and the truthfulness of theology by bringing into focus the energies of God, a category ignored by Western theology.

In regard to truth in the theological speculations of the leaders of Christian New Perspective, that evaluation is much harder to arrive at and may be impossible this side of heaven. Truth in theology is often confused and equated with agreement with one's confessional theology.

---

4. Ibid., 268.

As a Catholic young man in the 1960s, I was sure that Catholic theology was 100 percen biblical, true, and complete. This included the officially sanctioned theology of St. Thomas Aquinas, which held to the concept of transubstantiation, which many Protestants loathed. Too bad for them!

But as a matter of fact several months before St. Thomas died he had a visionary experience while celebrating Mass that left him stunned. Here is a description of what happened from the authoritative Catholic *Butler's Lives of the Saints*:

> On the feast of St. Nicholas [in 1273, Aquinas] was celebrating Mass when he received a revelation that so affected him that he wrote and dictated no more, leaving his great work the *Summa Theologiae* unfinished. To Brother Reginald's (his secretary and friend) expostulations he replied, "The end of my labors has come. All that I have written appears to be as so much straw after the things that have been revealed to me." When later asked by Reginald to return to writing, Aquinas said, "I can write no more. I have seen things that make my writings like straw."[5]

I love going to Holy Communion and have received many blessings from that sacrament. However, I now understand transubstantiation as a speculative idea that may be either close to the truth or entirely wrong. Its degree of truth or falsity does not affect the grace of the sacrament.

Having said this, it seems that earnest theological debate, and its inherent speculations, is pleasing to God as it indicates our desire to seek the truth. In this regard, the Fox-Sanford theory that Jesus' bloody sweat is related to the forgiveness of mental sins is insightful and helps appreciate our Savior's work in the atonement, but I will not have an argument about it with a Christian brother. I find Glenn Clark's theory of Jesus' blood giving out vibrations less attractive.

> If the spirit that is at work among a people operates as a spirit of love to God and man, it is a sure sign that it is the Spirit of God.[6]

No one can consider the leaders of Christian New Perspective as anything but loving and sacrificial Christians. Recall Agnes Sanford's week of fasting and travail prayer for Harry Goldsmith. Recall her years of travel in healing missions that left her exhausted. Recall also Glenn

---

5. Thurston, *Butler's Lives*, March 7.

6. Cited from Goen, *Great Awakening*, 253. This is an abbreviation of Edwards' points in section 2 of *Distinguishing Marks*.

Clark risking his life to bring his prayer insights to the high altitudes of the Colorado YMCA, which could have killed him.

From personal observations at CFO and OSL events from over thirty years, I can testify that the spirit of love the Christian New Perspective pioneers left in those institutions continues to hold strong and vibrant. Strangers come to gather, pray together, and fellowship as if they have been together years. Praying for one another in the power of the Holy Spirit does that. Christian love is the chief characteristic of these meetings. The same may be said of the two organizations that inherited Mrs. Sanford's teaching legacy: Christian Healing Ministries and Elijah House.

Edwards' criteria point to the fact that Mrs. Sanford and her companions indeed performed a great work of God, one that continues to work its good fruit throughout modern Christendom.

Bibliography

Adamnan. *Life of St. Columba, Founder of Hy.* Edited by William Reeves. Edinburgh: Edmonston and Douglas, 1874.

Albert, David Z., and Rivk A. Galchen. "Was Einstein Wrong? A Quantum Threat to Special Relativity." *Scientific American,* March 2009. Online: http://www.sciam.com/article.cfm?id=was-einstein-wrong-about-relativity.

Alexander, Brooks. "Mind Power and the Mind's Eye." *SCP Journal* 9/3 (1999) 8–20.

Albrecht, Daniel E. "Carrie Judd Montgomery: Pioneering Contributor to Three Religious Movements." PNEUMA 8 (Fall 1986) 101–19.

Alder, Vera Stanley. *The Fifth Dimension.* London: Rider, 1940.

Altizer, Thomas J. J., and Mark Taylor, *Living the Death of God.* Albany: State University of New York Press, 2006.

Ameneompe. Instructions of Ameneompe. Online: http://www.maat.sofiatopia.org/amen_em_apt.htm#3a.

Anonymous. *The Way of the Pilgrim.* Translated by R. M. French. New York: Seabury, 1965.

Applebaum, Yoni. "Publishers Gave Away 122,951,031 Books During World War II." *The Atlantic,* September 10, 2014. Online: http://www.theatlantic.com/business/archive/2014/09/publishers-gave-away-122951031-books-during-world-war-ii/379893/.

Arends, Carolyn. "A Both/And Path to Truth." *Christianity Today,* August 15, 2011. Online: http://www.christianitytoday.com/ct/2011/august/bothpathtruth.html.

Arnold, Carrie. "New Science Shows How Maggots Heal Wounds." *Scientific American* 308/4, March 19, 2013. Online: http://www.scientificamerican.com/article/news-science-shows-how-maggots-heal-wounds/.

Ash, James L., Jr. "American Religion and the Academy in the Early Twentieth Century: The Chicago Years of William Warren Sweet." *Church History* 50 (December 1981) 450–64.

———. "The Decline of Ecstatic Prophecy in the Early Church." *Theological Studies* 37 (June 1976) 227–52.

Athanasius. *Life of Antony.* Translated by Carolinne White. London: Penguin, 1998.

Augustine. *On the Sermon On the Mount.* Translated by William Findlay. Nicene and Post-Nicene Fathers, Second Series 6. Buffalo: Christian Literature, 1888

———. *The City of God.* Edited by R. V. G. Tasker, translated by John Healy. New York: Dutton, 1945.

———. *The Retractions.* In *Augustine: Earlier Writings.* Selected and Translated by John H. S. Burleigh. Philadelphia: Westminster, 1953

The Baltimore Catechism. No. 3. 1941 rev. ed. Paterson: St. Anthony Guild, 1949.

Baltz, Francis B. "Agnes Sanford: A Creative Intercessor." MA thesis, Nashotah House, 1979.

Banks, John Gayner. *The Gospel of Power.* San Diego: St. Luke's, 1946.

———. *Manual of Christian Healing.* 14th ed. San Diego: St. Luke's, 1965.

———. *The Redemption of the Body.* Mountain Lakes: Christian Healing Foundation, [1931].

Barna Group. "Americans Describe Their Views about Life after Death." October 21, 2003. Online: http://www.barna.org/barna-update/article/5-barna-update/128-americans-descr.

Barr, Steven M. *Modern Physics and Ancient Faith.* Notre Dame: University of Notre Dame, 2003.

Barrow, John D., Frank J. Tipler, and John A. Wheeler. *The Anthropic Cosmological Principle.* New York: Oxford University, 1988.

Bates, J. Barrington. "Extremely Beautiful, but Eminently Unsatisfactory: Percy Dearmer and the Healing Rites of the Church, 1909–1928." *Anglican and Episcopal History* 73 (June 2004) 196–207.

Beard, Rebecca. *Everyman's Search.* New York: Harper, 1950.

Bell, Robert B. H. *Intelligent Living.* Pasadena: Western Art, 1950. 1st ed. 1937.

———. *The Life Abundant: A Manual of Living.* Milwaukee: Morehouse, 1927.

Bell, Robert B. H., Helen Peck, and Ethel M. Campbell. *The Live Abundant Cook Book: Suggestions for the Preparation of Natural Food.* Wilmington: Carolina Printing and Stamp, 1935.

Belloc, Hilire. *The Great Heresies.* London: Catholic Book Club, 1938.

Bennett, Dennis. *Nine O'Clock in the Morning.* Plainsville: Logos, 1970.

Bennett, Dennis, and Rita Bennett. *Trinity of Man.* Plainsfield: Logos, 1979.

Bennett, Drake. "Easy = True." *Boston Globe,* January 31, 2010. Online: http://marketingpedia.com/Marketing-Library/CognitiveFluency/Easy=True-CognitiveFluency-BostonGlobe_013110.pdf.

Bennett, Rita. *How to Pray for Inner Healing for Yourself and Others.* Old Tappan, NJ: Revell, 1983.

Bentley, Philip J. "Uncertainty and Unity." *Journal of Judaism* 33 (Spring 1984) 1919–201.

Berg, Stefan. "Luther's City Revisits the Reformation" *Spiegel Online,* October,28, 2008. Online: http://www.spiegel.de/international/germany/the-protestant-rome-luther-city-revisits-the-reformation-a-586439.html.

Bergner, Mario. *Setting Love in Order.* Grand Rapids: Baker, 1995.

Briggs, John. "The Genius Mind." *Science Digest* (December 1984) 74–77, 102.

Blom, Philipp. *A Wicked Company: The Forgotten Radicalism of the European Enlightenment.* New York: Basic, 2010.

Bloom, Allen D. *The Closing of the American Mind.* New York: Simon and Shuster, 1987.

Bonaventure, *Meditations on the Life of Christ*. Translated by Isa Ragusa and Rosalie B. Green. Princeton: Princeton University, 1961.

Bottum, Joseph. "The Death of Protestant America." *First Things*, August–September 2008, 23–33.

Boom, Corrie Ten. *Tramp for the Lord*. Old Tappan, NJ: Revell, 1974.

Bovon, Francois. "Beyond the Book of Acts: Stephen, the First Christian Martyr in Traditions Outside the New Testament Canon of Scripture." *Perspectives on Religious Studies* 32/2 (Summer 2005) 93–107.

Boman, Thorleif. *Hebrew Thought Compared with Greek*. Translated by Jules Moreau. Philadelphia: Westminster, 1961.

Boyd, Greg "Learning Imaginative Prayer." *Leadership Journal* 29 (Winter 2008) 63.

Braden, Charles S. *Spirits in Rebellion: The Rise and Development of New Thought*. Dallas: Southern Methodist University, 1963.

Bradshaw, David. "The Divine Energies in the New Testament." *St. Valdimir's Theological Quarterly* 50/3 (2006) 189–223.

Brierlen, Michael. "Honest to God." *Modern Believing* 46/3 (July 2005) 82–83.

Brown, Candy Gunter. *Testing Prayer: Science and Healing*. Cambridge, MA: Harvard University Press, 2012.

Brown, Harold O. J. *Heresies: The Image of Christ in the Mirror of Orthodoxy and Heresy from the Apostles to the Present*. Garden City, NY: Doubleday, 1984.

Bultmann, Rudolf. *Kerygma and Myth: A Theological Debate*. Edited by Hans Werner Bartach, translated by R. H. Fuller. London: SPCK, 1957.

Buckley, James M. *Christian Science and Other Superstitions*. New York: The Century, 1899.

Buckley, William F. *God and Man at Yale: The Superstitions of "Academic Freedom"*. Chicago: Henry Regency, 1951.

Bundy, David. "Pentecostalism as a Global Phenomenon: A Review Essay of Walter Hollenweger's *Pentecostalism: Origins and Developments Worldwide*." *PNEUMA* 21/2 (Fall 1999) 289–303.

Burkhardt, Jacob *The Age of Constantine the Great*. Basil, 1853.

Burns, R.M. *The Great Debate on Miracles*. London: Associated University, 1981.

"The Call to Holiness: A Statement of Evangelicals and Catholics Together." *First Things*, March 2005, 23–26. Online: http://www.firstthings.com/article/2005/03/the-call-to-holiness.

Caddy, Emilie. *Lessons in Truth*. Kansas City: Unity School of Christianity, 1941.

Calvin, John. *Institutes of the Christian Religion*. Translated by John Allen. Philadelphia: Presbyterian Board of Publication, 1941.

Camp, Claudia V. "The Wise Women of 2 Samuel: A Role Model for Women in Early Israel." *Catholic Biblical Quarterly* 43 (January 1981) 14–29.

"The Camp Farthest Out." Untitled brochure. N.p., [1931].

Campenhausen, Hans von. *Ecclesiastical Authority and Spiritual Power in the Church of the First Three Centuries*. Stanford, CA: Stanford University Press, 1969.

Capra, Fritjof. *The Tao of Physics*. Boulder, CO: Shambhala, 1975.

Cary, Benedict. "Long-Awaited Medical Study Questions the Power of Prayer." *New York Times*, March 31, 2006.

Casel, Don Odo. *The Mystery of Christian Worship and Other Writings*. Edited by Berkhard Neuheuser. Westminster: Newman, 1962.

Casey, Robert P., et al. *Quantulacumque: Studies Presented to Kirsopp Lake*. London: Christophers, 1937.

Cassian, John. *The Conferences*. Translated by C. S. Gibson. Nicene and Post-Nicene Fathers, Second Series 11. Buffalo: Christian Literature,1894.

Castaldo, Chris. "Catholics Come Home?" *Christianity Today*, January 19, 2010. Online: http://www.christianitytoday.com/ct/2010/januaryweb-only/13-22.0.html.

Catechism of the Catholic Church. New York: Doubleday, 1997.

Chardin, Teilhard de. *The Phenomenon of Man*. Translated by Bernard Hall. New York: Harper & Row, 1959.

Chappell, Paul G. "The Divine Healing Movement in America." PhD diss., Drew University, 1983.

Chauncy, Charles. *Seasonable Thoughts on the State of Religion in New England*. Boston: Roger & Fowle, 1743.

Clarence H., and Thomas H. Johnson, editors. *Jonathan Edwards: Representative Selections*. New York: American Book Co., l935.

Clark, Glenn. *Correspondence Course in Spiritual Healing*. St. Paul: Macalester Park, 1953.

———. *From Crime to Christ*. St. Paul: Macalester Park, 1948.

———. *The Holy Spirit*. St. Paul: Macalester Park, 1954.

———. "The Holy Spirit." Audio recording from the 1954 New Mexico CFO. St. Paul: Cutler Memorial Library, n.d.

———. *How to Find Health through Prayer*. New York: Harper, 1940.

———. *I Will Lift Up Mine Eyes*. New York: Harper , 1937.

———. *Man's Reach*. St. Paul: Macalester Park, 1977.

———. *The Man Who Talks with Flowers*. St. Paul: Macalester Park, 1939.

———. *Power in Athletics*. St. Paul: Macalester Park, 1935.

———. *The Power of the Spirit in the Athletic Field*. [St. Paul]: privately published, 1929.

———. "The Soul's Sincere Desire." *Atlantic Monthly*, August 1924, 167–72.

———. *The Soul's Sincere Desire*. Boston: Little, Brown, 1928.

———. *The Thought Farthest Out*. St. Paul: Macalester Park, 1930.

———. *The Three Mysteries of Jesus: The Cross, the Blood, the Name*. St. Paul: Macalester Park, 1942.

———. *Water of Life*. St. Paul: Macalester Park, 1931.

———. *The Way, the Truth, and the Life*. New York: Harper, 1946.

Clark, Miles. *Glenn Clark: His Life and Writings*. Nashville: Abingdon, 1975.

Clifford, Richard. *The Wisdom Literature*. Nashville: Abingdon, 1998.

Collins, Gary. *The Magnificent Mind*. Waco: Word, 1985.

Colson, Charles. "The Post-Neuhaus Future of Evangelicals and Catholics Together." Interview by Susan Wunderink. *Christianity Today*, January 23, 2009. Online: http://www.christianitytoday.com/ct/2009/januaryweb-only/103-51.0.html.

Conkin, Paul K. *Cane Ridge: America's Pentecost*. Madison: University of Wisconsin, 1990.

Cousins, Norman. *Anatomy of an Illness as Perceived by the Patient*. New York: Norton, 1979.

Cromartie, Michael. "Freud Analyzed: A Conversation with Paul Vitz." *Books & Culture*, January–February 1999, 30–33.

Crosby, Robert C. "A New Kind of Pentecostalism." *Christianity Today*, August 3, 2011. Online: http://www.christianitytoday.com/ct/2011/august/newkindpentecostal. html.

Crowder, John. *The New Mystics*. Shippensburg, PA: Destiny Image, 2006.

Cullis, Charles. *Faith Cures: Or, Answers to Prayer in the Healing of the Sick*. Boston: Willard Tract Repository, 1879.

Cunningham, Raymond J. "The Impact of Christian Science on the American Churches, 1880–1910." *American Historical Review* 72 (April 1967) 885–905.

D'Andrade, Hugh. *Charles Fillmore: Herald of the New Age*. New York: Harper & Row, 1974.

Daily, Starr. *Release*. New York: Harper, 1942.

Danielou, Jean. *The Theology of Jewish Christianity*. London: Darton, Longman & Todd, 1964.

Dayton, Donald W. *Theological Roots of Pentecostalism*. Metuchen, NJ: Scarecrow, 1987.

Dearmer, Nan. *The Life of Percy Dearmer*. London: Book Club, 1941.

Dearmer, Pearcy. *Body and Soul: An Enquiry into the Effect of Religion upon Health*. 2nd ed. New York: E. P. Dutton, 1923. 1st ed. 1909.

———. *The Power of the Spirit*. London: Humphrey Milford, 1919.

De Arteaga, William L. "F. W. Fuller: A Scribe for All Seasons." *Sharing*, May 1992, 7–11.

———. *Forgotten Power: The Significance of the Lord's Supper in Revival*. Grand Rapids: Zondervan, 2002.

———. "Glenn Clark and the CFO." *Sharing*, November–December, 1992, 13–19.

———. "Glenn Clark's Camps Farthest Out: Schoolhouse of the Charismatic Renewal." *PNEUMA* 25/2 (Fall 2003) 265–88.

———. "The Hunters' Revolution in Healing Prayer." *Anglican Pentecostal* blog, May 8, 2013. Online: http://anglicalpentecostal.blogspot.com/2013/05/the-hunters-revolution-in-healing.html.

———. "Is Calming Tornadoes a Christian Ministry?" *Anglican Pentecostal* blog, June 1, 2013. Online: http://anglicalpentecostal.blogspot.com/2013/06/is-calming-tornados-christian-ministry.html.

———. "John MacArthur's Strange Fire as a Parody of Jonathan Edwards' Theology." *Pneuma Review*, November 3, 2013. Online: http://pneumareview.com/john-macarthurs-strange-fire-as-parody-of-jonathan-edwards-theology-by-william-de-arteaga/.

———. *Quenching the Spirit: Discover the Real Spirit behind the Charismatic Controversy*. 2nd ed. Lake Mary, FL: Creation House, 1996.

———. "Making Healing Respectable: The OSL." *Sharing*, January 1992, 9–13.

———. *Past Life Visions: A Christian Exploration*. New York: Seabury, 1983.

———. "Pearcy Dearmer: A Priest for All Seasons." *Sharing*, June–July 1992, 22–26.

———. "The Rev. John L. Nevius: The Holy Spirit Gives a Lesson in Chinese." *Pneuma Review*, May 10, 2014. Online: http://pneumareview.com/the-rev-john-l-nevius-the-holy-spirit-gives-a-lesson-in-chinese/.

De Arteaga, William L., and Carolyn De Arteaga. "An Indicator of Inner Healing as Grace: The Fido Factor." *Journal of Christian Healing* 13 (Summer 1991) 11–13.

Decker, Ed, and Dave Hunt. *The God Makers*. Eugene, OR: Harvest House, 1984.

"A Dissenting View of God's Creation: Faith in the Crucible of the New Physics." *Christianity Today*, February 1, 1985.

Doniger, Simon. editor. *Religion and Health: A Symposium.* New York: Association Press, 1958.

Dresser, Horatio. *A History of the New Thought Movement.* New York: Thomas Y. Crowell, 1919.

———. editor. *The Quimby Manuscripts.* New York: Thomas Y. Crowell, 1921.

Eddy, Mary Baker. *Christian Healing: A Sermon Delivered at Boston.* Boston: First Church of Christ Scientist, 1908.

———. *Christian Science Versus Pantheism.* Boston; First Church of Christ Science, 1898.

———. *Retrospection and Introspection.* Boston: First Church of Christian Science, 1892.

———. *Science and Health with Key to the Scriptures.* Boston: Christian Science Publishing Society, 1906.

———. *Yes and No.* Boston: First Church of Christ Science, 1908.

Edwards, Jonathan. *The Distinguishing Marks of a Work of the Spirit of God,* 1741.

———. *A Faithful Narrative of the Surpring Work of God in the Conversion of Many Hundred Souls in Northampton.* Boston: J. Loring, 1831.

———. *Some Thoughts Concerning the Present Revival of Religion in New England.* Edinburgh, T. Lumisden, 1743.

Einar, Thomasen. "Orthodoxy and Heresy in Second-Century Rome." *Harvard Theological Review* 97/3 (July 2004) 54–58.

Elbert, Paul. "Calvin and the Spiritual Gifts." *Journal of the Evangelical Theological Society* 22/3 (September 1979) 235–56.

Ellenberger, Henri. *The Discovery of the Unconscious.* New York: Basic Books, 1957.

Elliot, John H. "Paul, Galatians, and the 'Evil Eye.'" *Currents in Theology and Mission* 17/4 (August 1990) 262–73.

Espiritu Santo, Diana. "The Powers of the Dead: Spirits, Socialism, and Slaves in an African-Cuban Universe." *Fieldwork in Religion* 3/2 (November 2008) 161–77.

Erdozain, Dominic. *The Problem of Pleasure: Sport: Recreation and the Crisis of Victorian Religion.* Suffolk: Woodbridge Boydell, 2010.

Evans, W. E. *Mental Medicine: A Theoretical and Practical Treatise.* Boston: Carter and Pettee, 1874.

Fareley, Edward. *Theologia: The Fragmentation and Unity of Theological Education.* Philadelphia: Fortress, 1983.

Farrar, F. W. *Mercy and Judgment.* New York: E. P. Dutton, 1881.

"The Fate of Catholic Europe: The Void Within." *The Economist,* August 5, 2010. Online: http://www.economist.com/node/16740795.

Faust, Clarence H., and Thomas H. Johnson, editors. *Jonathan Edwards: Representative Selections.* New York: American Book Co., l935.

Fillmore, Charles. *Atom-Smashing Power of Mind.* Lee's Summit, MO: Unity School of Christianity, 1949.

———. *Christian Healing.* Lee's Summit, MO: Unity School of Christianity, 1909.

———. *The Twelve Powers of Man.* Kansan City: Unity School of Christianity, 1941.

Finney, Charles *Memoirs.* New York: A. S. Barnes, 1872.

Flegg, Columba Graham. *Gathered Under Apostles: A Study of the Catholic Apostolic Church.* Oxford: Clerendon, 1992.

Foller, Oskar. "Martin Luther on Miracles, Healing, Prophecy and Tongues." *Studia Historia Ecclesicticas* 31/2 (October 2005) 333–51.

Foster, David Kyle. "Conversation with Francis and Judith MacNutt." *Pneuma Review*, March 20, 2014. Online: http://pneumareview.com/conversation-with-francis-and-judith-macnutt/.

Foster, James D., and Glenn T. Morgan. "Piaget and Parables: The Convergence of Secular and Scriptural Views of Learning." *Journal of Psychology and Theology* 13 (Summer 1985) 97–103.

Fox, Emmet. *The Sermon on the Mount.* New York: Harper & Row, 1934.

———. *Ten Commandments: The Master Key of Life.* New York: Harper & Row, 1934.

Freeman, James Dillet. *The Household of Faith: The Story of Unity.* Lee's Summit, MO: Unity School of Christianity, 1951.

Frodsham, Stanley Howard. *Smith Wigglesworth: Apostle of Faith.* Springfield, MO: Gospel Pub., 1990.

Frost, Evelyn. *Christian Healing.* London: Bradford & Dickens, 1940.

Gamow, George. *Thirty Years That Shook Physics.* Garden City, NY: Doubleday, 1966.

Gay, Peter. *The Enlightenment, an Interpretation: The Rise of Modern Paganism.* New York: Knopf, 1966.

Gardner, Rex. "Miracles of Healing in Anglo-Celtic Northumbria as Recorded by Venerable Bede and His Contemporaries: A Reappraisal in the Light of Twentieth Century Experience." *British Medical Journal 257* (December 1983) 24–31.

Gaze, Henry. *Emmet Fox: The Man and His Work.* New York: Harper, 1952.

Genovese, Eugene. "The Question." *Dissent*, Summer 1994, 371–76.

Gerostergios, Asterios N. "The Religious Policy of Justinian I and His Religious Beliefs." PhD diss., Boston University School of Theology, 1974.

Gibbon, Edward. *The Decline and Fall of the Roman Empire.* 1776.

Gilman, James E. "R. G. Collingwood and the Religious Sources of Nazism." *Journal of the American Academy of Religion* 54/1 (Spring 1986) 111–28.

"The God Is Dead Movement." *Time*, October 22, 1965. Online: http://content.time.com/time/magazine/article/0,9171,941410,00.html.

Goen, C. C., editor. *The Great Awakening.* New Haven, CT: Yale University Press, 1972.

Goldberg, Jonah. *Liberal Fascism: The Secret History of the American Left from Mussolini to the Politics of Meaning.* Garden City, NY: Doubleday, 2010.

Goldsmith, Harry. "Anatomy of a Healing." *Sharing* 57/3 (1989) 30–36.

Gonzales, Justo, and Catherine Gunsalvus Gonzales. *Heretics for Armchair Theologians.* Louisville: John Knox, 2008.

Gordon, A. J. *The Ministry of Healing in All Ages.* Boston: H. Gaunett, 1883.

Gottschalk, Stephen. *The Emergence of Christian Science in American Religious Life.* Berkley: University of California Press, 1973.

Gowing, Peter G. "The Legacy of Frank Charles Laubach." *International Bulletin of Missionary Research* 7/2 (April 1983) 58–42.

Grant, Ulysses S. *Personal Memoirs.* 2 vols. New York: C. L. Webster, 1885, 1886.

Graves, Robert, editor. *Strangers to Fire: When Tradition Trumps Scripture.* Woodstock, GA: Foundation for Pentecostal Studies, 2014.

Gray, Donald. *Percy Dearmer: A Parson's Pilgrimage.* Norwick: Canterbury, 2000.

Greeley, Andrew. *Unsecular Man: The Persistence of Religion.* New York: Schocken, 1972.

Greene, Brian. *The Elegant Universe: Superstrings: Hidden Dimensions, and the Quest for the Ultimate Theory.* New York: Random House, 2003.

———. "Hanging by a String." *Smithsonian*, January 2015, 21–27, 88–90.

Greenspan, Freedrick E. "Why Prophecy Ceased." *Journal of Biblical Literature* 108/1 (1989) 37–49.

Gregory of Nyssa. *On the Christian Mode of Life.* In *Ascetical Works*, edited and translated by Virginia Woods Callahan. Washington, DC: Catholic University of America Press, 1967.

———. *The Life of St. Macrina.* In *Ascetical Works*, edited and translated by Virginia Woods Callahan. Washington, DC: Catholic University of America Press, 1967.

Gribbin, John. *In Search of Schrodinger's Cat.* Toronto: Bantam, 1984.

Gross, Don H. *The Case for Spiritual Healing.* New York: T. Nelson, 1958.

Grubbs, Norman. *Rees Howells, Intercessor.* Fort Washington, PA: Christian Literature Crusade, 1952.

Gumprecht. Jane. *Abusing Memory; The Healing Theology of Agnes Sanford.* Moscow: Canon, 1997.

———. *Holistic Health: A Medical and Biblical Critique of the New Age Deception.* Moscow: Ransom, 1986.

Gusmer, Charles W. "Anointing of the Sick in the Church of England." *Worship* 4/5 (May 1971) 263–72.

Gussai, Hemchand. "The Old Testament: A Heresy Continued?" *Word and World* 8/2 (April 1988) 150–57.

Hagin, Kenneth. *Laying on of Hands.* Tulsa: Kenneth Hagin Ministries, 1983.

———. "Living the Life of Faith, Part 1." *Word of Faith* (June 1986) 2–4.

Halberg, Fred. "Barrou and Tipler's 'The Anthropic Cosmological Principal.'" *Zygon* 23/2 (June 1988) 139–57.

Harding, Glenn. *The Saga of Glenn Clark and the Camps Farthest Out.* N.p.: privately printed, n.d.

Harnack, Adolph von. *Marcion: The Gospel of the Alien God.* Translated by John E Sleely. Durham, NC: Labyrenth, 1989.

Harkness, George. *Mysticism: Its Meaning and Message.* Nashville: Abingdon, 1973.

"Hath Made Thee Whole." *Time*, June 16, 1924. Online: http://content.time.com/time/magazine/article/0,9171,718509,00.html.

Hejzlar, Pavel. "John Calvin and the Cessation of Miraculous Healing." *Communio Viatorum* 49/1 (2007) 31–77.

High, Stanley. "More Things Are Wrought by Prayer . . ." *Reader's Digest*, June 1957.

Hillman, Eugene. *Polygamy Reconsidered: African Plural Marriage and the Christian Church.* Maryknoll, NY: Orbis, 1975.

Hiltner, Richard. *Religion and Health.* New York: Macmillan, 1943.

Hoffman, Bengt R. *Luther and the Mystics.* Minneapolis: Augsburg, 1976.

Hocken, P. D. "Charismatic Movement." In *The Dictionary of Pentecostal and Charismatic Movements*, edited by Stanley M. Burgess and Gary B. McGee. Grand Rapids: Zondervan, 1988.

Holmes, Fenwicke L. *How to Develop Faith That Heals.* New York: Robert M. Bride, 1925.

Honner, John. "Unity-in-Difference: Karl Rahner and Niels Bohr." *Theological Studies* 46 (September 1885) 490–506.

Hume, David. An Enquiry Concerning Human Understanding. Edited by Eric Steinberg. Indianapolis, Hachett, 1977.

Hunt, Dave. *Beyond Seduction: A Return to Biblical Christianity.* Eugene, OR: Harvest House, 1987.

————. *A Woman Rides the Beast: The Roman Catholic Church and the Last Days.* Eugene, OR: Harvest House, 1994.

Hunt, Dave, and T. A. McMahon. *The Seduction of Christianity.* Eugene, OR: Harvest House, 1986.

Hunter, Charles, and Francis Hunter, *How to Heal the Sick.* Kingwood, TX: Hunter Ministries, 1981.

Hutchison, William R. "Protestantism as Establishment." In *Between the Times: The Travail of the Protestant Establishment in America, 1900–1960,* edited by William R. Hutchson. New York: Cambridge University Press, 1989.

Hynek, J. Allen. "The UFO Phenomenon: Laugh, Laugh, Study, Study." *Technology Review* 83/7 (July 1981) 1–9.

Ignatius of Loyola. *The Spiritual Exercises of St. Ignatius.* 1524. Online: http://www.ignatianspirituality.com/ignatian-prayer/the-spiritual-exercises/.

Jaggers, O. L. *Everlasting Spiritual and Physical Health.* Dexter: privately printed, 1949.

Jaki, Stanley L. *The Road of Science and the Ways of God.* Chicago: University of Chicago Press, 1978.

James, William. The *Varieties of Religious Experience.* New York: Modern Library, 1902.

Jenkins, Philip. *The Jesus Wars: How Four Patriarchs, Three Queens, and Two Emperors Decided What Christians Would Believe for the Next 1,500 Years.* New York: HarperCollins, 2010.

Jeremais, Jorchim. *The Parables of Jesus.* New York: Scribner, 1955.

Jewell, John. *The Long Way Home.* Nashville: T. Nelson, 1982.

Johnson, Elizabeth. "Does God Play Dice? Divine Providence and Chance." *Theological Studies* 57/31 (March 1991) 2–18.

Johnson, Thomas C. "Historical Consensus and Christian Science: The Career of a Manuscript Controversy." *New England Quarterly* 53/1 (March, 1980) 3–22.

John of the Cross. *The Ascent of Mount Carmel.* Translated by David Lewis. London: T. Baker, 1906.

Jones, Ilion. "Is Protestant Christianity Being Sabotaged from Within?" *Christianity Today*, January 7, 1966, 3–6.

Judah, J. Stillson. *The History and Philosophy of the Metaphysical Movement in America.* Philadelphia: Westminster, 1967.

Justin Martyr. *Dialogue with Trypho.* Edited by Michael Slusser, translated by Thomas B. Falls. Washington, DC: Catholic University of America, 2003.

Kallas, James. *The Satanward View: A Study of Pauline Theology.* Philadelphia: Westminster, 1956.

Keller, Ernst, and Marie-Luise Keller. *Miracles in Dispute.* Translated by Margaret Kohl. Philadelphia: Fortress, 1969.

Kelsey, Morton. *Dreams: The Dark Speech of the Spirit.* Garden City, NY: Doubleday, 1968.

————. *Healing and Christianity.* Minneapolis: Augsburg, 1973.

Kerin, Dorothy. *The Living Touch.* Tunbridge Wells: Courier, 1961. 1st ed. 1914.

Kester, Aaron "The Charismata in Crisis: The Gifts of the Holy Spirit in the Reformation Church of England." PhD diss., Miami University, 1990.

Kimmel, Jo. *Steps to Prayer Power.* Nashville, Abingdon: 1972.

King, James G. "Thomas Aquinas and Prophecy." *PNEUMA* 1/2 (Fall 1979) 50–58.

Kluger, Jeffrey. "The Biology of Belief." *Time*, February 12, 2009. Online: http://content.time.com/time/magazine/article/0,9171,1879179,00.html.

Knolly, Hanserd. "Michael Haykin, (c. 1599–1691) on the Gifts of the Spirit." *Westminster Theological Journal* 54/1 (Spring 1992) 99–113.

Knox, *Ronald. Enthusiasm: A Chapter in the History of Religion*. New York: Oxford University, 1950.

Krüger, Günter. "Johann Christoph Blumhardt (1805–1880): A Man for the Kingdom." *Currents in Theology and Missions* 23/6 (December 1996) 427–41.

Kydd, Roland A. N. *Charismatic Gifts in the Early Church*. Peabody, MA: Hendrickson, 1984.

————. *Healing Through the Centuries: Models for Understanding*. Peabody, MA: Hendrickson, 1998.

Lambert, Frank. *Pedlar in Divinity: George Whitefield and the Transatlantic Revivals, 1737–1770*. Princeton, NJ: Princeton University Press, 1994.

Lane-Gay, Julie. "Direction for the Gardiner: Wise Advice from a 17th-Century Savant." *Books & Culture*, August 9, 2010. Online: http://www.booksandculture. com/articles/webexclusives/2010/august/directionsgardiner.html.

Landsberg, Mitchell. "Claremont Seminary Reaches Beyond Christianity." *Los Angeles Times*, June 27, 2010. Online: http://articles.latimes.com/2010/jun/27/local/la-me-claremont-20100629.

Langstaff, Beth Y. "Temporary Gifts: John Calvin's Doctrine of the Cessation of Miracles." PhD diss., Princeton Theological Seminary, 1999.

Larsen, Timothy. "St. Flo: The Improbable Life of Florence Nightingale." *Books & Culture*, November–December 2008, 16–17.

————. "Imagine There's No Christendom. Secularization and the 1960s." *Books & Culture*, March–April 2010, 20–21.

La Shell, John K. "Imagination and Idol: A Puritan Tension." *Westminster Theological Journal* 49 (1987) 305–34.

Laubach, Frank. *Channels of Spiritual Power*. Westwood, NJ: Revell, 1954.

————. *How to Teach One and Win One for Christ*. Grand Rapids: Zondervan, 1964.

————. *Prayer, The Mightiest Force in the World*. Old Tappan, NJ: Revell, 1946.

Lefebure, Leo D. "The Wisdom of God: Dialogue and Natural Theology." *Christian Century* 111/30 (October 26, 1994) 984–88.

————. "The Wisdom of God: Sofia and Christian Theology." *Christian Century* 111/29 (October 19, 1994) 951–56.

Leslie, J. "How to Draw Conclusions from the Fine-Tuned Universe." In *Physics, Philosophy, and Theology*, by Robert J Russell et al., 297–312. Vatican City: Vatican Observatory, 1988.

Lewis, C. S. *God in the Dock: Essays on Theology and Ethics*. Grand Rapids: Eerdmans, 1970.

————. *The Space Trilogy*. New York: Macmillan, 1975.

Lilla, Mark. "Our Libertarian Age." *New Republic*, July 17, 2014. Online: http://www. newrepublic.com/article/118043/our-libertarian-age-dogma-democracy-dogma-decline.

Loren, Julia. "Healers of the Wounded Soul." *Charisma*, August 31, 2005. Online: http://www.charismamag.com/entertainment/413-j15/features/spiritual-pioneers/1677-healers-of-the-wounded-soul.

Lubac, Henri de. *The Drama of Atheist Humanism*. Translated by Edith Riley. New York: Sheed & Ward, 1950.

Lundin, Roger. "Old Pieties No Longer Sufficed: Emily Dickinson and the Loss of Belief." *Books & Culture*, September–October 2009, 17–19.

Luther, Martin. *Letters of Spiritual Counsel*. Translated and edited by Theodore G. Tappert. Library of Christian Classics 43. Philadelphia: Westminster, 1955.

MacArthur, John. *Strange Fire*. Nashville: T. Nelson, 2013.

MacNutt, Francis, *Deliverance from Evil Spirits: A Practical Manual*. Grand Rapids: Chosen Books, 1995.

———. *Healing*. Notre Dame: Ave Maria, 1974.

———. *Homosexuality: Can It Be Healed?* Jacksonville, FL: Christian Healing Ministries, 2001.

———. *Overcome by the Spirit*. Old Tappan, NJ: Chosen Books, 1990.

———. "A Proposed Solution to the Re-Baptism Dilemma." *Ministries* 3/2 (Spring 1975) 58–61.

———. "Sharing God's Love." Audio recording. Ardmore: Lord's Own Tape ministry, n.d.

MacNutt, Judith. *Angels Are for Real*. Minneapolis: Chosen Books, 2012.

MacNutt, Sylvester F. *Gauging Sermon Effectiveness*. Dubuque, IA: Priory, 1960.

Maloney, George A. *The Mystic of Fire and Light: St. Symeon the New Theologian*. Denville, NJ: Dimension, 1975.

Manuel, David. *Like a Mighty River: A Personal Account of the Charismatic Conference of 1977*. Orleans, MA: Rock Harbor, 1977.

Matharaj, Rabi R., and Dave Hunt. *Death of a Guru*. Nashville: A. J. Holman, 1977.

McKinley, E. H. *A History of the Disciplined Order of Christ, 1945–1990*. Nashville: DOC, 1990.

Maeterlink, Maurice. *Buried Temple*. London: Allen, 1902.

Mansfield, Stephen. *Derek Prince: A Biography*. Lake Mary, FL: Creation House, 2005.

Manis, Andrew M. *Macon Black and White*. Macon, GA: Mercer University, 2004.

Marshall, Catherine. *Something More*. New York: Avon, 1976.

Martin, Malachi. *Hostage to the Devil*. New York: Reader's Digest Press, 1976.

Martin, Walter. *Christian Science*. Minneapolis: Bethany House, 1957.

Mason, David. *Apostle to the Illiterates*. Grand Raids: Zondervan, 1966.

Mathews, Shailer. *The Spiritual Interpretation of History*. Cambridge, MA: Harvard University Press, 1920.

Mathews-Green, Gregory, and Federica Mathews-Greene. "Eastern Orthodoxy: A Gallery of Impact Pray-ers." *Church History* 57 (1997) 15–18.

McCance, Dawn W. "Physics, Buddhism, and Postmodern Interpretations." *Zygon* 21 (Spring 1986) 287–96.

McConnell, D. R. *A Different Gospel: A Historical and Biblical Analysis of the Modern Faith Movement*. Peabody, MA: Hendrickson, 1988.

McDermott, Gerald R. "The Great Divider: Jonathan Edwards and American Culture." *Books & Culture*, January–February 2010, 8–10.

McDermott, Mary Shidler. *The Theology of Romantic Love: A Study in the Writings of Charles Williams*. Grand Rapids: Eerdmans, 1962.

McDonnel, Kilian, and George T. Montague. *Christian Initiation and Baptism in the Holy Spirit*. Collegeville, MN: Liturgical, 1994.

McKeon, Joan Rogers. *Trinity Church: An Anniversary History, 1937–1987*. Moorestown: privately printed, 1987.

McLain, Wayne. *A Heavenly View: The Best of Rufus Moseley.* St. Paul, MN: Macalester Park, 1993.

———. *A Resurrection Encounter: The Rufus Moseley Story.* Minneapolis: Macalester Park, 1997.

Mead, Harriet. "History of the International Order of St. Luke the Physician." *Sharing,* January 1984, 8–13.

Melanchthon, Philipp. *Loci.* [1543].

Merton, Thomas. *Seven Storey Mountain.* New York: Harcourt, Brace, 1948.

Meyerhoff, Steven. "Andover Seminary: The Rise and Fall of an Evangelical Institution." *Presbyterian* 8/2 (Fall 1982) 13–24.

Midgley, Mary. *Evolution as Religion: Strange Hopes and Stranger Fears.* London: Methuen, 1985.

———. *Science as Salvation: A Modern Myth and Its Meaning.* London: Routledge, 1992.

Miller, Stephen M. "How We Got Our Bible: A Gallery of Mavericks and Misfits." *Christian History* 43 (1994) 18–22.

Missildine, Hugh W. *Your Inner Child of the Past.* New York: Simon and Schuster, 1963.

Montgomery, John Warwick. *The Suicide of Christian Theology.* Minneapolis: Bethany House, 1970.

Moseley, Rufus. *Manifest Victory.* Rev. ed. New York: Harper, 1947. 1st ed. 1941.

———. *Perfect Everything.* St. Paul, MN: Macalester Park, 1949.

Nee, Watchman. *The Spiritual Man.* New York: Christian Fellowship Publishers, 1968.

Nevius, John. *Demon Possession and Allied Themes.* New York: Revell, 1896.

Nielson, Charles M. "The Loneliness of Protestantism." *Christian Century,* September 15, 1965, 11–21.

Neyfakh, Leon. "What Playfulness Can Do for You." *Boston Globe,* July 20, 2014. Online: http://www.bostonglobe.com/ideas/2014/07/19/what-playfulness-can-for-you/Cxd7Et4igTLkwpkUXSr3cO/story.html.

Nietzsche, Fredrich. *The Gay Science.* 1887.

Noll, Mark, and Bruce Hindmarch. "Rewriting the History of Evangelicalism: W. R. Ward, 1925–2010." *Books & Culture,* March/April 2011, 8.

Oakes, Edward T. "Unauthorized Freud: Doubters Confront a Legend." *First Things,* January 1, 1999. Online: http://www.firstthings.com/article/1999/01/001-the-man-behind-the-curtain.

Osburn, Vivian. "Koronis." *Fellowship Messenger,* April 1985, 2–4.

Ostling, Richard N. "Most Improbable Dialogue." *Christianity Today,* October 30, 2009. Online: http://www.christianitytoday.com/ct/2009/november/11.23.html.

Pagels, Elaine H. *The Gnostic Paul: Gnostic Exegesis of the Pauline Letters.* Philadelphia: Fortress, 1975.

Palladius. *Lausiac History.* Translated by Robert T. Meyer. Westminster, MD: Newman, 1965.

Parke, John H. "The Reawakening: A Brief History of the OSL." *Sharing,* March 1989, 22–29.

Parker, Gail Thain. *Mind Cure in New England.* Hanover, NH: University Press of New England, 1973.

Parkhurst, Genevieve. *Glorious Victory through the Healing of Memories.* St. Paul, MN: Macalester Park, 1973.

Payne, Leanne. *The Broken Image: Restoring Personal Wholeness through Healing Prayer.* Westchester, IL: Cornerstone, 1981.

———. *Healing the Homosexual.* Westchester, IL: Crossway, 1985.

———. *Heaven's Calling: A Memoir of a Soul's Steep Ascent.* Grand Rapids: Baker, 2008.

———. *Real Presence: The Holy Spirit in the Works of C. S. Lewis.* Westchester, IL: Cornerstone, 1979.

Peale, Norman Vincent. *The Power of Positive Thinking.* New York: Prentice-Hall, 1952.

Peck, M. Scott. *People of the Lie.* New York: Simon & Schuster, 1983.

Peel, Robert. *Spiritual Healing in a Scientific Age.* San Francisco: Harper & Row, 1987.

Pentuc, Eugen J. "A Self-Offering God and His Begotten Wisdom (Proverbs 8:22–24)." *Greek Orthodox Theological Review* 46 (Fall–Winter 2001) 255–265.

Peters, Thomas J., and Robert H. Waterman Jr. *In Search of Excellence.* New York: Harper & Row, 1982.

Pigott, Robert. "Dutch Rethink Christianity of a Doubtful World." BBC News, August 5, 2011. Online: http://www.bbc.co.uk/news/world-europe-14417362.

Polkinghorne, John C. *The Faith of a Physicist: Reflection of a Bottom-Up Thinker.* Princeton, NJ: Princeton University Press, 1994.

———. *From Physicist to Priest: An Autobiography.* London: SPCK, 2007.

———. "The Life and Work of a Bottom-Up Thinker." *Zygon* 35 (December 2000) 947–53.

———. *One World: The Intersection of Science and Theology.* London: SPCK, 1986.

———. *Quarks, Chaos, and Christianity.* London: SPCK, 1994.

———. *The Way the World Is.* Grand Rapids: Eerdmans, 1984.

Popper, Karl R. *Conjectures and Refutations: The Growth of Scientific Knowledge.* New York: Harper & Row, 1968.

———. *The High Tide of Prophecy: Hegel, Marx, and the Aftermath.* Vol. 2 of *The Open Society and Its Enemies.* New York: Harper & Row, 1963.

———. *The Logic of Scientific Discovery.* London: Hutchinson, 1959.

———. *Objective Knowledge: An Evolutionary Approach.* Oxford: Clarendon, 1979.

———. *The Spell of Plato.* Vol. 1 of *The Open Society and Its Enemies.* New York: Harper & Row, 1963.

———. *Unended Quest: An Intellectual Autobiography.* La Salle, IL: Open Court, 1976.

Poterfield, Amanda. "Native American Shamanism and the American Mind-Cure Movement." *Horizons 11* (Fall 1984) 276–89.

Poulain, Augustine. *The Graces of Interior Prayer: A Treatise on Mystical Theology.* Translated by Lenora L. York-Smith. St. Louis: B. Herder, 1910.

Powell, Katherine L. "Remembering Ethel Banks." *Sharing,* December 1991, 12–14.

Powell, L. Mark. "There's Healing in Holy Communion." *Logos,* November–December 1979, 54–57.

Public Broadcasting Atlanta (PBA). "Wise Heart: The Growth of a Great University in the Deep South." TV broadcast, February 6, 2012.

Price, Alfred. *Ambassadors of God's Healing, and, An Adventure in the Church's Ministry of Healing.* Irvington, NJ: St. Luke's, n.d.

Puller, F. W. *The Anointing of the Sick in Scripture and Tradition.* London: SPCK, 1910.

Pusey, Edward B. *An Eirenicon.* London: Rivingtons, 1865.

Quimby, George A. "Phineas Parkhurst Quimby: Biography." *The New England Magazine* 6/23 (March 1888) 269–76.

Rad, Gerhard von. *Wisdom in Israel.* Nashville: Abingdon, 1972.

Rae, Alister. "Extrasensory Quantum Physics." *New Scientist* 27 (November 1986) 36–39.

Rae, Rusty. "The Extraordinary Becomes Ordinary: A Profile on Francis and Judith MacNutt." *Sharing*, May 1988, 22–25.

Rahner, Hugo. *The Spirituality of St. Ignatius Loyola: An Account of Its Historical Development.* Translated by Francis John Smith. Westminster: Newman, 1953.

Rawson, F. L. *Life Understood: From a Scientific and Religious Point of View, and the Practical Method of Destroying Sin, Disease, and Death.* London: The Crystal, 1917. 1st ed. 1912.

Rhys, J. Howard. "The School of Pastoral Care." *The Living Church* 162/22 (May 30, 1971) 8–9.

Richardson, Don. *Eternity in Their Hearts.* Ventura: Regal, 1981.

Robie, Joan Hake. *Devotion in Motion.* Lancaster: Starburst, 1981.

Robinson, John A. T. *Honest to God.* London: SCM, 1963.

Ross, Bobby. "The Workers Are Few." *Christianity Today*, August 2007, 18–19.

Rothman, Tony. "A 'What You See Is What You Beget' Theory." *Discover* 8, May 1987, 90–99.

Ruthven, Jon Mark. "Are Pentecostal Seminaries a Good Idea?" *PNEUMA* 26/2 (Fall 2004) 339–45.

———. *On the Cessation of the Charismata: The Protestant Polemic on Postbiblical Miracles.* Rev. ed. Tulsa, OK: Word & Spirit, 2010.

San, Faith Annette. *Prayers of Faith: On Learning to Trust the Lord.* Pasadena, CA: Hope Pub. House, 1996.

Sandford, John. "The Blessedness of Brokenness." Audio recording. Spokane, WA: Elijah House, n.d.

———. "A Sensible View of Exorcism." Audio recording. Spokane, WA: Elijah House, n.d.

Sandford, John, and Paula Sandford. *The Elijah Task.* Plainfield, NJ: Logos, 1977.

———. *Healing the Wounded Spirit.* South Plainfield, NJ: Bridge, 1985.

———. *The Transformation of the Inner Man.* South Plainfield, NJ: Bridge, 1982.

Sanford, Agnes. *Behold Your God.* St. Paul, MN: Macalester Park, 1958.

———. *Creation Waits.* Plainfield, NJ: Logos, 1978.

———. "The Forgiveness of Sins." Audio recording from the Ardmore, Oklahoma CFO, September 1966. Ft. Myers: Lord's Own Tape Ministry.

———. *The Healing Light.* St. Paul, MN: Macalester Park, 1947.

———. "Healing of Memories." Audio recording. Richardson Springs, CA: Springs of Living Water, n.d.

———. *The Healing Gifts of the Spirit.* Philadelphia: J. B. Lippincott, 1966.

———. *Healing Power of the Bible.* Philadelphia: J. B. Lippincott, 1969.

———. "How to Receive the Healing of Memories." Audio recording. Fort Myers, FL: Lord's Own Tape Ministry, n.d.

———. "Illumination." Audio recording. Richardson Springs, CA: Springs of Living Water, n.d.

———. *Let's Believe.* New York: Harper, 1954.

———. *Lost Shepherd.* Philadelphia: J. B. Lippincott, 1953.

———. *Melisa and the Little Red Book.* St. Paul, MN: Macalester Park, 1976.

———. *Oh, Watchman.* Philadelphia: J. B. Lippincott, 1951.

————. *A Pasture for Peterkin*. Illustrated by Ted Sanford. St. Paul, MN: Macalester Park, 1956.

————. "Power in the Body of Christ." Audio recording. Ft. Myers, FL: Lord's Own Tape Ministry, n.d.

————. "Power to Become Sons of God." Audio recording. Richardson Springs, CA: Springs of Living Water, n.d.

————. "Prayer of Healing." Audio recording. Ft. Myers, FL: Lord's Own Tape Ministry, n.d.

————. "The Real Meaning of Redemption." Audio recording. Ft. Myers: Lord's Own Tape Ministry, n.d.

————. "Redemption of Our Bodies." Audio recording from the Ardmore, Oklahoma CFO, September 1966. Ft. Myers: Lord's Own Tape Ministry, n.d.

————. *The Rising River*. Philadelphia: J. B. Lippincott, 1968.

————. *Route 1*. Plainfield, NJ: Logos, 1975.

————. *Sealed Orders*. Plainfield, NJ: Logos, 1972.

————. *The Second Mrs. Wu*. Philadelphia: J. B. Lippincott, 1965.

————. "There is Now No Condemnation." Audio recording from the Ardmore, Oklahoma CFO, Sepembert 1966. Ft. Myers: Lord's Own Tape Ministry, n.d.

————. "Trinity of Man." Audio recording. Ft. Myers: Lord's Own Tape ministry, n.d., audio cassette.

————. *Twice Seven Words*. Plainfield, NJ: Logos, 1971.

Sanford, Edgar L. *God's Healing Power*. Englewood Cliffs, NJ: Prentice-Hall, 1959.

Sanford, John A. *Dreams and Healing*. New York: Paulist, 1978.

————. *Healing and Wholeness*. New York: Paulist, 1977.

Satlow, Michael. *Jewish Marriage in Antiquity*. Princeton, NJ: Princeton University Press, 2001.

Schmid, Ulrich. "In Search of Tatian's Diatessaron in the West." *Vigiliae Christianae* 57/2 (2003) 176–99.

Schmidt, Leigh Eric. *Restless Souls: The Making of American Spirituality*. New York; HarperCollins, 2005.

Schaafs, Werner. *Theology, Physics, and Miracles*. Translated by Richard L. Renfield. Washington, DC: Canon, 1974.

Segré, Gino. *Faust in Copenhagen: A Struggle for the Soul of Physics*. New York: Viking, 2007.

Senor, Dan, and Saul Singer. *Start-Up Nation: The Story of Israel's Economic Nation*. New York: Twelve, 2009.

Shalit, Wendy. *A Return to Modesty: Discovering the Lost Virtue*. Old Tappan, NJ: Free Press, 1999.

Slee, Colin B., editor. *Honest to God: Forty Years On*. London: SCM, 2004.

Shlemon, Barbara Leahy. *Healing the Hidden Self*. Notre Dame, IN: Ave Maria, 1982.

————. *Healing Prayer*. Notre Dame, IN: Ave Maria, 1980.

Siegal, Robert. "Straight at the Blue." *Christian Century* 22/1 (September 23, 1987) 783.

Sloan, W. B. "China Inland Mission." In *Ecumenical Missionary Conference, New York, 1900*, vol. 2, 277–79. New York: America Tract Society, 1900.

Smith, James K. A. "Thinking in Tongues." *First Things*, April 2008. Online: http://www.firstthings.com/article/2008/04/003-thinking-in-tongues.

Sommerville, C. John. "Happy in the State of Denmark." *Books & Culture*, May–June 2010, 19.

Spong, John Shelby. *Why Christianity Must Change or Die: A Bishop Speaks to Believers in Exile.* San Francisco: Harper One, 1998.

Spurling, Hilary. *Burying the Bones: Pearl Buck's Life in China.* London: Profile, 2010.

Stafford, Tim. "The Kingdom of the Cult Watchers." *Christianity Today*, October 7, 1991, 18–23.

Stapleton, Ruth. "Her First CFO Experience." Audio recording. St. Paul, MN: Cutler Tape Library, 1974.

———. *Power Through Release.* St. Paul, MN: Macalester Park, 1968.

Stapleton, Ruth Carter. *The Experience of Inner Healing*, Waco, TX: Word, 1977.

———. *The Gift of Inner Healing.* Waco, TX: Word, 1976.

Stephanou, Eusebius A. "The Charismata in the Early Church." *Greek Orthodox Theological Review* 21 (Summer 1976) 125–46.

Sweet, William Warren. *The Story of Religion in America.* New York: Harper, 1930.

Synan, Vinson. *An Eyewitness Remembers the Century of the Holy Spirit.* Grand Rapids: Chosen, 2010.

———. "The Role of the Holy Spirit and the Gifts of the Spirit in the Mystical Tradition." *One in Christ* 10/2 (1974) 193–202.

———. *The Holiness-Pentecostal Movement in the United States.* Grand Rapids: Eerdmans, 1971.

Tapscott, Betty. *Ministering Inner Healing Biblically.* Houston: Tapscott Ministries, 1987.

Thurston, Herbert, and Donald Attwater, editors. *Butler's Lives of the Saints.* Vol. 1. London: Burns and Oats, 1956.

Tillich, Paul. "Heal the Sick, Cast Out Demons." *Union Seminary Quarterly* 11/1 (November 1955) 6–9.

———. "The Relation of Religion and Health." In *Religion and Health: A Symposium*, edited by Simon Doniger, 185–205. New York: Association Press, 1958.

Tompkins, Peter. *The Secret Life of Plants.* Scranton, NJ: Harper Collins, 1973.

Trine, Ralph Waldo. *In Tune with the Infinite.* New York: Dodd & Mead, 1921.

Unity School of Christianity. *Prayer in the Marketplace.* Lee's Summit, MO: Unity School of Christianity, 1952.

Underhill, Evelyn. Mysticism: A Study in the Nature and Development of Man's Spiritual Consciousness. New York: Dutton, 1911.

Van Dyke, Dick. *My Lucky Life In and Out of Show Business.* New York: Crown Archetype, 2011.

Vaskuil, Dennis. *Mountains into Goldmines: Robert Schiller and the Gospel of Success.* Grand Rapids: Eerdmans, 1983.

Ward, W. R. *Early Evangelicalism: A Global Intellectual History, 1670–1789.* Cambridge: Cambridge University Press, 2006.

Warfield, Benjamin B. *Counterfeit Miracles.* New York Scribner's, 1918.

Wells, Andrew F. *The Cross Cultural Process in Christian History.* Edinburgh: T. & T. Clark, 2002.

Westminster Larger Catechism. 1788. Online: http://www.epc.org/document.doc?id=106.

White, Agnes. "The Waste of It." *The Silhouette* 16 (1918) 58.

White, Ann. *Healing Adventure.* Plainfield, NJ: Logos, 1969.

White, Hugh Watt. *Demonism Verified and Analyzed.* Yencheng, China: Presbyterian Committee of Publication, 1922.

———. *Jesus, the Missionary.* Shanghai: Presbyterian Mission Press, 1914.

Wilson, B. R. "The Origins of Christian Science: A Survey." *Hibbert Journal* 62 (1958–1959) 161–70.

Wilson: Henry B. *Does Christ Still Heal?* New York: Dutton, 1917.

———. *Ghosts or Gospels: The Methods of Spiritualism in Healing Compared with the Methods of Christ.* Boonton, NJ: Nazarene, 1923.

———. *God's Will for the World.* New York: Dutton, 1923.

Winner, Lavern F. "Art for God's Sake." *Christianity Today,* March 24, 2010. Online: http://www.christianitytoday.com/ct/2010/march/23.43.html.

———. "Cleanliness and Godliness." *Books & Culture,* July 23, 2009. Online: http://www.booksandculture.com/articles/2009/julaug/cleanlinessandgodliness.html.

Winquest, Charles E. "Thomas J. J. Altizer in Retrospect." *Religious Studies Review* 8/4 (October 1982) 337–42.

Wolf, Fred Alan. *Taking the Quantum Leap: The New Physics for Nonscientists.* San Francisco: Harper & Row, 1981.

Wolfe, Paul B. "Scripture in the Pastoral Epistles: Pre-Marcian Marcianism?" *Perspectives in Religious Studies* 16/1 (Spring 1989) 5–16.

Woodward. Kenneth L. "Sister Ruth." *Newsweek,* July 17, 1978, 58–60.

Yancey, Philip. "Insight on Eternity from a Scientific View of Time." *Christianity Today,* April 6, 1984, 26.

Yerxa, Donald A. "On the Road with Christianity: Interview with Andrew Walls." *Books & Culture,* May 1, 2001. Online: http://www.booksandculture.com/articles/2001/mayjun/6.18.html.

Zimany, Roland. "Divine Energies in Orthodox Theology." *Diakonia* 11/3 (1976) 281–85.

Zukav, Gary. *The Dancing Wu Li Masters: An Overview of the New Physics.* New York: W. Morrow, 1978.

Subject Index

A History of the English Church and People, 46
A Pasture for Peterkin, 228
A Treatise Concerning Religious Affections, 74
Abstinence, 94
Abusing Memory, 272
Active Service, 98
Affirmation/negation, 109, 161
Africa, 104, 44, 123, 135, 186, 266
Agnes Scott College, 189
Agnostic, 72, 152, 242
AIDS, 74, 165
Alcoholics Anonymous, 108, 142
Alexander, Brooks, 124, 181, 282
Altizer, Thomas J. J., 75, 294–96
Ambrose, Isaac 115
America, 26, 54, 60–6, 76, 78–81, 96, 118, 123, 139, 252
American Great Awakening, 70
American Holiness, 70
American transcendentalists, 90
An Eirenicon, 124
An Enquiry Concerning Human Understanding, 50
Ananias, 14
Andover, 287
Angels, 52, 110, 252
Angley, Ernest, 289
Anglican, 6, 47–8, 63, 105, 123–29, 134, 187, 204, 227, 293

Anglo-Israelism, 97
Anglo-Saxon, 97
Anointing of the Sick in Scripture and Tradition. The, 125
Anointing with oil, 34–6, 43, 124–5
Anointing, 35, 47–8, 76, 124–25, 192, 249–50, 254, 278
Anthropic principle, 100
Apologists, 16, 31, 51
Apostles, 1, 12–6, 30, 40
Aquinas Institute, 243
Aquinas, Thomas, 40, 44, 100, 301
Archangels, 110
Aristotle, 33, 40, 45
Ascension of Moses, 12
Ashram, 163
Asia, 123
Athanasius, 20
Atheist, 50, 54, 62, 139, 189, 287, 291, 293
Atlantic Monthly, 142–3, 149
Augustine, 29–35, 39, 41, 43–4, 115
Avatars, 91
Azusa, 75–6, 283

Baker, Mary Morse 84
Banks, John Gaynor, 4, 129, 131, 158, 192
Baptism of the Holy Spirit, 6, 137, 221, 223, 230, 243, 245–49, 253, 267–68

Baptism, 13, 31, 174, 188, 198, 236, 243, 255, 282

Baptist, 75, 89, 92, 94, 160, 183, 186, 218, 282

Barth, Karl, 294

Beard, Rebecca, 151

Behavior of matter, 101

Behold Your God, 225, 227, 229, 232, 234, 273, 298

Bell, Robert B. H., 180, 183, 275

Belloc, Hilaire, 54

Benjamin of Nitria, 20

Bennett, Dennis, 264, 286

Bernard of Clairvaux, 43

Bernard, St. 127

Bernstein, Eduard, 58

Beyond Seduction, 265

Bible Study (Mrs. Sanford's) 185–89, 225, 229, 244

Bible, 18, 144, 155, 167, 174, 177, 198, 210, 219, 223, 232, 234, 246, 268–69, 270, 277–78, 283, 286, 292, 300

Biblical accountability, 149, 155, 161

Big Bang, 100, 193

Biology, 277

Bishop's Book, The, 47

Blood sacrifice, 86

Blood, 32, 109, 164, 190, 193, 210, 213, 223, 301

Blumhardt, Johann, 52–3,

Blumhardt, John Christopher, 127

Bob Jones University, 292

Body and Soul, 127–28

Body of Christ, 92, 155, 210–11, 273

Bohme, Jakob, 71

Bohr, Niels, 101–2, 148

Bonaventura, 112

Book of Acts, 14, 239

Book of Common Prayer, 47–8, 124

Book of Job, 154

Book of Jubilees, 12

Book of Mormon, 84

Book of Revelation, 11

Bradshaw, David, 195

Breast cancer, 31, 35

Bride of Christ, 69

Broken Image, The, 272

Brother Lawrence, 141, 145, 148, 157, 167–68

Brown, Harold, 26

Brown, Roland 158, 163, 167

Brown, Roland and Marcia, 158, 163

Bucket List, The, 290

Buckley, James, 76–7, 265

Bultmann, Rudolf, 52–3, 110

Burden bearing, 210, 251

Buried Temple, 139

Butler's Lives of the Saints, 301

Caddy, Emily, 94

Calvin, John, 29, 39–45, 69, 100, 114–15, 256

Calvinism, 54, 104

Calvinist, 54–9, 70, 82, 114, 231, 268, 278

Cambridge, 105, 124, 132

Camps Farthest Out, 137, *See* CFO

Cancer, 31, 85, 211, 290

Candler Seminary, 295

Capitalist, 58

Capra, Fritjof, 103–4

Carter Stapleton, 219, 252, See Stapleton, Ruth

Carter, Jimmy, 219

Carver, George Washington, 240

Cassian, John, 20–1

Cast out demons. See deliverance

Casting out of demons, 13

Catholic Apostolic Church, 70

Catholic Charismatic Renewal, 3, 22, 217, 254

Catholic Homiletic Society, 253

Catholic mystics, 140

Catholic, 2–5, 17, 21–2, 29, 33, 36, 38–51, 78, 89, 92, 95–6, 112–19, 124–27, 140, 165–66, 197, 199, 204, 210, 213, 223, 230–32, 245, 253–55, 264, 270–71, 299–301

Celibacy, 27, 187–88, 289

Cessationism, 1–2, 18, 30–1, 39–48, 50, 53–5, 62, 69, 76–82, 87–9, 110, 115, 122, 134, 138, 146, 149, 167, 175, 182, 222, 228, 230, 232, 240, 256, 275–76, 286, 292, 300

CFO, 2, 6, 78, 131, 137–39, 147–68, 193,
214–22, 227, 234–36, 240, 245,
249, 252, 275, 282, 298, 300–2
Channels of Spiritual Power, 157
Charcot, Jean-Martin, 83
Charismatic Renewal, 2–4, 22, 24–27,
64, 122, 133, 138, 163, 167, 203,
217, 225, 235, 243–45, 248, 254,
264–66, 287, 290
Charismatic, 22–3, 125, 138, 165,
167–68, 191, 200, 203, 213, 220,
223, 230–33, 237, 242–45, 249,
254–56, 263–64, 272, 287, 292
Chaucer, 35
Chauncy, Charles 72, 74, 76
Child of God, 93, 152, 198
China, 79, 173–75, 178–80, 228
Christ the Healer, 179
Christ, 4, 18–20, 34, 46, 50, 86, 95, 107,
155, 164, 182, 195, 211, 213,
217, 229, 241, 249, 267, 274, 279
Christian Advocate, 76
Christian Apologetics, 227
Christian apologist, 31, 105, 222
Christian Broadcasting Network, 243
Christian Healing Ministries, 252, 256,
271, 302
Christian healing revival, 192
Christian mysticism, 140–41, 210
Christian New Perspective, 4–7, 71, 75,
79, 122, 151, 173, 197, 199, 278,
283, 297–302
Christian prayer, 37, 112, 144–45, 210
*Christian Science and Other
Superstitions*, 76
Christian Science, 5–6, 59–62, 76, 81–
101, 117, 122–26, 131–34, 145,
149, 151, 160–61, 229–231, 263,
266, 274, 282–83
Christian Socialist Union, 126
Church of England, 123, 126
Church of the Healing Christ, 96
City of God, 31
Clark, Glenn, 4, 6, 79, 82, 98, 111, 138–
39, 146–53, 155–67, 185, 187,
193, 195, 203, 215, 219, 243,
275, 282–86, 290, 301

CNP, 122, 134, 151, 173, 193, 197, 231,
274, 282, 284
Collective unconscious, 213
Colwell, Hollis 180–184
Command healing, 199–200
Communism, 54, 56, 58, 62
Compassion, 30, 75, 126, 189, 193, 277
Complementarity, 100, 103
Comte, Auguste, 57
Conferences, The, 20
Confession, 156, 204–7, 273, 300
Congregationalist, 55, 84
Constantine, 11
Copenhagen interpretation, 97, 102–3
Copenhagen, 101
Corinth, 15
Council of Nicaea, 15
Counterfeit Miracles, 77
Cousins, Norman, 151
Cox, Harvey, 284
Creation Waits, 6, 242
Creation, 100, 103, 105, 177, 193, 279
Creatives, 137, 168
Creator, 104, 110–11, 240
Cullis, Charles, 75–6, 290
Cult, 78–9, 87, 90, 114, 131, 150, 154–
55, 161, 202, 269
Czechoslovakia, 207

Daily, Starr, 155–6, 158, 163–65
Dante, 153
Darwinian evolution, 264
Darwinism, 77
David, 145
Day, Albert E., 162
Dearmer, Percy, 125, 126–29, 135, 276,
284
Death of God, 5, 62, 294 See DOG
Deification, 195
Deism, 286–87
Deliverance from Evil Spirits, 254, 299
Deliverance, 2–3, 5, 20, 35, 38–9, 42,
136, 138, 166–68, 235, 245,
249–55, 271, 291, 298–99
Demonic, 19, 39, 45, 81, 92, 94, 155,
158, 186, 196, 218, 230, 237,
243–44, 255, 268, 275, 293–94
Demonism Verified and Analyzed, 176

Demythologizing, 52, 55, 226, 299
Denmark, 54, 101
Depravity, 44
Depression, 179, 181–82, 185, 204, 209,
        212, 215, 233, 246, 294
Derek Prince, 245, 249, 253
Destiny, 56, 69, 105, 122
Devil, 39, 45, 250 *See* Satan
Discernment, 6, 43, 45, 75, 176–77, 182,
        185, 188, 230, 270, 275–76, 295
Disciples of Christ, 55
Disciples, 13–4, 17–19, 34, 36, 58, 109,
        117, 199, 232, 240, 293
Disciplined Order of Christ, 162
*Distinguishing Marks of a Work of the
        Spirit of God,* 72, 116
Divine Comedy, 153
Divine healing, 76, 78, 126
Divine Science, 95
Divinity, 229, 286, 291
Docetists, 26
DOG, 61–4, 103, 122, 186, 290, 293–95
Dominican, 2, 253–54
Doniger, Simon, 292
Drury, Edith, 246
Dunamis, 34
Dutch, 51, 70
Dysfunctional, 249, 294

"Each one, teach one", 156–57
Eastern mysticism, 103
Eastern Orthodox Church, 22, 182, 229
Eastern religions, 82, 92
Ebola, 153
Eddy, Mary Baker, 59, 82–97, 108, 117,
        123, 157, 161, 164, 201, 274, 281
Edict of Milan, 11
Eggleston, Louise, 151, 158, 168
Egypt, 20, 24–5, 41, 278
Einstein, Albert, 60–1
Elders, 34, 69, 172
Electromagnetic radiation, 90
Elijah House, 250, 252, 271, 302
Elijah, 94–5, 299
Elisha, 32–3, 108–9
Elliot, Norman, 167
Emerson, Ralph Waldo, 82–3
Emory University, 295–96

Emotional, 62, 72, 74, 83, 135, 193,
        204–6, 112, 276, 295
Energia, 34–6
Energies of God, 33–4, 109, 192, 194–
        95, 226, 266, 300
Energy, 32, 60, 98, 100, 105, 125, 130,
        140, 165, 187, 193–95, 205, 223,
        229, 243
England, 48, 64, 97, 122, 142, 207, 277
Enlightenment, 48–51, 55–6, 92
Epilepsy, 31
Episcopal, 76, 122–24, 129–33, 158,
        187–88, 198, 204, 209, 210–11,
        234, 245, 264, 294
Epistle of Barnabas, 12
Epistles, 14–5, 26, 140
Equation, 60–1, 100–1, 213
Essence, 33–4, 91, 194
Eucharist, 181, 228, 251
Europe, 20, 49–54, 58, 62, 71, 84, 114,
        207, 209
Evangelical, 32, 44, 53, 70–1, 75, 83,
        87–8, 97, 139, 155–56, 159, 166,
        174, 195, 199, 202, 211, 219,
        227, 230–31, 248, 251, 256, 264,
        269–72, 289, 292, 296, 299
Evans, Warren Felt, 81, 83
Everlasting Spiritual and Physical Health,
        200
Exorcism, 3, 14, 16, 18, 22, 32, 35, 42,
        51, 158–59, 174–75, 199, 233,
        244–45, 271, 298–99
Exorcist, The, 35
Experience of Inner Healing, The, 219
Extraterrestrial, 227

Faintings, 72, 74
Faith Cure, 62, 75–9, 203, 266, 274
Faith healer, 94
Faith of a Physicist, The, 106
Faith, 107–8, 109–12, 117, 119, 135–36,
        140, 143, 147, 150, 156, 158,
        175, 180–84, 189–90, 199–200,
        213, 223, 228–34, 274, 285, 292
Faithful Narrative, 72
Fallings, 74–5
Fascism, 56, 107
Fasting, 20, 210, 212, 301

Fear of the Lord, 16, 279, 283–84

Fear, 74, 83, 85, 108, 134, 148–50, 156, 158, 198, 201–2

Fellowship of St. Luke, 130

Filioque, 229

Fillmore, Charles, 93–5, 222

Finney, Charles, 162

Fire, 63, 95, 112, 241–42, 275

Fitch, 89

Florida, 224, 243, 252, 271

Fogg, Wilber, 248–49

Ford, Arthur, 283

Forgiveness of sins, 193, 298, 213–14, 217, 219, 298

Forgiveness, 204, 212–17, 219, 301

Fox, Emmet, 4, 95–7, 127, 183, 208, 301

Francis of Assisi, 240

Free-will, 282

Freud, 58–9, 62, 83

Fruit, 73–5, 123, 134, 167, 183, 195, 204, 243, 274, 283, 302

Fruits of the Spirit, 165, 223, 243

Full Gospel Business Men's Fellowship International, 168

Fuller Seminary, 292

Fundamentalism, 292, 97

Fundamentalist, 78, 97, 283

Galatian Bewitchment, 17, 19, 22, 35–6, 50, 54, 117, 165, 255–56

Gangrene, 207

Gardner, Rex, 46, 51

Gehazi, 108–9

Genesis, 106, 177

Gentile, 25

German Idealism, 89

Ghosts or Gospels, 129

Gifford Lectures, 105

Gift of healing, 36, 95, 229

Gift of Inner Healing, The, 219, 271

Gift of tongues, 139, 165, 224, 244, 284

Gift of wisdom, 277

Gifts of the Holy Spirit, 14, 161–62, 165, 221, 225, 243–44

Global South, 300

Gnostic, (Gnosticism) 12, 15, 81, 87, 92–6, 152, 154–55, 199, 295

God Makers, 265

God the Father, 298

God's energies, 33, 186, 196

God's healing power, 187, 189, 199, 201, 205, 230

God's kingdom, 141

Goldsmith, Harry, 205, 207, 228, 230, 235, 272, 301

Good Business, 96

Gordon, A.J., 76

Gospel of James, 12

Gospel of John, 209

Gospel of Thomas, 12

Gospels, 12, 14–5, 17, 25–7 30–1, 35, 37, 41, 45, 50–4, 97, 110, 112, 132–33, 145, 150, 162, 164, 182–83, 225, 248, 283, 299

Gout, 31

Grace, 21, 34, 36, 39, 42, 44–5, 54, 82, 122, 131, 154–56, 163, 222, 230, 248, 251, 267–68, 276–77, 289, 298, 301

Graves, Augusta, 176

Gray Lady, 1–2, 188, 207–8, 228

Great Awakening, 70–5, 117, 265, 276, 286

Great Depression, 118, 147, 180

Great Pharisee, 72, 76–7

Greely, Andrew, 64

Gregory of Nyssa, 22, 95

Gregory of Palamas, 195

Gregory of Pontus, 239

Gross, Don H., 287–89

Guideposts, 96

Guild methodology, 290–91

Guild of Health, 63, 128–29

Gumprecht, Jane, 272–73

Harding, Glenn, 148, 167

Harvard, 132, 140, 142, 160, 253, 286–87

Healing explosions, 200

Healing Gifts of the Spirit, The, 217, 225, 244, 267

Healing light, 34, 192, 194, 197, 226

Healing Light, The, 2, 6, 187–88, 192–206, 210, 215, 221, 229, 233, 255, 286, 298

Healing lines, 76, 217

Healing pioneers, 282, 290
Healing Power of the Bible, The, 225
Health food, 135–36, 183, 188, 275
Heat, 194
Heavenly language, 77
Hegel, 56, 85, 89
Henry VIII, 47, 129
Heresies, 263
Heretic, 4, 15–6, 23–7, 34, 58, 71, 78, 80,
        82, 86–87, 111, 190, 275
Hernia, 31
Herodotus, 51
Heterosexuality, 273
Hill, Howard, 167
Hindu, 154, 265
Hippy, 245
Hitler, 270
Holiness, 20, 38, 68, 78, 177, 283
Holland, 54
Holmes, Fenwicke L., 118
Holy Communion, 17, 131, 197, 301
Holy Ghost, 222, 223, 225, 267
Holy Rollers, 75, 134, 297
Holy Spirit, 4–6, 13–9, 19, 27, 30, 55, 64,
        69, 70, 80, 119, 137, 145, 161–
        67, 205, 221–2, 224–25, 229,
        233, 242–45, 250, 253, 255, 267,
        275–76, 278, 282–83, 285–86,
        298, 302
Holy Spirit, The, 165
Homeopathic, 75, 84
Homer's *Odyssey,* 153
Homosexual, 237, 272
Honest to God, 63
Hour of Power, 98
House of Saul, The, 182
How to Find Health Through Prayer, 149,
        151, 159, 298
How to Heal the Sick, 200
Howells, Rees, 211–12
Huguenots, 48
Human mind, 45, 58, 83, 111, 119
Hume, David, 50–3
Humility, 31, 36, 154, 201, 281
Hunt, Dave, 4, 219, 252, 265–71
Hunter, Charles and Francis, 200
Hurricane Katrina, 243
Hurricane Rita, 243

Hurricane, 242–43
Hutchinson, Abigail, 72, 74
Hypnotism, 82–3
Hypotheses, 61, 103, 283

I Will Lift Up Mine Eyes, 147, 187
IBM, 146
Idealism, 5, 82–3, 85, 88–9, 97, 110–11,
        143, 145, 152
Idealist sects, 81–2, 87, 90, 93, 95
Idolatry, 25, 114–17, 268
Ignatius of Loyola, 114, 270
Illumination, 223, 225
Imagination, 112–13, 115–16, 141, 145,
        216, 270
Imperialism, 62
In Tune with the Infinite, 118, 143
India, 153, 212
Inner healing ministry, 6, 218–19, 237,
        250, 255, 272, 276
Institutes, 41–2
Instructions of Ameneompe, 278
INTA, 91, 94
Intelligent design, 264
Intelligent Living, 135
Intercession, 36, 117, 210–14, 251, 272
Intercessory prayer, 77, 85, 188, 209,
        215, 248
International Conference on the
        Church's Ministry of Healing,
        133
Irenaeus, 18
Irving, Howard, 287
Irvingites, 70
Israel, 87, 97, 278
Italy, 54

Jaggers, Otis L., 200
Jairus' daughter, 88, 109
James, William, 128, 140, 152, 160, 289,
        292
Jefferson, Thomas, 75
Jesuit, 64, 113, 125, 264
Jesus People, 245
Jesus Prayer, 182
Jesus, 12–5, 25–7, 30, 32–7, 46, 50, 70,
        73, 85–8, 92–6, 105–17, 132–33,
        145–47, 154–59, 162–66, 176,

179, 182–85, 188, 190, 193,
198–200, 210–14, 222–27, 229,
230–33, 239–43, 251, 255–59,
275–77, 279, 281, 286–87, 291,
295
Jewish, 4, 12, 25, 30, 71, 174, 197, 207,
212
John of the Cross, 21
John the Baptist, 94–5
Jonathan Edwards, 112, 116, 222, 268,
270, 286, 297
Jones, E. Stanley 162
Jones, Rufus, 140
Journal of Christian Healing, 255, 277
Joy, 41, 113, 141–42, 146, 157, 162, 223,
233
Judaism, 27, 71
Jung, Carl, 60, 218, 237, 284, 294
Jungian psychology, 218, 237, 272

Kabbalah, 71
Kansas City, 244, 263
Kelsey, Morton, 218, 237, 239
Kennell, Ruth, 152
Kenyon, E. W., 163, 138
Kierkegaard, Soren, 53, 101
Kimmel, Jo, 253, 300
King James Version, 34
King Solomon, 182, 277–78
Kingdom of God, 49, 78, 119, 136, 146,
149, 163, 193
Knowledge, 16, 42, 45, 223, 277, 299
Kuhlman, Katherine, 288

Lady Wisdom, 278
Lake Idi Hopi, 151
Lake Koronis, 147–48
Lake, Kirsopp, 143
Laselle House, 234
Latin America, 254
Laubach, Frank 156–58, 163, 167, 284
Laughter, 151
Law of the Spirit, 251
Laying on of hands, 34–5, 42–3, 76, 128,
133–34, 202, 214, 256, 272
Legalism, 68–9, 281
Lesson in Truth, 94
Let's Believe, 225, 228

Lewis, C. S., 210–11, 227
Liberalism, 58, 122, 287
Life Abundant, The, 134–35, 180, 184
Life Understood, 140–41
Light, 2, 6, 60, 100–1, 105, 193–98, 201,
208, 225
Liturgical, 13, 198
Living the Death of God, 294
Logic of Scientific Discovery, The, 61
Logos International, 203
London Daily Mail, The, 98
Lord's Prayer, 36, 98, 119, 143
Lord's Supper, 210
Lost Shepherd, 210, 228
Love, 53, 63, 69, 73, 111, 118, 142, 157,
193, 196–97, 204, 208, 212, 252,
302
Lovekin, Marion, 224
Luke, 28, 109–10
Luther, Martin, 27, 29, 38–9, 42–5, 49,
54, 85
Lutheran, 54–5, 60, 78, 101, 144, 282

Macalester Park, 146, 166, 192, 203
MacArthur, John, 300
MacNutt, Francis, 2, 6, 22–3, 217, 245,
252–55, 263, 272, 299, 300
MacNutt, Judith, 252, 256
Macon Daily Telegraph, 161
MacPherson, Aimee Semple, 220
Macrina, 95
Maeterlink, Maurice 139
Maggots, 207
Manual of Christian Healing, 131, 133
Marcion of Sinope, 26
Marcion Shove, 5, 64, 71, 79, 126, 263,
266, 278
Martyr, Justin, 16
Marx, Karl, 57–8, 201
Marxism, 6, 55, 60–1, 107
Mary, 12, 36, 256
Mashal, 145, 215, 219
Materialist worldview, 107
Matharaj, Rabi R., 265
Mathews, Shailer, 153
McDonnell, Killian, 287
Meditations on the Life of Christ, 112
Megalomania, 85

Melanchthon, Philipp, 40
Merton House, 254
Merton, Thomas, 253
Messer, Anton, 83
Messiah, 13, 25
Metaphysical, 57, 80, 117, 152–59, 197,
    199, 205, 229, 266, 269, 282
Methodist, 55, 70, 76, 81, 89, 131, 134,
    179, 219, 275, 295–96
Middle Ages, 35, 49, 113, 127, 131, 195,
    223
Mind of Christ, 107
Mind-Cure, 81, 87–8, 91, 131
Miraculously healed, 31
Mirandola, Giovanni Pico della, 71
Missionaries, 77, 79, 123, 156, 175–76,
    240, 283
Mokansan, 178, 253
Monasticism, 19, 43
Monotheists, 87
Monrovia, 239, 241–45
Montanists, 70
Moorestown New Jersey, 179–80, 225,
    238–39, 244
Moravians, 55, 70
Mormon, 84, 265
Moros, 157
Moseley, Rufus, 111, 159–65, 219, 222,
    283–84
Muslim, 184
Mysteries, 125
Mysticism, 16, 103, 140–41, 210
Myth hermeneutic, 52, 286

Natural theology, 25, 104, 106, 109
Nature ministry, 3, 239, 241–42
Nazarene, The, 129
Nazis, 207, 212
Nazism, 54, 56, 153
New Age, 4, 79, 92, 197, 270, 273
New England, 83, 87, 97, 211, 334, 335
New Jerusalem, 70
New Lights, 75
New Orleans, 243
New Testament, 4, 5, 11–7, 25–8, 32–4,
    45, 70–1, 87, 108, 194–95, 199,
    232, 235, 276, 284, 286

New Thought, 4, 138, 140–43, 145–49,
    152–67, 180–85, 197, 200, 203,
    205, 263, 272, 281–84
Newsweek, 220
Nicholson, Jack, 290
Nietzsche, Friedrich, 56, 62, 187, 294
Nuns, 43, 197, 204, 211
Nutrition, 134

Occult revival, 269
Occult, 4, 57, 71, 76, 93, 103, 186, 212,
    240, 266, 269–70, 278, 283–84
Oden, Thomas, 285
Oedipus, 59
Oh Watchman!, 228
Old Orchard Beach, 76
Old Testament, 12, 15–9, 24, 26–30, 88,
    108, 226, 230
On Religion, 52
On the True Religion, 30
Once born, 152
Oracles of Memander, 25
Oral Roberts University, 245, 293
Order of St. Luke, 2, 64, 79, 130, 133,
    158, 187
Original sin, 44
Osage Indian, 247
OSL, 2, 79, 131, 134–35, 152, 179, 188,
    192, 198, 214, 222, 227, 234,
    237, 245, 253, 283, 298–99, 302
Osteomyelitis, 207

Pacifism, 95
Pantheism, 86, 266–67, 295
Pantheistic, 75
Parables, 145, 228, 300
Paracelsus, 71
Parapsychology, 230
Parham, Charles, 77
Parkhurst, Genevieve, 168, 218
Particle physics, 97, 105
Particle, 100–2, 110
Pascal, Blaise, 222–23
Pastoral Care Ministries, 237
Paul, 11, 13–22, 25, 27–8, 30, 32, 34,
    45, 69, 77, 92, 94, 104, 106, 140,
    144, 167, 174, 194–95, 211, 242,
    275–79, 289, 293

Payne, Leanne, 237, 272

Peabody College, 160

Peace Institute, 176

Peale, Norman Vincent, 96

Penance, 36, 70, 131

Penicillin, 207

Pentecost, 14–5, 282–3

Pentecostal Revival, 76

Pentecostal, 2, 5–7, 55, 62–4, 75–9, 87,
122, 128, 150, 155, 159–68, 200,
226–25, 231, 242–43, 254–56,
263–66, 271–75, 283–85, 292,
293, 297–300

Pepuza, 70

Perfect Everything, 163

Pharaoh, 24–5, 278

Pharisaism, 72, 81, 122, 286, 300

Pharisees, 5, 25, 70, 75, 81, 266, 281

Philosophy, 18, 29, 32–3, 40–1, 82, 107,
225, 294

Pietists, 55, 70

Pilgrimages, 32, 35, 39

Pineal, 222–3

Pituitary, 222–3

Placebo, 84, 88

Planck, Max 100

Planck's constant, 100, 105, 119

Plato, 160

Platonic, 27

Plotinus, 29

Polio, 194

Politics, 56

Polkinghorne, John C., 105–6

Polygamy, 48, 174

Pope John XXIII, 253

Popper, Karl R., 60–1, 201, 274, 281, 291

Positive thinking, 94, 96, 134, 153,
231–32

Positivism, 5, 57

Powell, Lyman, 90

Power of God, 96, 110, 183, 190, 192,
201, 226, 274, 286

Power of Positive Thinking, The, 96

*Power of the Spirit in the Athletic Field,
The,* 146

Power Through Release, 219

Practice in prayer, 235

Practicing the Presence of God, 141, 148

Pragmatism, 89

Praise, 155, 166, 200, 224

Prayer language, 283

Precognitive, 230, 248

Predestination, 282, 39, 45, 282

Pre-existence, 232, 264

Premodern, 288, 290–91

Presbyterian, 55, 70, 87, 89, 134, 139,
173–76, 198, 204, 253, 282,
286–87

President of the United States, 158

Preternatural, 230

Price, Alfred W., 131–33, 253, 288

Princeton, 77, 156, 245

Proctor's School for Boys, 178–79

Prophecy, 42, 69, 77

Prophetic, 21, 27, 68, 128, 150, 177, 200,
230, 241, 248–49, 275

Prosperity, 97, 118, 299

Protestant, 1, 5, 17, 23, 29, 36, 40, 43–5,
48–55, 64, 71, 76–8, 87, 92–3,
111, 114–17, 122, 138, 140–41,
146, 153, 155–56, 168, 199, 202,
247, 256, 286–87, 291, 298, 300

Protoevangelium of James, 12

Proverbs, 278–82

Pseudo-science, 5, 60–2

Psychic, 102, 230–31, 248, 264, 283, 292

Psychology, 44, 54, 60–2, 115, 130, 175,
177, 210, 218, 268, 272, 287

Psychosomatic, 52, 54, 76, 83

Puller, Frederick W., 124–7, 276

Puritan, 6, 115, 119, 186

Pusey, Edward, 124

Quakers, 55, 95, 142

Quantum mechanics, 98, 102–11, 201

Quantum physics, 5, 88, 97, 99, 287–88

Quantum theology, 106

Quark, 105

Quimby, Phineas, 82–5, 87–8, 92, 117

Rawson, Frederic L., 96–9, 103, 107,
140–42

Redemption of the Body, The, 131

Redemption, 211–12, 234

Redemptive suffering, 19–20

Reformation, 12, 40, 43, 44, 47–9, 70,
    76, 113–14, 232, 283
Regent University School of Ministry,
    293
Reincarnation, 13, 94–5, 155, 232
Relics, 32–5, 39, 117
Relinquishing prayer, 159
Repentance, 90, 111, 198, 251
Resurrection, 45, 52, 93–4, 226
Resuscitation, 14, 33, 29, 46, 108–9, 199
Revelation knowledge, 223
Revisionist, 58, 128
Revival, 62, 64–5, 69–77, 79–80, 112–
    13, 116–7, 122, 162, 177, 192,
    200, 211, 283, 286, 291, 293
Rheumatic fever, 202
Rhys, Howard, 235–37
Rhys, Howard, 3, 235–37
Robinson, John A. T., 63
Robinson, Pat 242
Robinson, Ruth, 167
Roman Empire, 11
Roman Vestal Virgins, 12

Sacrament, 35–6, 41–3, 47, 124, 188,
    196–98, 203–6, 210, 217, 255–
    56, 301
Sacramental confession, 205–6, 217
Sadducaic, 2, 53–4, 62, 64, 122, 143,
    289, 291, 296
Sadducees, 5, 52, 81
Saint Stephen's Church, 187, 256
Saints, 5, 14, 18, 32–6, 117, 127, 241
Salvation, 14, 17, 38, 58, 72, 85, 176, 251
Sammy, 189–90
Samuel, 231
San Andres Fault, 242
Sanctification, 251, 195
Sanctified, 22, 33, 36, 72, 113
Sandford, John, 6, 211, 218–19, 237–38,
    299
Sandford, Paula, 247, 218
Sanford, Edgar, 228
Sanford, John, 248, 26
Sanford, Ted, 209, 238
satan, 42, 73, 295, 298
Savior, 73, 88, 141, 301
Schizophrenia, 158

Schleiermacher, Friedrich, 51–2
Schlemon, Barbara, 240
School of Pastoral Care, 186, 210, 233,
    234, 237–39, 248, 250, 254
School of Theology and Missions, 293
Schrodinger, Erwin, 101, 104
Schrodinger's cat, 101
Schuller, Robert, 96
Science and Health with Key to the
    Scriptures, 84, 87
Science and Health, 84, 89, 117, 83
Scientific, 87, 97, 99, 101, 105–7, 140–
    41, 193, 201, 203, 240, 280–82,
    284, 288, 291
Scopes Trial, 53
Scotland, 117
Scottish Presbyterian Revival, 74
Scottish Reformed, 117
SCP Journal, 270
Sealed Orders, 3, 241, 264
Séance, 185–86, 275
Seasonable Thoughts on the State of
    Religion in New England, 74
Second coming, 95, 274
Second Great Awakening, 75, 276, 286
Second Mrs. Wu, The, 228
Secret Life of Plants, 240
Seminary, 61, 64, 75, 93, 227, 283,
    285–96
Sermon on the Mount, 30, 96, 183, 208
Seven Storey Mountain, The, 252
Sexual liberation, 59
Shakarian, Demos, 168
Shaman, 265–68, 270
Sharing, 129–30, 192
Shepherd of Hermes, 12
Shingles, 184
Shoemaker, Sam, 130
Shunamite, 108–10
Siam, 51
Sin consciousness, 273
Sin-bearer, 95, 154–55
Sister Ruth, 220
Slain in the spirit, 252
Social service, 62
Society of Saint John, 148
Society of the Nazarene, 129–30
Sofia, 279

Solzhenitsyn, Alexander, 152
*Some Thoughts Concerning the Present
    Revival of Religion in New
    England,* 74
Son of God, 13, 53, 73, 92, 140, 154,
    182, 185, 298
Soul's Sincere Desire, The, 143–48, 165,
    286
Southern Baptist, 218, 282
Southern California Metaphysical
    Institute, 118
Spain, 54
Spirit guides, 270
Spirit of history, 56–8
Spirit of infirmity, 35
Spirit, See Holy Spirit
Spirit-filled Christians, 165
Spirit-filled, 200, 217, 222, 244, 248,
    250, 256, 264–65, 271, 283, 294
Spiritism, 186
Spiritual authority, 13, 16
Spiritual Counterfeits Project (SCP),
    269
Spiritual Frontiers Fellowship, 283
Spiritual Interpretation of History, The,
    153
Spiritualism, 36, 94, 154, 186, 188, 196,
    270
St Bartholomew's Day Massacre, 49
St. Anthony, 19–20
St. Augustine. See Augustine, Bishop of
    Hippo
St. John's Church, 129
St. Stephen's Church, 132–36, 179
St. Vladamir's Theological Quarterly, 195
Stalinist Russia, 58
Stapleton, Ruth Carter, 167, 218–20,
    252, 263, 271–73
STD, 62
Stephen, 14, 32–3
Stoic, 19
Strange Fire, 300
Subatomic, 99, 102, 105
Supernatural, 5, 31, 52–3, 62, 143, 193
Superstitious, 11, 32
Sweet, William Warren, 78
Sylvester, 185–86
Syrophoenician woman, 87

Tao of Physics, The, 103
Teilhard de Chardin, Pierre, 264
Ten Lost Tribes of Israel, 97
Thecla, 95
Theodult, 36
Theophostic, 7
Theory of relativity, 60
Third World, 157
Thirty Years War, 49
Thorn in the flesh, 19
Tillich, Paul, 291–92
Time magazine, 64, 295
Titanic, 59
Tongues, 77, 139, 162, 164–65, 217, 224,
    243–44, 249, 283–84
Tooth ache, 87
Tornadoes, 243
Tozer, A.W., 219
Transatlantic Evangelical Revival, 70
Transcendent, 198–99, 295
Transcendentalism, 82
Transformation of the Inner Man, The,
    211, 219, 251–52, 265, 286
Transubstantiation, 301
Travail prayer, 210–14, 228, 301
Treaty of Westphalia, 49
Trine, Ralph Waldo, 118, 143
Trinitarian, 20, 119, 163
Trinity Episcopal Church, 179, 185, 188
Trinity School of Ministry, 293
Trinity, 29, 34, 229, 276
Tuberculosis, 75, 93
Tulloch, Ethel, 139
Tumor, 85
Tuppan, 277
Turkey, 70, 279
Twice born, 152
Twice Seven Words, 234
Tyson, Tommy, 23, 219, 253–54

Unction, 42–3, 125, 256
Underhill, Evelyn, 140
Unforgiveness, 189–90, 204
Union Theological Seminary, 156, 173,
    292
Unitarian, 82, 287
United Kingdom, 71

United Prayer Tower, 165
Unity Christianity, 81, 122, 155, 187, 197
Universalists, 92
Universe, 57, 91, 99–104, 110, 193, 227, 279, 288
University of Chicago, 153, 161
Unsecular Man, 64

Varieties of Religious Experience, 127, 152, 160, 289–90
Venerable Bede, 46
Veterinarian, 277
Vibration, 91, 164, 193–95, 223, 301
Victorian England, 322
Vienna, 60
Vietnam War, 62, 288
Vineyard, 271
Virtue, 34, 195
Visualization, 88, 112–13, 117–19, 135, 181, 197, 199, 202, 215, 219, 231, 268–71, 276
Voltaire, 49, 53

Walk on the water, 107
Wallace United Church of Christ, 249
Ward, William R., 71–2
Warfield, Benjamin B., 77
Watchman Nee, 249, 264
Water of Life, 153, 155
Watson, Tom, 146
Wattage, 100, 107, 119
Wave, 91, 100–1, 105, 193, 223
Way of exchange, 211
Way, the Truth, and the Life, The, 298

Weed, Fr., 204
Welsh Revival, 211
Wesleyan, 68
Westborough, 224–27, 234, 242
Western Christian, 6, 194
Westminster Larger Catechism, 115
White, Agnes, 173, 176
White, Ann, 218
White, Hugh W. 173
Whitefield, George, 71–2
Wigglesworth, Smith, 199
Wildfire, 241–42
Will of God, 24, 143
Williams, Charles, 210–11
Wilson, Henry B., 129–30, 134
Wimber, John, 203, 271
Wisdom of God, 277–84, 290
Wisdom, 277–80, 282, *See also,* Lady Wisdom
Witchcraft, 36, 83, 230–31, 293–94
Woodstock, 62
Word of Faith, 300
Word-Faith, 138
World War I, 60, 98, 132, 153, 158, 161, 177
World War II, 1, 54, 62, 79, 178, 188, 192, 200, 207, 253, 288

Xenolalia, 283

Yale, 287
YMCA, 139, 146, 150, 302
Youth, 82, 92, 139, 227, 296

Zeus, 104